"THE REST OF US"

The Rise of America's Eastern European Jews

STEPHEN BIRMINGHAM

Futura

A Futura Book

First published in Great Britain in 1985 by
Macdonald & Co (Publishers) Ltd
London & Sydney

This edition published in 1987 by
Futura Publications, a Division of
Macdonald & Co (Publishers) Ltd
London & Sydney

ISBN 0 7088 3111 7

Printed and bound in Great Britain by
Cox & Wyman Ltd, Reading

Futura Publications
A Division of
Macdonald & Co (Publishers) Ltd
Greater London House
Hampstead Road
London NW1 7QX
A BPCC plc Company

"THE REST OF US"

Also by Stephen Birmingham from Futura:

For Harry Simons
in memory

Contents

Preface

Iᴛ was not my intention when I decided to write this book to write a book that would merely be "about rich people." There are some readers, of course, who will argue that this is what the book has become, since our American society inevitably measures success in dollars. But I was actually thinking of America's Eastern European Jews in terms of another kind of success — a social success, that of a mass migration of millions of people who have managed to become, within the lifespan of a single generation, an essential part of our social fabric and civic landscape.

The Jewish immigrants who came to America between 1881 and 1915 seemed, at first glance, to be culturally unadaptable: poor, hungry, ill-clothed, often sickly, speaking no English and in some cases illiterate, they were also steeped in a religious tradition that even America's older-established Jews considered barbaric and bordering upon fanaticism. Politically, they burned with ideas that most Americans had been taught were radical and dangerous. No culture could have seemed more alien to our shores. What could possibly be done with these people, these benighted escapees from a distant, despotic land? How and where would they ever fit in?

And yet, barely a hundred years later, here they are — as people of prominence and influence in every major American city, and in nearly every walk of life. They have survived anti-Semitism from both Christians and fellow Jews. And they have prospered — in a wide-ranging spectrum of businesses from Wall Street to Hollywood, as well as in science, education, politics, the professions, and the arts — and their prosperity has contributed to the prosperity of America at large. Theirs has been a success story in what the sociologists call assimilation.

It would be simplistic to say that this is a story that could have happened "only in America." America did not offer the Eastern Europeans much of anything to begin with, beyond a chance to be lucky. But, with the inner resources these Jews were possessed of, that chance was enough. Throughout the world, and throughout history, Jews had been punished and persecuted whenever and wherever they seemed to outstep their bounds and threaten, economically, the Christian majority. In fifteenth-century Spain and Portugal, the Catholic monarchs expelled the Jews simply because they had become too important, too necessary. Similar Christian illogic was behind the czarist pogroms of Russia. For a time, for instance, Russian Jews were permitted to be bartenders and inn-keepers, and to work in the liquor trade. But when they proved to be good at it, and prospered at it, allegations arose that the Jews were plotting to take over Russia, using vodka as a weapon to befuddle innocent Russian Christian minds, and a harsh reaction followed. Fears that Jews were usurping more than their rightful share of Europe's money and power were also behind Hitler's grisly plan to "cleanse" Europe of its Jews. But in America, to its credit, as the Russian Jews prospered, this did not happen, though there were plenty of mutterings of "too much Jewish power" from certain quarters. It didn't happen, perhaps, because we are a nation of immigrants, a nation of gamblers — what greater gamble is there than immigration itself ? — and in our hearts we all believe that everyone deserves that chance to be lucky, and this is what we mean when we talk about freedom.

But when assessing the success of the Eastern European Jews in the United States, it is important to keep matters in perspective, and to remember that for all their financial prosperity no American Jewish families have ever come remotely close to equalling the fortunes of the wealthiest non-Jews. The canard that Jewish money dominates the country is just that. No American Jew has ever amassed a personal fortune equal to that of, say, J. P. Morgan, Henry Ford, Henry Clay Frick, Andrew Carnegie, or Howard Hughes. Among contemporary non-Jewish families, the Mellon and du Pont families are each worth between three and five billion dollars. The Getty and Daniel K. Ludwig families are worth between two and three billion, and the Rockefellers between one and two billion.

By contrast, the richest Jewish family in America is the Pritzker family of Chicago, collectively worth between seven hundred million and one billion dollars. The founding father, Nicholas J. Pritzker, came from Kiev at age nine in 1880, in the first wave of Russian immigrants. The basis of the family fortune is Chicago real estate, which Pritzker began acquiring in the early 1900s when the city was still young and raw. "Never sell your land — lease it," was his advice to his sons, and they followed it. Today, the Pritzker real estate holdings are worth, conservatively, half a billion dollars, and other Pritzker investments include Hyatt Hotels, the Cerro-Marmon Corporation, the Hammond Organ Company, the W. F. Hall Printing Company, Continental Airlines, and a number of trucking companies. The Chicago law firm of Pritzker and Pritzker has no clients other than itself, and has not accepted a new client in over forty years because of potential conflicts of interest with the family's other, far-flung enterprises.

The second-wealthiest Jewish American family is that of the late Samuel Irving Newhouse of New York, who, with his two sons, built a communications empire worth between six and seven hundred million dollars — twenty-one daily newspapers, five magazines, six television stations, and twenty cable-television systems. The patriarch of this family fortune was born in 1895 on New York's Lower East Side, the eldest of eight children of Russian and Austrian immigrants. Though Newhouse was in the business of pleasing the reading and viewing public, he had no use for personal publicity. Invited many times to be listed in *Who's Who in America*, he refused to fill out the necessary forms. He was, however, intensely devoted to the welfare of his relatives, and was one of the most nepotistic of American employers. At one point, some sixty-four Newhouse sons, brothers, cousins, and in-laws were on the Newhouse payroll. His most visible philanthropic gift has been the Mitzi E. Newhouse Theatre at New York's Lincoln Center, honoring his wife.

Next in line in the roster of Eastern European fortunes in America is that of Walter Annenberg and his seven sisters. Since the stock of Triangle Publications — the parent corporation that publishes *TV Guide*, *Seventeen*, the *Philadelphia Daily News*, and the

Daily Racing Form, and that owns six television and nine radio stations, plus twenty-seven cable-TV franchises — has long been family held, the size of the Annenberg fortune has long been a matter of guesswork, but is probably in the three- to four-hundred-million-dollar range. To make sure that his private golf course at Sunnylands, his four-hundred-acre estate outside Palm Springs, would always have water, Walter Annenberg bought the local water company. Though Annenberg and his wife are solidly respectable citizens — he a former ambassador to the Court of St. James's, she a former U.S. chief of protocol, and both friends of Presidents Nixon and Reagan — the family fortune is clouded by its founder, Walter's father, the late Moses L. Annenberg, who made his money from a telegraphic news service for bookie joints that carried information between racetracks across the country. In 1939, the senior Annenberg was convicted of income tax evasion, fined eight million dollars, and sentenced to three years in prison.

Less well known, perhaps, but on an equal financial footing with the Annenbergs is the Blaustein family of Baltimore. The founding father, Louis Blaustein, was born in Lithuania in 1869, and came to America in his teens. He started out as a kerosene peddler, and devised a then-novel way of transporting fuel — in a steel drum, mounted on wheels, with a spigot at the bottom, the forerunner of the tank truck. Next, he opened America's first drive-in gas station. Up to then, gasoline had been sold at curbside, a clumsy operation. At the time, motorists had to take a station attendant's word as to how much gasoline it took to fill their tanks, and more often than not, a station proprietor added a few gallons to the sale for good measure. At Blaustein's station, this sharp practice was eliminated, and a ten-gallon jar was affixed to the top of each pump with the gallonage marked off on its side, so the motorist could see how much he was getting. It was the forerunner of today's metered pumps.

But his most sophisticated innovation was his development of the first special antiknock motor fuel, which revolutionized the gasoline and automobile industry, and made possible the use of the high-compression engine. Blaustein's gasoline was called then, as it is now, Amoco. Louis Blaustein died in 1937, and his company was taken over by his son, Jacob. In 1954, Jacob Blaustein negotiated the sale of Amoco to Standard Oil of Indiana for stock that made the Blaustein family the largest shareholders in that company. Today, the Blausteins own some 5,250,000 shares of Indiana Standard, worth on a good Wall Street day between $315,000,000 and $400,000,000.

Interestingly, those Russian Jews who chose to seek their fortunes in the most unorthodox and riskiest ways wound up, though hardly poor, in financial strata considerably below the Pritzkers, Newhouses, Annenbergs, or Blausteins. From a long, charmed life as a mastermind of organized crime, Meyer Lansky died worth between $100,000,000 and $150,000,000. And the flamboyant movie producers from Hollywood's golden era did even less well, despite the power they once wielded. Perhaps this was because they moved in a world where excessive spending became almost de rigueur, a kind of overhead that had to be figured into the cost of doing business, and where everyone was expected to die broke in the Old Actors' Home, which Louis B. Mayer had foresightedly helped endow. But Mayer himself, once the highest-salaried individual in the United States, died worth only $10,000,000.

From such figures, however, it is clear that the Russian-Jewish immigrants, while they did not create fortunes equal to those of the Christians, did not do badly, either. And whereas before the arrival of the Russians, the Germans had been the dominant Jewish economic group, the Russians quickly eclipsed the Germans in both numbers and sheer buying power, a continuing source of hard feelings between the two groups — the German Jews of "old" money, and the spectacularly arisen Russian *nouveaux*.

In some ways, the careers of the Russian-Jewish entrepreneurs I have chosen (rather arbitrarily) to write about, and their twentieth-century success stories, call to mind the sagas of the notorious Christian robber barons of the century before — the first-generation Fricks, Goulds, Carnegies, Vanderbilts, Harrimans, Hills, and Rockefellers, all of whom proved that "new money" and "bad manners" did not rule each other out. The newer Jewish barons shared many characteristics with their older Christian counterparts — brashness, energy, vast egotism, a certain rapacity, and an almost touching absence of humor. All viewed "business" as a deadly, fascinating, zero-sum game with only one winner on any field, and a joyful opportunity to outmaneuver the federal government. All were intelligent, even highly so, but few were the least bit intellectual. None seemed to enjoy their money very much when they got it in such huge quantities. Their tastes in pleasure remained simple, fleshly, and inexpensive.

And so what is different about the twentieth-century American Jewish entrepreneurs from Eastern Europe? Simply put, they were more honest. Almost without exception (and including Meyer Lansky), they believed in giving good weight. They were exceptionally careful about customer opinion. Few Russian Jews have been known to cry, "The public be damned!" — the curse that was uttered by William Henry Vanderbilt. There is Talmudic tradition in this. The Talmud itself enjoins against sharp practice, and cautions against, say, a Jewish cobbler's placing his shop in too close proximity to the shop of another Jewish cobbler. The direct competition is to be given elbow room, and space in which to breathe and flourish. Perhaps these ethical standards explain why, for centuries, the ruling courts of Europe preferred to conduct their most important and sensitive business affairs with Jews. They could be trusted.

This significant difference also helps explain why, on the whole, Russian-Jewish business success in America has been accepted by the rest of the populace with equanimity and respect, without envy or rancor. The robber barons of old were feared and hated by the public, and vilified by the press. Even today the name of Jay Gould is a household word synonymous with ferocious greed and fiscal skulduggery. But who today has anything ill — or anything at all — to say about the business activities of a Nicholas Pritzker or a Louis Blaustein? Their public image has remained benign, if they have any public image at all.

The collective success stories — against such seeming odds — of the Russian Jews in America also illustrate a point well made by Emerson in *The American Scholar:* "If the single man plant himself indomitably on his instincts, and there abide, the huge world will come round to him." (Disraeli, a Jew, put it a little differently: "Everything comes if a man will only wait.") Bringing with them from the Old World so little culture that was usable in the New, that's what these Jewish men and women had — instincts: instincts that told them to fight and survive.

Which is not to say that the majority of Eastern European Jews in America were fighters and instinct players. Most had no such ambitions, opportunities, talents, or temptations to conquer. Most made a living, paid their taxes, died, and were buried to the words of the Kaddish. But those who fought, fought well and fairly.

But, as I have said, this book is not intended to be just about people getting rich. And, impressive as the business successes of such as the Pritzkers, Newhouses, Annenbergs, and Blausteins may be, this is not a book about the rise of these particular families. Rather, it is about the rise of men and women who have intimately affected the way we live and think and view and enjoy ourselves — who have, in the process of their American successes, left their imprint on our culture in terms of the news and entertainment media, the fashion and beauty industries, the arts and music, who have shaped our tastes in our living and even in our drinking habits. The book is inspired, if that is not too pompous a word, by a persistent suggestion. Having written two other books about earlier Jewish migrations to America — the proud Sephardic families who arrived many years before, and whose sons fought in, the American Revolution, and the German-Jewish banking and merchant families who came to the United States in the mid-nineteenth century — I felt it was appropriate to take up the third, and greatest, wave of Jewish immigration, which began in the 1880s and reached flood stage by 1910. "When," Russian-Jewish friends kept asking me, "are you going to write a book about the rest of us?"

Here it is, and here they are.

S.B.

Part One
BEGINNINGS: 1880-1919

1

UPTOWN FIREBRAND

In the early summer of 1906, a huge and unruly mob of screaming Jewish women and children suddenly descended on a number of public schools on New York's Lower East Side and began hurling stones and brickbats at the buildings. The riot extended from Rivington Street to Grand Street, and from the Bowery to the East River, with the greatest violence concentrated in the most easterly sections. Windows and door panels of the schoolhouses were smashed, and certainly many frightened teachers — cowering within their classrooms — would have suffered bodily harm if a police task force, wielding nightsticks, had not quickly appeared and been able to quell the mob. It was not immediately clear, furthermore, what the uprising was all about.

The year 1906 was one of militancy by women. The charismatic Jewish-American anarchist Emma Goldman, then thirty-seven, had just founded her publication, *Mother Earth*, with her beloved "Sasha," Alexander Berkman, who had recently been released from prison for attempting to murder the steel magnate Henry Clay Frick in the Homestead Strike of 1892. The *London Daily Mail* had coined the term "suffragettes" to describe women like Emmeline Pankhurst and her daughters, Christabel and Sylvia, who were campaigning for woman suffrage. And the Lower East Side was by then no stranger to scenes of social unrest. The rent strikes of 1904 had been particularly disquieting and that same year, in the so-called Children's Strike, more than a hundred young women, many in adolescence, most of them Jewish, who had been earning pennies for piecework in a local paper-box factory, marched to protest a pay cut of ten percent. The irony was that their employer was one Mr. Cohen, a Jew.

Meanwhile, from the trickle of Jewish emigration from Eastern Europe — Russia, Poland, Rumania, Austria-Hungary — that had begun in 1881, there had grown a flood. By 1906, nearly two million Jews — roughly a third of the Jews of Eastern Europe — had left their homes. Over ninety percent of these had come to the United States, and most of them had settled in New York City, where Ellis Island was attempting to process as many as fifteen thousand immigrants a day. The Lower East Side was bursting at its seams. Yet none of these turbulent forces seemed immediately to account for the violent outburst of the women and children against the East Side public schools.

When the dust had settled, however, it turned out that a rumor had somehow billowed in the ghetto to the effect that doctors were murdering children in the schools by slashing their throats and then burying their bodies in the schoolyards. And blame for the incident — later labeled the Adenoids Riot — was laid at the doorstep of a much beleaguered lady educator named Julia Richman, the district school superintendent, who was herself Jewish.

In fact, it was a case of a Julia Richman program that had backfired. Among other innovations, Miss Richman had introduced seasonal smallpox vaccinations for East Side children. There had been much resistance to this at first, from immigrant parents who couldn't understand why their children were being pricked with needles, which resulted in sore arms. But eventually the vaccination program had been accepted. In 1906, however, at one school — P.S. 100 at Broome and Cannon streets — the vaccinating physicians had discovered that a number of children suffered from adenoids, or swollen lymph-node tissue at the back of the throat, which could be removed by simple surgery. The principal of P.S. 100, one Miss A. E. Simpson, had sent home carefully worded notes to the parents of the affected children, explaining that, if possible, parents should have their own doctors perform the operation. If not, Miss Simpson explained, Board of Health physicians would do the work at the schools at no cost, and if they wished this, parents were asked to sign forms and releases, giving the board their permission. Unable to read English, not knowing what they were signing, but doing their best to comply with strange

new American customs and procedures, many parents had dutifully
signed the forms. Thus it was the routine snipping of adenoids
that had led to the throat-slashing stories.

The Christian press, typically, blamed "excitable, ignorant Jews,
fearing Russian massacres here, knowing nothing of American
sanitary ideas and the supervision exercised over school children
by the Health Board," for the riots. The *New York Tribune*, among
others, praised the police for their "vigorous application of the
slats to the most convenient section of the nearest 'Yiddisher.' "
But for the Lower East Siders it was another case of unwanted
interference from Miss Richman.

Julia Richman was, in the somewhat disparaging phrase of the
day, an "uptown do-gooder." She followed in the noble tradition
of women like Lillian Wald, a German-Jewish young woman who
had come from a family of comfortable means, had gone into
nursing, and, in 1893, had gone to the Lower East Side to devote
her life to the healing of the sick and needy. With the financial
backing of the German-Jewish philanthropist Jacob H. Schiff,
Lillian Wald had established the Henry Street Settlement, where
thousands of immigrant Jews were welcomed after their long journey in steerage, where they were fed, housed, and cared for —
deloused, dusted off, taught rudimentary English, and otherwise
eased through the shock of entering a new culture.

A number of prominent uptown Christians had also become
involved, as volunteers, with settlement house work. Just as it had
become fashionable for every New York lady to support a "favorite
charity," a favorite settlement house was adopted — the Henry
Street, the University Settlement, and so on. The aim of the settlement houses was to form a bridge between the old and new
worlds — to instill within an immigrant population a sense of
personal purpose and spiritual fulfillment in American democracy.
It was true that the settlement houses tended to concentrate their
efforts on children and young people. There was a strong feeling
that children were often "held back" in the Americanization process by immigrant parents who were too fixed in their Old World
ways to adapt to a different society, or too timid or shy to try. But
if children could be persuaded to influence parents, the theory
went, the parents too might be persuaded to see the light. There
were, however, no overt efforts to Christianize children, but only

attempts to make them feel comfortable in a predominantly Christian American world. The settlement houses provided courses and lectures on everything from American politics to American sports, from manners to modes of dress. They were, in other words, trying to supplement and augment what Julia Richman was doing in her schools.

And in many ways they were successful. But there were still stirrings of unrest and distrust about these incursions by Christians and Jews who were "different" among the Jews of the Lower East Side.

Lillian Wald — in her off-duty hours, a least, when not teaching tenement dwellers how to unstop drains, dispose of garbage, deal with rats, or swallow unpleasant-tasting medicines — affected a rather grand and patrician manner, favoring large flowered hats and face veils. Still, she came to be much loved on the Lower East Side, and as her legend grew she was transformed into something of a latter-day Florence Nightingale. Had there been candidates for sainthood in the Jewish faith, she would have been one of them. Not so Miss Richman, whose goals — helping the new immigrant to assimilate — were essentially the same. It was probably the difference in the two women's personalities that accounted for the different ways in which their activities were regarded. Lillian Wald was soothing, motherly, comforting, a hand-holder. Julia Richman was a whip-cracker, with no patience for sloth and inefficiency, a woman of easily elicited opinions, with no hesitancy about saying exactly what was on her mind, on almost any subject.

And of course the two women's fields of expertise set them apart, from the point of view of the people they were both trying to serve. Lillian Wald's concerns were more concrete and immediate — healing the ailments of the human body. Julia Richman's bailiwick was more subtle and elusive — Americanizing the immigrant mind.

Like Lillian Wald, Julia Richman grew up in a world of moderate affluence. Her family, who had emigrated from Germany two generations earlier, had prospered to the point where they were solid city burghers. Her father owned a paint and glazing business and had, among other things, supplied all the original glass for the old Cooper Institute, a particularly lucrative contract. The family was also very ancestor-proud, and could trace itself back to 1604, to the city of Prague, in what was then Bohemia, and Julia liked to note that her family tree was studded with illustrious physicians, teachers, and rabbis.

She had been born October 12, 1855, the middle child of five, in New York City, where the family lived at 156 Seventh Avenue, in the heart of the then-fashionable Chelsea district. She had attended P.S. 50 and then, after the family's move to suburban Long Island, Huntington High School. At Huntington, though she got excellent grades, she was known as something of a tomboy and a show-off. With her long skirts pinned between her legs, she would climb tall trees and swing from their branches. She was also a bit of a troublemaker, and was famous for her imperious manner and quick temper. At age twelve she discussed the future with a young contemporary, and the following exchange is reported to have taken place:

The friend: "Julia, I'm pretty, and my father is rich. When I finish high school I'll marry a rich man who will take care of me."

Julia (indignantly): "Well, I am not pretty, my father isn't rich, and I'm not going to marry, but before I die all New York will know my name!"

Growing up in a rigidly disciplinarian Jewish household, Julia and her sisters were instructed in the domestic arts by an exceptionally demanding mother. Each girl, for example, was required to take her turn at setting the table for family dinners — no small chore, considering the fact that the dinners consisted of six courses and involved seven place settings. Once, after setting the table as instructed, Julia called her mother into the dining room to inspect the results. Mrs. Richman circled the big table slowly, checking each item. All the silver and glassware, china and napkins were properly placed, but Julia's mother spotted one discrepancy. The lace tablecloth hung a bit lower on one side of the table than the other. "Julia," said her mother, "take everything off the table, put it all back in the drawers and cupboards where it came from, straighten the cloth and start over." Julia did as she was told. It was a lesson, she liked to recall in later years, that had taught her the importance of "exactness."

She was more independent, however, when it came to choosing a career. Much to her parents' dismay, she announced, at age fourteen, that she intended to become a schoolteacher. Her Victorian father was particularly distressed at this decision, since teaching inevitably meant spinsterhood; in those days, a teacher's pregnancy was grounds for dismissal. But Julia prevailed, and, at fifteen, she enrolled at New York's Normal College.* She graduated in 1872, after completing what was the standard two-year teaching course, but because she was not yet seventeen years old — the minimum age for a teacher then in New York — her license to teach had to be withheld until her birthday.

Julia Richman's first teaching assignment was in a classroom full of boys, where, since many of her pupils were her own age and older, she had certain difficulties instilling the kind of discipline she had in mind. Soon, however, she was transferred to girls' classes, and here she did considerably better. Presently it was being said of Julia Richman that she was "born to command," and as her reputation grew so did her executive ability — and, no doubt, her ego. She began moving steadily upward in the public school system — first to vice-principal of P.S. 73 and then, in 1884, to principal of the girls' department. She was not yet thirty, and she was the youngest principal in the city's history, as well as one of the first women — and the only Jewish woman — principals.

She was already a woman to be reckoned with. As an extracurricular task, she had volunteered to teach the Sabbath school at her family's temple, Emanu-El. Here she found herself obliged to deliver religious instruction to one particularly obstreperous young man. She took her problem to her supervisor, recommending that the youth be suspended or punished. Her supervisor wrung his hands and said to her, "But we can't do anything about *him*. Don't you realize he's the son of one of our richest members?" Miss Richman handed in her resignation on the spot.

In 1903, Julia Richman was appointed district superintendent of schools, and here were more firsts. She was the first woman school superintendent in Manhattan, again one of the youngest of either sex, and again the first Jewish woman to hold such an exalted position in the city's school system. Her prediction was beginning to come true, and all New York was beginning to know her name.

Miss Richman was now regarded with no small amount of awe in educational circles. As a result, she was given the almost

*Later to be renamed Hunter College.

unprecedented option of selecting her own school district to supervise, and after considering several others, she made a choice that was as audacious as it was dramatic and newsworthy. She chose the most difficult and challenging district of all: the Lower East Side, the ghetto of Jewish poverty, where older and tougher male superintendents had dreaded being assigned.

Here, under the mantle of her stewardship, would fall the education of some twenty-three thousand children, along with the supervision of six hundred teachers, and the running of fourteen different day and night schools. The "children," meanwhile, were of all ages — from six-year-olds to men in their twenties and thirties who were just starting to do the equivalent of first-grade work. What made teaching on the Lower East Side especially difficult, of course, was that most of the pupils could not speak English.

Immediately, Julia Richman began to impose upon her district her own personal style. She was an early advocate of "progressive education" — a concept that was then quite new — but her vision went beyond that. She saw the combined role of her schools as extending farther than the limits of the classroom walls, and out into the East Side community at large. She believed that her schools' influence should be stretched out into the crowded streets and tenements and little shops. She believed that the daily lives of the East Side poor — not just the children but their parents and grandparents as well — should be embraced by the school system. In addition to academic subjects, she decided that her pupils would be instructed in such matters as hygiene, sanitation, table manners and etiquette, the importance of learning American customs, the American legal system, and civil obedience. She even — though the notion shocked her fellow educators whenever she brought it up — toyed with the idea of introducing sex education into the curriculum.

She swept aside everything and anything that smacked of pro forma ritual. "It is much easier," she once said, "and so much prettier to teach the oath of allegiance to the flag than to teach a community to keep the fire escapes free from encumbrances." At the same time, she exercised her passion for "exactness," and her surprise visits of inspection to her schools were dreaded throughout the district. Her beady eye caught everything — improperly washed blackboards, broken pieces of chalk, unsharpened pencils. One of her staff moaned, "Every time she visits a school it is like Yom Kippur!" — the Day of Atonement.

Naturally, with a role as broad and sweeping as the one she assumed for herself, a woman such as Julia Richman was bound to make enemies. And make them she did. But along the path of her career she had also managed to make friends in high places. Under the umbrella of her superintendency, for example, she had gathered the New York Police Department, and one of her targets became community vice. A particular bane was a group of young men who, in the idiom of the day, were called "cadets" (pimps) and who were charged with being in the business of leading young girls into "lives of degradation." The cadets and other young hoodlums hung out in and around Seward Park, and Miss Richman was soon spearheading a cleanup of that area. In at least one Richman-inspired raid, two hundred fifty truants from her schools were arrested, along with a quota of cadets. At the same time, she busied herself with other good works. She rented a house in the ghetto and had it converted into a social center for her teachers. She made an incursion into Lillian Wald's territory, and supervised the conversion of an old ferryboat into a floating sanitarium for consumptives, who were believed to profit from fresh salt air. In her spare time, she helped found the National Council of Jewish Women, an organization whose original purpose was to protect young Jewish girls from white slavers, who, lying in wait for them at the docks, had their own plans for degradation. She was also the first president of the Young Women's Hebrew Alliance, and for a number of years she edited a magazine called *Helpful Thoughts*. *Helpful Thoughts* was directed at the children of Jewish immigrants, and devoted its contents to what its title promised — helpful thoughts by which children could be Americanized and could assimilate as quickly as possible. She lectured tirelessly, and wrote magazine articles on her educational theories. None other than Louis Marshall — the foremost Jewish lawyer in New York, who, along with Jacob Schiff, was the leader of the German-Jewish community — had praised Julia Richman for her "years of acknowledged usefulness."

Mr. Marshall, however, was very much an outside observer, and had spent no time on the receiving end of Miss Richman's "usefulness." To those who had, she seemed more like a martinet. By 1906, the year of the Adenoids Riot, Miss Richman was very much an authority figure on the Lower East Side, and for this she was in no small way resented. With her clipped, precise speech, her imposing bosom, her carefully marcelled mane of dark red hair, in her spotless white gloves and expensively tailored if understated suits, she was also a commanding physical presence. At fifty-one, she was definitely in her prime, if not at the height of her popularity, and in the wake of the riot there were allegations that somehow her school district could have prevented the misunderstanding; as there had been in the past, there were a number of noisy demands for her replacement or resignation. But Miss Richman moved on to another useful — if unpopular — project: free eye examinations for all her pupils and, if necessary, free corrective eyeglasses. (Jewish immigrants were particularly fearful of eye examinations; those who failed to pass them at Ellis Island had been refused entry.) As usual, she ignored her critics.

At the time, Julia Richman was living at 330 Central Park West on the Upper West Side — a neighborhood that was directly antipodal to her school district — and her address was certainly a part of her problem. (By contrast, Lillian Wald had settled in a fifth-floor walk-up on Jefferson Street, asking only for the luxury of a private bathtub.) Where Miss Richman lived was also a ghetto of sorts, but it was a ghetto of affluence. The western flank of Central Park and the side streets leading off it had become a wealthy German-Jewish residential district. The development of the passenger elevator had led to the building of a number of tall, imposing apartment houses on the Upper West Side with grand-sounding names, such as the Chatsworth, the Langham, the Dorilton, and the Ansonia, and the apartments they offered were unusually spacious with high ceilings, commanding views of the city in all directions, and many servants' rooms. New York's Christian upper crust might still prefer their Upper East Side town houses, but the city's German-Jewish elite — historically leery of investing in real estate — tended to choose apartment living. (It was not until many years later that luxury apartment houses were built on the Upper East Side.)

At addresses like Julia Richman's lived families who had been poor immigrants themselves a little more than a generation earlier, but who now wore top hats and frock coats to their Wall Street offices. In the years during and after the Civil War, former rural foot peddlers had made the great transition into banking, retailing, and manufacturing. Their names were Guggenheim, Lehman, Straus, Sachs, Altman, Loeb, and Seligman. For years, the little knot of families had intermarried with one another, and by the early 1900s they composed a tight network of cousins and double cousins. Within the group, of course, there were stratifications. The German Jews of Frankfurt origin considered themselves superior to the Jews of Hamburg, but the Jews of Frankfurt *and* Hamburg considered themselves superior to those of Munich, or anywhere in the south. The Seligmans thought of themselves as better than the Strauses, since the Seligmans had become international bankers while the Strauses, of Macy's, had remained "in trade." The Guggenheims, who were Swiss Jews, were a problem. They were the richest of the "crowd," but they were considered socially somewhat gauche. Julia Richman's family belonged very definitely to this small set, which called itself the "One Hundred," to distinguish itself from the Christian "Four Hundred" of Mrs. William Astor. Julia's sisters, furthermore, had all made proper in-the-group marriages — Addie Richman to an Altman, whose family ran what was considered to be New York's finest department store, and Bertha Richman to a Proskauer, whose family included prominent lawyers.

By 1906, the dividing line between "uptown" (German) Jews and "Lower East Side" (Eastern European) Jews had become the source of much hard feeling, and Julia Richman was, in both manner and appearance, very uptown. Her uptownness was assumed to account for her heavy emphasis on discipline and correctness, and for her high-handed habit of involving herself in matters — such as the police force — that had previously been considered out of the jurisdiction of the schools. Lillian Wald at least seemed sympathetic to the East Siders' most pressing needs. Julia Richman seemed more interested in getting the East Siders to conform to her own exacting standards, in imposing her own toplofty values, in changing centuries-old ways of thinking, seeing, living, being.

To complicate matters further, the Lower East Side had become something of a fashionable cause, or Cause, in New York City. Rich Christian ladies, such as Mrs. Oliver H. P. Belmont and Miss Anne Morgan (sister of J. P.), made sable-clad forays into the Lower East Side to dispense their Christian charity to the "poor, deserving Jews." These Lady Bountifuls were distrusted and suspected of being missionaries bent on conversion, and it was hard to distinguish Julia Richman, in her stone marten scarves, from one of these.

It was also suspected that her efforts at uplifting were — like those of her family and social set — self-serving, and based essentially on a bad case of embarrassment. The Eastern European Jews were especially sensitive on this point, and with good reason. Julia Richman's values were seen as those of the wealthy few, and she seemed to be trying to force-feed her notions to the hungry masses, who, in their own eyes, already had perfectly acceptable standards of their own, which they saw no need to change. Marching into their midst with her pronouncements on the importance of clean fingernails and lessons on how to curtsy, this uptown woman not only came from enemy territory, she also symbolized capitalism, a force that traditionally oppressed rather than uplifted the poor. She lived on a street that was already being called the Jewish Fifth Avenue.

On top of everything else, she represented a form of Judaism that the Eastern Europeans did not fully understand and were not ready to accept. She actually practiced a religion very different from theirs. As early as 1845, thirty-three young German-Jewish immigrants who had arrived in Manhattan just a few years before banded together to establish a Reform congregation, which they named Emanu-El. The very term "Reform," of course, indicated that these Germans felt that there was something about traditional Judaism that needed updating and correcting. Reform had had its seeds in Germany, but had come into full flower in the United States, where it was regarded — by the German-American Jews, at least — as an essential step toward assimilation into the American culture.

Reform Judaism was touted as "the dominion of reason over blind and bigoted faith," but it really represented the new dominion of America over the Old World. Among the revisions advocated by Reform was that houses of worship no longer be called synagogues, but instead be known as temples. The principal day of worship was shifted from Saturday to Sunday, to conform with the religious habits of the American majority. The use of Hebrew was virtually dropped from the order of service, in favor of English. Keeping kosher households was deemed both archaic and impractical — as well as un-American. (The great American leader of the Reform movement, Rabbi Isaac Mayer Wise, had shocked the Jews of Cincinnati by putting on a banquet at which shrimp and crawfish were among the delicacies offered.) In fact, inside the new Reform temples, with their pulpits and pews and chandeliers, where hatted women worshiped alongside unhatted men and not in separate curtained galleries, the atmosphere was often indistinguishable from that of an American Christian church. The strictly Orthodox, kosher-keeping Russians, Poles, Lithuanians, and Hungarians viewed all these developments as examples — sinister and shocking ones — of how quickly the faith could erode in America if one were not ever watchful.

In Russia, rabbis had long warned their congregations that Westernization of the religion would spell its undoing. Steeped in centuries of Orthodoxy, the Men of the Book had spent their days bowed at the eastern walls of their synagogues, endlessly studying the Talmud, dissecting its exhortations, preparing commentaries on the Holy Word, and commentaries upon commentaries — often at the expense of any other kind of labor or scholarship. In most Eastern European congregations, the reading of secular books had been banned — for how could the words of mere men be allowed to compete with the Word of God? From this had grown the belief, which the Eastern Europeans had brought with them to America, that work other than Talmudic scholarship was unworthy of the Jew, that poverty was the pious Jew's lot, that pursuit of Mammon was unrighteous. That the uptown German-Jewish businessmen had not only grown rich, but had also tailored their religion to fit more easily into the Christian mode in the process, seemed sheer apostasy. To the Germans, who saw themselves as "Americanized," this attitude merely seemed unenlightened — backward, ignorant.

Simple statistics also offered an explanation for the increasing East-West, German-Russian mutual antipathy. In 1870, the number of Jews in New York City had been estimated at eighty thousand, or less than nine percent of the city's population. With the exception of a handful of crusty, aristocratic, and ingeniously interrelated Sephardic families who had been living in the city since the mid-seventeenth century, most of these families had come originally from Germany — driven out not so much by religious persecution (though there was some of that) as by taxation and the threat of conscription into the German armies. Since their numbers were small, their arrival in New York had been a nonevent, and their presence in the predominantly Christian city went relatively unnoticed. They lived very quietly, almost deliberately so, preferring inconspicuousness to ostentation. They worked hard and, in the process, had gained a reputation for probity. As bankers, they had established valuable international connections with such powerful British and European firms as Hambro's and the House of Rothschild. During the Civil War, while amassing considerable fortunes of their own, they had helped establish the Union's credit overseas at a time when President Lincoln's treasury desperately needed it.

As merchants, the Strauses of Macy's, the Rosenwalds of Sears, Roebuck, and the Altmans of Altman's had provided the city with high-quality merchandise at fair prices. As publishers, the related Ochses and Sulzbergers offered a newspaper that was responsible, even essential. As families, they kept to themselves, and if they had any desire to storm the gates of Mrs. Astor's Christian circle they were too proud to show it. (Indeed, the German Jews often left the impression that *theirs* was the more difficult social sphere to storm.) They projected just the opposite wish — to leave the established structure of Christian society exactly as they had found it. The German Jews, in other words, were assimilationists only *up to a point*, and had prudently not tried to push beyond that point. It might be added, too, that many of the German Jews were blond, fair-skinned, and blue-eyed. In appearance, they did not stand out against the prevailing look of the population. They flowed pleasantly — not with it, but alongside it.

And yet, by 1906, nearly ninety thousand Jews were arriving in New York City *every year*, most of them from Russia and Poland. (Because the Russians and the Poles seemed indistinguishable, all these immigrants were grouped as "Russians.") Now the Jewish population of the city stood at close to a million, or roughly twenty-five percent of the total population, and by 1915 there would be nearly a million and a half, or twenty-eight percent. In sheer numbers, the Jews of New York seemed to be overtaking the non-Jewish population. And, massed together on the Lower East Side, they were nothing if not conspicuous.

They arrived looking like bindle stiffs — hobos with their worldly possessions slung over their shoulders in gunnysacks. The men were swarthy skinned, often bearded and side-curled. They were poor, and looked it: ill-clothed, ill-shod, often sickly. They were nearly always in need of baths and fumigation — and smelled it. They looked, and were, frightened — and what is more alarming than a look of terror in a stranger's eyes? There was something even more off-putting in their collective appearance: they looked not only fearful, but defiant, wary, suspicious. They looked poor, and yet they did not look *abject*, the way Americans tend to think poor people *ought* to look. The immigrant Jews from Eastern European lands conformed to no previous immigrant image. As a group, they were not beggars. There were no outstretched Jewish hands asking for alms. At the same time, though poor, they seemed curiously proud. There were certain means of livelihood that, though readily available to them, they were unwilling to perform. Immigrant Italians, Irish, and Swedes lined up for jobs helping to dig the tunnels for New York's subway system, and lay its tracks; not the Jews. Irish girls happily took positions as cooks, parlor maids, and children's nurses for rich families, but not the Jews. Scotsmen worked as coachmen, footmen, and chauffeurs, and Englishmen worked as butlers, but the Jews would have none of these occupations. It was not that they had no taste for hard, physical labor. Jewish newsboys raced through the streets night and day delivering papers; Jewish girls toiled long hours in sweatshops working at sewing machines, and brought piecework home with them at night. A Jewish youth seemed to have no reluctance to work as a singing waiter in a restaurant; why did he refuse to buttle in a rich man's house? Why would he not join the police force or the fire department the way the Irish did? Was there something innately repugnant about wearing a *uniform?* It was all very perplexing. The phrase "doing one's own thing" had not yet come into the language, but that was what the Eastern European Jews seemed bent on doing, and through it all, they seemed buoyed up by some inner strength or fire. They were feisty, fractious, independent, argumentative — bickering shrilly and incessantly with one another. They seemed almost to wear a collective chip on the shoulder.

To make understanding these newcomers more difficult, they had names that were unpronounceable. How was one to deal with a name like Yaikef Rabinowski, or Pesheh Luboschitz? They spoke a language, Yiddish, that sounded a little like German but was written in Hebrew characters — backwards, from right to left. Even the German Jews described Yiddish as a "vulgar jargon," despite the fact that Yiddish, which is Judeo-German, was a language comprehensible to native Germans, from the lowliest peasant to the members of the kaiser's court. In short, these new arrivals appeared exactly to fit Emma Lazarus's description of immigrants in "The New Colossus," which was inscribed on the base of the Statue of Liberty in New York Harbor — "wretched refuse" of Europe's teeming shore. And they kept coming.

The newspapers, reporting on this strange new breed of immigrants, did not help speed their welcome. The Eastern European Jews were "ignorant" and "primitive," and "the dregs of society." Whenever the newspapers ventured into the Lower East Side — which they did periodically with scented handkerchiefs pressed to the journalistic nostrils — there emerged stories of "horrible conditions in the Jewish quarter," and of overcrowding in filthy tenements, vivid descriptions of vermin, garbage, marital disorders, insanity, violence, gangs of "cigarette-smoking street toughs" (cigarette smoking was regarded as a certain sign of depravity), alcoholism, starvation, prostitution, and crime. The newspapers were soon speaking of the Lower East Side in terms of "the Jewish problem," and it was a problem the self-respecting, quasi-assimilated German Jews could have done without. The Eastern Europeans were giving all Jews a bad name, and they threatened the Germans' carefully acquired "Americanization."

A generation or so earlier, the German-Jewish immigrants had started out as peddlers, and the later-arrived Russians had come to the logical conclusion that peddling was a good Jewish way to earn a living in America. But times had changed somewhat. The Germans — usually on foot, but sometimes with the luxury of a horse and wagon — had done their peddling in the rural reaches

of New Jersey, Pennsylvania, and the South, where they provided
a much-needed service to farm families who lived miles away from
the nearest villages and stores. The nineteenth-century Jewish
peddler with his wares — thimbles, watches, underwear — had
been a welcome figure on the horizon. At the various farms where
he stopped he was often given food and shelter and other forms
of hospitality. But now, in the twentieth century, thanks to men
like Julius Rosenwald and his invention — the Sears, Roebuck
mail-order catalogue — plus the introduction by the U.S. Post
Office of rural free delivery in 1903 and parcel post ten years
later, the rural foot peddler had become obsolete. So the new
Jewish peddler now took to the streets of New York.

This new breed of peddlers, with their ramshackle carts — most
of them homemade or adapted from cast-off baby buggies — ped
dled mostly to each other. Certainly no uptowners came to the
Lower East Side in search of pushcart bargains, though occasional
tourists ventured down just for a look at the raucous scene. The
Jewish Lower East Side, furthermore, was a strictly defined area
between Houston Street on the north, Monroe Street on the south
the Bowery on the west, and the East River docks and warehouses
on the east. These bordering streets were literally battle lines. To
the south of the Monroe Street boundary — or frontier — lived
the hostile Irish. West and north lived the equally hostile Italians
and German Catholics. As more immigrants arrived, much as the
"Jewish quarter" tried to press outward, the more tightly it became
compressed. Its narrow streets contained not only tenements but
synagogues, factories, warehouses, and shops, and the area con
tained only one tiny park. Soon this wedge-shaped piece of real
estate had more than seven hundred inhabitants to the acre and
by the turn of the century, it was reported that the population
density of this strip of land had exceeded that of the worst, most
crowded sections of Bombay. Into this scene of extreme congestion
pushed the pushcarts. The Lower East Side became a massive
traffic jam of peddlers' pushcarts, laden with everything from soiled
rags to fresh chicken soup. One didn't stroll on the Lower East
Side; one shouldered one's way through the pushcarts and the
massive crowd of pushing humanity. Vehicular traffic was impos
sible, and the East Side air was redolent of the commingled odors

of pushcart merchandise. By 1906, the pushcarts had become a
civic nuisance, a "disgrace" to the great city. They were even, by
a jump of the imagination, made to sound morally dangerous.
Because the pushcarts filled the streets from one side to the other,
so the argument went, Jewish youngsters were deprived of the only
outdoor spaces they might have otherwise had for play. Thus deprived, it followed, the Jewish youth turned naturally to crime,
the girls to prostitution, and it was true that in an area so tightly
packed with people, Jewish prostitutes did offer their services out-
of-doors.

And the pushcart scene did seem — to the uninitiated outsider,
at least — to be full of fury and violence. Again, this had a great
deal to do with the fiery and passionate Russian personality. The
Germans, as a group, were staid and taciturn. In their businesses,
deals were concluded with a nod or a handshake. The Russians,
by contrast, were noisy, brash, assertive, and high-strung. They
shook their fists and beat their breasts to make their points. Unhappy with a price, they didn't merely shrug; they wailed. And
since many of the pushcart vendors were women, who became the
family breadwinners in order to leave their husbands to the higher
calling of Talmudic study, this added shrillness to the already
high decibel level in the streets. When not hawking their wares
through Hester Street at the top of their lungs, the vendors seemed
to spend their time vociferously disagreeing with one another in
the little East Side coffeehouses. While physical fighting was rare,
there seemed to be an excessive amount of verbal conflict — all
of it, from the German point of view, quite unseemly.

The Russians had also developed their own brand of grim, self-
mocking street humor, which the Germans found more than a little
vulgar. Bits of doggerel were set to music and sung in the streets
and coffeehouses, reflecting the Russians' way of life and their
wry views of it. One such, translated from the Yiddish, went:

> *Rent money and landlord,*
> *Rent money and landlord,*
> *Rent money and landlord,*
> *You have to pay your rent.*
> *When the landlord comes,*

> *you doff your hat;*
> *Won't pay your rent?*
> *Then out with your furniture!*

At the same time, the Yiddish theater was filled with agony, passion, and wild laughter at the Jewish comedians. Uptown, of course, the Germans preferred to be entertained by the calming strains of Strauss, Mendelssohn, and Mozart.

A final difference between the two breeds of Jews was political. The Russians had arrived with their souls afire with socialism, with the stirrings of the Bolshevist movement, and were already struggling to form trade guilds and unions to do battle with the "bosses." But the Germans by now were contented capitalists, conservative supporters of President Theodore Roosevelt. The Russians appeared to pose a real threat to the American way of life as the Germans had learned to enjoy it, and it seemed essential that this Jewish radicalism be nipped in the bud, that the Russians be retrained in the "proper" way of American political thinking. To this end as well, Julia Richman and her ilk had set their high-minded goals.

Of course, on the surface, it might seem that it would have been easier on the Germans if they had simply ignored the increasingly embarrassing presence of their very visible coreligionists from Eastern Europe — to have disowned these people who claimed to be their spiritual cousins. And no doubt there were many who would have preferred to do just that. But, led by men like Schiff and Marshall, who argued that the Talmudic principle of *zedakah*, or righteousness, was involved, the German-Jewish uptowners, with an almost audible collective sigh, decided to take up the philanthropic burden of the unpopular unfortunates. The most palpable initial problem appeared to be urban overcrowding; and for a while the United Hebrew Charities and the Baron de Hirsch Fund — a $2,400,000 trust established by the German capitalist for the specific purpose of helping Jewish immigrants to settle peacefully in America — embarked on several programs designed to persuade Europeans to settle elsewhere than in New York City.

These organizations, trying their best to sound charitable, pointed out that the "country air" in New Jersey and the Catskill Mountains, or even farther away on the western plains, would surely benefit the immigrants. A plan was devised whereby boats carrying Jewish immigrants would be diverted to the Southwest, to such Gulf ports as Galveston. But nothing quite worked. The Russian Jews were an urbanized people — even the rural *shtetls* were organized as tightly packed minicities — and were unused to farming, physically and psychologically ill-suited to becoming cowboys or ranchers. Besides, they wanted to settle where their own like-speaking and like-thinking friends and kin had settled, and that was inevitably New York.

In 1888, as a result of the Germans' charitable efforts, two hundred Jews were actually shipped back to Europe in cattle boats. But what were two hundred out of hundreds of thousands? Merely a tiny dent in what was increasingly described in warlike terms as an "invasion." Uptowners, more and more alarmed, attempted to have laws passed in Washington to restrain further immigration, and Public Health Service standards for admission to the United States became more and more stringent. But the tide could not be stopped.

The only solution, it seemed, was for the Germans to try, if possible, to reshape these shabby people along what the Germans considered acceptable lines. The United Hebrew Charities began providing free lodging, meals, medical care, and counseling for new immigrants. It sponsored uplift-intended lectures and classes — on the English language, on American morals, manners, modes of dress, on the dangers of socialism — all designed to teach the poor Russians the unwisdom of their former ways. To support these programs, the Germans dug deeply — if at times begrudgingly — into their pockets because, as usual, Louis Marshall and Jacob Schiff were setting the stiff-upper-lip, noblesse oblige example, and insisting that others do the same. When refugees overflowed Castle Garden* and the rooming houses nearby, the New York commissioner of emigration opened the Wards Island buildings, and Schiff personally contributed ten thousand dollars for an aux-

---

*Until Ellis Island was opened as an immigration center in 1892, immigrants were received at Castle Garden, a onetime fort and sometime concert hall that stood on an island — since connected to Manhattan by landfill — just off the Battery.

iliary barracks. Together, Schiff and Marshall established small-loan societies to help the immigrants get into businesses other than pushcart vending.

But of course gratitude is a notoriously difficult emotion to arouse in the breasts of charity's recipients, particularly when the gift is bestowed in the spirit of rebuke. And the most galling, to the Germans, thing about their philanthropy was that the Russians didn't seem grateful at all. In fact, when they accepted it, they seemed to accept it resentfully, angrily. Given out of hard feelings, it was taken with feelings that were even harder.

The fact was that the conditions on the Lower East Side that the Germans found so "appalling" did not seem so bad to the Russians. That the Germans should have judged them so the Russians at first found puzzling, and finally found infuriating. To be sure, living conditions were not that much better than they had been in the old country, but they were not that much worse, either. In their urban ghettos and in the *shtetls* of the Pale of Settlement — that 386,000-square-mile area stretching from the Baltic to the Black Sea, which included the Ukraine, Byelorussia, Lithuania, and much of Poland — the Russians had spent generations learning how to live with overcrowding, and how to live, as it were, in layers and in shifts. A people can deal with a lack of elbow room in one of two ways: by lashing out at one's neighbors, or by huddling against them for warmth and comfort like mountaineers lost in a winter blizzard. The Russians had found it practical to do the latter. With the resilience and ingenuity that often emerge among a people confronted by a common enemy, the Russian Jews had learned to adapt their lives to uncomfortable situations, to turn disadvantages into advantages.

There was something to be said, after all, for three generations of a family — from frail grandparents to nursing infants — all living together under one low roof. You learned to know very well whom you could trust and whom you could not. There might be family bickering, but at least you were bickering with someone you *knew*. There might be little privacy, but at least there was intimacy. Even lovemaking was an experience shared by the entire family. Chores and responsibilities could be parceled out according to talents, and the occasional presence in a family of a *luftmensh* — literally, someone who lives on air and does no work at all — or a *shlemiel* could be tolerated. In getting to know your neighbors only too well, you also got to know whom you could turn to in time of need, and whom you could not. To settle disputes, there was always the rabbi, with his book of answers to every question, and his infinite wisdom.

What mattered about America was not that the kitchen sink was also the family bath- and washtub, or that an entire tenement was served by a single common toilet that often didn't work. What mattered was that one no longer lived in dread of the gloved fist pounding on the door at night, of one's barely adolescent son being conscripted into the czar's army, never to be seen again, or of being forced to stand by helplessly as one's mother or sister was raped and disemboweled by drunken cossack soldiers. No wonder the Russian Jews had learned to dread the coming of the Christmas holidays, and had carried that dread with them to America. That season, and again at Easter, was when the czar's soldiers were handed bonuses and sent off on leave and when, as like as not, they would decide to charge, in an orgy of violence, into the Jewish quarter. No wonder the Lower East Side Jews were baffled to learn that the uptown Germans, increasingly, celebrated Christmas with toys under a tree.

At least, in New York, the old uncertainties were in the past. It was for this reason that the raucous cries of the pushcart peddlers had a curiously joyous ring. It was this sort of feeling that, years later, would prompt Senator Jacob Javits to say that, having had a mother who was a pushcart vendor, he had always felt himself to be a member of a particular elite — of a choosy and exclusive club. The strong emotional attachment that East Side families felt toward their individual pushcarts was something that the uptown Jews simply could not understand.

German-Jewish anti-Semitism had begun to express itself when Rabbi Kaufmann Kohler of Temple Emanu-El, touting German superiority, declared from his pulpit that German roots meant "peace, liberty, progress, and civilization," and that German Jews were freed of the "shackles of medievalism," that their minds were "impregnated with German sentiment . . . no longer Oriental." By a queer rationale, the Germans began to speak of the Russians as something akin to the Yellow Peril, and Russian "Orientalism" along with bolshevism became a repeated theme. The German-Jewish uptown press echoed this, speaking of "un-American ways" among the "wild Asiatics," and referring to the Russians as "a piece of Oriental antiquity in the midst of an ever-progressive Occidental Civilization."

The *American Hebrew* asked: "Are we waiting for the natural process of assimilation between Orientalism and Americanism? This will perhaps never take place." It was a paraphrase of Kipling's "East is East, and West is West, and never the twain . . ." The *Hebrew Standard*, another journal that printed the uptown view, put it even more strongly: "The thoroughly acclimated American Jew . . . has no religious, social or intellectual sympathies with them. He is closer to the Christian sentiment around him than to the Judaism of these miserable, darkened Hebrews." Because many Russian and Polish names ended in *ky* or *ki*, the mocking terms of "kikey" and "kike" came into use — a German-Jewish contribution to the American vernacular.*

Miss Julia Richman, meanwhile, continued to sail undaunted through these troubled waters, head held high, serenely convinced of her own infallibility. With her hair sweeping elaborately upward from her wide forehead in carefully measured rows of waves, she had emerged unscathed from the Adenoids Riot, and continued, relentlessly, in her efforts to homogenize the East Siders into the American mainstream. Her new target became the Hebrew language. As early as 1894, she had drafted a report to the Hebrew Free School Association, urging that the teaching of Hebrew be discontinued, or at least de-emphasized, arguing that one new language was sufficient for an immigrant child to have to struggle with. It was a sensible enough point. But it was lost on immigrant parents, who had always stressed the teaching of Hebrew in their religious schools. How else would a Jewish child be able to read the sacred texts? Miss Richman was unmoved.

For her stands on matters like this, Julia Richman was vili-

---

*The *i* or *y* suffix means "resident of." Thus, a Pinsky is someone from Pinsk and a Minsky someone from Minsk. But there is even more in an Eastern European name than that. Immigrants from Russia proper considered themselves superior to those from Russian Poland. Therefore, it was better to have a name ending in *y*, indicating Russian, than *i*, indicating Polish. Similarly, a name ending in *ov* (the Russian style) carried more prestige and cachet than an *off* (the Polish).

fied — to the extent that many of her more important contributions, revolutionary for her time, were overlooked. She had, for example, inaugurated special classes for retarded students. She instituted regular meetings between parents and teachers, and helped to organize parent groups on a school-by-school basis long before anyone had heard of the PTA.

Immigrant children obviously faced special problems in terms of learning. If, for example, a fourteen-year-old boy, fresh off the boat and knowing no English, was enrolled in a public school, he might easily be placed in a class of first-graders who were learning the alphabet and their first sums. Needless to say, the fourteen-year-old felt miserably awkward and out of place. Miss Richman looked for new and imaginative solutions to such situations. Under her aegis, special classes were set up for cases like this. The fourteen-year-old would thus spend three or four months in a special class learning the rudiments of English, and then be shifted to a class with his own age group. Miss Richman also knew that children learn from other children, and so youngsters who had mastered the language were enlisted to help instruct those who had not. It was a method that worked as well as any; that is, those who were eager to learn did very well, and those who were not did not.

Her approach to the first stumbling block, language, was clear-headed and commonsensical. A 1907 syllabus for English classes in Miss Richman's district read:

Spoken language is an imitative art — first teaching should be oral, have children speak.

Teach children words by having them work with and describe objects.

Words should be illustrated by means of pictures, toys, etc.

Presentation of material should keep pace with the pupil's growth in power.

A bright pupil should be seated next to one less bright, one should teach the other.

In copying, the purpose is language, not penmanship.

By 1905, ninety-five percent of the students in the thirty-eight schools of the Lower East Side were Jewish, and in at least one school in Miss Richman's district — P.S. 75 on Norfolk Street — the student body was one hundred percent Jewish. It was perhaps natural, then, that Miss Richman should have instructed her teachers — a great many of whom were Irishwomen — in what was "special" or "different" about a Jewish child. On the plus side, she reminded her staff, were such traits as the Jew's idealism and "thirst for knowledge." But she also cited "other characteristics" of Jews in general and Russians in particular that teachers might encounter, and might find alien and off-putting. Among these were "occasional overdevelopment of mind at expense of body; keen intellectualism often leads toward impatience at slow progress; extremely radical; many years of isolation and segregation give rise to irritability and supersensitivity; little interest in physical sports; frank and openminded approach in intellectual matters, especially debatable questions."

In order to encourage "interest in physical sports," and to try to keep the children off the crowded streets, Miss Richman's schools and playgrounds were kept open on afternoons, evenings, and over weekends. Because she felt that the Eastern European Jewish mentality was more pragmatic than reflective, she introduced a course called "Practical Civics," which studied the way the American city, state, and federal governments actually worked, and replaced standard courses in American history — with their emphasis on memorizing the dates of wars and the names of generals and the birthdates of Presidents — with this. One point of Practical Civics was to show that American capitalism and the free-enterprise system actually *worked*.

Miss Richman's East Side students were also instructed in manners, morals, hygiene, etiquette, and grooming, and understandably, these lessons were less palatable to her students. In a world where meals at home were seldom eaten with more than a single wooden spoon, it was hard to grasp the importance of knowing which fork to use at an elaborate table setting. (Years later, to be sure, many former students educated under the Richman regime would ruefully admit that they were grateful to her for their knowledge of how to conduct themselves in a more polite society than had once been theirs.) On her periodic surprise visits to her schools,

Miss Richman was a stickler for little politenesses and courtesies, and the children would be put through their paces: "Good morning, Miss Richman. How are you today? . . . Fine, thank you. . . . Yes, ma'am. . . . No, ma'am. . . . Yes, please. . . . Thank you very much. . . ."

Richman students were expected not only to learn English, but also to learn to speak it correctly, another onerous chore for the immigrants, who had difficulty with certain English constructions. There is, for example, no equivalent in either Russian or Polish for the English *ng* sound, and in both languages consonants preceding vowels are given hard emphasis. Thus, words like *singing* and *belonging* tended to come out as *sin-ging* and *belon-ging*. There was also trouble with the *th* sound, which exists only in Greek, English, and Castillian Spanish, so that *this* came out as *dis*, and *cloth* as *clot*. Nor is there an equivalent to the letter *w* in the Russian alphabet, so that *water*, for example, was pronounced *vater*. The New York speech that Americans today call a "Brooklyn accent" is directly descended from the immigrants of Eastern Europe, but Miss Richman's students were not supposed to talk that way. There were actual cases when her students were denied their diplomas until they could properly say "Long Island," and not "Lon Gisland."

The phrase "de facto segregation" did not exist in 1906, but Miss Richman realized that this was the situation that existed in her mostly-Jewish schools. And in determining to do something about it she raised more hackles. In an effort to achieve a greater ethnic balance, a proposal was drawn up to bus children from the East Side to less crowded schools on the West Side. Reaction to the idea of busing was strong even then, and there was an immediate angry outcry from Jewish parents. The *Jewish Daily Forward* inveighed against Miss Richman, pointing out that she was a German Jew, of the enemy camp, who was bent on destroying the fabric of East Side family life. East Side parents, it seemed, felt much more comfortable sending their children to schools that were close to home, and where they could be with other Jewish children. It made the whole immigration and Americanization process seem much less terrifying. The busing proposal failed, but it left a great deal of anger and distrust in its wake.

Nonetheless, Julia Richman's name was known throughout the

city, and her position seemed secure. In 1908, however, she very
nearly came to grief. That was the year when, perhaps unwisely,
she had the temerity to step boldly outside the realm of public
education into the raffish world of the pushcart vendors. This was
the most sensitive of areas, and however well-intentioned she may
have been, she demonstrated that she did not understand one
simple fact of Jewish immigrant life: the synagogues and the Hebrew language might be the spiritual bulwarks of the Lower East
Side, but the pushcarts had become the immigrants' temporal
anchor in the New World.

By then, of course, many New Yorkers would have agreed with
her that the Jewish pushcarts were an abomination and a blight
on the city's landscape. And even before Miss Richman decided
to deal with the problem single-handedly, there had been efforts
made to bring it under control. The city required that each pushcart
vendor purchase a fifteen-dollar license, and it issued only four
thousand of these licenses at a time. But at least ten thousand
additional unlicensed vendors were plying their wares about the
streets, and as a rule, a few dollars in bribes could be counted
on to persuade the police to look the other way. At the same time,
there was a great deal of worried talk in the press about "Jewish
crime in the streets," though the stories failed to mention that a
vast majority of the arrests were for pushcart violations.

In 1908, Julia Richman went to Police Commissioner General
Theodore Bingham and demanded that he vigorously enforce the
pushcart license laws. At first, Bingham was reluctant. "You don't
want to be too hard on the poor devils," he told her. "They have
to make a living." Miss Richman replied frostily, "I say, if the
poor devils cannot make a living without violating our laws, the
immigration department should send them back to the country
from which they came."

Her retort was widely quoted, and immediately the East Side
erupted in fury. Considering the powerful emotional attachment
of the vendors to their carts, she had struck a raw nerve. Immediately, Miss Richman's resignation was again demanded, to which
Miss Richman replied, as usual, that she had no intention of
resigning. Once more it was declared that Miss Richman should
be reassigned to a school district as far from the East Side as
possible. But Miss Richman was nothing if not stubborn. Instead

of trying to temper her inflammatory statement, or retracting it, she repeated it, insisting that pushcart violation was grounds for deportation.

At this point, Julia Richman might well have been in fear of her physical well-being if, by sheer coincidence, an event had not occurred that managed to deflect the criticism from her to the shoulders of another scapegoat. An article appearing in the *North American Review*, titled "Foreign Criminals in New York" and written by none other than Commissioner Bingham himself, stated that, though Jews comprised only twenty-five percent of New York's population, they accounted for fifty percent of the city's crime. Among other things, Bingham said:

It is not astonishing that with a million Hebrews, mostly Russian, in the city (one-quarter of the population) perhaps half of the criminals should be of that race when we consider that ignorance of the language, more particularly among men not physically fit for hard labor, is conducive to crime. . . . They are burglars, firebugs, pickpockets and highway robbers — when they have the courage; but though all crime is their province, pocket-picking is the one to which they take most naturally. . . .

On the heels of these incendiary remarks, all Miss Richman's deportation comments were forgotten, and the focus of East Side fury became Theodore Bingham. It was recalled that this was not the first time the commissioner had made anti-Semitic statements and allegations. The previous year, in an article for *Harper's Weekly*, he had claimed that twelve hundred out of two thousand pictures in his department's rogues' gallery were of Jews.

While the Yiddish newspapers on the Lower East Side fumed in print over the commissioner's statements, demanding that Bingham be fired, there was an almost eerie silence from the drawing rooms and offices of such wealthy uptown Jews as Jacob Schiff and Louis Marshall. Where, the *Jewish Daily News* — or the *Tageblatt*, as it was known in Yiddish* — wanted to know, were the voices of these powerful men who claimed leadership of the Jewish community? Years earlier, the *Tageblatt* reminded its readers, in 1877, when one of the uptowners' own German kind, the banker Joseph

---

Tageblatt literally translates as "Daily Page."

Seligman, had with his family been turned away from Saratoga's Grand Union Hotel (where the Seligmans had vacationed for years) on the grounds that the hotel no longer wanted Jewish guests, there had been such a public outcry nationwide among the Jewish mighty and well-heeled that the hotel had been forced out of business. Where, in the face of this latest insult, was the outcry now? Was the difference the fact that the maligned this time were *Russian* Jews?

Schiff and Marshall, it seemed, preferred to resolve the matter without an outcry — or to assume an ostrich attitude in the hopes that, if ignored, the matter would go away. Finally, however, and under pressure, Marshall did issue a rather cautious statement. He did not, he said, wish to refute Bingham's remarks "by any sensational methods." Instead, he had met privately with New York's Mayor George McLellan and the deputy police commissioner. A carefully worded retraction was worked out, and delivered to the press a few days later. In it, Commissioner Bingham admitted that his statistics were in error. Rather lamely, he blamed the mistake on unnamed "sources" outside his office who had got their numbers wrong — though why the police commissioner's office would not have correct crime statistics at its fingertips, and would have needed to turn to outside sources, was left unexplained. The outside sources had turned out to be unreliable. The commissioner was very sorry about the whole thing.

But on the East Side the Jewish press was far from mollified. As the *Tageblatt* remarked, the East Side was proud of "a Jacob Schiff and a Louis Marshall," and considered these men a credit to American Jewry. But the East Side also wanted "self-recognition. . . . We wish to give our famous Jews their honored place in an American Jewish organization in the measure that they have earned it. But we wish them to work with us and not over us." The *Tageblatt* also said, "We have a million Jews in New York. Where is their power? Where is their organization? Where are their representatives?"

Here, of course, was a pivotal question. How *could* such a large and diverse population organize and form any sort of coalition of power? It was not just a question of German versus Russian, or uptown versus Lower East Side. The Lower East Side itself was seething with differences and factions. Some of the populace were

Russians, some were Poles, some Hungarians, some Slavs, some
Latvians, some Lithuanians, some Czechs, some Galicians. They
all spoke Yiddish, but in accents so varied that it was often difficult
for one group to understand another. The Russians disliked the
Poles, the Poles disliked the Russians, the Russians and Poles
collectively disliked the Lithuanians, and everybody who was not
Hungarian found the Hungarians toplofty and condescending. In
the *Jewish Daily Forward,* the letters-to-the-editor page, called
Bintel Briefs, became a kind of forum for dispute, and one 1906
letter — signed simply "The Russian Mother" — tells just part
of the story:

> Dear Mr. Editor:
>
> My own daughter, who was born in Russia, married a Hungarian-
> Jewish young man. She adopted all the Hungarian customs and not
> a trace of a Russian-Jewish woman remained with her. This would
> not have been so bad. The trouble is, now that she is first-class
> Hungarian, she laughs at the way I talk, at my manners, and even
> the way we cook. . . . Not an evening passes without . . . mockery
> and ridicule.
>
> I therefore want to express my opinion that Russian Jews and
> Hungarian Jews should not intermarry; a Russian Jew and an Hun-
> garian Jew are in my opinion two different worlds and one does not
> and cannot understand the other.

Some East Side Jews were budding Marxists, some were socialists, some were Zionists. Some were Orthodox, some were
atheists. The Jews of Warsaw could not see eye to eye with those
from Krakow. Already the phrase was being quoted: "If you get
two Jews together, you have three arguments." Some European
Jews were already declaring themselves thoroughly disillusioned
with the United States, cursing America for what they saw as an
overly legalistic society. As one East Sider complained, "In the
old country, if you did something that was wrong, the policeman
would tell you that it was wrong. If you said you did not know that
it was wrong, the policeman would say, 'Well, now you know, so
don't do it again.' Here, if you do something that is wrong, they
just arrest you and fine you or throw you into jail." The American
concept that ignorance of the law is no excuse appeared, to many
immigrants, cruel and unjust.

The only possible means of unifying all the unhappy and disputatious elements on the Lower East Side seemed to be to get them all somehow to embrace America as an abstract ideal, to make them feel that they were loyal Americans first, Jews second. It was a large order — large, even, for a woman of Julia Richman's stubborn, iron-willed ambitions.

To the disinterested outside visitor, the Lower East Side in the early 1900s would have appeared utterly chaotic, and nothing been foreseen to come out of it except disaster — or, at the very least, some sort of violent social upheaval or revolution. And yet that is not what happened at all. Instead, out of it came artists, writers, lawyers, politicians, entertainers, and businessmen, like Irving Berlin, Jacob Javits, Samuel Goldwyn, David Sarnoff, Jacob Epstein, Eddie Cantor, Danny Kaye, and Edward G. Robinson. Out of this and similar ghettos came a premiere American architect named Emery Roth, a fashion photographer named Richard Avedon, a designer named Ralph Lauren, a cosmetics queen named Helena Rubinstein, a movie mogul named Louis B. Mayer, another named Adolph Zukor, and a liquor tycoon named Samuel Bronfman — and many, many, more, including a pretty New York girl named Betty Joan Perske, who, after being educated at the high school on Second Avenue and Sixty-seventh Street that was eventually named in Julia Richman's honor, went on to Hollywood and Broadway stardom as Lauren Bacall.

2

WHY THEY CAME

THE routes the Eastern European Jews took to come to America were circuitous, difficult, and tricky. No two tales were exactly alike, though there was a common theme — escape. And all required a common element — bravery.

Shmuel Gelbfisz, for example, had been born in the Warsaw ghetto, probably in 1879. Later, he would give 1882 as the year of his birth, and since he arrived in New York with neither a passport nor any other documents, there was no way his claim could be gainsaid. His father had been a Man of the Book, and spent most of his hours endlessly studying the Talmud. But his mother was a moneylender and, as such, was a woman of some importance in the community, if not always a popular one when she knocked on the door to call in her loans. She was also unusual in that she could read and write, and earned additional money writing letters for her friends and neighbors to their relatives in the United States. But despite these advantages, her son was a restless boy who had grown impatient with his father's strict Orthodoxy. In 1896, when he was either fourteen or eleven, he decided to run away from home and head for the land of golden opportunity. He discreetly "borrowed" one of his father's suits, had a tailor friend cut it down to his size, and with a small amount of money he had saved, plus a few rubles — borrowed again — from his mother's cash box, he set out more or less on foot — begging a ride wherever he could — for the German border.

At the border, he paid the customary bribe to a guard who promised to spirit him across. The guard took his money, but then

betrayed him, and threatened to send him back. Using the excuse
that he needed to use the toilet, Gelbfisz found himself in a bathroom with a high window overlooking the Oder River. He climbed
to the window, flung himself out into the river, and swam across
to Germany, where he made his way to Hamburg.* By the time
he reached Hamburg, his money had run out. While wandering
the streets wondering what to do next, he noticed a shop with a
name on it that he thought he recognized. He spoke to the shopkeeper in Polish, and discovered that he had found a countryman.
When young Gelbfisz explained his plight, the fellow Pole left his
shop and scurried around the neighborhood collecting money for
the refugee. Within a few hours, this kindly soul had collected
enough money for Shmuel to book passage on a boat to England.

In London, penniless again, Gelbfisz spent three days and nights
in Hyde Park, where his address was a bench just opposite the
entrance to the old Carlton House, from which he watched the
hotel's guests arriving and departing in their glittering finery through
the great glass doors. On the fourth day, however, he was picked
up by a charitable Jewish group, which, with some difficulty,
managed to locate some distant Gelbfisz relatives who were living
in the city of Birmingham. The Birmingham relatives were less
than overjoyed to receive him, though they helped him find a job
hauling coal. Finally, to be rid of him, they gave him sufficient
carfare to get him to Liverpool. It was only about seventy-five miles
away, but at least it was on the sea.

In Liverpool, Gelbfisz learned that steerage passage to Canada
had just gone up from four pounds six shillings to five pounds. At
the end of his rope, he finally took to the streets as a beggar until
he had raised the fare. Then, after the steerage crossing, he was
deposited in Halifax, Nova Scotia, and made his way to the United
States border, entering illegally in 1896. This was also the year
that Thomas A. Edison's "Marvelous Vitascope" — a forerunner
of motion pictures — was first shown to a New York audience,
though the coincidence would not be noted until long afterward.

Years later, whenever he traveled to London, he always made
a point of putting up at the Carlton House. Though he could not
play a note, a grand piano was always ordered placed in the suite.

*Later, he would boast that he had managed to swim the Oder even though he had never learned
to swim.

But the major requirement was that the suite overlook the park, so that he could look down on the particular park bench that had once been his home. By that time, of course, Shmuel Gelbfisz had changed his name twice, and had become Samuel Goldwyn of Hollywood.

In some ways, to be sure, Shmuel Gelbfisz's emigration from Russian Poland was not typical. He set off for America of his own free will, out of a sense of dissatisfaction and restlessness. Others who left Eastern Europe at the same time did so out of desperation — to flee conditions that had become unbearable and to escape from lives that had become unlivable.

In the synagogues of the Pale of Settlement it had been customary, as part of the regular order of service, to include a special blessing for the good health and long life of the czar. This blessing was sincere enough, but the sentiments that accompanied it were less affectionate than fatalistic. One wished the czar good health and long life because at least one had a fair idea of the sort of terrors and confusions that *this* czar was capable of bringing down upon one's head. It was the *next* czar — this one's successor — who loomed as the dreadful question mark.

Life for the Jews of Russia had never been exactly easy. And one of the greatest hardships that had to be endured was the fact that, throughout the eighteenth and nineteenth centuries, conditions had alternated violently back and forth between periods of relative tolerance and calm and periods of reaction and repression, depending upon who occupied the throne. In the mid-eighteenth century, with things in her country going well, Catherine II had started her rule as a relatively benign monarch. She had felt that Jewish merchants and bankers would be good for her economy, and had welcomed them into the trades and professions. For a while it seemed as though Jews might one day gain the status of ordinary Russian citizens. But then the empress had a change of heart, and a period of restrictive policy followed.

The reign of Nicholas I, between 1825 and 1855, had been particularly savage. Under Nicholas, more than six hundred specifically anti-Jewish edicts were written into law. These ranged from the mildly annoying — censorship of Jewish texts and newspapers, rules that restricted the curricula of Jewish schools — to the monstrous: expulsion from homes and villages, confiscation of property, and a decree that bound young boys between the ages of twelve and twenty-five to service in the Russian army for twenty-five years. These boys were marched on foot to training camps hundreds of miles from their homes, often in Siberia, and many died along the route. Once in the camps, they were subject to Christianized training, and were forbidden to practice any Jewish ritual. Those who refused were beaten, tortured, or killed. The object of the "Iron Czar" was to remove all traces of Judaism from his czardom, to purify and Christianize it. Furthermore, he called what he was doing "assimilation" of the Jews. It was no wonder that the word had a sinister ring to the Russians when the German Jews talked of the importance of assimilation in America.

Tales of the lengths the young Russian-Jewish youths would go to in order to avoid the long military ordeal under Nicholas I — an ordeal that was tantamount to a death sentence — became legion. In Samuel Goldwyn's Warsaw, two young brothers had faced each other with pistols. One shot his brother in the arm, to cripple him, and the other shot his brother in the leg. One boy poured acid over his legs. The burns never really healed, he never walked again, and he spent the rest of his life with the lower part of his body wrapped in bandages. But pistols and acid were luxuries, unaffordable in most Jewish households. And so a popular way to render oneself unfit for conscription into the Russian military was to chop off the index finger of one's right hand — the trigger finger — with a kitchen cleaver. Many of the young men who arrived at Ellis Island had been self-maimed in that way.

During his reign of terror, Nicholas I was also successful at persuading Jews to turn against, and betray, their fellow Jews. In each community, at least one Jew was given special officer status — and, of course, pay — to function as a *khaper*, or "grabber." The *khaper*'s job was to identify the Jewish boys to the military police, who then snatched them from their schoolyards, from the streets, and even from their houses.

No wonder the accession of Alexander II — whom Disraeli called "the kindliest prince who ever ruled Russia" — came as a relief. Alexander permitted a few Jewish youths to enter Russian universities. Certain Jewish businessmen whom he found useful were permitted to travel in parts of Russia where they had previously been prohibited. Special Jewish taxes were eased somewhat, and Alexander reduced the compulsory conscription period for Jews to five years. In his army, too, it was possible for a Jew to rise to officer rank without becoming a *khaper*. Then, on March 1, 1881, Alexander II was assassinated by a band of revolutionaries. With his successor, Alexander III, came disaster.

The new czar's tyranny over the Jews became legalized under the May Laws of that year, which prohibited Jews from owning or renting land outside towns and cities, and discouraged them from living in villages. The increasing economic pressures triggered the "spontaneous" outbreaks of 1881, the massacre of Kishinev in 1903, and the massive and brutal pogroms that followed. In 1891, thousands of Jews were expelled without warning from Moscow, Saint Petersburg, and Kiev, and six years later, when the government seized and monopolized the liquor traffic, thousands of Jewish innkeepers and restaurateurs — not to mention malt, grain, and corn dealers — were thrown out of business.

The reason behind Alexander III's persecution of the Jews was the same as Nicholas I's: a fanatical resolve to create a homogeneously Christian country, which meant the eradication of Judaism as a religious entity. As one of Nicholas I's edicts had explained, "The purpose in educating Jews is to bring about their gradual merging with the Christian nationalities and to uproot those superstitions and harmful prejudices which are instilled by the teachings of the Talmud." For "uproot," the czar might have substituted "kill." It was certainly an uprooting process more furious and brutal than anything that had been attempted since the Inquisition, four hundred years earlier, and it would not be surpassed until the Hitler era.

But another, more palpable reason — though it was never as clearly spelled out — behind the pogroms, both the official and the "spontaneous" ones, was the desperate, and largely unsuccessful, attempts by Jewish workers to organize trade and labor unions. In 1897, the General League of Jewish Workers in Russia, Poland, and Lithuania — Der Allgemeiner Jiddisher Arbeiter Bund — was organized, and over the next three years, led several hundred strikes of cobblers, tailors, brush makers, quilters, locksmiths, and weavers, who had been working eighteen hours a day for a wage of two to three rubles a week. Many of these strikes were marked by violence, bloodshed, and arrests. In the first years of the twentieth century, thousands of persons were arrested for political reasons, most of them Jews. In 1904, of thirty thousand organized Jewish workers, nearly a sixth were thrown into prisons or exiled to Siberia. The Pale of Settlement had become a hotbed of secret revolutionary activity. Then the revolution of 1905, a failure, seemed to erase all hope. It appeared that the only solution was to escape to America, the land of the free.

Needless to say, emigration was a painful step to take in itself, and an enormous gamble. But the decades of persecution had had at least one positive effect — a Darwinian principle had been proved, and only the hardest and toughest had survived. Years of common martyrdom had instilled common strengths. Proud and cynical, those Jews who had made it through the pogroms had begun to see themselves as a kind of aristocracy of endurers, and had even developed a certain hard-boiled sense of humor about their situation. If one can turn terror into a joking matter, there is strength in that. And there was certainly a touch of grim amusement in Russia as the downtrodden continued to offer up blessings for the czar's long life.

But pride and humor were put to the test with emigration. Emigration was an admission of failure. It meant an inability to endure any longer. As a result, some of the older rabbis stubbornly counseled their congregations not to emigrate — that emigration meant that the Jewish backbone had finally been broken, that a noble cause was being given up, the white flag raised. Thus, many Jewish families left their homes filled with a sense of shame, believing that the act of leaving marked them as cowards. Thus, many of the arrivals in the New World stepped off the boats in a thoroughly complicated and confused state of mind, not knowing whether they were spineless fools or heroes.

At the same time, the Jewish immigrant had often left behind him a seriously divided family. If, for example, a young man finally made up his mind to leave for America, he usually had the support of his mother, who saw nothing but hopelessness for her son's future in Russia. His father, on the other hand, was often opposed. The Jewish father, who in many cases was the Talmudic scholar and spiritual head of the household, had heard tales of young Jews' losing their faith in profligate America, and also argued that a son's duty was to remain at home to help support his family. Often the domestic bitterness that the young immigrant left behind him never healed, which only added to his guilt at having abandoned his homeland.

But abandon it they did, by the hundreds of thousands.

In the forlorn little Jewish settlement of Uzlian, deep in the province of Minsk — where to live in a house with a wooden floor instead of one of dirt was a sign of enormous affluence — a child was born on February 27, 1891. Only years later would he reveal one of his most vivid childhood memories. Beginning in 1881, with the ascension of the despotic Alexander III, Jews of the region had been fleeing in increasing numbers every year, and he could recall standing with his mother at the Minsk railway station with throngs of Jews, waiting for the train that would take them to the port city of Libau. Nearby a political demonstration of some kind was taking place. Suddenly a company of cossack soldiers came charging down on horseback, and commands were barked out ordering the crowd to disperse. Whether the soldiers were acting on orders from above or merely on a whim there was no way of knowing. No one moved. Then the mounted soldiers tore into the crowd, wielding long whips, trampling screaming mothers and children under their horses' hooves, while the terrified little boy clung to his mother's skirts.

When he and his family finally made it to New York, via Canada, in 1900, he was nine years old. His name was David Sarnoff, the future founder and board chairman of the Radio Corporation of America. Other Russian Jews would have memories similar to Sarnoff's. Some would try to erase them from their minds, and never speak of them. Others would cling to their memories obsessively, and repeat the stories to their children and grandchildren, reminding them that such things could, and did, happen.

There were two ways to leave Russia: legally and illegally. Both courses were fraught with problems and frustrations, and they were equally expensive. To leave legally required costly visas, exit permits, and other bureaucratic travel documents, which often took months — even years — to acquire. Minsk was a popular gathering point for refugees waiting for permission to cross over into Poland, and another was Odessa, on the Black Sea. Sometimes families were delayed for so long in these cities while they waited for their necessary documents that children were conceived and born in the process, thus requiring additional permits and papers for the new babies. Today, many Russian-Jewish families who identify themselves as "from Minsk," or "from Odessa," actually represent families who had traveled long distances from tiny villages in the interior of the country. An illegal exit attempt was, obviously, riskier, but if successful it could also be much quicker. But one had to be prepared to bribe police, soldiers, and border guards at every step of the way.

In general, there were four principal routes out of Russia. Jews from southern Russia and the Ukraine usually tried to cross the Austro-Hungarian border illegally, and then make their way to Vienna or Berlin, and from there northward to German or Dutch port cities. From western and northwestern Russia and Poland, another illegal crossing was required into Germany — the route Shmuel Gelbfisz had chosen — where the immigrants regrouped and made their way northward to the sea. From the Austro-Hungarian Empire it was somewhat easier, and Jews were able to make a legal crossing into Germany, and on to Berlin and the north. From Rumania, the preferred route was through Vienna, Frankfurt, and Amsterdam.

Though a few who could afford to do so traveled some of these distances by train, most covered the long miles on foot, and these treks often involved swimming across border rivers, and inevitably involved dealing with members of patrols who profited handsomely from the refugees' plight. For weeks before departure, young Jewish men and women not only saved their money but also practiced walking long distances to toughen their bodies for the ordeal ahead.

Once in the European port cities, more confusion awaited them. Long lines of people waited for days at dockside to board loading ships, only to be told in the end that no space was available. In Bremen, Hamburg, Rotterdam, and Amsterdam thousands of people slept huddled in doorways, on the streets, and in parks, railway stations, and public toilets. By day, most of those waiting tried to find odd jobs, and a few — but surprisingly few — resorted to begging. Daily, the signals kept changing. One Jewish group, which had made it from Amsterdam to London, was told by an immigration official that "the committee" would help them. But when they arrived at the address of the committee, they were told that the committee had gone out of existence. There were always bureaucratic delays to contend with. One young man, emigrating from Lithuania in 1882 when in his mid-thirties, was named Harris Rubin. He told this story: After weeks of waiting in various lines, he had finally obtained that precious piece of paper: a steerage ticket for passage on a waiting boat. But when he arrived at the dock and presented his documents to the passenger agent, he was curtly told that, because he was traveling alone, and had left his wife and children behind him, he could not board. Only those traveling as families were being accepted. A few days later, however, seeing that the boat had not yet departed, Rubin decided to try again. Apprehensively, he saw that he was going to have to confront the same passenger agent. But this time the agent merely waved him aboard.

Then there were the rigors of the steerage crossing, which cost between twenty and twenty-four dollars, depending on the cupidity of the ship's owner, and which lasted from four to six weeks, depending on the weather. The men and the women were separated by sex into two large holdlike rooms, stacked with bunks, below the water line. The bunks were narrow and short, arranged in tiers about two feet apart, and made of wood. There were no mattresses, blankets, or, needless to say, sheets. One's sack of belongings became one's pillow, and since belongings consisted of pots and pans and perhaps an extra pair of shoes, it was usually a lumpy one. One toilet served as many as five hundred people, and whether, or how often, one was allowed above decks for air depended on the arbitrary policy of the ship's officers.

Aboard ship, since most of the steerage passengers had never experienced ocean travel, seasickness was epidemic and sanitation was largely left in the hands of the passengers. As a rule, however, food was plentiful — no captain was eager to have reports of deaths at sea appear on his manifest — though not very appetizing. A typical daily menu consisted of bread, butter, salted herring, cake, and potatoes in their skins. But even those who felt well enough to eat were reluctant to touch the food, which they had been assured was kosher, but which they suspected — with good reason — was not.

It was no wonder that the Jewish immigrants arriving at Ellis Island looked spent and wasted. They had been sustained on the

crossing mostly by hope. And yet, before they could debark, the
master of a ship routinely required each immigrant to sign a document testifying that he had been well fed, well treated, well cared
for medically, and was in excellent health. To their credit, these
documents helped many sickly immigrants pass through the United
States Immigration Department's health inspections.

Then there was the first view of America: the turreted, mosque-
like towers of the main immigration building at Ellis Island, rising
out of the waters of the harbor like a fairy-tale castle surmounted
with quaint domes and finials. Though the interior of this building
was starkly institutional — cavernous processing rooms, where
immigrants were shunted through a maze of corral-like iron fences
from one set of inspections to another, meals served at long trestle
tables with wooden benches in whitewashed mess halls —
it must have seemed like paradise in comparison with steerage.
In the vast, barrackslike dormitories filled with row after row of
double-decker beds, there were at least clean white sheets, blankets, and fat down-filled pillows.

Processing at Ellis Island could take several days. Most dreaded
were the eye examinations for trachoma, a contagious form of
conjunctivitis, which the *New York Times,* in rather an alarmist
style, described as "a sweeping plague — especially on the east
sides of our cities — of European importation [that] would surprise
no medical man familiar with foreign conditions and in touch with
the swollen tide of immigration flowing towards us from sources
beyond the jurisdiction of modern sanitation." Anyone suspected
of suffering from what the *Times* called this "insidious and dis-
abling eye disease" was sent back to Europe on the next boat. In
1904, twenty thousand immigrants were rejected because of trachoma.

Finally, there was the culture shock upon arrival in the city
itself. Each immigrant's experience was different, of course, but
there were a few common themes. A number complained, for
example, of rude stares and jeers — particularly from children
and teenagers. But most immigrants found that, compared with
what they had endured, they were treated surprisingly well, though
there were some aspects of America for which they were unprepared. Here, for example, are some of the impressions of one Isaac
Don Levine. Later a successful journalist, Levine was born in

Byelorussia in 1892, and came to the United States as a youth of nineteen.

He was astonished, for one thing, by the "skyscrapers," and craned his neck backward to count up to sixteen floors of one building before being overcome by dizziness. Levine also marveled at the letter boxes, the mechanics of which he had a bit of trouble figuring out, and at the frequency of mail collections and the speed of delivery. In Kiev, he noted, a letter might travel for twenty-five years before reaching its destination. At first, he was startled by the sight of policemen carrying clubs instead of wearing sabers, and their habit of swinging their clubs as they walked about he at first found frightening. Later, he decided that this was just a mannerism, and not a threatening gesture. He noted that American policemen tended to be very tall.

Young Levine also observed that America appeared to be "the land of companies," and that even a poor shoemaker whose shop was one basement room had hung out a shingle proclaiming himself to be the "Brockton Shoe Repairing Company." There were other surprises. Back home in Russia, a number of foreign currencies had circulated interchangeably. But when Levine tried to pay his streetcar fare with a ten-kopeck coin, it was refused. He was also astonished to find, when he produced the correct fare in American money, that he was not given a ticket. Instead, the conductor simply pulled a chain and rang a little bell. Furthermore, the conductor made no attempt to cheat or overcharge him — did not even try to extract a bribe — as had been commonplace back home. He was struck by the speed and efficiency of the American railroads. A trip from Boston to Kansas City, he learned, took only forty-eight hours, and involved only one change, in Chicago. At home, to cover a similar distance between Vilnius and Orenburg took six days, and involved changing trains no fewer than eight times. On the trains and streetcars, he admired the "two rows of leather straps hanging on both sides of the car for the convenience of the standing public," and added, "I cannot understand why they should not have at home the same useful device."

Levine found the prices of clothes — "American clothes lack grace and elegance, but provide comfort" — low by comparison with those at home, and the rent "not as high as it sounds at first." He noted that most American schools were taught by women, not men — "old maids with kind hearts, but not pretty looks" — and when he finally screwed up sufficient courage to try to enroll in a public high school in order to improve his English, he was surprised to find that the principal who interviewed him was a man dressed in an ordinary business suit, not an officer in a military uniform. Perhaps Levine's most astonishing discovery of all was the American public library system. Here he found that after filling out a simple form he was given two cards — one for fiction, one for nonfiction — good for four years. With these, he could remove as many books as he wished "without a penny's expense on my part," and was left wondering "how it is possible that no money deposit should be made." He saw that there were no policemen patrolling the stacks of books, that "no suspicious eye follows you," and that some library patrons were so relaxed in their surroundings that they actually slept in their chairs. On the other hand, he was disappointed to discover that the young woman who issued his library card appeared to be illiterate. She had asked him how he spelled his name. "In our country, I said, a girl who could not spell would not command such a position." Levine asked his friend Hyman about this, and Hyman confirmed that many highly placed Americans could not spell. The doctor whom Hyman had consulted about his wife's rheumatism had also asked him to spell his name. "Just think of it," wrote Levine in a letter home: "the doctor, a university man, and cannot spell."

There were new curiosities daily. Like most Russian immigrants, Isaac Levine had never seen a Negro. But here, he wrote, "You meet colored people everywhere, and they seem to be more numerous than the whites. Most of them are very poor and ignorant." He also noticed an odd practice among American males involving their legs. When sitting down, in a streetcar or at a restaurant table, men hitched up their trousers at the knee, exposing much more ankle and calf than would have been acceptable at home. Men also seemed to think nothing of pulling up their trousers, sitting back in their chairs, and tossing their feet up on tabletops or windowsills — behavior for which they would have been arrested in Russia. For a long time Levine watched with fascination, through an open window, a man who was seated beyond it with his feet up on the sill. The upper portion of the man's body was obscured behind the newspaper he was reading, and as he read his body seemed to sway backward and forward. Later, Levine discovered the explanation for this extraordinary motion — an American invention called the rocking chair.

Levine was impressed with the fact that every American home, "except very old ones," had a bathroom, but other conveniences were more distracting. In Russia, for instance, he had been told that all American houses were lighted with electricity. But in New York he found that the poorer homes were still lighted by gas. Though he was shown how to light and extinguish the gaslight in his room, he had also heard that many American suicides were accomplished by taking gas. He was more than a little nervous, when he lowered his lamp, "over this dangerous [ether] flowing in a pipe not far from [my] bed."

Levine was also unprepared for the American gum-chewing habit. Sitting next to a young woman on a streetcar who was "making queer motions with the muscles of her mouth," he wondered "what kind of mouth disease she possesses." Learning that Americans chewed a chicle concoction for pleasure, he was nonplussed. He was equally put off by Americans' use of tobacco: "On every step you meet a pipe sticking from the mouth of a venerable citizen, a common pipe, at the look of which decent people at home would be horrified." Of American food, he was impressed by the eggs, which he discovered "are absolutely oval and if you possess that steadiness in your hand — they can be made to stand erect on either of its ends," something that the small round eggs of Russia could not be made to do. As for American drinking habits, Levine was of two minds. He complained that "vodka, real, real strong vodka, for which the hearts of some of our country men here long so much . . . is not to be found here." On the other hand, while admitting that the "American drunkard is usually a peaceful dove," he also found it "more disgusting to see it in a nicely dressed, civilized being than in a tattered, illiterate peasant," and was appalled by the number of saloons — "some of the streets are literally covered with them" — and the fact that he had been told that American consumption of alcohol "beats Russia." He added, "The people begin to realize the great harm caused by it and the prohibition movement is gaining ground."

Obviously, Isaac Levine was a fairly resilient young man, who quickly learned to take the ways of the New World in his stride, and looked on the bright side of things. Passing an American schoolhouse, he would observe that it was "rather large, surrounded by a spacious, clean yard, but ugly looking." It reminded him of "a jail at home or of a soldiers' quarterhouse." But over it "the American flag was waving . . . and my aesthetic feelings were fully satisfied looking at it. I think it is the most beautiful banner in the world."

Still, an element of homesickness could not be ruled out. In an old photograph, taken by Lewis W. Hine around 1910 and showing a group of Jewish women and children working on piece goods in a Lower East Side tenement, there is an odd detail. Though the scene is one of hardship and even squalor, a photograph is shown hanging prominently on the wall of the shabby room. It is of Czar Nicholas II — the last of the czars — and his family.

In the single decade between 1900 and 1910, more than eight million immigrants poured into the United States, most of them from Eastern Europe, a heavy percentage of these Jewish. The record of 1,000,000 immigrants in a year was first broken in 1905, was broken again in 1906, and reached an all-time high in 1907 with 1,285,000. Not all of these people, of course, became rags-to-riches success stories. But an astonishing number of them did. By the early 1900s, a new aroma seemed to be wafting across the air of the Lower East Side — barely detectable, perhaps, from the outside, but there nonetheless — the heady, intoxicating smell of Prosperity.

Though certainly overcrowded, the entire Tenth Ward could no longer be viewed as a single, unmitigated slum. Already "better neighborhoods" had begun to carve themselves out of the confusion of narrow streets. The poorest street, with the worst overcrowding, the most people to a room, was probably Cherry Street. But, by contrast, just a few blocks away was East Broadway, a wider thoroughfare, which had become the Lower East Side's best address. On East Broadway lived the rabbis, doctors, shopkeepers, and families who had secured white-collar jobs in the city's bureaucracy. A 1905 census revealed that one out of every three families living in the apartments on East Broadway employed at least one servant.

In 1903, the *Jewish Daily Forward*, which always closely scru-
tinized these trends, reported that a new word had entered the
Yiddish language: *oysesn*, or "eating out." To dine out — not at
a friend's or relative's house, but at an actual *restaurant* — had
been unheard-of in the old country (and up until that point, even
in the new), but the *Forward* noted that this stylish habit was
"spreading every day, especially in New York." And, a little later,
the newspaper commented that vacations in the country "have
become a trend, a proof of status."

The *Forward* had begun carrying advertisements for resort hotels
in the Catskills as early as 1902, when at least three such establishments offered their services, stressing kosher meals and farm-
fresh eggs and vegetables. Their greatest attraction, of course, was
clean mountain air and escape from the muggy heat of New York
summers. In the beginning, these "resorts" were primitive affairs — hastily and cheaply converted farmhouses that had been
divided up into tiny, cell-like rooms, or barns that had been filled
with beds for dormitory-style living. For four or five dollars a week,
children half-price, they seemed a bargain. But it wasn't long
before hotels in the Catskills began offering more amenities —
electric light, hot and cold running water, telephones, billiard
tables, bowling alleys, and even nightly entertainment. And in
less than two decades' time the great Jewish resort palaces —
Grossinger's, the Concord — would make their appearance, upon
which the whole idea of Miami Beach would soon be modeled.
The mocking phrase "Borscht Belt" would be born, and Jewish
comedians and performers — trying their wings for Broadway and
the movies — would make wicked fun of their new-rich audiences'
fancy airs and pretensions, to their audiences' great and unblem-
ished delight.

Meanwhile, on the Lower East Side, another trend was noted
by the ever-watchful *Forward*. Suddenly, it seemed, everybody on
the East Side had to own a newfangled contraption called a Victrola, and the *Forward* complained vociferously about the noise
created by them. In 1904, the paper editorialized:

God sent us the Victrola, and you can't get away from it, unless you
run to the park. As if we didn't have enough problems with cockroaches
and children practicing the piano next door. . . . It's everywhere, this

Victrola: in the tenements, the restaurants, the ice-cream parlors, the candy stores. You lock your door at night and are safe from burglars, but not from the Victrola.

Pianos? By 1904, owning a piano was yet another symbol of Jewish status. According to the *Forward:*

There are pianos in thousands of homes, but it is hard to get a teacher. They hire a woman for Moshele or Fennele and after two years decide they need a "bigger" teacher. But the "bigger" teacher, listening to the child, finds it knows nothing. All the money — down the drain. Why this waste? Because Jews like to think they are experts on everything.

Granted, the *Daily Forward* tended to exaggerate cases (*thousands* of pianos?) and, in its generally cranky tone, liked to scold its Jewish readers for not doing exactly as the *Forward* thought best. An opinionated paper, it preferred to see immigrant Jewish noses pressed firmly to the grindstone, and Jewish money not frittered away on such frivolous frills and luxuries as meals in restaurants, holidays in the mountains, phonographs, pianos, and piano lessons for the children. (No matter that the pianos were usually bought "on time" from secondhand dealers, or taken over from previous tenants who couldn't afford to move them.) Still, it was clear that the immigrants had money to spend, or waste, depending upon how one looked at it, and were determined to spend it exactly as they wished.

Some immigrant Jews were doing even more extraordinary things. Some were even marrying Christians.

3

A JEWISH CINDERELLA

Of course not all the Jews who escaped from czarist Russia made straight for the Lower East Side. Some, having made it as far as England, settled there, and an Eastern European enclave developed in the Whitechapel section of southeast London. Others, having crossed the Atlantic in English vessels to Canadian ports, settled there, in such cities as Montreal and Toronto, both of which now have large Jewish populations. Others, having cleared Immigration at Ellis Island, quickly made their way to join family or *landsleit* — countrymen — who had settled in the American Midwest or Southwest. Rose Pastor's family had settled in Cleveland, where no one would have suspected that she would create a national news sensation in 1905 in faraway New York.

The spring of that year had not been a particularly momentous or exciting one. Aside from the record-breaking immigration figures, no great events were shaking the earth, no burning issues consumed the public consciousness midway through the peaceful first decade of the twentieth century, which had been named the "Century of Progress." The popular and colorful Teddy Roosevelt was comfortably into his second term at the White House, having been reelected the year before by an unprecedented majority. That year, through Roosevelt's initiative, delegates from the empires of Russia and Japan had met at Portsmouth, New Hampshire, and agreed upon terms for peace that would end the Russo-Japanese War, and for this achievement, Roosevelt would later receive the Nobel Peace Prize.

The battle lines, meanwhile, were being drawn between Americans who insisted that they would never forsake their horse-drawn landaus and victorias and those who were taking to the highways in the noisy new motorcars with their internal-combustion engines. Obsolete carriage horses were being turned loose — into the streets of cities like New York, where they quickly died, creating a certain sanitation problem — in favor of Packards, Reos, and Wintons, while stables were being converted into garages, and coachmen into chauffeurs.

In the world of fashion, huge wide-brimmed hats surmounted with arrangements of silk flowers, artificial fruits and vegetables, even stuffed birds, were coming into vogue, and with them came the flaring gored skirts that swept the street on all sides. The artist Charles Dana Gibson had portrayed a number of tiny-waisted, fresh-faced girls wearing bosomy pleated and ruffled shirtwaists, and the shirtwaist would dominate fashion for nearly a generation as part of the Gibson Girl look. In Manhattan's garment district, the shirtwaist business was booming, and the Jewish girls who worked in these factories were known as "shirtwaist girls." The term "sweatshop" was not yet in common use, and would not be until the tragedy of the fire at the Triangle Shirtwaist Company in 1911, in which 146 people, most of them shirtwaist girls, lost their lives.

Then, in the middle of what had been an uneventful spring, the American reading public was treated to banner headlines detailing what was billed as a real-life "Cinderella story."

It all began on April 5, 1905, when the staid and stately *New York Times* — which never put engagement announcements on its front page except in the cases of European royalty or international celebrities — broke its long-standing precedent. Obviously, the *Times* felt that the news of this particular betrothal was of unusual significance. Its front-page headline read:

J. G. PHELPS STOKES
TO WED YOUNG JEWESS

*Engagement of Member of Old
New York Family Announced*

BOTH WORKED ON EAST SIDE

An entire new century, after all, was now under way, a century that seemed filled with golden promise and limitless possibilities, in which anything could happen, and in which the newsboy heroes of Horatio Alger's tales — "Tattered Tom" and "Ragged Dick" — were regarded as inspirational. Fairy tales, it seemed, could indeed come true, and the story certainly seemed to contain all the necessary elements of a fairy tale.

The backgrounds of the engaged pair, the *Times* pointed out, could not possibly have been more dissimilar. The young Jewess in question — and in its choice of phraseology, even from the Jewish-owned *Times*, there was a hint of condescension — was not even a member of one of New York's proud uptown Jewish families (such as the Ochses and Sulzbergers). She was, of all things, a Polish immigrant, and poor.

This Cinderella's name was Rose Harriet Pastor, and she was on many counts an extraordinary young woman. At the time of her engagement to Mr. Stokes she was twenty-five years old — not technically beautiful, but slender and petite with delicate features including a thin, patrician nose, pale skin, green eyes, and an impressive mane of Titian hair that she wore, in the Gibson Girl fashion of the day, pulled back at the nape of her neck in a loose chignon. She had been born in a tiny village called Augustów, near Suwalki, on what is now the Russian-Polish border, in the Jewish Pale of Settlement, the daughter of Jacob and Anna Weislander. When Rose was still an infant, her father died and her mother remarried, and Rose took her stepfather's surname of Pastor. As thousands of Jewish families were doing to escape the pogroms, the Pastors emigrated from Poland in 1881, when Rose was two, and settled in London's Whitechapel. Here, in the East End ghetto, the little girl helped her mother sew bows on ladies' slippers for the next ten years. But, when the time came, she was also sent to school, which would give her a distinct advantage when the family was able to afford its next move, in 1891, to America. By that time, English had become Rose Pastor's first language, and she spoke it with a pleasant British accent.

Once in the United States, the family traveled to Cleveland, where they had distant relatives. Soon afterward, Rose's stepfather died, and this, as it would turn out, would also be indirectly to

her advantage. Though it forced her, at age twelve, to go to work
to help support her mother and the younger children, it also made
her her family's mainstay, and made her grow up quickly. For the
next twelve years she worked fourteen hours a day in a Cleveland
cigar factory, in a production line, rolling wrappers around cigars.

Since cigars are rolled when wet, it was damp, messy, and
unpleasant work. And it was also monotonous. To relieve the
monotony, she read. She discovered that she could sit at her
worktable, rolling cigars with one hand, with a book in her lap,
turning the pages with the other. Whenever her supervisor moved
along the line, inspecting the girls' work, Rose would tuck the
book under her apron.

She read constantly, avidly, whatever she could get her hands
on. Had her Orthodox stepfather lived, this sort of behavior would
never have been condoned. Bookishness was considered dangerous
for Jewish girls, who, in any spare time they had, were supposed
to study the womanly arts of housekeeping for future Jewish husbands. But Rose spent all her spare time reading. Indeed, the fact
that she had not married by the age of twenty-five indicated that
she had become something of a bluestocking.

She had also begun to write poetry. Her verse was light and
airy and simple, much influenced by Emily Dickinson. In one
poem, called "My Prayer," she wrote:

> *Some pray to marry the man they love,*
> *My prayer will somewhat vary:*
> *I humbly pray to Heaven above*
> *That I love the man I marry.*

While the sentiments in Rose Pastor's verses did not bear much
heavy analysis, they were unquestionably pleasant ones, and she
began to submit her poetry to the *Tageblatt*. After a few initial
rejection slips, the paper began to buy and publish her verse.
Then, in 1903, the *Tageblatt* invited Rose to come to New York
to write an advice-to-the-lovelorn column on its English-language
page, offering her a salary of fifteen dollars a week. This was a
princely sum in an era when an Irish chambermaid might, if she
were lucky, earn that much in a month, and when a copy of the
Tageblatt itself sold for one cent. It was much more than Rose
was making rolling cigars, and much more interesting work. Rose

Pastor accepted the job eagerly, and her family followed their breadwinner to the East Coast, where she, her mother, and brothers and sisters took a small flat on Wendover Avenue in the Bronx.

Interestingly, in view of Rose Pastor's later career, the *Tageblatt* was the more politically conservative of New York's two leading Jewish dailies. Its rival, the *Forward*, was often fierily and outspokenly socialist and trade unionist, which, as we shall see, Rose Pastor herself would one day become. But the *Tageblatt* took the stance that socialism was "ungodly," and often tried to convince its readers that Jewish labor organizers like David Dubinsky and Sidney Hillman were actually Christian missionaries in disguise. The *Tageblatt* also devoted much space to the uptown do-gooder activities of Jacob Schiff and Julia Richman. Naturally, the *Tageblatt* received more approval and support from the uptown capitalists than the *Forward* did.

Meanwhile, there was nothing at all political about Rose Pastor's early *Tageblatt* columns. Under the title "Ethics of the Dust Pan," they were not so much advice to the lovelorn as collections of sentimental homilies:

> Life is a riddle to which love is the answer.
>
> You suffer today because you have sinned yesterday.
>
> A broken heart is better than a whole one where love has never crept in.
>
> Who is too anxious to please pleases not at all.

Or little jokes and plays on words:

> Good men become better by traveling, bad men, worse.
>
> When a man is in a pickle, even his sweetheart *jars* him.

In addition to her regular column, Rose was occasionally assigned to do an interview or a feature story, for which she was given even larger by-lines. For one of these she was asked to investigate the phenomenon of the handsome young aristocrat named James Graham Phelps Stokes, who was doing volunteer social work for the University Settlement House on the Lower East Side. She was also asked to find out if there was any truth to rumors that, as a result of a disagreement with the board of governors, Mr.

Stokes was about to withdraw his support from the University Settlement and move on to a new post.

From Stokes, Rose Pastor obtained a denial of the rumors, which the *Tageblatt* — with a certain penchant for making up stories out of whole cloth — had actually started. But it was also clear, from her story when it appeared, that she had been very much taken with Mr. Stokes personally. Breathlessly, and even a bit incoherently, she wrote:

Mr. Stokes is a deep, strong thinker. His youthful face "takes" by virtue of its fresh, earnest, and kind expression. One glance at his face and you feel that Mr. Stokes loves humanity for its own sake, and as he speaks on with the sincerity which is the keynote of his character you feel how the whole soul and heart of the man is filled with "Weltschmerz." You feel that he "has sown his black young curls with bleaching cares of half a million men."

Mr. Stokes is very tall, and, I believe, six feet of thorough democracy. A thoroughbred gentleman, a scholar, and a son of a millionaire, he is a man of the common people, even as Lincoln was. He is a plain man, and makes one feel perfectly at ease with him, nor does he possess that one great fault that men of his kind generally possess — the pride of humility. He does not flaunt his democracy in one's face, but when his democracy is mentioned to him, he appears as glad as a child who is told by an appreciative parent, "You have been a good boy to-day."

There was a great deal more in this vein, and later Rose Pastor would blame careless cutting and editing for the odd syntax and incomplete sentences, but even after deep cutting it was a two-column story, and, reading it, her editor could not resist saying to her teasingly, "If I thought as much of Mr. Stokes as you seem to do, I would take care not to let anybody know it."

She had, however, already let Graham Stokes know it. He had asked to see her copy before it was printed, and she had submitted the story to him for his approval. Clearly, he not only approved of it but was also more than a touch flattered by it. The story, and its author, made such an impression on him that, instead of returning her pages to her in the mail, he personally carried them back to her by hand. Then he invited her to dinner.

Later, Rose Pastor would confess that it was a case of "love at first sight."

The object of her affections, meanwhile, possessed all the qualities of a Prince Charming. James Graham Phelps Stokes, who was known to his friends as Graham, was thirty-one, Yale '92, over six feet tall, darkly handsome, with the profile and athletic build of a Greek god. He sailed, he rode horses, and at college he had been a track and tennis star. For years he had been regarded as one of New York's most eligible bachelors. He belonged to all the city's most exclusive clubs, including the City Club, the Knickerbocker Club, the Riding Club, the University Club, the National Arts Club, the Century Association, and the Saint Anthony Society, which was Yale's most elite fraternity. He was High Church Episcopalian. He and his family were firmly ensconced in the New York *Social Register,* and had been since the inception of that publication. The family had had its portraits painted by John Singer Sargent.

Though the *Times* and other newspapers, reporting the singular engagement, persisted in calling Graham Stokes a "millionaire," young Stokes himself modestly denied this. On the other hand, there was no question that his father was. Graham was one of nine children of the banker Anson Phelps Stokes, and the Stokes family mansion at 229 Madison Avenue on the crest of Murray Hill, the city's most fashionable address, was one of New York's great showplaces. For a country place, Anson Phelps Stokes had built Shadowbrook, in Lenox, Massachusetts, a hundred-room turreted granite castle that occupied an entire mountaintop and was second in size only to the Vanderbilts' Breakers at Newport among America's great resort "cottages." Once, when he was a student at Yale, one of Graham Stokes's brothers had wired to their mother at Shadowbrook, ARRIVING THIS EVENING WITH CROWD OF NINETY-SIX MEN. Mrs. Stokes had wired back, MANY GUESTS ALREADY HERE. HAVE ONLY ROOM FOR FIFTY.

And young Graham Stokes himself could hardly have been poor. He was president of the State Bank of Nevada, and he also owned a railroad, albeit a small one, the Nevada Central, with rolling stock consisting of only three locomotives and one passenger car.

Graham Stokes's lineage was as imposing as his family's wealth; he was "a descendant of families prominent in the Colonial history of New England," as the newspapers put it, in a day when New England ancestors mattered mightily to status-conscious New

Yorkers. Both the Phelps and Stokes families had been early settlers in the Massachusetts colony, and when they were joined by marriage in the early nineteenth century, it became a family tradition to use both names in the surname, where the words "Phelps Stokes" were spoken with an audible, if not an actual, hyphen. In addition to James Graham Phelps Stokes, there were also Caroline M. Phelps Stokes, Ethel Phelps Stokes, Mildred Phelps Stokes, and Isaac Newton Phelps Stokes. The names had been further glorified through distinguished membership in the clergy. One of Graham Stokes's younger brothers, the Reverend Anson Phelps Stokes, Jr., was secretary of Yale University, and pastor of New Haven's most fashionable church, Saint Paul's Episcopal. Finally, there were even connections with the British aristocracy. Through her marriage to an English viscount, Graham's sister Sarah Phelps Stokes had become the Baroness Halkett.

This, then, was the dazzling young man who had asked the hand of a Polish immigrant ex–cigar roller in marriage.

The young bridegroom-to-be had already attracted a certain amount of attention in New York because of his choice of lifestyle. After graduating from Yale, he had earned a medical degree from Columbia University's College of Physicians and Surgeons. But, rather than practice medicine, and while maintaining his banking and railroad interests along with his *Social Register* listing and uptown club memberships, he had chosen to move out of the family mansion and become a resident worker at the settlement house on Rivington Street. Other well-heeled uptowners, such as Mrs. O. H. P. Belmont and Miss Anne Morgan, had visited the Lower East Side to dispense largess. But young Stokes had chosen to work and *live* there. This was taken as an indication of his unusual dedication and sincerity — that his interest in the betterment of the poor was not that of a dilettante, even though he continued to keep a well-shod toe in the doorway of New York's uptown society.

In the weeks that followed the *Times*'s astonished front-page announcement of the engagement, Rose Pastor and Graham Stokes were trailed by reporters and photographers from scores of American newspapers and magazines. The vast social, economic, and religious gulf that yawned between the pair was the subject of much interest and comment. Their every move was chronicled, and every detail of their lives, past and present, that could be uncovered was reported on. The Cinderella aspect of the story was dwelt on at length, and soon the Stokes-Pastor romance was being treated as though it were the greatest love story of the new century. Avid readers were told what the couple wore, where they dined, what they ate. They were besieged with requests for interviews. One of the few granted by the heroine of the tale was to a reporter from *Harper's Bazaar* (or *Bazar*, as it was spelled then), which was then, as now, one of the bellwethers of fashion for the American upper crust.

"She might have been the model for Rosetti's Beatrice," wrote the *Bazar*, "or for the quiet and dreamy maidens in a Burne-Jones drawing." Upon seeing her, the *Bazar* reporter wrote, "there grew into my consciousness, as one gains clear sight after darkness, the certainty of her essential womanliness; her eye was gentle, her movement graceful, her manner restful; she had poise, that inevitable accompaniment of character." The *Bazar*, however, was not too awed to forget to remind its readers of the essential incongruity of the situation, and that "the groom [was] a Yale graduate, a clubman, a banker, a member of one of the oldest and most exclusive American families, heir to fortunes multiplied at will . . . and the bride, an East Side Russian Jewess of humble origin, who has spent years in a cigar-factory. It was hard to imagine Hymen's torch kindled at the altar of more dissimilar lives."

The pair were asked all the most obvious questions. Hadn't Mr. Stokes's old and most exclusive parents disapproved of the match? Graham Stokes issued a manly statement to the *Times:* "I wish the Times would correct two serious errors in the published accounts of my engagement. The first is that there is serious opposition on the part of my family. That is entirely false. There is nothing but the utmost cordiality and delight. The second error is that there is a difference in religious belief between Miss Pastor and myself. She is a Jewess, as the Apostles were Jews — a Christian by faith." As proof of family solidarity behind the union, Graham Stokes announced that his clergyman brother would perform the marriage ceremony in an Episcopal service.

Rose Pastor also adopted the Jews-and-Christians-are-the-same argument, saying that she believed Judaism to be an "inspired religion," and so did her fiancé. However, she added, both of them believed that, added to the tenets of Judaism, were "many additional truths" of Christianity. She pointed out that both Moses and Paul were Jews, and that Jesus "came not to destroy the law of the prophets but to fulfill." After all, weren't both the Old and New Testaments bound between the same hard covers? Both she and Mr. Stokes, she said, "accepted the teachings of Jesus unqualifiedly, regarding Him as a divine teacher and guide." *Harper's Bazar* also tried to sort out this tricky matter, saying, "The only difference between them is a matter of ancestry. Her ancestors were of the Jewish race, his were not. It is a question of race and not religion. [She] is a Christian woman, and has all the impulses, beliefs, strength, and sweetness which characterize the ideal Christian character."

These theological rationalizations might satisfy *Harper's Bazar* and its largely Christian readership, but they sat not at all well among members of the Old World Orthodox-Jewish community in which Miss Pastor had been raised, who greeted her statements with outrage and dismay. She could not, her Lower East Side countrymen insisted, have it both ways. A Jew was a Jew. A Christian was a Christian. And though the word *conversion* had been carefully avoided in describing Miss Pastor's religious high-wire balancing act, it was pointed out that Episcopalian marriages were not performed unless both parties had been baptized. In other words, Rose Pastor was converting to Christianity, and trying to hide the fact behind a smoke screen of obfuscation and Judeo-Christian double-talk.

Others pointed out that if there had been a good Jewish father in the picture, such goings-on would not have been tolerated. No one, meanwhile, had asked Rose Pastor's mother how she felt about the matter. Perhaps this was because Anna Pastor's limited English would have made her a difficult interviewee. Or perhaps the poor woman was too overwhelmed by what was happening to her family to think coherently about it. In any case, for a readership more titillated by the ways of the rich than those of the poor, the press was much more interested in what the Stokes family thought about the unusual alliance. But if any of them had misgivings, they kept very stiff upper-class upper lips and refused to show it.

Of Rose Pastor's social zeal, the *New York Times* commented, "As she talks on the uplifting of the poor, her face lights up." At the same time, one of her friends — unidentified — was quoted describing her as "very interesting, very sincere, but somewhat of a dreamer."

The Jewish press, however, remained cynical and unconvinced of her sincerity. The *Tageblatt*'s rival, the *Daily Forward,* was always looking for ways to embarrass the *Tageblatt* or one of its staff, and the *Forward* was quick to pick up one juicy bit. Not many months before the engagement was announced, the *Tageblatt* had run an editorial that had inveighed heavily against intermarriage between Christians and Jews. The editorial had taken to task Israel Zangwill, the British writer, for marrying a Christian woman. And who had been the author of that polemic? Why, none other than Miss Rose Pastor herself! But now, when it suited her, Miss Pastor endorsed interfaith marriages.

Miss Pastor, meanwhile, continued to insist that the couple's common interest in the poor overrode all their differences, and that the Stokes family's money had not been a consideration in her decision. Of her own self-education, she said, "It was a hard struggle. I read much, and I only read books that I thought would be useful to me, and then I began to write. My efforts to obtain an education were all due to a desire to be of service, not because I had any desire to rise above the station I then occupied in life."

As the early summer progressed, the news and magazine stories about the romantic pair continued, and both complained that they could not leave their homes or offices without running a gauntlet of photographers and reporters. In response to repeated questions about what she and Mr. Stokes expected to accomplish on the Lower East Side, Rose replied, "If our life and our united deeds do not speak for us, I feel we should be silent." What deeds, the *Daily Forward* wanted to know? Everyone knew that New York's Christian community wanted to Christianize the newly arrived Jewish immigrants. So, secretly, did the uptown Jewish merchant-banker class — those of Julia Richman's ilk — many of whom had already converted.

These stories of threatened conversions frightened the Lower East Side Jews. Down through the centuries had come horror stories, such as the account of how King Manuel of Portugal, in order to solve the Jewish "problem," had all the Jewish children in his realm kidnapped on the first day of Passover in 1497, taken to churches, and forcibly baptized. Then, their parents were given the choice of baptism or exile. Conversion-scare stories also sold papers, and the *Tageblatt* countered with a report of a Jewish man who had been accosted on a New York street by a Christian, and forced to eat oysters. The man became violently ill and died. Later, the *Tageblatt* admitted that the story was a fiction.

While all this was going on, a date for the "wedding of the century" was set. It would take place on July 18, 1905, the bride's twenty-sixth birthday, at the Point, another summer home of the bridegroom's parents, in Noroton, Connecticut, overlooking Long Island Sound. (The Stokeses, it seemed, spent July at the shore, and August in the mountains.) To minimize the publicity, only the immediate families and a few close friends were invited. Of course this attempt at privacy only whetted the press's appetite, and on the day of the wedding there was more publicity than ever. Some reports had it that the bride looked radiant, others that she looked sad and worried and drawn. One said that Mrs. Anson Phelps Stokes, Sr., heaved a great, mournful sigh when her son uttered the words "I do." But the fact was that the Point was so thoroughly cordoned off by police that none of the press was able to see either the bride or the groom, or witness any part of the ceremony. Nor would the family go so far as to reveal what the bride wore.

Two days later, Mr. and Mrs. James Graham Phelps Stokes boarded the White Star liner *Cedric* for a three months' honeymoon in Europe. Though they had come aboard early, in order to avoid detection, they were recognized by a photographer as they strolled on the deck. The photographer's head and shoulders were covered with a black cloth, and to foil him, Graham Stokes blocked his lens with a corner of his coat. Unable to see what was the matter with his camera, the photographer darted back and forth underneath his drapery. Finally, Stokes tapped the man on the shoulder and politely asked him not to take any pictures.

The newlyweds did, however, grant a shipboard interview to a *New York Times* reporter in their stateroom. They would visit England, France, Switzerland, Hungary, and southern Italy, they announced. From Budapest, they would also journey northward to the little Polish *shtetl* where Rose Pastor Stokes had been born

Otherwise, said Mr. Stokes, "we have no definite plans. We avoided
making any. Both of us are tired, and we are looking for a rest.
When we reach London, and we are going there first, we will be
met by my mother's automobile and our first run will be through
Scotland. All our travel will be by automobile. We have had too
much publicity. A great deal has been said about what my wife
and I propose to do in uplifting the fallen. The fact that the people
of the East Side are as self-respecting as we are seems to have
been overlooked. What we want to do now is just to go away quietly
and have a restful time." (In its headline on the Stokes departure
story, the *Times* commented somewhat tartly, "Not So Bent on
Uplifting," seemingly missing the point of Mr. Stokes's statement.)

The *Times* reported that Mrs. Stokes wore a white shirtwaist, a
gray walking skirt, and a wide-brimmed straw hat with a large
black ostrich feather. Mr. Stokes wore a light suit, a "negligee
shirt," white canvas shoes, and a straw hat. It was also noted that
the Stokes stateroom on the *Cedric*'s promenade deck was "comfortable but not overluxurious," though certainly it was more luxurious than the steerage quarters in which the bride had first sailed
to America.

There were one or two more ominous notes. The only people to
arrive at the pier to see the Stokeses off were two young girls with
whom Rose Stokes had worked. No members of either of their
families had come to wish them bon voyage, and the curious
absence of any flowers, candy, fruit baskets, wine, or other of-
ferings that might have been expected in a honeymoon stateroom
drew comment.

The newlyweds were well out to sea when the first blistering
attack upon them appeared. On July 20, 1905, an editorial prepared by the *Hebrew Standard*, and headlined "The Climax of
Apostacy" (*sic*), which the paper would publish the following day,
was distributed in advance to other American newspapers. The
article took it for granted that Rose Pastor's Christian marriage
implied the bride's denunciation — as well as renunciation — of
her inherited faith, and said, among other things:

The christological influence the young millionaire and his newly Chris-
ianized bride will exert over the children with whom they will come

into contact will be distinctly harmful. They are Jewish children, and
any teaching which will create a gulf between them and their parents
must certainly be regarded with suspicion.

Notwithstanding the statement that all the work the gentleman in
question will do on the east side will be of non-sectarian character, we
find that he is a Director of the Federation of Churches, which is doing
distinctly Christian work on the east side. Consequently we may safely
presume that the work both he and his newly-made wife will be engaged
in among Jewish children will be of a non-Jewish character, and to this
we strenuously object.

That this Christian gentleman and Jewish girl should have married is
their own business, that the lady should have adopted another religion
is a matter for her own conscience, but the announcement that they are
to work on the east side among the Jewish children is certainly the
business of the community. We may say quite frankly and openly that
they would have shown far better taste had the young couple quite frankly
and openly said that they would leave the east side alone and continue
their uplifting work among other sections of the population in greater
need of it than the Jewish community.

Interestingly, the *Hebrew Standard* had also editorialized that
the uptown German Jews were "closer to the Christian sentiment"
around them, and had nothing in common with the "Orientalism"
of the East Side's "miserable darkened Hebrews." Was the *Standard* addressing itself to a "white" Jewish readership? Or was this
just another indication of the kind of Jewish schizophrenia that
seemed to be sweeping the country? In any case, it was another
dark omen that the Cinderella Story, and the Romance of the
Century, might in the end turn out to be something else again.

"Fame!" Rose Pastor had written in one of her verses for the
Tageblatt:

> Fame!
> What's in the name
> To make men hurry and scurry so;
> To make them hanker and worry so;
> Rushing forever past friend and foe
> Rushing so madly through maddening crowd,
> Heedless of human hearts crying aloud;
> Hearts that are hungry — and still theirs are proud!

Passing the true for profitless gain;
Giving up all for the naught of a name —
  For fame!

But now, of course, Rose Pastor Stokes herself was famous, and her marriage — giving up her Jewishness for the naught of a name — had provided a whole generation of East Side Jewish girls with a romantic idyll of how, with a simple "I do," it was possible to leap out of grinding poverty into success and luxury. Upon returning to New York from their summer-long honeymoon in Europe, Rose and Graham Phelps Stokes set themselves up in a top-floor apartment in a building on the corner of Grand and Norfolk streets on the Lower East Side, just nine blocks east of the Bowery. They had chosen this far from fashionable address, Rose explained to an interviewer from *Harper's Bazar*, for a variety of reasons. For one thing, it was close to the University Settlement, where both planned to continue to work. For another, it was hard by the teeming Eastern European Jewish ghetto, and the poor whom they intended to uplift. To her interviewer, Rose dismissed the apartment as "tiny," though it had a comfortable quota of six rooms — a library, a dining room, a sitting room, a large and well-equipped kitchen, and two bedrooms — and a bath. The building had an elevator, run by "a German woman in a blue calico gown." Rose pointed out that the apartment rented for "only" thirty-eight dollars a month. But the interviewer noted that, though Rose Stokes described her decor as "simple," there were "finely bound books" on the bookshelves of the library, a piano in the sitting room, "handsome vases" filled with fresh flowers on the tables, some bronze pieces, Oriental rugs on the floors, and Millet etchings on the walls. Mrs. Stokes explained that she had "literally" no servants, "the only help being the janitress, who is called in on sweeping-days."

The Stokes apartment, and its location, also had a symbolic significance, Rose explained. With it, she hoped to demonstrate how, with a few simple touches, even the most cramped dwelling place in the ghetto could be made pleasant and attractive. Rose explained how, with little economies, it was possible to live on a modest budget. For example, she used very little meat, substituting "eggs cooked in innumerable ways." She used lots of uncooked

vegetables, plenty of milk, good bread and butter and fruit, but
neither coffee nor tea. Another economy was to eliminate table
linen. Instead of napery — "quite an item in the household expenses" — she used "pretty Japanese napkins" of white paper,
which could be bought at twenty cents the hundred, disposed of
after each meal, and "which entirely eliminate laundry work." She
went on to say that she hoped her apartment would have a second
symbolic function: that it would "arouse public interest, and force
more general recognition of the unfair condition of life and labor
that weighs down our neighbors." This was why she was taking a
reporter from *Harper's Bazar*, and a photographer, on a tour of the
place.

But which was it to be? An example of how the poor could get
by with substituting eggs for meat, using paper napkins instead
of linen, milk instead of coffee or tea, and thus be able to afford
Oriental rugs and fresh flowers? Or a demonstration of the fact
that the rich lived better than the poor — a fact that few of the
poor had not grasped? Rose Pastor Stokes seemed not to have
realized that she could not have it both ways; that her elevator
building, her janitress, her six rooms with private bath, her steam
heat and electricity were amenities that would have seemed in-
comprehensible to the average tenement dweller down the street
where a family of five lived in a single windowless cell, a single
fetid toilet served an entire building, the family bathtub was the
kitchen sink where only cold water ran, and a fire escape in good
weather provided the luxury of a second room. She seemed not to
realize that, for a family bringing in only six or seven dollars a
week, an apartment costing "only" thirty-eight dollars a month
would have been out of the question. This appeared to be at the
heart of Rose's problem. Now that she was indeed famous, she
seemed not quite to know what to do with her fame.

As the year 1905 drew to a close, meanwhile, there was a certain
amount of speculation within the upper reaches of New York society as to whether the new Mrs. James Graham Phelps Stokes
would be listed in the next edition of the *Social Register*. Or
whether, for having married a Jewess, Mr. Stokes would be dropped
from the little list of who mattered in New York's white, Anglo-
Saxon, Protestant upper crust.

These questions were duly answered when the 1906 issue of

the *Register* made its annual autumn appearance. Both newlyweds were listed, along with their prestigious clubs, at the unlikely address of 47 Norfolk Street, close to what was now their joint settlement-house work — though they also indicated a more pre-possessing summer address: a place called Caritas Island, off the Connecticut shore near Stamford. Thus, Rose Pastor earned another distinction of sorts. She had become the first person of known Jewish descent to be included in New York's official "stud book," unless one counted August Belmont, who "passed."

That Rose would have been included in the *Social Register* was interesting for several reasons. For one thing, she had obviously gone to the trouble of filling out the necessary little form, which asked listees to supply their "Christian name." For another, it indicated to some degree her endorsement of the values represented in America's first attempt to catalogue and codify its upper class (*Who's Who in America* would not appear until several years later), a class into which she had so recently and magically been elevated. Was there any ambivalence, any feeling of duplicity here? Apparently not, because for the next two decades Rose and Graham Stokes's names would appear in Capitalism's official gazetteer.

Many young Jews had left Russia with their souls afire with socialism, yearning for the day when the hated czars would be deposed and leadership would be assumed by the working classes. Many still carried with them their keys to *das alte Heim* — the old home — even though they had seen with their own eyes the old home put to the torch, and knew that the old village had been scorched from the face of the earth and erased from the map. Some even dreamed of going back to Russia someday, when a new order had finally been established.

But the ferocious pogrom of 1903 in the city of Kishinev, in southern Russia — in which forty-nine people were murdered and more than five hundred maimed and mutilated — had been a grim reminder that life in the old home continued to be a perilous game of Russian roulette. In the wake of Kishinev, there was also apprehension in New York that another great wave of emigration to America would be set off, further flooding the already crowded labor market — which was exactly what happened. American Jews were torn between compassion for their beleaguered countrymen

and fears that their gains in the New World would be placed in
new jeopardy. Finally, when the attempted Russian revolution of
1905 failed dismally, most Jewish immigrants resigned themselves
to the idea that America would be their home for the rest of their
lives, and probably the rest of their children's lives as well. The
question then became: could they work within the existing system,
or did the system itself have to be changed?

There was evidence to show that the American system worked.
The former tinker now had his own scrap-metal business. The
itinerant cobbler now had his own shoe-repair shop with his name
in gold letters on the door, and could afford a vacation in the
Catskills. The tailor now had his own dressmaking business, and
had bought his family a piano. Rose Pastor had, in the Jewish
expression, "made all her money in one day," and was now listed
in the ranks of New York's society ladies. But she didn't behave
like one. She was one who claimed the system ought to be changed.

Not long after her return from her grand tour of Europe, Rose
Pastor Stokes announced that she had become a socialist. Her
mission, she revealed, would not be to Christianize East Side
children. Instead, it would be to free the workers of the world from
the shackles of "the bosses." From an improvised platform in Union
Square, she spoke of the thousands of other immigrants who were
still locked within the confines of the ghetto, who worked long
hours at low wages, who did piecework at home by gaslight until
they went blind, who offered up their young lives at the golden
altar of capitalism, while their employers grew fat and rich. Rose
Pastor, it seemed, had found a new calling, as a rabble-rouser.

By 1910, while still living like a capitalist on Norfolk Street,
Rose had announced that *both* she and her husband were members
of the Socialist party. In any strike or demonstration, Rose could
be found marching, chanting, making fiery speeches. Though she
and her husband often dined out in restaurants, she joined the
Hotel and Restaurant Workers' strike, protesting low wages and
poor working conditions. In one way or another, she kept herself
in the public eye, choosing, for the most part, unpopular causes.
In 1914, Margaret Higgins Sanger introduced the phrase "birth
control," and had to flee to England to escape federal prosecution
for publishing and mailing "Family Limitation," a brochure that
dealt with contraception. Rose Stokes immediately took up the

cause of birth control, and became one of the leaders of the American movement. With Helena Frank, she translated Morris Rosenfeld's "Songs of Labor" and other poems from the Yiddish. She turned her hand to pencil drawings, all of them depicting the harsh injustices inflicted upon workers by the American capitalists. With a young Russian-Jewish playwright named Elmer Reizenstein (later Elmer Rice), she became involved in the Proletarian Theatre movement, and wrote a never-produced play, *The Woman Who Wouldn't*, about a charismatic female labor leader who campaigns tirelessly against the "bosses," in which character she doubtless saw traces of herself. "For the future — not the distant future — belongs to us," she wrote to her friend Eugene V. Debs, an unsuccessful Socialist candidate for President in 1912. It began to seem as though Rose Stokes's chief claim to fame would be as a backer of lost, or losing, causes.

Still, the Jewish socialist movement was slow to get under way in the United States. For one thing, who had the energy left over for politics at the end of a working day? Where was the time to attend speeches and rallies, and mount demonstrations? What was the point in organizing strikes, when inexpensive thugs could be hired to break them up, and scab labor was so cheap? The answers to all these questions were negative, and adding to the gloomy outlook was a kind of traditional Jewish cynicism and pessimism: after all, for centuries — and not just in disenfranchised Russia — the Jews had been struggling for some kind of political recognition, but without success. Why should their chances be any better in America? True, there were hundreds of thousands of Jews in New York City, but they were still in the minority. Even if every Jew in the United States proclaimed himself a socialist tomorrow — a distinct unlikelihood — the Jewish socialists would still be enormously outweighed by the rest of the population. A *worldwide* socialist movement might prevail someday, but never a Jewish one.

Still, a few Jewish socialist leaders emerged during the early years of the century — Meyer London, Morris Hillquit. In 1900, the International Ladies Garment Workers Union had been organized under Joseph Barondess, and a few scattered strikes for higher wages and better working conditions had been staged in the Jewish-owned "needle trades," but without much in the way of results. Workers — most of them women — in the garment industry still labored for three or four dollars a week, and strikes were quickly broken up by hired Irish, Italian — and some Jewish — thugs who charged the picket lines and frightened the women.

Then, in 1909, there began to be talk of a "general strike" in Local 25 of the ILGWU, which was the shirtwaist makers' union. Thanks to Charles Dana Gibson, it seemed as though every American woman wanted a whole wardrobe of shirtwaists, and by 1909 New York's production of shirtwaists had reached fifty million dollars annually. At the same time, the young women who pieced the goods together and fitted them with ruffles, bows, and trimmings were required to pay for their own needles, thread, and fabrics, while for every ten-dollar shirtwaist a seamstress turned out, she was paid two dollars. The girls had to rent the chairs they sat in, and had their pay docked if they were more than five minutes late to work. The general strike was an ambitious idea, considering the fact that when it was proposed, Local 25 could boast of only about a hundred members, and had a little less than four dollars in its treasury.

Still, a meeting to discuss the matter was called for November 22 at Cooper Union. Apparently the timing was right, for thousands turned out — not only the shirtwaist makers, but all sorts of rank and file from the men's and women's clothing, fur, hat, glove, shoe, and trimmings industries. Rose Pastor Stokes was there in her blazing coif of red hair, shouting, "Arise! Unite! Down with the bosses!" The labor leader Samuel Gompers was the keynote speaker, and he was followed by others. But as the evening wore on, and speaker followed speaker, a mood of torpor and lethargy began to pervade the audience. Jewish pessimism was setting in again; like so many other rallies, this one appeared to be coming to naught, and between rounds of halfhearted applause a few people began sneaking out to head home for the night. Then all at once a teenage girl named Clara Lemlich sprang to her feet and raced to the stage. Speaking in Yiddish, she cried out, "I am a working girl, one of those striking against intolerable conditions. I am tired of listening to speakers who talk in generalities. What we are here for is to decide whether or not to strike. I offer a resolution that a general strike be declared — now!" To a hushed audience, she swore, "If I turn traitor to the cause I now pledge, may this hand wither from the arm I now raise."

This spunky performance seemed to galvanize the audience. Suddenly it was on its feet, stamping, shouting, cheering, waving fists. Then it was out into the street with more shouting, cheering, hand-clapping, and singing of songs. The next morning, the strike was on.

Something about the idea of a major strike being led by a seventeen-year-old girl caught the fancy of all New Yorkers. Even Rose Stokes had been upstaged, and no work stoppage in the city had ever received so much publicity. Well publicized, too, were the working conditions in the shirtwaist factories that the girls were protesting. Most shops closed, and when scabs were sent in, workers from other unions joined the Jewish girls to help fight them off. Hundreds of strikers were arrested, but rich and social people from uptown — including the regulars, Alva Belmont and Anne Morgan — provided money for their bail. Checks poured in from all over the country to help the strikers, and the students of Wellesley College in Massachusetts sent a check for one thousand dollars to the strike fund. Week after week the strike went on, and every day there was a new report in the newspapers, usually dealing with the young girls' stamina and bravery in the face of their merciless employers. In the *New York Sun*, McAlister Coleman wrote:

The girls, headed by teen-age Clara Lemlich, described by union organizers as a "pint of trouble for the bosses," began singing Italian and Russian working-class songs as they paced in twos in front of the factory door. Of a sudden, around the corner came a dozen tough-looking customers, for whom the union label "gorillas" seemed well-chosen.

"Stand fast, girls," called Clara, and then the thugs rushed the line, knocking Clara to her knees, striking at the pickets, opening the way for a group of frightened scabs to slip through the broken line. Fancy ladies from the Allen Street red-light district climbed out of cabs to cheer on the gorillas. There was a confused melee of scratching, screaming girls and fist-swinging men and then a patrol wagon arrived. The thugs ran off as the cops pushed Clara and two other badly beaten girls into the wagon.

I followed the rest of the retreating pickets to the union hall, a few blocks away. There a relief station had been set up where one bottle of milk and a loaf of bread were given to strikers with small children in their families. There, for the first time in my comfortably sheltered, upper West Side life, I saw real hunger on the faces of my fellow Americans in the richest city in the world.

Official New York took a stand of pious disapproval of the shirtwaist-makers' strike, and denounced the act of striking itself as un-American, immoral, and even unholy. In sentencing a striker, one city magistrate declared, "You are on strike against God and Nature, whose firm law is that man shall earn his bread in the sweat of his brow." But public sympathy — and that of the press — prevailed. Bail costs for the strikers ran as high as twenty-five hundred dollars a day, but somehow they were met, and the strike continued until February of the following year — nearly three full months.

When it was finally settled, though, it was hard to tell whether there had been a victory or not. A number of improvements in working conditions were promised by the shirtwaist companies, but the strikers' principal demand — that the ILGWU be recognized — was denied. In the course of the strike, however, membership in the union had swelled from a hundred to more than ten thousand. From that point onward, the ILGWU would have to be reckoned with as a force in the garment trade.

Throughout the rest of 1910, and into the winter months of 1911, strike seemed to follow strike among the Jewish trade unions — not only those within the garment industry but also those of the bakers', printers', and painters' unions. On March 25, 1911, the Triangle Shirtwaist Company fire provided the union movement with powerful new impetus.

If none of the strikes of this period had quite the impact and drama and appeal of the one led by Clara Lemlich, they had another unexpected side effect — a kind of collective search of the Jewish conscience. Many of the owners of the struck businesses were themselves Jewish, and were aware, painfully, that the long series of strikes was only furthering the Christian notion of Jewish contentiousness — that one reason why Jews had trouble assimilating into American life was that they could not even get along with one another. Owners of Jewish businesses were also increasingly sensitive to accusations of Jewish avarice and Jewish acquisitiveness — the "pound of flesh" syndrome — and to an impression that was being created that Jews exploited their own kind. Was this sort of thing, as they said, good for the Jews? Was this the way Jews wanted to present themselves to the rest of the community — as a breed of hagglers, backbiters, complainers, bullies? A Jewish labor writer, Will Herberg, tried to deflect this sort of criticism when he wrote in the *American Jewish Year Book* that Jewish employers and employees shared "a common social and cultural background," and within it "an age-old tradition of arbitration, of settling their often bitter disputes within the Jewish community. . . . They shared too, as a heritage of centuries of self-enclosed minority existence, a marked concern for the *reputation of the Jewish community with the outside world* [italics added]."

True enough. Still, feelings of Jewish guilt cannot be entirely credited for the fact that the multitude of Jewish-on-Jewish strikes were eventually settled, and that the settlements generally, little by little, left the workers better off. But ethnic guilt did make the settlements more painful and personal.

Rose Stokes, meanwhile, had become an increasingly vocal spokeswoman for the Jewish radical Left. She took eagerly to the lecture platform, and traveled about the country expounding her doctrine of socialism, while her more publicity-shy husband stayed behind in New York with his work at the University Settlement. Now Rose would be in Chicago, now Pittsburgh, now Saint Louis, and wherever she went she created headlines. Her press, now, was almost always openly hostile, which provided Rose with another outlet for her bewildering energy — writing letters of clarification and denial to editors of newspapers, a practice that, as we shall see, would soon get her into deep trouble. If Rose had a fault it was that she was passionately sincere — well-meaning, theatrical, and usually in over her head.

Audiences in goodly numbers usually turned out to hear what Rose Stokes had to say. After all, by virtue of her marriage, the Jewish Cinderella had become something of a national celebrity, and many people were simply curious to have a look at her. But the trouble was that Rose had a slight credibility problem. It was hard to take her all that seriously. Here she was, after all, with a rich husband — a doctor to boot, who could practice medicine if he chose, but didn't because he didn't have to work — who owned a railroad, who'd provided her with an apartment in the city and a house in the country on Long Island Sound. And she was railing against intolerable working conditions and the venality of bosses. The feeling was: yes, there were problems, and yes, the problems were serious ones, but they were hardly Rose's problems anymore. What was this privileged lady, this creature of capitalism, *kvetching* about?

One woman who was not impressed by Rose's oratory was Miss Julia Richman, who, when she referred to Rose at all, called her "That Woman," or "That Crazy Russian." After all, Rose was trying to stir up dissent against the very form of government that Julia Richman was trying to get her students to embrace. Still, by 1912, Miss Richman had begun to feel that much of her life's mission had been accomplished. The Great Pushcart Era of the Lower East Side was coming to an end, for one thing. Though this was the result of immigrants' moving steadily into the middle class, Miss Richman tended to believe that she deserved personal credit for this development. Feeling that hers was a job well done, she announced her retirement that year "to make room for a younger woman."

She was fifty-six years old, but foresaw many years of public service and general usefulness ahead of her in other fields. She planned, for example, to continue lecturing and writing articles. In 1908, her book *Good Citizenship* — a civics textbook designed for fourth-graders in an urban setting — had been published by the American Book Company. It dealt primarily with how city fire, police, and sanitation departments did their jobs, and its moral tone was high. She reiterated her familiar themes. On the importance of keeping fire escapes clear, she wrote: "[The fire]* taught the folly and the awful danger of blocking up fire escapes so that they are impassable when needed most." Turn-of-the-century sweatshops had often been unfairly blamed for periodic epidemics of contagious diseases, and Miss Richman echoed the quaint medical theories of the day:

---

*Miss Richman's fire was fictional. Three years after they were written, the Triangle fire made her words seem prophetic.

The desire to save money often leads men to break the law. . . . Rather than pay more rent for extra space in which to place his workmen, the manufacturer of clothing, for example, gives out a portion of his work to be done elsewhere. . . . Most of the workers are poor foreigners. . . . A single case of [a] disease among the workers in a sweat shop, will throw off enough germs to infect all the other workmen. . . . The contagion does not end here, unfortunately. Not only may each man who becomes ill carry the disease into his own home, but the germs in the workroom may fall upon the clothing made there, and they are carried with it into the stores where it is sold, and from there into the homes of the people who buy it.

And of course the pushcarts did not escape her ire:

Worse even than the slovenly housekeepers are the men who sell fish and vegetables from wagons or push carts and drop the refuse from their stock upon the pavements. Yet they are the very ones who should be most careful to keep the streets clean, since they do business in them, free of charge, to save paying rent as others must do for a store. . . . Scattering refuse in the street is a sign of bad breeding; it is also forbidden by law.

In 1912, with Ernest H. Lehman, she was working on another book, about methods of teaching Jewish ethics, which the Jewish Chautauqua Society of Philadelphia planned to publish. Among her other projected plans was the establishment of a correspondence course for teachers in religious schools. Her memoirs, to be titled *Forty Years in the New York Public Schools*, had been promised to the Macmillan Company.

In June, Miss Richman sailed for Europe with a group of friends, intending a summer holiday. At the outset of the trip, with her usually splendid constitution, she felt fine. But during the crossing she felt increasingly ill. Seasickness was blamed, but when she landed at Cherbourg her condition was so poor that she was rushed by train to the American Hospital in Paris. There her condition was diagnosed as appendicitis, with "complications."

It was of these that she died a few days later.

4

AN OCCUPATION FOR GENTLEMEN

DESPITE the well-intentioned efforts of the do-gooders and re-formers, and a general improvement in the immigrants' eco-nomic status, there was still plenty of crime on the Lower East Side. It was almost inevitable in an area so densely packed with humanity. East Siders grew accustomed to hearing the periodic sounds of human screams rising from tenement streets and win-dows, and quickly learned to ignore them. The scream might mean a simple domestic argument, or it might mean that someone was being murdered, but in any case it was wisest not to become involved. If one did, and the police came, the innocent bystander was often hauled off to jail with the offender. Much of the crime was youthful hooliganism. Certain blocks were considered Irish territory, others were Italian, and still more were Jewish. None of the three groups got along with the others, but the Irish and Italian street gangs, being Catholic, tended to side together against the "Christ-killers." The Jewish youths rarely carried knives, but the Irish and Italians did, and taunts and insults between the gangs frequently led to fights, stabbings, killings, followed by vendettas of revenge.

In the summer months, each ethnic gang had staked out a particular strip of East River shoreline where the boys swam naked from the docks. These preserves, however, were always being invaded by bands of youths from enemy territory, and there were water fights and drownings. Jewish youths, instilled from the time of infancy with the idea that education was the best avenue out of the ghetto, were not often truants. But the Irish and Italians were

less scrupulous about school attendance, and the Jewish youth
forced to walk home from school through a hostile neighborhood
often found himself confronted with a knife-wielding band of Irish
boys demanding that he drop his trousers to show whether or not
he was circumcised. If he were not circumcised "enough," the
enemy gang would try to perform the operation for him. Doughtier
Jewish boys soon learned to give out as good as they got. If you
could put up a good fight, after all, you earned for yourself that
intangible asset, respect.

It had been discovered that there was money to be made out of
this touchy ethnic situation. For a few pennies a day, a beleaguered
Jewish boy found that he could purchase the "protection" of an
older or tougher Italian or Irishman. Or the tougher Jew might
hire out to protect a frailer coreligionist, and become, in effect,
his bodyguard. The protection notion quickly spread to involve
the business community as well, and the shopkeeper and café
owner learned that hiring a protector on a monthly basis was
practical insurance against having his premises looted or vandal-
ized. On this level, the protection business became quite lucrative,
and many Jewish entrepreneurs — as well as Italians — became
involved in it. No one seems to have given much thought to the
legality of the protection business — or racket, as some called it.
Paying protection was a nuisance, but a necessary one, part of the
overhead and the cost of doing business, and the price was simply
passed on to the consumer.

The Jewish press of the Lower East Side in the early 1900s
tended to overlook Jewish crime. The press was aware of it, of
course, but preferred to underplay it. It was an embarrassment,
and to make too much fuss about it might fan the embers of anti-
Semitism, that ominous presence that always hovered close by in
the Jewish consciousness. Meanwhile, Jewish parents worried lest
their children be attracted by the flamboyant and obviously expensive life-styles of some of the more successful Jewish criminals.

Hundreds of Jewish girls, unable or unwilling to work in the
garment-industry sweatshops, had turned to prostitution. One particularly poor area, not far from the old Third Avenue elevated,
was notorious for its "houses of iniquity," as pious Jews preferred
to call them. Pretty Jewish girls also openly walked the streets in
fancy dresses, servicing their customers from tiny rented rooms

or, for a lower fee, on stoops or while draped across garbage cans in back alleys. Percentages of their earnings were collected by Jewish pimps, also well dressed, a number of whom were said to have murdered girls who cheated them. Running gambling operations was by no means an exclusively Italian occupation. A number of Jews ran illicit gambling parlors in tenement basements or on rooftops. And along a certain section of Delancey Street the crap games were played in the open air on the sidewalk. Periodically, the police came through and broke them up, but within half an hour the games would be proceeding as enthusiastically as before the interruption.

In fact, when a Jew and an Italian could put aside their religious differences to become partners in a gambling venture, they frequently made an unbeatable combination. In other words, Jewish crime — and it is important to remember that it was often not thought of as crime, but as a business dedicated to fulfilling certain human needs — was just another way to get ahead in the New World. It was simply one of the high-risk, high-return investment businesses that the Eastern Europeans tended to prefer.

In a sense, the Eastern Europeans were all gamblers, inured for generations to the come-and-go, win-or-lose philosophy. Life in Russia had always been a gamble, with the whims of the czar the numbers on the wheel of fortune. And when at last Lady Luck ran out for the Jews, with the odds stacked impossibly high against them, there was emigration — another gamble. The risks and the dangers for the emigrant were incredibly high, but the rewards for the winners were even higher. This gambling nature was another thing the uptown German Jews found alien and unattractive — even though the Germans had taken the same gamble two or three generations earlier, and had become successful in fields that were essentially gambling operations: stockbrokerage and retailing. But the Eastern Europeans seemed, to the Germans, to be becoming successful in all sorts of endeavors that, according to most American business standards, were most "unbusinesslike." The tailors and seamstresses of the old country were going into the fashion business. What could be riskier or more unpredictable than the whims of fashion? Yet it was apparent that some East Side cloak-and-suiters were prospering. It made no sense. (What was overlooked was that the former Russian tailors had brought with them the concept of *sizing*, which was already revolutionizing the garment industry; before the Eastern Europeans, all men's or women's ready-to-wear was sold in one or two, or at the most three, sizes.) Talented songwriters, musicians, and performers, in the tradition of the Yiddish theater, were journeying to the Borscht Belt in hopes of establishing careers that would lead them to Broadway or Hollywood. (The Yiddish theater, outlawed in Russia, had simply gone underground; it flourished anew in New York.) Others were becoming theatrical agents and producers. But what could be riskier than show business? In Russia, where Jews could not own real estate and where banks could not be trusted, Jews had tended to invest in precious stones, gold, furs, and other portables, which could be hidden from the tax collector and packed up quickly when the time came to move. In America, these people gravitated toward the fur and jewelry businesses, either as retailers or as auctioneers. Again, these were high-risk endeavors, subject to wildly fluctuating commodity prices and the fickle whims of fashion; but for those who succeeded, the returns were also high.

And crime, of course, carried the highest risks of all. It was a business so unbusinesslike that it could not properly be called a business at all, and yet the Lower East Side would also produce some of the most successful and powerful gangsters in the world. One of these arrived at Ellis Island in April, 1911, as a ten-year-old boy named Meyer Suchowljansky.

The Suchowljanskys had come from the town of Grodno, in Russian Poland, where, at least until the time of the Alexandrine pogroms, the family had been reasonably prosperous, dealing in furs, spices, and rice. Though there was ice on the walls of their house in winter, and the streets of the town ran with mud in spring, the house was built of wood and had a wooden floor — signs of status. Then the pogroms had come. Meyer Suchowljansky's father emigrated to New York first. A few years later, he was able to send for his wife and son.

From Grodno, young Meyer Suchowljansky brought with him two vivid and violent memories. One was of a local rabbi who had been walking home one night across a field and stumbled on the body of a Christian girl who had been raped and bludgeoned to death with a stone. Unfortunately, the rabbi took the unwise course of running to tell the authorities what he had found. To his further misfortune, the authorities he notified were two Russian Orthodox priests. The priests, arriving at the site, immediately decided that the rabbi himself had committed the act, and that his purpose was to use the girl's blood in making Passover matzos.* The rabbi was arrested, taken to prison, and tortured for two years. For a time, he was kept in a dungeon beneath the church. Finally, in a public ceremony, his body was cut in quarters while he was still alive, and the quarters were hung on display on the walls of Grodno. Only after a number of weeks was the Jewish community given permission to cut him down and bury him.

The second memory was of a visit to Grodno by a young Jewish revolutionary who had held a meeting at Meyer's grandfather's house. Young Meyer remembered the revolutionary soldier's words: "Jews! Why do you just sit around like stupid sheep and allow them to come and kill you, steal your money, kill your sons and rape your daughters. Aren't you ashamed? You must stand up and fight. You are men like other men. I have been a soldier in the Turkish army. I was taught to fight. A Jew can fight. I will teach you how. We have no arms, but it doesn't matter. We can use sticks and stones. Even if you're going to die, at least do it with honor. Fight back! Stop being cowards. Stop lying down like stupid sheep. Don't be frightened. Hit them and they'll run. If you are going to die, then die fighting. Protect your beloved ones. Your womenfolk should be able to rely on you."

Fight back. This would become the principal watchword in Meyer Suchowljansky's life.

Physically, however, Suchowljansky was far from prepossessing. As a scrawny child of twelve, he looked three or four years younger than his age. But he had large, bright, intense eyes that flashed dangerously when he was angry, and he soon earned a reputation in his neighborhood as a boy who, even when he was outweighed and outnumbered, never ran away from a fight. When attacked by older bullies, little Meyer would fight back with his teeth and fingernails, as well as with his knees, elbows, feet, and fists. Even when he lost a fight, his performance was impressive, and it had

---

*The charges of Jewish ritual murder of children, and cannibalism, date back to pre-Christian times, along with the bizarre claim that human sacrifice is condoned by the Talmud. The canard has been repeated throughout the centuries, and in the fourteenth century even made its way into Chaucer's "Prioress's Tale": "O yong Hugh of Lincoln, slayn also/ With cursed Jewes, as it is notable/ For it is but a litel whyle ago,/ Preye eek for us."

to be admitted that the little fellow was no coward. For this, he earned no small amount of admiration and respect.

He was also a bright boy — particularly good at mathematics — and, though he remained a dutiful Jewish son, he also very quickly became wise to the ways of the East Side streets. One of his weekly chores was to carry his mother's freshly made *cholent* — the meat and vegetable pie traditionally served on the Jewish Sabbath — to a nearby bakery to be slow cooked (his mother's oven was too small). To pay the baker for this service, five cents was scrupulously set aside each week. Meyer's route on this Friday errand took him along Delancey Street, where the noisy sidewalk crap games took place, and he would watch with fascination as the excited players exhorted their dice to fall in the desired combinations, and listen to their whoops of delight when they won and gathered up their take. One day, when he was about twelve, Meyer decided to throw the baker's nickel into the game. He immediately lost it. He was then forced to return home with the uncooked pie and tell his mother that there would be no *cholent* for the Sabbath meal.

His mother's reaction was one of such utter desolation — she did not scold or punish him, but simply sat silently weeping — that Meyer that night made a solemn promise to himself. It was not, as his mother might have hoped, never to gamble again. Instead, he promised himself that the next time he gambled he would win.

For the next few weeks, standing at a little distance from the play, he studied the crap games. He soon noticed that some of the regular players were obviously shills, or come-ons. He also observed the tactics of the "mechanics," as they were called — men who could conceal as many as six dice in the palm of a hand, and by gently rubbing the indentations of the cubes with the tips of their fingers, could toss them in any combination they wanted. He noticed that whenever a greenhorn joined a game he was usually allowed to win — for a while. Then, when his excitement reached such a pitch that he tossed in his whole weekly paycheck, he lost. Circulating among the players, Meyer also became aware of the loan sharks, who offered loans to losing players — at who knew what elevated rates of interest — to encourage them to stay in the game. Finally, he realized that the men who acted as bankers in the street games were not the actual bankers at all. Certain well-dressed men, most of whom appeared to be Italian, were always found not far from the action in the street. These men never gambled. They might have been casual observers or passersby. But they watched the games very closely, and from time to time scribbled little notes on scraps of paper. These were the men who ran the games, who rented the sidewalk space, and periodically they approached the bankers and collected their lion's share of the take.

Having determined the proper moment to enter as well as to leave a game, Meyer ventured another *cholent* nickel, and won. He then wandered on to another game, waited for the right moment, and won again. Soon he would never have to worry about losing the money for his mother's *cholent* again, because he had a considerable wad of cash stuffed into a hole in his mattress. It was at that point, he would declare later, that he decided his life's career would be as a gambler, but as a gambler of a special sort. Never, he would caution friends, gamble with money that you cannot afford to lose, because, in the end, the gambler always loses. No winning streak can last forever. In gambling, the only one who consistently wins is the man who runs the gambling house, who owns the roulette wheels, the crap tables, the blackjack tables, and the slot machines. And the beauty of the gambling business is that, though the owner might extend a bit of judicious credit here and there, it is otherwise cash, all cash.

With this philosophy Meyer Suchowljansky, with his name abbreviated to Meyer Lansky, would go on to become the guiding genius of Las Vegas, to become the king of casino gambling in Havana and, later, the Bahamas, and to reach the point where he would be one of the richest men in America and regarded as the unquestioned financial linchpin of the mob.

The young Shmuel Gelbfisz had found that in America his Polish name was an unpronounceable mouthful, and so it was first modified to Samuel Goldfish. But under whatever name he used he was at heart a gambler; in later years an entire file cabinet in his office would bear the label GAMBLING and be filled with the records of his wins and losses, and scribbled IOUs for huge sums from such Hollywood tycoons as Louis B. Mayer, Irving Thalberg, David

Selznick, and Harry Cohn. In the beginning, however, he was just a young man on the make, looking for a chance to grab the brass ring from the merry-go-round whenever it might appear.

His first job in New York was as a telegraph delivery boy, and his first address was a rooming house in the Bronx. In the evenings he attended public night-school classes to learn English, and supplemented these lessons by reading old newspapers he fished out of trash cans. His scholarship was desultory, and his mastery of the language was imperfect, at best. But he had not been delivering telegrams long before, in one of his secondhand newspapers, he ran across an ad for a job as a glove cutter in upstate Gloversville, New York, then the glove-making capital of the country. He decided to journey there.

Gloversville — originally called Stump City — was a drab little factory town dominated by mills and tanneries that turned out silk and leather gloves and mittens. But the glove and other subsidiary industries had made a number of local families reasonably rich. And, as he had been from his park bench outside London's Carlton House, Sam Goldfish was awed by the visible trappings of wealth and power. Gloversville's premier hotel was the Kingsborough, and in his off-work hours, Goldfish spent much time outside the hotel's gilt-and-glass doors, watching the well-dressed guests pass in and out of the ornate lobby and chandelier-hung dining room.

But the glove-cutting job itself turned out to be mechanical and boring, and Sam decided that the real excitement — and money — in the glove business was in selling. He persuaded his employer to lend him, in return for a cash deposit, a batch of gloves, and set off as a traveling salesman, given as his territory the Hudson River Valley between New York and Albany. In this role, he quickly discovered his true talent — as a master of ballyhoo. Spreading open his sample case, gesticulating wildly with his hands — a lifelong mannerism — he would wax rhapsodic over the virtues of his gloves, while moaning and clapping his hand to his forehead over the folly of retailers whose orders he deemed too small. Nor was he averse to a bit of bribery. For placing larger orders, buyers got not only bigger discounts but also little gifts of cash.

Within a year, Sam Goldfish was his company's top salesman, and was earning ten thousand dollars in annual commissions, a princely income in turn-of-the-century dollars. Still, on his trips back to Gloversville to place his orders, he somehow felt himself "not good enough" to pass the inspection of the haughty doorman and headwaiter of the Kingsborough Hotel. Like many immigrants, Sam distrusted banks. A man whom he had befriended in New York, who happened to be the stationmaster at Grand Central Station, handled his money for him, and acted as his banker, paying him a little interest on his funds. This was convenient because, on his selling travels, Sam Goldfish was always passing through Grand Central. It was also habit-forming, and later on he would set the style for other movie moguls who, like royalty, never carried cash.

Sam Goldfish's entry into show business was quite accidental. In 1912, when he was admitting to being thirty but may actually have been thirty-three,* he met a young Russian-Jewish girl named Blanche Lasky, who called herself an actress and had been playing at one of the little Catskill resort hotels that lay along Sam's selling route. Blanche Lasky was half of a moderately successful vaude-ville musical team with her brother Jesse. Jesse Lasky played the violin and Blanche played the piano. They also sang and danced, and Jesse Lasky had a tap-dance routine that he performed while warbling on a cornet. The Laskys' was an up-and-down life of one-night stands, but the glove salesman was immediately stagestruck. He married Blanche Lasky later that year, and moved into the apartment that she, her brother, and mother shared in Brooklyn.

One Sunday afternoon not long afterward, Sam and his new wife and brother-in-law went to see a film at a movie house on New York's Thirty-fourth Street. It was a first for Sam Goldfish. One of the shorts on the program happened to include a pillow-fight sequence featuring a young actress named Mary Pickford. Sam Goldfish found himself captivated by Miss Pickford's image on the screen, and, simultaneously, by the notion of making his own motion pictures. It was obvious that audiences were delighted with

---

*More than personal vanity may have accounted for the uncertainty about Sam's real age, and there may have been a more poignant explanation. In Russia, Jewish parents often falsified the ages of their male children, in order to postpone for as long as possible the age of forced conscription into the czarist army. In one community near Kiev, the Jewish congregation actually burned down its own synagogue to destroy birth records. It seemed that more girl children than boys had been born that year, and the congregation feared official reprisals if the shortage in the supply of males was discovered.

the primitive new medium of the "flicker show." Among other things, the early movies appealed to immigrants of any variety. The plots were simple, obvious, scary, or funny in a slapstick sort of way, and no language barrier stood in the way of understanding what was going on in the silent shorts. And they were cheap: admission to the movies cost only a few pennies.

That evening, Sam, Blanche, and Jesse went home to his mother-in-law's house, and sat down with Mrs. Lasky to talk about the possibility of a movie-making venture. Blanche, who had been brought up in a small town in southern California and preferred the climate there, pointed out that more and more movies were being made on the West Coast because of the clearer air and longer hours of sunshine. Also, not having to heat a studio in winter was an important cost consideration.

The next question was money. Sam had saved some ten thousand dollars through his Grand Central banker, and offered to put this in. Jesse Lasky also had some savings, and so did his mother. The kitchen-table meeting in Brooklyn had not even reached the stage of deciding what sort of film they were going to produce when Jesse Lasky asked, "Who will we get to direct?" Sam said, "What about Cecil?"

Cecil was a young and footloose sometime playwright, sometime actor named Cecil Blount DeMille, with whom Sam and Jesse regularly shot craps on Saturday nights at the Lasky-Goldfish home. Cecil DeMille had dabbled in a number of other business ventures, none of them successful, and lived in the shadow of an older brother, William C. DeMille, who, before the age of thirty-five, had written and produced a number of hugely popular plays with David Belasco and was now quite rich. Perhaps, it was suggested, if Cecil DeMille were brought on the team, William DeMille might be persuaded to invest in the venture, since it was known that Cecil had trouble making his rent.

Cecil DeMille had never directed a motion picture, but he was immediately enthusiastic. Furthermore, he proposed that the new partnership should not content itself with making a simpleminded little one-reeler of the sort that were being shown all over town in the vaudeville houses, interspersed with live acts and performing dogs. DeMille wanted to produce a full-length film that told a real *story*, something that had never been done before. Though none of the three partners had had any experience whatever at making films, they were all charged with enormous optimism. As Goldfish said to Lasky, "We've never produced a picture, and DeMille has never directed one. We should be *great!*"

Together, the fledgling group managed to round up a total of twenty-five thousand dollars, in bits and pieces, with Sam Goldfish supplying the major share, to capitalize their film. Cecil DeMille had asked his brother for five thousand, but William, who had staked Cecil in too many other, fruitless enterprises, declined. (Had he been more foresighted, William DeMille could have become a one-fifth owner of Paramount Pictures, which was what, as a result of later mergers and acquisitions, the Goldfish-Lasky-DeMille organization eventually evolved into.) The group then paid ten thousand dollars — a staggering sum in those days — for the film rights to a stage play called *The Squaw Man*, and hired a popular young stage actor named Dustin Farnum to play the title role.*

Just before shooting was to start, Goldfish suggested that DeMille take a quick trip to upstate New York, where another film was being made, just to get the hang of how movie directing was done. A last-minute crisis almost prevented DeMille's trip. It seemed that his grocer was pressing him for a twenty-five-dollar delinquent bill. But Goldfish paid that, and DeMille was off.

DeMille spent an hour or so lurking around the shooting location, and returned to New York to tell his partners that his crash course in filmmaking had shown him that there was nothing to it. All one needed was a pair of riding boots, jodhpurs, and a megaphone. Then Goldfish, Lasky, DeMille, their star, and their script boarded a train and headed west.

The making of *The Squaw Man* was as confused and haphazard as the creation of the little company. They had planned to shoot the film in Flagstaff, Arizona, which no one had told them was in the mountains. Arriving in Flagstaff in the middle of a blinding blizzard, they quickly reboarded the train and continued to Los Angeles. En route, DeMille had hired, as his assistant director, a man who sold Navaho jewelry along the aisles of the Santa Fe trains. Once in California, the group rented a barn in Santa Monica

---

*After whom Dustin Hoffman's star-struck mother named her son.

for a studio (today, ironically, the giant CBS Television studios occupy the site), and, to save money, DeMille cast both his wife and his young daughter in the picture.

The initial results were not "great," exactly. When the first print of *The Squaw Man* was shown, the images jumped chaotically all over the screen. The actors seemed to slide off the edges of the frames. Reshooting was out of the question. All the money was gone, and Dustin Farnum, whose final paycheck had bounced, was threatening to sue. In desperation, Sam Goldfish carried the print back east with him to a Philadelphia filmmaker who thought he might be able to fix it. Repairs were made, which involved trimming the edges of the frames, even though this meant that, in certain scenes, actors' arms and legs and even faces had to be cut off.

Sam Goldfish then arranged a publicity campaign for the film's opening in New York. On opening night, however, both he and Lasky were too nervous to make a public appearance, and instead sneaked into the theater near the end of the picture. To their amazement and enormous relief, the audience was laughing and cheering. *The Squaw Man* was a hit, and during its run would earn more than twice the amount of money the partners had put into it. The crazy gamble had paid off.

The Squaw Man would also earn a place, of sorts, in motion picture history. Though D. W. Griffith's *Birth of a Nation* is usually cited as being the first "long" movie ever produced, *The Squaw Man*, which came to the screen in 1914, predated *The Birth of a Nation* — or any other American film of four reels or longer — by more than a year.

The success of *The Squaw Man* brought the Goldfish-Lasky group to the attention of another newly arrived West Coast filmmaker, Adolph Zukor. By 1914, both Adolph Zukor and Samuel Goldfish were reasonably rich and successful film men. Like Goldfish and Lasky, Zukor was an Eastern European Jew, born in Hungary in 1873, who had come to America in the usual fashion, by steerage, with forty dollars sewn into the lining of his second-best waistcoat for safekeeping by his thrifty mother, which amount was to stake his future in the New World. Zukor, too, had got into the movie business almost by accident. He had made his way to

Chicago, where he had gone into the fur business with a man named Morris Kohn. By 1899, Kohn and Zukor had prospered sufficiently in furs to open a branch office in New York. There, Zukor's principal contact was another furrier, Marcus Loew, whom Zukor knew from many fur-selling trips between New York and the Midwest. Zukor and Kohn, figuring that it would be politically prudent to discuss their New York move with Mr. Loew — whose territory they were in a sense planning to invade — sought him out. Loew was surprisingly helpful. He not only offered to initiate the two Chicagoans into the New York fur fraternity, but he also helped the two men and their families find apartments in the city. Mr. Loew found an apartment for Mr. Zukor in the same block as his own, and the two men and their wives became friends — for a while, at least.

In the meantime, while the Zukors and Kohns were moving to New York, one of Morris Kohn's cousins was pestering his family and friends for money to open a penny arcade. He had found one financial backer in a former peddler from Buffalo named Mitchell Mark, who had branched into the penny arcade business and owned two arcades in Buffalo and one in Harlem. In 1899, a vacant dairy kitchen on Fourteenth Street near bustling Union Square — then one of the chief shopping areas of the city (Tiffany's was right down the street) — had caught Mr. Mark's eye, and he was eager to turn it into yet another arcade, in which he would offer one-reeler flicker shows. But the owner of the Fourteenth Street property was leery of leasing his store in such a high-class neighborhood to a man of unproven worth — and credit — like Mitchell Mark. So, using Morris Kohn's cousin as an intermediary, Mark persuaded the two "respectable furriers," Kohn and Zukor, to be his front men in the deal, with their presence providing at least psychological reassurance that the rent would be paid. In return for this favor, Zukor and Kohn were given a share in the business, which they named the Automatic One Cent Vaudeville Company. The long, narrow arcade was lined solidly on both sides with machines where, for a penny, the viewer could watch primitive little movies with such titles as "A Ride on the 'L,' " "Creeping Jimmie," and "French High Kickers." Thus, the two furriers found themselves in show business. Soon the fur business would be no more than a memory.

The Fourteenth Street arcade was an immediate success. It did not, as might have been expected, add a touch of sleaziness to a fashionable shopping district. On the contrary, it had the atmosphere of a well-run toy store and attracted a well-heeled clientele. Matrons who lived on Murray Hill could leave their children there, with pocketfuls of pennies, while they shopped the "Ladies' Mile," or Broadway from Twenty-third to Eighth streets, at Altman's, Arnold Constable, Lord and Taylor, and Siegel-Cooper. The Automatic Vaudeville featured, as a free attraction, a clever little contraption that had been Morris Kohn's brainchild. This was a miniature electric train that circulated among the various coin machines. As it passed, the pennies from the hoppers of the machines were automatically dumped into its freight cars. As many customers lined up to watch the little train as did to play the machines, and the constant clatter of falling coins added the kind of excitement usually associated with a gambling casino.

One of the men who came to see the train at its work was Marcus Loew. Later, Loew would admit that the sight of all that money tumbling in made him also decide to get out of furs and into penny arcades. He decided it was time for Zukor and Kohn to repay the favor that they owed him. He wanted a piece of the Automatic One Cent Vaudeville Company.

Since Zukor, Kohn, and Mark had already embarked on ambitious plans to expand their operations into Philadelphia, Boston, and Newark, they were delighted by the possibility of a new injection of capital and quickly agreed to let Loew buy shares in their enterprise. At first, it seemed a winning combination. But once all four men were in partnership together there was trouble. As in any all-cash business, employee theft was a constant problem. The men who operated the flicker shows and the toy train had to be watched like hawks, and presently the four partners were all snooping on one another. Each began keeping his own set of books, and needless to say, no two sets agreed. By 1904, Loew and Zukor were bickering over the ledger sheets, accusing each other of stealing from the company, and disagreeing about who deserved what share of the burgeoning business. Both had agreed that twenty-five hundred dollars a year was a reasonable take-home pay for each, but, as Loew put it later, "Adolph didn't think I was worth twenty-five hundred a year, and I had the same opinion of him." Loew, who had been the last to join the quadrumvirate, became the first to withdraw his investment. In 1905 he opened his own arcade, which he called People's Vaudeville, in what had been a vacant storefront on the corner of Seventh Avenue and Twenty-third Street.

Next to pull out of Automatic Vaudeville was Morris Kohn, taking his electric train with him. He, too, set up shop elsewhere. Mitchell Mark, meanwhile, was considered a foolish dreamer. He foresaw a far more dazzling future for motion pictures than any of the others did, and insisted that customers for movies, instead of standing in front of glass-windowed boxes in penny arcades, would one day settle themselves into plush-covered seats in front of giant screens in movie palaces with golden carved cherubs on their ceilings. He withdrew from Automatic Vaudeville in 1905 to concentrate on building theaters. The culmination of his dream, which was not far off, was the opening of the Mark Strand Theatre at Broadway and Forty-seventh Street, a thirty-three-hundred-seat showplace in the heart of the theater district.

That left Adolph Zukor with what was left of Automatic Vaudeville, which, with its principal crowd-pleaser, the train, removed, was not much. The five-year collaboration also set a pattern for internecine warfare and distrust that would dominate the motion picture business — which would become an almost exclusively Eastern European business — for the next half-century and more.

For a while, Adolph Zukor operated a nickelodeon, next door to the old Fourteenth Street location, which did well enough — as did anything, it seemed, that offered the magic flicker shows. Then, with more breezy self-confidence than anything else, he formed what he called the Famous Players Company, the purpose of which, according to Zukor's slogan, was to produce "Famous Plays with Famous Players." His windy press releases, however, failed to mention that he owned no famous plays, nor did he have any famous players under contract.

It was another gamble. But the gambler must allow for luck, and in 1911 Luck reached out and touched the shoulder of the thirty-eight-year-old Adolph Zukor. A French silent film, called *Queen Elizabeth*, had been exhibited with success in Europe. It starred "the divine" Sarah Bernhardt, the most famous actress in the world at that time. Its subtitles were in French, which was the only language Miss Bernhardt could perform in, and this fact had persuaded American impresarios that *Queen Elizabeth* was not exportable for American audiences. The American rights to the film were therefore both available and cheap. But Zukor knew that, on earlier American tours, Bernhardt — speaking in French in such stage vehicles as *Camille* and *Fedora* — had left audiences cheering and standing on their seats at the end of her performances, even when no one had understood a word she had said. The French subtitles could easily be redone in English. Would it matter that the words on the screen would not exactly coincide with the movements of the Divine Sarah's lips? Zukor decided not. The audience would be paying more attention to Bernhardt's exaggerated gestures, the wild tossing of her head, the beating of her breast, and to her famous blazing eyes.

Zukor acquired the rights to *Queen Elizabeth,* and the subtitles were translated. He then arranged for a celebrity-studded premiere in the summer of 1912 in a first-rate legitimate theater — the Lyceum on Broadway. The offering was a huge critical and popular success, and Adolph Zukor was hailed as a production genius. And so, when Zukor approached Goldfish and Lasky in 1914 and proposed a merger, it sounded like another wonderful idea. It would be a pooling of both talent and money. The resulting company was named Famous Players–Lasky. Zukor was president of the new company, Goldfish was chairman of the board, and Lasky was vice-president.

Almost immediately, however, Zukor found Sam Goldfish as difficult to deal with — as stubborn, temperamental, and unpredictable — as any of his previous partners. The two men couldn't agree on who was running the company, or who was to make decisions. The movie business had become — as it remains today — a curiously bifurcated business, with a certain basic clumsiness built into it. It operated on two coasts, the East and the West. Production was all done in California. But the largest audiences were in eastern cities, along with the newspapers and critics that mattered the most. Even more important, the banks and investment houses, upon whom the movie companies relied for financing, were all in New York. Everything that was done in Hollywood, then as now, was predicated on "what New York says." Then as now, motion picture producers were constantly having to shuttle back and forth between the East Coast and the West.

When Sam Goldfish was in New York talking to the money men, and Zukor was in California trying to grind out movies, Goldfish took over policymaking. And when Goldfish was in California, and Zukor was in New York, the opposite happened, and Goldfish took over production — and even the direction — of the films. The limbo periods — those four or five days it took to travel across the continent by train, and whoever was traveling was incommunicado — were worst of all, when each man was convinced that the other was scheming diabolically behind his back.

To make matters even worse, Sam Goldfish and Jesse Lasky were crossing swords. The problem was Blanche Lasky Goldfish's complaints about her husband. Blanche, it seemed, even though she now had a young daughter to care for, felt very much pushed into the background by the two most important men in her life, her brother and her husband. She felt, with some justification, that if it had not been for her, the two men might never have come together in their filmmaking venture. Now she was being ignored on the sidelines of their mounting success. "If I hadn't suggested the flickers that afternoon in New York, where would they be?" she complained. Blanche also considered herself a performer, and whereas men like Cecil B. DeMille put their wives and other relatives into their films, Blanche had never been cast in a single Goldfish picture. On top of it all, she suspected that now that Sam was in show business, he had formed a fondness for younger showgirls, and she may have been right. Sam's office door was often locked while he conducted lengthy interviews with aspiring actresses. On his transcontinental trips, he was frequently accompanied by female "secretaries." And there was no doubt that Sam Goldfish was fond of beautiful women. His film "discoveries" were invariably female, and he spent a great deal of time fussing over his actresses' hairstyles, makeup, and dress. Blanche was developing a full-scale case of classic wifely jealousy. There were the customary bitter accusations, recriminations, scenes. Sam Goldfish, meanwhile, a big, barrel-chested man with a bullet-shaped head, the wide, square jaw of a fighter and a temper to go with it, was not the sort of man to be bothered by the whinings of a mere woman. The more Blanche complained and demanded, the more he cut her off with a door slammed in her face.

Blanche took her complaints to her mother, who naturally sympathized with her daughter. Blanche also complained to her brother, who found himself very much in the middle. He was unhappy about his brother-in-law's presumed philanderings, but there was little he could do about the situation. Sam, after all, was not only the chairman of the board of the company; he was also the major stockholder in it, and in a very real sense, Jesse Lasky was Sam's employee. The fact that for a number of years Sam, Blanche, Jesse, and Mrs. Lasky had lived under the same roof only made matters stickier.

At her mother's suggestion, Blanche Goldfish hired a private detective to monitor her husband's activities, and the detective's findings seemed to confirm her suspicions. Confronted with this, Sam flew into a towering rage, and when his wife left their house to consult a lawyer, he had all the locks changed and refused to let her back in. The ensuing divorce proceedings were bitter and acrimonious on all sides, with a great deal of ugly name-calling, and with Sam, among other things, claiming that his small daughter, Ruth, was probably not his own child. One result of the divorce would be that Ruth, custody of whom was given to her mother, would not learn for twenty years who her father really was.

Inevitably, the domestic upheavals *chez* Goldfish had an effect on the already uneasy partnership. His problems at home seemed to make Sam even more irascible and autocratic at the office, and during one of Sam's out-of-town trips Adolph Zukor flatly told his board of directors that he could no longer work with Mr. Goldfish. Either he or Goldfish would have to go. When Sam returned from his travels, he faced a chilly board of directors who asked for his resignation. Huffily, he resigned, uttering, according to legend, his famous ultimatum, "Include me out!" Later, he would disclaim this comment, saying only, "I didn't think it was a very nice thing for them to do." But it was not an altogether un-nice thing for Sam Goldfish. To help persuade him to relinquish his chairmanship, he was given an even million dollars' worth of stock in Famous Players–Lasky.

Now on his own, like so many others of his competitive and rising generation, Sam Goldfish turned his back on both Zukor and his former brother-in-law, and went scouting for new partners with whom to invest his money. Soon he found them — two brothers named Edgar and Archibald Selwyn, who had been successful producers of legitimate plays on Broadway — and with them formed the Goldwyn Pictures Corporation, a name taken from the first syllable of Sam's last name and the last syllable of the Selwyns'. Into this new arrangement, Sam brought his million dollars, and the Selwyns brought a healthy clutch of stage plays ready to be turned into movies.

In 1918 Sam Goldfish petitioned the New York courts to have his name legally changed to Goldwyn. There had been titters among audiences, he had heard, when the words PRODUCED BY SAMUEL GOLDFISH appeared on the screen, and Sam was no longer a man who took titters lightly. Since Sam, for corporate reasons, had taken the precaution of having the name Goldwyn copyrighted, consent was required from the copyright holder. But since the copyright holder was Sam himself, who was also president of the company, this technicality presented no problem. Permission was granted by the court. As Judge Learned Hand put it, "A self-made man may prefer a self-made name."

5

HEROES AND HEROINES

L EAH SARNOFF liked to describe her four sons — David, Lew, Morris, and Irving — in terms of superlatives. One was "the handsomest." Another was "the smartest." The third was "the kindest." But David — "Ah, David," his mother would say, "David has all the luck."

Within four days of his arrival in New York, David Sarnoff had found a job selling newspapers on Grand Street on the Lower East Side to help support his younger brothers and sisters. He was nine years old, and the secret of his success as a newsboy was not so much luck as speed. When Sarnoff began hawking copies of the *Tageblatt* in 1900, which happened to be the year Rose Pastor began submitting her wistful romantic verses to the same paper, it was necessary for the newsboy to snatch his bale of papers as it tumbled off the conveyor belt, snap its binding wire with a jackknife, and run with the papers, shouting "Extra! Extra!" through the streets. The papers were not returnable, and if a newsboy did not dispose of his quota quickly, the business would go to his competition. David Sarnoff was a small, wiry, intense boy with large dark eyes, jug ears, and a ski-jump nose. He was also quick on his feet, and soon realized that he could be even quicker and more efficient if he were mobilized. Taking his cue from the push-cart vendors, he fashioned a makeshift cart out of a packing crate and four mismatched bicycle wheels picked up on the street. With this contraption he was able to build up a route along which he sold as many as three hundred *Tageblatt*s a day. His profit was a penny for every two newspapers sold — fifty percent, since the

Tageblatt retailed for a penny a copy — and this could add up to earnings of $1.50 a day, or $7.50 a week (the paper did not publish on the Sabbath). He was also able to earn an additional $1.50 a week singing soprano in the synagogue choir. This, it might be pointed out, was a princely income, compared with what older children were being paid for long hours of work in the sweatshops, and David's working day was seldom more than two hours long. This left him time to go to school.

It was not long before the enterprising new newsboy in town caught the attention of a group that called itself the Metropolitan News Company. Metropolitan News was a commercial distributor, or jobber, that bought newspapers in bulk and delivered them to newsstands, candy stores, and other retail outlets, using a horse and wagon. As the *Tageblatt*'s biggest customer, Metropolitan got the first papers off the presses, before anyone else. Sarnoff's business was street sales and some home delivery, but it looked attractive enough to Metropolitan for them to approach him with an offer to buy his route. At first, their offer was ten dollars, but Metropolitan's price rose steadily until it reached the staggering figure of twenty-five dollars, which was almost an offer he could not afford to refuse — more than a month's earnings for one little route. But, instead of accepting, Sarnoff took a gamble and made a counterproposal. Metropolitan could have his route — he could always build up another — for nothing. In return, Sarnoff asked only for the first three hundred copies of the daily press run, enough to give his cart a head start. The deal was accepted. Within weeks, he had built up a new route, and, as he had expected, Metropolitan was soon after him again with an offer to buy that one.

David Sarnoff could probably have gone on parlaying his paper routes into cash until Metropolitan controlled the entire Lower East Side, which, of course, was what it wanted. But there was danger here. In 1902, a rival Yiddish publication had been founded by an enterprising young Russian immigrant named Abraham Cahan. This was the *Jewish Daily Forward,* and since it offered a more socialistic, less uptown-establishment editorial point of view, it had quickly become popular with New York Jews who had been forced to leave Russia for reasons more political than anything else. Circulation wars between American dailies had become commonplace, and these had been known to be unpleasant, even bloody, with the newsboys of the competing papers most often the victims of the bloodshed. Sarnoff was wise enough to see that he could not go on expecting Metropolitan News to pay him cash for his routes forever; they might easily resort to more forceful methods. Besides, he had another idea.

He was thirteen now, and had begun to think about owning his own newsstand. With his own stand, he could sell both *Tageblatt*s and *Forward*s. He would be buying from Metropolitan News, instead of selling to them. Two of his brothers, Lew and Morris, were now old enough to help out, and their mother could fill in while the boys were at school. There was a small stand for sale uptown, at the corner of Forty-sixth Street and Tenth Avenue. It was hardly the best neighborhood in town. It was also enemy territory, in that it was largely Irish Catholic. In fact, that particular section of the West Side was already known as Hell's Kitchen. Still, the idea of newsstand ownership appealed to him, but the price — two hundred dollars — made it seem out of the question, though he could not help talking about it, and how he would run it, if only two hundred dollars could somehow miraculously be delivered into his hands. It was then that a strange stroke of luck occurred.

Returning home one evening, David noticed a mysterious stranger standing near the doorway of the Sarnoffs' tenement house. It was a woman, and she did not seem to be from the neighborhood — she was too well dressed, and her English was too precise — but she engaged him in conversation. Was it true that his father was too ill to work? (Never in good health, Abe Sarnoff had literally starved himself while working at his trade as a painter in order to send for his wife and children, and was now bedridden as a result.) Was it true that the thirteen-year-old David was now supporting his entire family? Was it true that he sang in the synagogue choir, and picked up an extra dollar or two singing at weddings and bar mitzvahs? Was it true that he needed two hundred dollars to buy a newsstand? When he had answered all these questions in the affirmative, the woman handed David Sarnoff an envelope, and then slipped quietly away into the night. In the envelope was exactly two hundred dollars. Was it a miracle, or luck, or a bit of each? David Sarnoff would not know the answer until many years later.

As the proprietors of their own newsstand, the Sarnoffs moved out of their Monroe Street tenement into slightly larger quarters, closer to their new business, on West Forty-sixth Street. And now that his mother and brothers were set up in business, with David himself making twice-daily rounds with his cart to collect his papers for his stand, he decided that this might be the moment for him to secure a regular salaried job. Schooling for him was over, and in those days there were no working-paper requirements for someone his age to take a full-time job. While peddling newspapers he had learned a great deal about the power of the press, and had even used this knowledge to good advantage at Stuyvesant High School. In an English class, his teacher had been discussing *The Merchant of Venice*, and had held up the character of Shylock as "typical" of Jewish cruelty and greed. David Sarnoff had protested this interpretation, and had been hauled into the principal's office for disrupting the classroom. The principal had tried to smooth things out between David and the teacher, but the teacher had been adamant: either David Sarnoff would be banned from his classroom or he, the teacher, would resign. With that, David mentioned that some of the Jewish newspapers, with whom he had connections, might be interested in the fact that New York's public schools were teaching anti-Semitism. Miraculously, the tables were turned. David was restored to his English class, and the teacher's resignation was accepted.

Experiences such as this had led Sarnoff to think about a career as a newspaper reporter. A reporter's life was considered an exciting and glamorous one in those days, when dozens of New York dailies competed fiercely with one another for scoops on the biggest stories, for circulation, and for advertising space. The newspaper reporter had to be quick and resourceful, and often had to involve himself in scrapes and daring adventures, as he kept his finger on the pulse of the big city. And so, one afternoon, Sarnoff took himself down to the offices of James Gordon Bennett's *New York Herald*, in Herald Square. Bennett, the father of sensationalist "yellow" journalism in America, had turned the *Herald* into one of the most powerful papers in town. Directed to the personnel department, Sarnoff was told that he could be used as a messenger at five dollars a week, plus ten cents an hour overtime, and was handed a uniform and a bicycle. There was only one problem: his new employer was not the *New York Herald* at all. It was the Commercial Cable Company, whose offices were next door. He had walked into the wrong building. Thus, through luck again or happy accident, the future board chairman of the Radio Corporation of America found himself, not in the newspaper business, but in the fledgling radio and electronics industry — the very industry that, in Sarnoff's lifetime, would help account for the demise of most of New York's newspapers, including the *Herald*.

As it happened, one of Commercial Cable's biggest subscribers then was the *Herald*, and much of Sarnoff's work involved delivering telegraphed dispatches to and from the newspaper. In order to understand the priority of the messages he was transporting, it behooved him quickly to learn the Morse code. He thus, while barely in his teens, became aware of the increasing importance of radiotelegraphy — "wireless," as it was called — as a medium for transmitting news. In his spare time, he began reading everything he could find on the new communications method, and during slow periods of the day he was permitted to practice on the telegraph key, and to tap out coded conversations between his Herald Square office and a young counterpart who worked in Commercial Cable's downtown office on Broad Street.

Great strides had been made in the field of radio communications since the turn of the century. In 1901, Guglielmo Marconi's brainchild had demonstrated its global possibilities when a faint signal, beamed across the Atlantic from the Cornish coast of England, was received at Saint John's, Newfoundland, and it was not long before actual voices and scraps of music were being transmitted, albeit often very indistinctly, across the primitive airwave frequencies in addition to dots and dashes. It did not take much imagination to realize that, as techniques were perfected, the airwaves might be used to transmit entertainment, and not just news, from one part of the world to another, and that this entertainment might have commercial value, much as the movies did.

The United States Navy had gone so far as to undertake a feasibility study to determine whether or not radio signals might one day be used to replace its flocks of carrier pigeons. But the commercial possibilities of radio had failed to catch the imagination of the general public — perhaps because the technology was so hard to envision. It was easy enough to understand how the human voice, or an electric current, could be made to travel through a wire. Every child, after all, had rigged a telephone of sorts using two paper cups and a string, and the use of business and residential telephone service was expanding rapidly. But that sounds could also travel electronically through the empty ether was a difficult concept to grasp, as was the theory — which was being explored by scientists even then — that one day a system would be devised whereby the air could also be filled with thousands of invisible colored pictures, which could be picked up by millions of home receivers. To the public, radio remained an interesting little gadget, the bailiwick of a few scientists and operators scattered in a handful of stations in remote places, but of no significant social importance. When plans for the British White Star Line's great flagship, *Titanic*, were announced, and it was learned that the vessel would be equipped with a radio communications system, most people assumed that this was no more than a promotional gimmick. When David Sarnoff tried to explain radiotelegraphy and radiotelephony to his mother, Leah Sarnoff could not understand it, and so had no idea what her son's new job entailed. This embarrassed her. When friends asked Leah what young David was up to, she told them he had become a plumber, to which they replied, "That's nice!"

Plumbing, however, was about the only enterprise David Sarnoff was not involved in. Every morning, before reporting to work at Commercial Cable, he spent four hours collecting and delivering papers to the family newsstand. In the evenings, when he was not studying electronics, there was choir practice. In the year 1906, however, when Sarnoff was not quite sixteen, two interconnected events occurred that provided a temporary setback to his career. The Jewish High Holidays, Rosh Hashanah and Yom Kippur, were approaching, and Sarnoff asked his employer for these days off, without pay, explaining that he was needed in the choir. He was bluntly told not only that he could have the days off but that, for asking, he was fired. This was a double blow because, simultaneously, his usefulness to the choir as a boy soprano was also coming to an end for natural reasons. His choirmaster had already docked him a nickel off his wages for failing to reach high C.

It was not long, though, before he found another job, with the Marconi Wireless Telegraph Company of America. The job was lowly enough — as an office boy. And the starting pay was only $5.50 a week, with no allowance for overtime. But its importance was that he was now working for the inventor who held the first patent for wireless telegraphy using electromagnetic waves — Marconi himself, who had also developed the antenna principle. The successor to Marconi's company would be called the Radio Corporation of America.

For the next few years, Sarnoff worked for Marconi, steadily moving upward in the ranks: to an assistant radio operator, with a salary of sixty dollars a month, and then to full operator, for seventy dollars a month. Much of his time was now spent in a series of remote outposts and on ships at sea, as a "sparks" for shipping companies that had installed the Marconi systems. In the spring of 1912, he was back in New York, where the John Wanamaker department store had placed a radio station on its top floor. A similar station had been installed in Wanamaker's Philadelphia store, and the stated purpose of the two stations was to facilitate interoffice communications and ordering between the two branches. Actually, it was more of a public relations stunt. Wanamaker's had suspected that, like Morris Kohn's electric train, the presence of a radio station in the store would draw crowds, and they were right. Shoppers congregated outside the glass window of the little studio to watch young David Sarnoff briskly sending and receiving messages between New York and Philadelphia over the newfangled wireless. The station's top-floor location served a double purpose. The reception was better from there, but it was also true that, in order to see the show, Wanamaker's customers had to pass through all the other selling floors, which featured other temptations. It was one of the first commercial uses to which radio had been put.

In the early evening of April 14, 1912, David Sarnoff, wearing his headset and punching his little keys and buttons, was doing his routine job at Wanamaker's — a job that may have begun to seem a bit boring, and even somewhat demeaning, since he was essentially an entertainer performing for spectators. All at once he received a faint and alien signal. It came, he quickly determined, from the S.S. *Olympic*, fourteen hundred miles away in the north Atlantic. Once he had asked that the message be repeated, its import was clear. The *Titanic*, bound for New York, had struck an iceberg at full speed, and was sinking fast. The

Olympic was steaming to its rescue. Immediately, Sarnoff focused his radio's full power on the *Olympic*'s signal, which repeated the SOS message again and again.

The *Titanic*, hailed as the crowning glory of the British shipbuilding industry and the pride of the White Star Line, was the largest, fastest, most luxurious ocean liner in the world. Its building and launching had been much publicized, and it had been touted as "unsinkable." This was its maiden voyage, and aboard it for the gala crossing were hundreds of prominent Americans and Europeans. One of the worst marine disasters in history was under way.

While trying to radio other ships that might be in the area, Sarnoff telephoned the newspapers, and within hours special editions were on the streets. As the night wore on, Wanamaker's kept its doors open, and crowds of friends and relatives of *Titanic* passengers, along with the merely curious, poured in, begging for news of survivors. Presently a police barricade had to be set up to protect Sarnoff from the mob, and give him the quiet he needed to transcribe his signals. Only a few special people were allowed into the studio with him — Vincent Astor, whose father, John Jacob Astor, was on the ship, and the sons of Isidor Straus, the head of Macy's, who was also aboard. Meanwhile, in Washington, President William Howard Taft ordered all other radio stations in the United States shut down so that nothing might interfere with the signals Sarnoff was receiving at Wanamaker's. At 2:20 A.M., Atlantic time, the news was heard that the *Titanic* had sunk.

For seventy-two hours, Sarnoff sat at his post listening, as, intermittently, the names of known survivors, who had been picked up by the *Olympic* and other radio-equipped vessels that had been in the vicinity, came trickling in. Then came the lengthening list of those known to have perished, and the word from White Star officials admitting a "horrible loss of life." John Jacob Astor's name was among the casualties. So was that of traction heir Harry Elkins Widener, who went down clutching a 1598 edition of Bacon's essays, and whose mother would donate the world's largest college library to Harvard in his memory.

Then came the tales of heroism and courage. Mr. and Mrs. Isidor Straus had each refused to enter a lifeboat without the other, preferring to go down together. Benjamin Guggenheim, of the copper-smelting family, had ordered his valet to dress him in his evening clothes, and refused to don a life jacket, since he wanted to go down like a gentleman.* There were tales of cowardice, too — of men who shouldered women and children aside to clamber aboard lifeboats first, of men who had dressed in women's clothing in order to do the same, of at least one man who had forced his way into a lifeboat wielding a pistol. In all, the total number of lives lost came to a staggering 1,513, and of the 2,224 aboard only 711 had been saved.

The *Titanic* disaster riveted public attention on the importance of radio. Many ships not equipped with radios had been much closer to the distressed liner than the *Olympic*, and had there been a means of contacting them the loss of life might have been far less. Quickly, the United States Congress passed the Radio Act, which required that all ships carrying fifty or more passengers be equipped with radios, and even those ships that carried fewer than fifty people hurried to install radios in order to stay in business. The *Titanic*'s sinking also riveted the world's attention on the Marconi system. But most of all it drew attention to the alert young hero of the day, David Sarnoff, who had manned the little station at Wanamaker's throughout the ordeal, and who now found himself an international celebrity, hero, and genius. The *Titanic*, David Sarnoff once said, "brought radio to the front, and incidentally me." Not quite two months earlier, he had celebrated his twenty-first birthday.

It was certainly the pivotal moment in his career, and one of the great moments of his life. His official biographer, Eugene Lyons (who also happened to be Sarnoff's first cousin, which may account for Lyons's occasionally awestruck tone as he describes his relative's accomplishments), tells us only that after the seventy-two-hour ordeal, without sleep, was over, Sarnoff treated himself to the luxury of a Turkish bath. But one may legitimately speculate about what may have been going through his head during those long hours. David Sarnoff was not the only man in New York who knew how to use a radio. Why, then, was he not relieved for three solid days? The fact seems to be that he refused to be relieved,

---

*The lady traveling with Mr. Guggenheim, who was not Mrs. Guggenheim, was rescued.

and so it would not be too cynical to ask: whose sense of personal drama was operating here? There he was, for example, the Russian-born lad from the ghetto, whose mother ran a newsstand and spoke little English, who had never finished high school, and yet who, with the passing of each suspenseful hour, was writing his own myth, creating his own American hero out of a fluke of fate.

Here he was in his little studio atop Wanamaker's, suddenly rubbing shoulders with Vincent Astor, heir to one of the greatest non-Jewish American fortunes, and the Straus brothers, scions of one of New York's proudest German-Jewish families — people whom, under ordinary circumstances, he would never have hoped to meet. It was not that Astor and the Strauses were more closely touched by the tragedy at sea than the hundreds of other anxious relatives of *Titanic* passengers who were being held at bay outside the studio by armed police. Nor were Astor and the Strauses in any way equipped to be of special help in the situation, nor were they there because they held high political office. Instead, these men had been admitted to David Sarnoff's studio under an unwritten subclause of the American Constitution, which provides that, in the land of equal opportunity, some people have more opportunity than others. These men were *important*. And David Sarnoff was important to them. Sarnoff's opportunity, as he sat tapping out and receiving his messages, was that he was offering an umbilical cord, a lifeline, between these important men and their important parents.

Following his Turkish bath, Sarnoff was rushed by taxicab — it may have been his first taxi ride — to Sea Gate, where radio communications were being set up between the mainland and the *Carpathia*, the ship that had finally collected all the *Titanic* survivors. By now, of course, he was the wunderkind of Wanamaker's, the man of the hour, and great cheers went up when Sarnoff arrived to take over the operation of the impromptu station. "He's here!" people cried. "He's here! Sarnoff is here!" as the flashbulbs popped.

The whole experience of having been elevated, so suddenly, to a position of power and importance must have had a profound effect on him. Certainly from that point onward David Sarnoff's life would take on something of the quality of a fairy tale, with all the curious twists of fate, irony, and coincidence associated with that genre — at least to hear him tell it. The luck of being in the right place at the right time to pick up the *Olympic*'s signals seemed to take on a mythic significance to him. He began to see himself as a kind of Horatio Alger hero — Ragged Dick, the poor newsboy, who had by chance been able to rescue the drowning millionaire, and had been rewarded with promotions into the highest ranks of commerce. As Sarnoff himself began his rise to the pinnacle of the American communications industry, he would supply his life with plot twists that an Alger might have envied — that seemed, in fact, almost too good to be true. In those seventy-two hours, the indefatigable Sarnoff had learned that America was the land of golden opportunity only when the opportunity was recognized, and seized. And that, once one has attained the spotlight and the center of the stage, one must cling to fame for dear life and never let it go.

Rose Pastor Stokes was still trying to cling to her own early fame, and, it began to seem, to cling to her marriage as well. Back in her *Tageblatt* days, Rose Pastor had written of

> Love —
> Oh, give me love!
> Love — the love that will always prove
> The beautiful force that will always move
> The life of the beautiful soul I love;
> A love that will flow from the heart I call,
> A heart from whose generous fountains fall,
> A love that is love and true love for all;
> But whose love, oh, joy! would be most for me.
> Then let fair fame be whatever she be,
> I fix my choice most profitably —
> On love.

Among the little homilies contained in her "Ethics of the Dust Pan" column had been, "The crowning glory of a woman's life is the attainment of love, not the object of it," and, "The woman's heart makes the home and the man makes the woman's heart," and, "Nothing endears two beings so much to each other as a quarrel." How, one might ask, was Rose Pastor Stokes's love life — how was her marriage faring — against the backdrop of all her political activities? There was increasing evidence that all was not well, and that quarrels were not endearing Rose and Graham Phelps Stokes to each other.

It was noted that, though Graham Stokes remained a member in good standing of the Socialist party, he was seldom seen marching beside his wife in the various strikes and demonstrations in which she so actively participated. Nor did Graham Stokes accompany his wife on her lecture tours as she, Debs, and Elmer Rice sought to spread the socialist doctrine across the country. Anzia Yezierska, a Russian-Jewish writer who knew the Stokeses, used their story as the basis for a novel, which she called *Salome of the Tenements*.

In the book, the wealthy, Christian character based on Graham Stokes is called John Manning, and the poor Jewish girl, based on Rose, is named Sonya Vrunsky. Here is the way Sonya Vrunsky describes her husband: "The Anglo-Saxon coldness, it's centuries of solid ice that all the suns of the sky can't melt." In an angry moment, Sonya calls her husband an *allrightnik* — that is, a materialist, a person of no sensitivity, and, most of all, a person with neither learning nor spiritual values. Of herself, however, Sonya declares, "I am a Russian Jewess, a flame — a longing. A soul consumed with hunger for heights beyond reach. I am the ache of unvoiced dreams, the clamor of unsuppressed desires. I am the unlived lives of generations stifled in Siberian prisons. I am the urge of ages for the free, the beautiful that never yet was on land or sea."

Whether such exchanges actually took place within the household on Norfolk Street is open to question, but in describing the Stokes marriage Miss Yezierska wrote that the two were "the oriental and the Anglo-Saxon trying to find a common language. The over-emotional Ghetto struggling for its breath in the thin air of puritan restraint. An East Side savage forced suddenly into the strait-jacket of American civilization. Sonya was like the dynamite bomb and Manning the walls of tradition constantly menaced by threatening explosions."

That Rose Stokes was indeed a highly emotional woman there can be no doubt. Once, strolling down a pushcart-crowded street, she had seen and spoken to an old woman selling candles from a basket set up on the doorstep of a store. As they were chatting, the man who owned the store appeared at the doorway and kicked the woman's basket, scattering her candles into the street. At the sight of this gratuitous cruelty, Rose wrote later, "I felt the deep world-sorrow; a flood of feeling overwhelmed me — I burst into tears and cried all the way home. It is a sad world, this; so much pain and sorrow; so much poverty and suffering is the lot of those who are, perhaps, God's best beloved. And, oh, how it clutches at the heart-strings — the thought that all this pain and misery is man's through his brother man." There is evidence that Rose Stokes wept easily. There is also evidence that she had an unusually quick temper.

Anzia Yezierska, meanwhile, the author of the roman à clef of Rose Stokes's marriage, had herself experienced the plight of her novel's heroine, and Rose's own. Miss Yezierska, too, had felt herself trapped between two cultures, and had made the mistake of dreaming that some fairy godmother's magic wand — some Prince Charming with a glass slipper — might appear to lift her out of the squalor of the ghetto into the perfumed world of American success. She did not understand — in fact, resented — the hard crash-course in assimilation that the ghetto offered; the ghetto in New York was like a school itself, in which each ill-clad newcomer — or greenhorn, as they were called — was treated like a freshman by upperclassmen, and hazed and taunted unmercifully until he or she adapted to the new rules or found, like David Sarnoff, some avenue of escape. On her first day of school in America, not speaking a word of English, Anzia Yezierska had found herself in a classroom where all the other students understood what the teacher was saying, and only she did not. Instead of trying to swim with the tide as best she could, as others had done, she was angry and humiliated and dropped out of school. America, she decided, was not as advertised.

To make matters worse, she had to endure an Old World patriarchal father who was a Talmudic scholar and spent his days with phylacteries and holy texts, and who railed at her because she was unmarried: "A woman alone, not a wife and not a mother, has no existence."

Anzia Yezierska had arrived in New York from Poland in 1901 at age sixteen, and, after the brief experiment with education, went to work as a housemaid for a wealthy Americanized Jewish family who refused to speak Yiddish with her, even though they spoke and understood it perfectly. After a month of scrubbing floors and doing laundry, she asked for her wages, and was shown the door. Her next job was in a sweatshop, where she attached buttons to blouses from dawn to dusk; when she finally protested the long working hours, she was dismissed. Her third job was in a factory, which at least gave her the luxury of evenings on her own.

After a dozen years in New York, she finally reached the point where she was thinking in English sentences. She began to write short stories, and to submit them to magazines. Her writing was amateurish and overwrought — "Here I am . . . lost in chaos, wandering between worlds" — but her theme, the immigrant experience on the Lower East Side, was one that struck some editors as strong and original, and her stories began to sell. At last, as a woman approaching middle age, she published her first novel on the immigrant theme, called *Hungry Hearts*.

Hungry Hearts earned her some respectful reviews, but very little money — only two hundred dollars in royalties. But then out of the blue, as James Graham Phelps Stokes had come to Rose Pastor, came Prince Charming in a golden chariot. It was none other than Sam Goldwyn of Hollywood, with an offer of ten thousand dollars for *Hungry Hearts*. Goldwyn, furthermore, wanted her to come to Hollywood to collaborate on the script, offering her a salary of two hundred dollars a week, plus all expenses. At last the American Dream had landed at her doorstep.

Off she dashed to Hollywood, followed by headlines that read IMMIGRANT WINS FORTUNE IN MOVIES; SWEATSHOP CINDERELLA AT THE MIRAMAR HOTEL; and FROM HESTER STREET TO HOLLYWOOD. At the Los Angeles railroad station, she was met by Goldwyn's publicity staff, who ushered her, terrified, into her first press conference. Then it was off to parties at the homes of such local luminaries as Will Rogers, Rupert Hughes, Elinor Glyn, Gertrude Atherton, and Alice Duer Miller. Paul Bern, who would later marry Jean Harlow, was assigned to direct *Hungry Hearts*, and her first illusion was shattered when she was told that her novel, intended as a heart-wrenching tragedy of poverty and despair, needed "laughs and a happy ending" to turn it into a successful motion picture. When she protested this butchery of her idea, she was told, "Screaming and yelling won't help. You've signed the contract that they can adapt the story as they think best. You were lucky that they used as much of your story as they did." She was shocked to meet a seasoned Hollywood writer who told her glibly that all the studio had used of his last story was the title. He told her that he was planning to change the title and sell the story again. Anzia Yezierska was given a large office at the studio, a big desk, and a secretary, and was told, "Write!" She found that she could not write a single word.

On the first day of shooting, Sam Goldwyn himself came on the set and sat down beside her. What was she working on now, he wanted to know. She explained that, so far, all she had come up with was the title for a new novel: it was to be called *Children of Loneliness*. Intrigued, Goldwyn asked Miss Yezierska to join him for lunch. She did not realize that this was an honor bestowed only on a very select few until, when the lunch was over, a number of very important people in the production, who had ignored Miss Yezierska up to then, suddenly seemed most eager to get to know her.

But the lunch with Goldwyn had not gone well.

"What's your new story about?" he asked her.

She replied that she had only written a few fragments of scenes, and could not really talk about the story until she got to the end.

"I don't know much about literature," Goldwyn said. "But I do know that the plot of a good story can be summed up in a sentence, and you must know the end of the plot before you begin."

Feeling helpless, Miss Yezierska replied that she didn't work this way. "My characters spin their own plots," she told him.

"But what's the plot," he insisted, "the suspense?"

"Suspense?" she said. "What greater suspense is there than the mystery of a guilty conscience?"

Miss Yezierska noticed the great producer's eyes beginning to look somewhat glazed. "Well, get to the point. What's the plot?" he repeated.

"The plot is the expiation of guilt," she said.

Now Goldwyn was looking as though his lunch was not agreeing with him, and Miss Yezierska then launched into a long, auto-biographical jeremiad: "I had to break away from my mother's cursing and my father's preaching to live my life; but without them I had no life. When you deny your parents, you deny the ground under your feet, the sky over your head. You become an outlaw, a pariah. . . ." The more she talked, the more Sam Goldwyn's apparent gastric disorder seemed to increase, and the more animated she became: "They mourned me as if I were dead. I am like Cain, forever bound to the brother he slew with his hate. . . ."

Mr. Goldwyn at that point remembered a pressing appointment, placed his napkin beside his plate, and excused himself. He had decided he was dealing with a madwoman.

And yet, because of all the publicity that had surrounded Anzia Yezierska's arrival in the movie capital, she was still regarded as a hot property in Hollywood. She was told that she had "a credit face" — that is, that she looked honest, that she had the kind of face that someone would extend credit to. Though she had written nothing at all since her arrival, William Fox of Fox Pictures approached her with a scheme to steal her away from Goldwyn, offering her an escalating contract to write for him — twenty thousand dollars for the first year, thirty thousand for the second year, and fifty thousand for the third. It was the kind of Hollywood contract that most film writers would have committed mayhem for. But, feeling bewildered, confused, totally out of her element, and beset by agonizing self-doubt — convinced that she could never produce anything worthy of such an imposing salary — she hesitated. She could not adjust to Hollywood's cynicism. She believed that she wrote from inspiration, and her muse had abandoned her. She was suffering from what today would be described as acute culture shock. In the end, she returned the Fox contract unsigned. "Who do you think you are?" William Fox asked her. "Joan of Arc, waiting for the voices?" She left Hollywood, never to return, and went back to New York and poverty.

Her next novel, *Salome of the Tenements*, fared commercially no better than her first. It was not bought for the movies. *Hungry Hearts*, as a film, did not do well at the box office. She was already a defeated woman. To her parents, she was a failure for not having married and had children. Later, as the Great Depression settled across the country, Miss Yezierska was able to find work with the WPA Writers' Project, where, to earn her paycheck, she was forced to grind out a prescribed number of words a day on a tourists' guidebook to New York City.

The story of Rose Pastor Stokes would end on a not much greater note of triumph. As World War I spread across the face of Europe, drawing the United States inexorably into the conflict — while President Wilson vacillated — Rose remained active, touring, joining picket lines, and making speeches for the cause of socialism. Until the early summer of 1917, Rose and her husband appeared to present a united front politically, but then the first signs of dissension were noted. This occurred after the Socialist party had officially denounced Wilson's war programs, when he had finally declared war on Germany in April of that year. Graham Stokes, who disapproved of the party's antiwar stand, announced that he was quitting it to join the army. This was followed by an announcement from Rose that she was also quitting.

But then, a few weeks later, she changed her mind, and announced that she was rejoining the Socialists. Within days, she was back in the political fray, attending Socialist meetings and rallies, chaining herself with handcuffs to striking workers. Late in 1917, she appeared to support a strike in the garment district, marching and chanting with the strikers. All at once, dozens of policemen descended, brandishing nightsticks. There were shouts, screams, and much general confusion at the confrontation, and then the policemen rushed the picket line, swinging. One of the striking women had been leading her small son by the hand. She was pushed aside, and a policeman began clubbing the child. Rose Stokes ran to protect the boy, and to throw her body across his. She was clubbed unconscious. It was the first of several brutal police beatings she would receive over the next ten years.

That was bad enough, but by 1919 Rose Pastor Stokes was in even deeper trouble. It was her fiery Russian style, as much as anything else, that lay at the heart of most of her difficulties. But here was a new spirit abroad in the land that also had to be taken into account. No sooner was the First World War over than there were outbursts of violence throughout the United States. It was a phenomenon that has been noted by historians and philosophers: in the wake of a great national conflict, with peace restored, a nation — its adrenaline level still high — frequently turns its feverish energy to identifying and unearthing enemies at home. The Versailles peace treaty was signed in June of 1919, but it seemed that civilian furies could not be demobilized as quickly as a platoon, and 1919 became the year of the zealot, an era of revenge against domestic foes, real or imagined. The Hun had been brought to his knees, but now it seemed that there were other heads to be bloodied.

In 1919, the anarchists Emma Goldman and Alexander Berkman were released from prison, and then deported, along with more than two hundred other "traitors," to Soviet Russia. An additional 249 Russian "undesirables" were shipped out aboard the S.S. *Buford*. A young special assistant to Attorney General Alexander Palmer was twenty-four-year-old John Edgar Hoover, whose job it was to handle deportation cases involving alleged Communist revolutionaries, and who would help Palmer organize federal raids on Communist party offices throughout the United States. In a New York post office, just before May Day, sixteen bombs were found addressed to prominent Americans, including John D. Rockefeller and Attorney General Palmer. Who was responsible for these was unclear, since America's list of enemies at home was growing — black anarchists, Red terrorists, the Jews, the Yellow Peril, the Roman Catholics, who, it was said, were conspiring to turn the country over to "Black Papism" and even to establish the pope in America. The Italians, too, were considered a dangerous element, and the groundwork was being set for the trial of two Italian-born anarchists named Sacco and Vanzetti, who would be executed for the alleged murder of a paymaster in South Braintree, Massachusetts.

May Day parades were broken up by the police. In the summer of 1919, race riots broke out in twenty-six American cities. On July 19, white soldiers in Washington, D.C., led a raid on the capital's black ghetto sections. On July 27, Chicago exploded when a disagreement at a Lake Michigan beach led to an armed foray into the city's Black Belt, at the end of which fifteen whites and twenty-three blacks lay dead, with hundreds of others seriously injured.

On the labor front, it was a year of chaos, with, all told, more than four million Americans either on strike or locked out. On September 9, the police of Boston went on strike, and Governor Calvin Coolidge reacted by ordering the Massachusetts State Militia into Boston, and firing all 1,117 of the striking officers. On September 22, steelworkers at the Gary, Indiana, plant of United

States Steel went on strike. The steel strike lasted 110 days, and ended with none of the workers' demands met.

The blacks, Catholics, Orientals, and Jews aside, it was apparent to most right-thinking and red-blooded Americans where the blame for all this unrest and mischief lay — on Communist Russia, the Bolsheviks. Everyone knew that the Bolsheviks had a long-range plan to take over the world and subject it to communism, and that free America was one of communism's principal targets. All at once, in 1919, the proliferation of strikes against American industry provided all the evidence that was needed that a Communist takeover was indeed at hand. In state capitals across the country, laws were passed against "seditious speech," and thousands were arrested and jailed for this offense, including a Socialist congressman from Milwaukee who was sentenced to twenty years in prison. In the state of Washington, the newly formed American Legion raided the headquarters of the International Workers of the World, and was roundly praised for this all-American action.

Each strike and riot of that year sparked a new Red Scare. Hundreds of people suspected of harboring Red sympathies were arrested, thrown into jail, and had their property confiscated. Informers abounded, ready with lists of Known Reds and Suspected Reds, on which they placed the names of all the people they didn't like. Innocent gatherings to hear lectures were translated as cell meetings. Because of a pointed finger and a cry of "Red!" a job could be lost and a reputation ruined. And if an employer could claim — and it was the easiest thing to do — that his employees' strike was "Red led" or "Red inspired," patriotism came to the fore, and the police could be brought in to break it up with fists and clubs and pistols.

Of course, this is not to deny that a number of the strikes *were* Communist led and Communist inspired.

From the time of America's entry into the war, meanwhile, the American Socialist party had been deeply divided between prowar and antiwar factions and, more important, between a moderate right wing and a radical left. The split had become formalized in 1919 when the Third International was founded in Moscow, dedicated to propagating the Communist doctrine throughout the world,

and with the stated purpose of producing a worldwide revolution
with the Comintern vowing to unite all Communist groups on a
global scale. During the war, Rose Stokes had aligned herself with
the left-wing Socialists. But by 1919, with the split complete, Rose
stopped calling herself a Socialist, and declared herself a Com
munist, helping to found the American Communist party. She
quickly became a member of its Central Executive Committee.

Her trouble, however, had begun the previous year. It had all
started innocently enough, in the early spring of 1918, when she
was invited to speak before the Woman's Dining Club of Kansas
City, Missouri, on March 16. By now, most of Rose's lecture
audiences regarded her as more of a national curiosity and celebrity
than as a political force — a poor Jewish girl who had married a
prominent Christian, a woman who, despite the wealth and luxuries
capitalist America had given her, still remained an avowed foe of
capitalism. In responding to the Woman's Dining Club invitation
Rose advised that she would be happy to accept, but warned that
if she spoke she would speak "as a Socialist." The club's board
of directors met to discuss this matter, and at least two members —
notably Mrs. Maude B. Flowers and Mrs. Florence E. Gebhardt —
vociferously opposed putting Rose on the program. America had
been in the war with Germany for less than a year, and socialism
smacked of anti-Americanism. But these ladies were in the mi
nority, and Rose's terms were accepted. She arrived in Kansas
City on the appointed date, and held forth on the dais for about
an hour and a half, including a question period.

She spoke, as she always did, extemporaneously, and in those
days before tape recorders, one of the problems would be that no
one who attended that meeting, including the lecturer herself
would ever be able to reconstruct verbatim just what Rose Pastor
Stokes had said to the ladies of Kansas City. As in any audience
different people remembered different things, but there was no
question that certain people found some of her remarks offensive
Some heard her say that she opposed the American war effort
Others inferred that she also opposed the drafting of young men
into the United States Army. A reporter from the *Kansas City Star*
who had attended the meeting, had his own version of what had
happened, which was published the following Monday, March 18

So she's back in socialism. Mrs. Stokes [is] for the government and anti-war at the same time. Mrs. Rose Pastor Stokes, whose address before the Business Woman's Dining Club Saturday night was characterized by a navy officer as disloyal and anarchistic, denied both charges today.

"As to my being 'terribly in favor of anarchy,' " she said, "I only wish Emma Goldman could hear that. How many, many times I have disputed that subject with her. I don't think that charge needs any further notice.

"As to the other things which have been published about the address Saturday night, even those who may have disagreed received it in a spirit of fairness and without any manifestation of disapproval. If there had been anything in it to warrant harsh criticisms, it seems strange that five hundred persons could have heard it through in such a spirit."

Mrs. Stokes said today that in the Saturday night address she emphasized the fact that America was forced into the war.

"Briefly," she said, "my statement was that while a very small minority of persons in America are in the war to make the world safe for capitalism, the overwhelming number of persons are in it to make the world safe for democracy. And that, ultimately, is the most significant issue of the great conflict."

Mrs. Stokes said today that she resigned from the Socialist party when the United States entered the war, because she disapproved of the anti-war platform of the party adopted at St. Louis, but a few weeks ago became a member again having decided the St. Louis platform, in the main, was right.

"I do not oppose the war, or its prosecution, in any sense," she said. 'I can see, at present, no way in which it can end except by the defeat of Germany. I believe the government of the United States should have the unqualified support of every citizen in its war aims. My misgivings are that, whatever the outcome of the war, the capitalistic interests of the world may use it to further their commercial exploitations of undeveloped and under-developed countries."

Certainly the *Star* reporter had got her to say a number of contradictory things — that she was both for the war and against it — with the result that the reader might conclude that she was a very confused woman. All might yet have been well, however, if Rose Stokes had been content to let the matter go at that. But she was not, and, carrying things farther, dashed off a letter to the managing editor of the *Star*, further clarifying her position, which was received the following afternoon, March 19:

> To the Star:
>
> I see that it is, after all, necessary to send a statement for publication over my own signature, and I trust that you will give it space in your columns.
>
> A headline in this evening's issue of the Star reads: "Mrs Stokes for Government and Against War at the Same Time." I am *not* for the government. In the interview that follows I am quoted as having said, "I believe the government of the United States should have the unqualified support of every citizen in its war aims."
>
> I made no such statement, and I believe no such thing. No government which is *for* the profiteers can also be for the people, and I am *for* the people, while the government is for the profiteers.
>
> I expect my working class point of view to receive no sympathy from your paper, but I do expect that the traditional courtesy of publication by the newspapers of a signed statement of correction, which even our most Bourbon papers grant, will be extended to this statement by yours.
>
> > Yours truly,
> > Rose Pastor Stokes

The managing editor of the *Star*, one Mr. Stout, ran the Stokes letter the following morning, March 20. He also sent a copy of it to the office of the United States district attorney because, as he put it later, "I felt it was a matter the government should have."

On June 15, 1917, the Congress of the United States had passed an act known as the Espionage Law. Based on the statements in her letter to the editor, and the fact that the *Star* had a circulation of 440,000, and was read by servicemen stationed in nearby military camps and cantonments who might presumably be subverted by Mrs. Stokes's views, Rose Pastor Stokes was promptly arrested and charged with three counts of sedition under Section 3, Title I, of the Espionage Law. Specifically, it was charged that she "did unlawfully, wilfully, knowingly and feloniously at Kansas City . . . attempt to cause insubordination, disloyalty, mutiny and refusal of duty in the military and naval forces of the United States in that she did, then and there prepare, publish and cause to be printed, published, distributed, circulated and conveyed in and by means of a certain newspaper . . . a certain communication," and so on. When the dismaying news reached Graham Stokes in New York, he hurried to his wife's side in Missouri, where she had been continuing her lecture tour.

In the trial that followed, two of the government's most important witnesses were the ladies of the Dining Club who had been most opposed to inviting Rose Stokes as a speaker. The more hostile of the two was Maude Flowers. Mrs. Flowers was asked by the prosecution to recall what Mrs. Stokes had said at the March 16 meeting, and she was quite specific:

She said that no thinking or well-informed person really believed that we were in this war for the sake of world democracy; that if we were sincere in our belief we would have entered the war when the neutrality of Belgium was violated, and we would most certainly have gone in when the Lusitania was sunk, but we did not enter the war until the U-boat became a menace to world trade, and threatened to isolate the Allies and threatened to cut off the munitions and our over-production that we sent to the Allies, and to threaten the vast loans the capitalists had already made to the Allies.

She said our men were in this war for what they believed was world freedom or world democracy; that in order to send our men, American men, into battle, they must have a principle to fight for, an ideal, and the capitalists and profiteers knew this and for this purpose the phrase was coined, "The world must be made safe for democracy." She said further that while our men entered the war in this belief, that they would become undeceived finally and that when they returned to this country it would be with a different belief and they would never take up life again on the old system. She said they would learn while they were abroad that they were not fighting for democracy but for the protection and safeguarding of Morgan's millions. That when they came back, or perhaps before, this country would be plunged into a revolution that had been for a long time pending, that we had been drifting towards an industrial revolution for a long time and this would most certainly bring it about.

She said further that the activities of the Red Cross, the activities of the Food and Fuel Administration and other war-created activities, were mere war camouflage. That is all, I believe, she said as directly bearing on the war.

Mrs. Flowers had brought along a friend, Miss Gertrude Hamilton, to attend the Stokes lecture, and Miss Hamilton was also called as a witness for the prosecution. Miss Hamilton repeated essentially what Mrs. Flowers had told the court, but added one small detail that was new. Miss Hamilton was certain that Rose Stokes had mentioned a poem that she had written, but that Miss Hamilton was quite sure Rose had not read to her audience, in which she had said that she was "thrilled by the sight of soldiers marching down the street." But now, Rose had said, after second thoughts, she regretted having written the poem and that "if she had the power to recall the poem she would do so."

Graham Stokes hired two prominent Kansas City attorneys, Seymour Stedman and Harry Sullivan, to handle his wife's defense in the case of *United States of America v. Rose Pastor Stokes*. Most of the trial work was done by Mr. Stedman. When Mrs. Florence Gebhardt was called to the witness stand for the prosecution, it began to seem as though she had heard an entirely different speech. Instead of a lecture that was anticapitalist, Mrs. Gebhardt had come away from the event convinced that she had heard a lecture that was pro-Russian. Asked to describe the talk, Mrs. Gebhardt stated:

She said that in Russia everything was free, that the land there being occupied was divided and the people were going to live on it as long as they wished, or could move off whenever they were ready; that the vaults and the banks were being broken into and the contents divided among the people to whom they rightfully belonged.

THE PROSECUTION: Did she say whether or not she approved of that?

There was an objection to the question from Mr. Stedman, which was overruled, and Mrs. Gebhardt was directed by the court to answer.

MRS. GEBHARDT: From her remarks I would say she approved of that.

All told, eleven witnesses were called for the government's side of the case, and following Mrs. Gebhardt's testimony the prosecution concentrated on what the witnesses thought the defendant had had to say, or felt, about Russia. Another Dining Club member, for example, Mrs. Margaret DeWitt, testified, somewhat ramblingly, that:

She spoke of the Bolsheviki as having taken possession of the land and of the country and of having taken possession of the money in Russia, and having taken possession of the land and allowing the principal land holder his fair ratio such as he could till, and that the rest of the land would be divided up among the Russian people, or among the people. And that theirs was an ideal government, that theirs was a true democracy and a pure democracy, and that they offered to the world this idea. . . .

I then asked a question. I asked why, if Russia were in this condition, and that she had come to this country and had profited by its institutions and developed here, why did she not return to Russia and give Russia the benefit of that — of her training. That was the time she mentioned the President. She said the President would not permit her. She said Emma Goldman had made that effort, but was not permitted, but she said, "I hope you do not class me with her."

The next witness was male, Mr. C. M. Adams, the husband of a Dining Club member, and his impression of the evening was not that Rose Stokes had wanted to disassociate herself from Emma Goldman, but that she had identified herself strongly with, and actually extolled, the famous anarchist. Said Mr. Adams, "Well, she mentioned about Emma Goldman being one of the greatest shining lights in her belief and only wished that she could express herself along the lines in as good fashion as she did."

The government had decided that its case would be given greater weight if an actual serviceman could be found who would testify on how Mrs. Stokes's remarks had affected him. Army Lieutenant Ralph B. Campbell, it seemed, had attended the lecture, and in his testimony he brought up the matter of the poem, which he insisted that Rose had actually read to her audience, thereby contradicting the earlier testimony of Miss Hamilton. Furthermore, Lieutenant Campbell stated, there had been a burst of applause after Rose Stokes read her poem, but that the defendant had "raised her hand to check the applause," indicating that she no longer agreed with the poem's patriotic sentiments. There was no testimony to corroborate this.

In his cross-examination of Lieutenant Campbell, Mr. Stedman tried to make order out of the confusion of exactly what the defendant had said, or had not said, on that fateful evening at the Woman's Dining Club of Kansas City.

MR. STEDMAN: I wish you would start out at the beginning of the address and state as much as you remember.

LT. CAMPBELL: Mrs. Stokes started her address with a resumé of industrial life of the world —

STEDMAN: Pardon me, state what she said. You are now giving your conclusions.

THE PROSECUTION: Oh no, he's not! He is stating the substance of what she said. Do you want him to use the exact words she stated?

STEDMAN: He stated the "resumé" and I assume it is a conclusion.

THE COURT: Well, of course, Lieutenant Campbell, you may state as far as you can the substance of what she stated there. The court doesn't understand by that, that counsel requires the explicit repetition of a long speech, but the substance of the various topics considered and what the subject matter was and her expressions relating to it.

LT. CAMPBELL: She mentioned the working conditions beginning with practically a written history; discussed the ancient guild system of workers —

STEDMAN (interrupting): That is not what I am asking for.

THE PROSECUTION: Yes it is.

THE COURT: Are you asking him to attempt to repeat the speech as near as he can verbatim?

STEDMAN: No. No man living could probably do that. . . . In substance what I am asking for is the language and not conclusions.

THE COURT: You may ask him for anything you see fit as near as he can recall. We are not going to take up time here to have an hour's speech recited by the witness.

STEDMAN: I am not trying to quarrel with Your Honor. . . .

THE COURT: Very well. You are at liberty to ask him about any portion of the speech you desire.

STEDMAN: I understand the court's ruling on this to be then that I cannot ask this witness the substance of that address?

THE COURT: I said that you could ask the substance of it but not to the extent of having him practically repeat in substance the entire speech which would amount even though not verbatim to something like an hour or more.

Throughout this interchange, the prosecution, in the person of the United States district attorney, remained silent, allowing Mr. Stedman and the judge to become further at loggerheads, and to work each other into the position of adversaries. Mr. Stedman seems to have been principally interested in "language" — as much direct quotation from the Stokes speech as the witness could remember — and the judge seems to have taken the position that this was asking the impossible. Meanwhile, it had probably begun to be clear to Stedman that no actual language would be forthcoming from Lieutenant Campbell. Mr. Stedman stepped away from the bench, saying, "Very well, to that I wish to take an exception and I do not care to cross-examine the witness any further."

All this testimony and cross-examination was very curious because, supposedly, the government's case against Rose Stokes was to be built upon the letter she had written and caused to be published in the *Star* on March 20, and not on the speech she had given to the Dining Club on March 16, about the content of which no two members of the audience seemed able to agree anyway. Still, there was one final, hostile witness from the Dining Club audience, Mrs. Eva J. Sullivan. Mrs. Sullivan testified that just before Mrs. Stokes had been introduced, the club's president had handed the defendant "a piece of paper" — presumably the check for her honorarium — saying, "I will have to take care of this, because it is your money," to which Mrs. Stokes had replied, "You may not want to give it to me after you have heard my talk." Mrs. Sullivan went on to say that the tenor of the talk had been that there were two classes of people who were interested in the war — one class for democracy, and the other for profit, and that the defendant had made the statement that she was "afraid the profiteers were getting control, and misleading the others."

As the trial progressed, it seemed to get farther and farther afield from the "wilful, felonious" act Mrs. Stokes had been charged with committing: writing the letter. Next, the prosecution brought in a witness to testify about an entirely different Stokes lecture, which she had delivered four days after the Dining Club talk, hundreds of miles away in the little town of Neosho, Missouri, in the southwestern corner of the state. Of what he could recall of this second lecture date on her Missouri tour, Mr. Frank D. Marlow said:

She said that the government at Washington was controlled absolutely by the moneyed class; that she believed that President Wilson was honest and sincere; that he was helpless for the reason that the government was controlled by the profiteers or the moneyed class. She said that she couldn't sanction and endorse the war because it was a war for the profiteer. She said that freedom of the seas meant freedom for the millionaires and she pointed to herself as one of those millionaires. She said that she couldn't advise nor urge men to fight in this war for the reason that it was a war for the profiteers.

All sorts of testimony was heard in the trial that probably would not be judged permissible in a court of law today. For example, one of Rose Stokes's arresting officers, Chief Deputy United States Marshal James N. Purcell, was allowed — over objections from the defense table — to describe his conversations with the defendant immediately after her arrest, when she would have been far wiser to have curbed her natural loquacity. She had told him, said Officer Purcell, that the United States government was controlled by the profiteers; that the war was between the capitalist classes on both sides, and that therefore it made no difference which side won as far as working people were concerned. She said that if Germany's winning the war would improve American working conditions, then she was all for Germany. As for what was going on in Russia, she said that the press accounts were not true, but were "censored to suit the people," as the vested interests in the Allied powers wanted them to be censored.

Shackled to the wrist of Officer S. W. Dillingham of the Justice Department's Bureau of Investigation, another of the arresting officers who was allowed to testify, she was as voluble as ever, and allegedly told him that she hoped that *both* Germany and the Allies would be defeated. The only victory she wanted to see was for the working classes. Mr. Dillingham said that he asked her, "Is it your point to cause a revolution in this country, as in Russia?" She replied, "Yes."

On March 29, while awaiting her arraignment, Rose Stokes was allowed to grant an interview to Mr. P. S. Dee, a reporter from the *Kansas City Post*. His testimony was that Mrs. Stokes had told him that the country had gone "war crazy," that "profiteers were getting such a strong hold on the government that after the war it would be absolutely impossible to jar them loose," and that she "feared for the working class, whose conditions were already so bad."

Only briefly did her letter to the *Star*, which constituted the entire basis of the prosecution, come into the proceedings. When the paper's managing editor, Mr. Stout, was cross-examined, Mr. Stedman tried to shift some of the blame onto Stout for publishing the seditious material, while at the same time turning it over to federal authorities. There was the following exchange:

STEDMAN: Did you think its [the letter's] possible effect was a violation of the Espionage Law?

STOUT: I was not familiar with the legal aspect, the technical aspect, but it seemed to me it was a subject the government should have.

STEDMAN: Did you think it might possibly create insubordination?

STOUT: I did not reason about it to that extent.

STEDMAN: Did you think that it was seditious?

STOUT: I thought it was disloyal.

STEDMAN: You thought it was disloyal?

STOUT: Yes. . . .

STEDMAN: You thought it was disloyal and you sent 440,000 copies to people who read your paper, did you?

STOUT: Yes.

One of the few members of the Dining Club who took the witness stand in Rose Stokes's defense was Mrs. Annette Moore, the club's president, who, after all, had engaged Rose as a speaker. Mrs. Moore said:

Her subject was "After the War, What?" and was purely problematical and apprehensive in every regard. Her whole thought seemed to be for the working class, and seemed to be that if — she precluded [*sic*] every remark with "if" — and if such and such were the fact, if the profiteers were permitted to charge such extortionate prices, such prices as the world had never known before, that in that event that when the boys came home from the trenches and found the democracy they had been fighting for had not been won, then we should have a social revolution in this country. . . .

She said as she saw these boys marching down Fifth Avenue, that she was thrilled at the sight of them, and she said that she was inspired to write this poem, and I believe — I am not quite certain on that point, but I believe she said that if the boys had not been fighting for democracy, and did not get what they had gone to fight for, that she would feel like recalling that statement.

Mrs. Moore's testimony was not exactly a powerful defense, but at least she did not mention anything about an endorsement of the Bolsheviks, which had seemed to obsess so many of the other witnesses.

Rose Stokes then took the stand on her own behalf. Once more, the subject was her remarks to the Dining Club, and not her letter to the editor, which was at issue. She began by stating at the outset that she had made no mention of the Red Cross on the evening of March 16, 1918. She then offered a summary of her lecture. Her summary was very long — too long, perhaps, because Rose was a woman who, given an audience to listen, always rose to the occasion — and the prosecution made no effort to interrupt her. This was what she told the judge and jury:

Now I said the war, at the bottom, was economic. . . . And I said that the United States, as other governments, had entered the war from vital pressures of vital interests; that no government ever declares war for purely idealistic reasons. . . .

I further said . . . that peoples had to have an ideal, that peoples on the contrary always went to war because of an ideal, and that therefore, if the people would fight at all, they must be stirred in their idealistic natures. Their hearts, their minds, are simple, pure, clean, and they desire to fight only for the highest things; and that when President Wilson uttered the great watchword of democracy, "We will make the world safe for democracy," the people arose to answer that call. And I said, "Can you imagine the people, who would die fighting for an ideal, fighting for purely economic reasons? Can you imagine the people fighting for such a thing as Morgan's dollars?" I said that when men fight they answer a great call, and that we could not get a baker's dozen, that is the very phrase I used, that we could not get a baker's dozen, if we had called out, "Come on, and fight," for instance, "for Morgan's dollars."

I said I had two brothers in the service, one in the army and one in the navy. I had persuaded my good mother, who hates war and who is so much opposed to killing that she would not have her boy go into the army, but he was eager to go and I wanted him to go, and I persuaded her and it took me a long time to persuade her, and finally she let him enter the navy and he is there now.

I said I was not opposed to the war; the war was upon us, it was here, we could not stop it. . . .

I never said our men were befooled. I said our men answered the call of democracy, believing they were fighting for democracy, and when they came home, when — if they found the things they fought for were not gained, that undoubtedly we should have both an industrial and social revolution in this country. . . .

I asked for questions and for a while we discussed further these matters and one question that was asked me was this: "Do I approve of the social revolution in Russia?" I said I approved of the ideal for which Russia was striving, and I approved thoroughly of the ideals of the Bolsheviki, the ideals they were striving for; that I knew them to be honest, sincere socialists who were working in the interests of the people; that they were socializing land and industry in Russia as fast as these could be socialized, and naturally there is always in great changes — great political, social or economic changes — some distress, just as there is in so-called peaceful times elsewhere; but that the newspapers, through the strict censorship, had not given us the truth about Russia, and I had reasons to believe through sources of information that I had, coming through such men as Colonel Thompson of the Red Cross, recently returned from Russia, and men like Lincoln Steffens, recently returned from Russia — that what I had learned from them gave me a different impression, and that President Wilson himself had heartily supported the ideas and aims of the Russian revolution.

Then, the question was asked me — the next question came from the same questioner, and that was: Did I approve of the taking from the banks the money of Russia? I said I did not know how much truth there was in this confiscation of wealth in Russia, but if they felt it necessary to take over wealth just as here, when we take over great aggregations of wealth for the common good — that if the people of Russia desired it, that perhaps it was right for them to do it and I would approve of it, if I felt it was in the interests of the whole people to socialize wealth.

Another question was put to me: why I did not go back to Russia if

I felt that conditions were not quite just here — and it was put indirectly. The question was asked, why don't those who have developed power and gained comforts and wealth here, who were not born in this country, why, if they do not like certain institutions and are criticising [sic] certain institutions, why don't they return to their own countries? Why not go back to Russia? And I arose to reply, and I said, "I presume, Madam, that you refer to me when you say that?" I said I was indeed very eager to go to Russia when the revolution took place because I did want to be helpful, and I had asked to go over, but that I was not permitted. And I instanced Emma Goldman, the case of Emma Goldman and Mr. Berkman, when they were first arrested and charged with certain violations of the law. This was before the last revolution in Russia. They were threatened by the authorities, as reported in our press, that they would be deported to Russia. This was before the revolution at all; this was before the czar had been deposed. They were threatened with deportation, and when later they were about to be tried and the revolution had occurred, they asked to be sent back — they asked to be deported to Russia, but the authorities, such was the report, refused to permit them to return.*

And I said further that I should answer still another part of my question. This was after I had seated myself and had recalled that the question was two-sided. I said you refer to me and ask why I, who have developed in this country and have grown up here to wealth and power and intelligence, why I should criticise — why I do not go back? Well, I will tell you why I criticise our institutions and perhaps you will feel that I have some — there is some justice in my criticism of these institutions. I told her that I came here when I was eleven years of age, that I still wanted to go to school but instead I was put into a factory, that my father worked very hard and yet did not earn enough to meet the needs of his growing family, that I was the oldest of seven children. I was ten years old when the next oldest came, that the other six as they grew were all little ones, that as I became grown up the great part of the burden of supporting the family fell upon me. I said for ten years I have worked and produced things useful and necessary for the people of this country, and all those years I was half starved, I never had enough to

---

*Emma Goldman and the Polish-American anarchist Alexander Berkman had founded the anarchist journal *Mother Earth* in 1906, shortly after Berkman's release from prison for attempted murder — the shooting and stabbing of Henry Clay Frick in 1892 during a strike at the Carnegie-Phipps steel mill in Pennsylvania. In 1917, *Mother Earth* was suppressed, and its editors jailed. A year after Rose Stokes's trial, both Goldman and Berkman were indeed deported to Russia.

eat, I never had a decent bed to sleep in, I sometimes slept on the floor. I was half naked; in the winter I never had a warm coat, I could not afford it. In the summer I never had a vacation, I could not afford it. For twelve years, day in and day out, for six days in the week and sometimes seven, and sometimes the whole season at a time, I worked at night in order to help out the family existence. I worked at doing useful work and never had enough. But the moment I left the useful producing class, the moment I became a part of the capitalistic class which did not have to do any productive work in order to exist, I had all the leisure I wanted, all the vacations I wanted, all the clothes I wanted — everything I wanted was mine without having to do any labor in return for all I have received. And I said, "Madam, do you think that conditions which can produce such an example as I now recite to you are conditions that are not worthy of criticism? Do you think that such conditions are just?" And she replied and shook her head and said, "No."

There were several odd points in her testimony that may have set the judge and jury wondering. Her charge of censorship in the press was of course offered without proof, and it was ironic that at the heart of the case were statements of her own that had been published, and perhaps *ought* to have been censored. And what had she meant by saying that in America it was often necessary to "take over great aggregations of wealth for the common good"? She may have been referring to income taxes, but it sounded rather threatening. And of course on at least one point she contradicted herself. She had started out by saying that she had not mentioned the Red Cross in her talk, but then said that the Red Cross had been mentioned, at least in passing.

On cross-examination, the government prosecutor asked her one question: What was her object in arranging a series of lectures to talk about the war? She replied: "My object was to bring the people to a realization that unless we who are left at home fight for democracy where we are, the boys in the trenches may perhaps come home and find they had not gained what they wanted. I believed that in going through that tour, stirring up people to consider the questions of democracy, we were doing our part to fight for the very things our boys have gone over to fight for."

With that, the defense rested its case.

The judge then turned to instruct the jury. His instruction was rambling, verbose, full of digressions, and consumed some twelve thousand words of court transcript, during the course of which there was much flag-waving and many appeals to red-blooded American patriotism. He began by reviewing the three counts of sedition with which Rose had been charged: attempting "to cause insubordination, disloyalty, mutiny and refusal of duty in the military and naval forces of the United States"; trying to "obstruct the recruiting and enlistment service of the United States"; and conveying "false reports and false statements with intent to interfere with the operation and success of the military."

The "false reports," of course, consisted of her letter to the *Star*. The court reminded the jury that the *Star*'s 440,000 papers in daily circulation not only went to thousands of Kansas City servicemen stationed at home and abroad, but was also going to young men of enlistment and conscription age — all men between the ages of eighteen and forty-five — as well as to younger men who would soon be of enlistment age. Furthermore, the newspaper circulated to the "mothers, fathers, wives, sisters, brothers, sweethearts, and friends of these men." The aggregate total of people who could be perverted by Rose Stokes's words, he seemed to imply, was staggering. Multiply this by the mothers, fathers, brothers, and sisters of the sweethearts and friends, and it was easy to see how Rose's thoughts could cause widespread insurrection across the face of the American continent. The court noted that an attempt had been made, during the trial, to show that the *Star*'s editor was equally culpable for printing the disloyal letter. This, however, the court forgave, reminding the jury that Rose had implored the editor to publish the letter, and that therefore the editor was simply being a gentleman by doing something that a lady asked. He added that, "People who . . . seek to promulgate their views through the press do so generally for the purpose of securing wide circulation and, if possible, adoption of those views" — no matter how dangerous or un-American those views might be.

The court embarked upon a long digression on the subject of Great Britain, and its treatment of its colonies, to which there had been a reference "in a rather slighting way." England, the court reminded the jury, was one of America's allies. So were France and Italy. England's colonies — Canada, Australia, New Zealand — though under no obligation to do so, had all rallied to the cause of the Mother Country and sent volunteers to aid England in its hour of conflict. English was the official language of America, yet the defendant had spoken slightingly of England. "Anything," the court said, "which leads to a lack of cooperation, anything which in any sense and from any source weakens the manpower and fighting power of that Ally, is a blow at ourselves, and to the success of our common venture."

The court then got to what it felt was the heart of the matter: the defendant's pro-Russian sentiments. "The present Bolshevist government, if it can be called a government," said the court, "is characterized by the defendant as ideal." The United States, on the other hand, had been characterized as a capitalistic system that oppressed the poor and enriched the middle and upper classes. "This would include," said the court, "all who, by industry and prudence, have made accumulation and provision for the future. The classes referred to embrace not only those of large wealth but those of modest fortune as well." In Russia, "the workers, so-called, are permitted arbitrarily to seize and divide up the land and wealth of the country, irrespective of former ownership. If such a system were to be applied to this country, not only the so-called rich, but the small land holder, and the small merchants would be called upon to divide their holdings on a per capita or similar basis. Such are the views of this defendant." One can only imagine that the conservative Middle Western burghers of Kansas City who comprised the jury were stabbed by fear at these dark words. Did America want its "banks and vaults broken into and the money divided among the people"?

American democracy, the court said, might not be perfect, but it was close to it, and agencies of the United States government were already hard at work on programs to improve the conditions of the poor. Now America was at war, and it was a time for Americans to present a united front to support that war. "Individualism must be put aside for the moment in this country," the court concluded. "We must now stand shoulder to shoulder . . . and that is true whatever may be her [the defendant's] opinion about different things, that may be settled here in times of peace and within our own domestic borders. Now the hand of that sort of criticism, and the tongue of that sort of criticism must be stayed until peace is restored and we can work these things out together, as we have always worked out problems here at home."

In short, the court appeared to be asking the jury to return a verdict of guilty.

And that was precisely what it did. The jury was out only twenty minutes before coming back with a verdict that found Rose Pastor Stokes guilty as charged on all three counts.

The judge then pronounced his sentence. The defendant was to pay the costs of the prosecution, and to be imprisoned at the Missouri State Penitentiary for ten years on each of the three counts. The only leniency provided was that the three ten-year terms could be served concurrently.

It began to seem as though the first Jewish woman in the *Social Register*, who may also have been the first Communist in the *Social Register*, might also be one of the first *Social Register* listees to go to jail.

In their eighty-nine-page brief for Rose Stokes's appeal, her attorneys were thorough, coolheaded, occasionally witty, and at all times incredulous about the way her trial had been handled. Messrs. Stedman and Sullivan claimed a total of 137 errors, which they proceeded to describe. The lawyers objected to the admission of unrelated testimony about Rose's second Missouri speech in Neosho; to admitting the testimony of Purcell and Dillingham, the two arresting officers; to the testimony of P. S. Dee, the newspaper reporter; to the question asked of Mrs. Gebhardt as to whether or not the defendant "approved" of what was going on in Russia; and to many other fine points of law. But most of the lawyers' objections centered on the fact that the trial had ranged far afield from the "crime" that Rose was accused of committing, which was writing to the editor and causing her letter to be published, and to the judge's extraordinarily biased and prejudicial instruction to the jury — "an appeal to the passion and prejudice of the jury . . . without relation to anything in evidence in the case, and persuasive as a whole to influence the jury to return a verdict of guilty.

"What the trial judge overlooked entirely, the gist of the whole matter," the lawyers wrote, "is that *the criminality charged* against this defendant is the effect of her single communication on other minds, with the results in military obstruction by the conduct of others." In other words, the lawyers contended, if the prosecution had been able to demonstrate that a single soldier had been insubordinate, or a single sailor had mutinied, as a result of Rose's little letter, it might have had a case. But instead all eleven of the witnesses were quizzed on what she might or might not have said in her lecture — an "attempt to prove one alleged crime by another."

Returning again and again to the letter, the lawyers pointed out that all Rose had said was that she was against the government. By this, they insisted, she meant that she was against the Wilson administration, "in the same sense in which every person who voted for candidates of the opposition last November was against the government." To vote for an opposition candidate, or to disapprove of what an administration was doing, was no crime. "Indeed," the lawyers wrote, *"we are against the government* . . . in fulfilling our professional obligations to Mrs. Stokes" by taking her case, in which the government was her adversary. "Only the high temper and passion of the war spirit could account for the writing of this indictment.

"Finally," the lawyers added, "as to the letter and its understanding, what impact in any reading could these insignificant little sentences have to pervert the general philosophy and patriotism of any reader? Mrs. Stokes is not for the government; she is in the opposition. This is not so startling a discovery as to disrupt the mental poise of a reader. . . . There was no scintilla of evidence of an obstruction of the recruiting service by this letter and its dissemination. There was no evidence . . . that her letter constituted in any respect an interference with the success of our military forces and an aid to the military forces of the enemy."

And what business, her counselors wanted to know, did the judge have in bringing in his hypothetical analysis of what would happen if Russian bolshevism were transported to America? "Why is any of this material included in the charge at all? . . . There was nothing about the Russians in the letter which is the basis for the indictment." The lawyers labeled this "a shocking example of judicial impropriety," and asked, "Under what sort of doctrine of judicial notice does the trial judge give to the jury the benefit of his certainty as to Russian events? This . . . was more than an appeal to the passions of the jurors. It took away from the trial the character of a decorous criminal prosecution under the genius and liberality of Anglo-Saxon jurisprudence."

Russia had nothing to do with her letter. Neither did the loyalty of Great Britain's colonies or the other Allies. In the course of what the lawyers termed a "meandering trial," the judge had allowed masses of testimony on extraneous matters, such as Rose's feelings "toward the war, the Red Cross, the Russian Revolution, Woodrow Wilson, patriotism versus internationalism, knitting socks for soldiers, and what not."

At the end of their brief, Rose's lawyers rather delicately brought up the matter of her rights of free speech, as guaranteed under the First Amendment to the Constitution. It was a tricky point, because a number of prominent American jurists and thinkers had already taken the stance that there were certain clauses in the Espionage Law itself that could be interpreted as an abridgment of free speech, and that the law itself was unconstitutional. Wisely, probably, Rose's lawyers decided to skirt this last issue, but they did note that the trial judge had stated that "individualism must be put aside for the moment in this country." Replied the lawyers, "If by 'individualism' the trial judge means the sum total of our individual liberties, then he sets aside the Constitution as a war measure, and this is beyond the remotest stretch of any act of Congress. We submit that it is the most vital function of the judiciary to serve an opposite role, to hold Congress jealously to the line of immunities and liberties preserved to the individual, in war as in peace, by the guarantees of the Constitution."

The labors of Messrs. Stedman and Sullivan were, in the end, successful. The guilty verdict against Rose Stokes was overturned by the United States Circuit Court of Appeals, Eighth Circuit, for the Western District of Missouri, and the government dropped its case. But much damage had nonetheless been done. The publicity surrounding the trial had left Rose branded in the public's mind as some kind of traitor or spy, involved in espionage, sedition, un-American and unpatriotic activities, against the war, opposed to the draft, in favor of a Bolshevist form of government, in favor of a similar revolution in America. Her lecture career — for which she had earned handsome honoraria — was over. Her name had become anathema.

Throughout the trial, James Graham Phelps Stokes had been a model of stoic, stiff-upper-lipped, upper-crust, if unhappy, supportiveness. He had obtained leave from his army duties to be with his wife, and appeared every day at her side — looking handsome in his captain's uniform, a walking advertisement for patriotic duty — and of course he paid the considerable legal bills that the defense of his wife had entailed. But the trial had been an emotional as well as a financial strain, and the signs of this showed in new lines of weariness on his good-looking face, as well as in the abrupt way he dismissed newspaper reporters' questions with, "No comment." After the appeal was won, both Stokeses did their best to withdraw from the limelight, and to retire to their private lives. But close friends and family members suspected that the ordeal of the trial had been a final test of the patience of Graham Stokes with his irrepressible Jewish wife, that the test had been failed, and that it was only a matter of time. . . .

For America's Eastern European Jews, 1919 would be a kind of watershed year. Three seemingly unconnected events — the outcome of the Russian revolution in 1917, the end of the First World War in 1919, and the advent of Prohibition that same year — would interweave and mesh in such a complex way, each event exerting a subtle but powerful force upon the others, that thousands of lives would be affected by their confluence.

The Russian revolution of 1917 took place in two stages — in February, when Nicholas II was overthrown, and in October, when the Bolshevist rule was established. Most Russian Jews greeted the news of the czar's downfall, when it reached America, with great jubilation. Of the Bolsheviks' takeover in October, there was less certainty and unanimity of approval. In New York, the conservative *Tageblatt* was disapproving, and editorialized that true freedom and order would not come to Russia until the Bolshevist movement had failed, and a representational democracy, on the lines of America's, had been adopted. But the socialist-minded *Daily Forward* was rapturous, and its managing editor, Baruch Vladeck, wrote: "Life is strange: my body is in America. My heart and soul and life are in that great wonderful land, which was so cursed and is now so blessed, the land of my youth and revived dreams — Russia."

America's entry into the war, meanwhile, effectively halted transatlantic immigration from Eastern Europe, and never again would there be such a tide of immigration as had been seen over the previous four decades.* Then, in the clamorous, almost hysterical spirit of jingoism that swept across America following the war, a flurry of increasingly restrictive United States immigration laws were passed that reduced immigration to a trickle, and virtually "froze" the American Jewish population at the figure where it then stood. These laws were drawn blatantly along racial and ethnic lines, and set strict quotas; they were accompanied by much patriotic breast-beating about eliminating "undesirables," "the foreign element," decrying "foreign ideologies," and calling for "one hundred percent Americanism."

It was as though America, having achieved victory in Europe, had decided that it must cleanse and purify itself and turn itself into not only the mightiest but also the most moral nation in the world. Vice and self-indulgence would be eliminated through prohibition of alcoholic drink. In the South, the Ku Klux Klan had been revived in the name of red-blooded Americanism, to show the black man who was boss, and even blacks who were war veterans were lynched. In this same mood, in Michigan, Henry Ford began publishing his *Dearborn Independent*, which immediately revealed strong overtones of anti-Semitism, and which would publish the spurious document *The Protocols of the Learned Elders of Zion*. (The *Protocols*, a proven fake, claimed to reveal an international Jewish conspiracy to take over the world's money.) For years after this, many Jews would refuse to buy a Ford car, and an embarrassed Mr. Vladeck of the *Daily Forward* would be chastised for accepting advertising from the Ford Motor Company, particularly since he had frequently refused to accept advertising from political parties with which he disagreed.

In the state of Tennessee, the teaching of the theory of evolution

*Between 1933 and 1940, about 140,000 Jewish refugees from the Nazis arrived in the United States, mostly from Germany and Austria. Then, after World War II, another 150,000 who had somehow managed to escape the concentration camps arrived. About 12,000 of these were from Eastern Europe, and were ultra-Orthodox Hasidic Jews, with their side curls, black hats, suits, and overcoats, who settled in the Williamsburg section of Brooklyn.

was outlawed as not being sufficiently patriotic and "Christian," even though the story of Creation was written in the Old Testament. Immediately following the Russian revolution, the Lower East Side had surged with prosocialist and antisocialist rallies and meetings, but by 1919 events — including Rose Stokes's trial — had made it clear that socialism was no longer an accepted American ideology. And a number of Eastern European Jews, remembering that the czarist pogroms had been aimed at stamping out anticzarist socialist dissidents as much as anything else, began to wonder uneasily if the same sort of anti-Jewish, antisocialist violence might not be about to erupt in the United States. Others, like Mr. Vladeck, may have simply felt that their hearts and souls were still in Russia. In any case, by 1920, some twenty-one thousand Jews had left America to return to their spiritual homeland, declaring themselves "Former Prisoners [of Capitalism]."

Meanwhile, by 1919, the Lower East Side had changed drastically — both cosmetically and demographically — from what it had been in Miss Julia Richman's heyday, and she no doubt would have approved of the changes. Rough-cobbled streets had been paved with asphalt. Old docks in the East River had been converted into swimming pools. A number of new parks had been created, and handsome new schools and other public buildings had been built. Furthermore, the "Jewish Quarter," or ghetto, could no longer be defined as existing between the boundaries of certain streets. The East Side was still a neighborhood of immigrants, but the Jews were moving out. By 1919, the pushcarts were all but gone, as the peddlers had moved indoors to shops, or to factories uptown. A few old-timers remained, not so much out of love as out of familiarity with their surroundings, but a new generation, American-born, had come of age since the 1880s, had gone to college, studied to be lawyers, doctors, accountants, teachers, architects, had prospered and had moved away. This generation of Jews would leave their memories of the ghetto behind them. They would also, as we shall see, shuck the strict Orthodoxy of their parents, in favor of a more modern, more American, more assimilationist Judaism.

There had been setbacks, to be sure, in this outward and upward process of mobility. In 1914, three popular Russian-Jewish banks on the Lower East Side, run by the brothers M. and L. Yarmulowsky, Adolf Mandel, and Max Kobre, had collapsed. These banks had been very casually set up by men who made their depositors big promises but who had little banking expertise, and whose loan policies were, to say the least, fly-by-night. In August of that year, responding to rumors that the banks were in an unsound financial condition, the New York State banking superintendent shut down all three. There was an immediate panic on the Lower East Side, and in the investigation that followed, the banking commission's worst fears were confirmed. The Yarmulowskys' bank, for example, owed $1,703,000, and had assets of only $654,000. The Mandel bank had $1,250,000 less than what it owed.

That the hard-earned savings of thousands of immigrants were wiped out in these bank closings was, of course, a tragedy. But on the other hand, it was impossible not to be impressed by the fact that these savings, in 1914, represented collectively more than ten million dollars. Also, those Jewish savers who had been wiped out did not accept their fate meekly or docilely, or even philosophically, as they might have done a generation earlier, or as they certainly would have done back home in Russia, where such disasters had been routine. They were fighting mad. M. Yarmulowsky and his family had to escape across rooftops to avoid the angry mob that had gathered outside his house. Reserves were called out to control the hundreds of demonstrators in front of Mandel's house. And the furious depositors marched to the district attorney's office, demanding satisfaction, in the American way, through legal action against the perpetrators of the fiscal malefactions. As a result, Mandel was convicted of embezzlement, Yarmulowsky was found guilty and given a suspended sentence, and Kobre committed suicide.

And yet, by 1919, the Eastern European Jews were back on their feet again, and moving steadily out of the ghetto. Some were moving to pleasant brownstones along Prospect Park in Brooklyn. In once-suburban Harlem, where many middle-class Jews had already moved, there was a postwar influx of poor blacks from the rural South, and in response to this, Jewish families made the next logical move northward, into the Bronx. Here, big, new, and roomy apartment houses — some red brick, some tan, some gleaming, expensive white — were rising along the wide street that was then known as Speedway Boulevard and Concourse. Both Harlem and the Bronx were becoming what sociologists call "entry neighborhoods," and they marked clear stages in the immigrants' passage out of poverty into some notion of respectability. Others moved to the Upper West Side, along Central Park West and West End Avenue, or, if they could afford it, to what by the 1920s had become the most fashionable Jewish address in the city, Riverside Drive, where there were big apartments with spacious views of the Hudson and the New Jersey Palisades beyond. From the affluence of Riverside Drive, it would seem only a step to the manicured lawns and gardens of Scarsdale, or to Georgian mansions on Long Island's South Shore, or to tennis courts and polo fields in Beverly Hills.

Part Two
GETTING OUT: 1920-1950

6

THE JEWISH LAKE
AND OTHER CREATIONS

THE uptown German Jews watched the emergence of the Russians as successful entrepreneurs with a curious commingling of emotions. On the one hand, there was a certain sense of relief and satisfaction: the "Jewish Quarter," downtown, was no longer an embarrassment of crowding, poverty, illness, and ignorance; the settlement houses and other social programs that the uptown moguls had helped institute had done their jobs, and the Russians, no longer eyesores, were moving into the mainstream of American life. At their uptown, exclusively German Temple Emanu-El, wealthy German hands were no longer beseeched to dig into ample German pockets to help "our miserable brethren" on the Lower East Side, and this development was welcomed. But, on the other hand, this had all happened so fast that it was almost dismaying. The Germans had complained so bitterly to themselves of the Russian burden they had shouldered that it was almost disappointing to have the burden removed so quickly — as someone who has enjoyed poor health for a number of years, and all the perquisites of illness, may feel a letdown when told that he has been miraculously cured.

It had taken the Germans two and in some cases three generations to reach their status of wealth and almost assimilation. It had taken the Russians barely one. Was it possible that the Russians were, of all things, cleverer? The banker Felix Warburg, who was Jacob Schiff's son-in-law, had actually met a few Russian Jews socially, and had announced, not without condescension, that he had found them "witty and interesting personalities." Among the mixed emotions, that of jealousy could not be ruled out. By

1920 — the year, coincidentally, of Jacob Schiff's death — it seemed uncomfortably possible that the Russians might one day eclipse the Germans, not only in terms of sheer numbers, but in terms of economic and social power. And it seemed possible that that day might not be far off.

Thus, the caste lines remained firmly drawn. The Russians did indeed seem enterprising; the Germans would admit that. But they also seemed brash, aggressive, pushy, loud, argumentative. They had not acquired the fine sheen of social polish that the Germans had striven so hard, and for so long, to possess. At a Jewish fund-raising gathering at Felix Warburg's Fifth Avenue house, a black-tie affair, two men were spotted who were not wearing dinner jackets. "They must be Russians," one of Mr. Warburg's sons whispered. The Russians, in other words, might have become successful, but they had not yet, in the Germans' eyes, become ladies and gentlemen.

Even more perplexing, perhaps, was the fact that Russian Jews were not going into endeavors that were considered solid and respectable, such as stockbrokerage and investment banking and insurance. They were going into chancier fields. Since many Russian men and women had arrived with some experience as tailors and seamstresses, they had gone into tailoring and dressmaking, and were now taking over the entire garment industry, and in the process turning it into what would become the largest single industry in New York City. Previously, nearly all the cloak manufacturers had been Germans, and prior to 1900, the average American woman had been very poorly dressed. Rich women shopped for fashions in Europe, or had dressmakers to copy the European designs that appeared in American fashion magazines. But poorer women dressed in what amounted to sacks, with neither fit nor style. But once the Russians entered the business, all that began to change. The Germans had been merely merchants, but the Russians were artists and artisans. In addition to the concept of sizing, they brought with them a knowledge and appreciation of the colors and textures and weights of fabrics. Having worked as tailors in Russia, they knew how a pleat should fall, how a hem should hang, where a gusset or a gore or a dart should be placed. Russian furriers understood the qualities of furs by the feel and by the smell of untreated pelts, and they knew how sections of kid could be pieced together to conform to the shapes of women's hands. Once they had mastered the mechanics of the garment industry — the machines that had been unavailable in the old country — they were able to introduce to it literally thousands of innovations, to perfect and revolutionize the industry. With the new techniques of mass production, they were able to offer women stylish, well-fitting clothes off the racks at low prices, and by 1920 fashion was available to even the lowliest waitress or shopgirl. They had invented American fashion.

Still, to the Germans, it seemed an unbusinesslike enterprise, for what could be chancier, more unpredictable, than fashion, which was subject to shifting tastes, whims, and sudden fads? Fashion, furs, diamonds, jewelry — all wildly fluctuating commodities, all even riskier than show business. But the Russian Jews seemed to thrive on risks.

Crime, meanwhile, could hardly be considered a business at all. What could be a more win-or-lose, go-for-broke career than a life outside the law? That the East Side had produced a number of criminals was well known, and the attitude toward these people among the Russian-Jewish community was somewhat ambivalent. On the one hand, Jewish parents did not point out these men to their children as examples of American success. And yet, at the same time, there was a certain grudging admiration for men who could buck the system and get away with it. The Jewish criminal wore snappy clothes, drove an expensive car, was good to his wife, and could afford to send his sons to Harvard instead of the City College of New York. There was a certain glamour about him, rather like a Hollywood movie star. Crime, after all, was another way out of the ghetto, and nobody could be faulted for wanting to get out. And, for some, it was proving a very *rapid* way out of the ghetto — as whirlwind a way as Rose Pastor's engagement and marriage. Also, for otherwise perfectly legitimate Jewish businessmen, it was often useful to have a friend with "connections" who could get things done expeditiously, without going through a lot of legal red tape. Union problems, for example, could often be handled with a little muscle from certain quarters. And so the Jewish criminal was not regarded, among Jews, as an enemy of society, but more as a part of the general American landscape. By 1920, Meyer Lansky had become part of this panorama.

There are at least two versions of how Meyer Lansky first became friendly with another tough young East Sider named Salvatore Lucania, later to become known as Charles "Lucky" Luciano. Lansky liked to recall that they had first encountered each other at what had threatened to become a Lower East Side street battle between the Italians and the Jews, and how Luciano had been attracted by the tiny — fully grown, he was only a few inches over five feet tall — Lansky's spunk and nerve. Luciano had called off the fight and later taken Lansky under his protection, gratis. Luciano would recall the initial meeting somewhat differently. Luciano had been earning extra pin money collecting pennies from Jewish youths for protection, but when he approached Lansky with the usual proposition, Lansky had replied, "Fuck you!" Impressed, Luciano had offered to supply Lansky with free protection, to which Lansky had replied, "Shove your protection up your ass!" Realizing that they were kindred spirits, the two became lifelong friends and business associates. This friendship, too, marked the beginning of a Jewish-Italian alliance against a common East Side enemy, the Irish.

Soon, into the Lansky-Luciano group came another, somewhat older Jewish youth named Benjamin Siegel. Siegel was a well-built, good-looking fellow who had quite a way with the ladies, and whose ambition in those days was to become a movie star. It was not such a farfetched notion, since one of his best friends was a young actor named George Raft. Raft had been a street fighter and gambler out of Hell's Kitchen, and had boxed his way up from a number of small-time clubs all the way to Madison Square Garden, where he realized that he hadn't the fighting ability to reach top boxing circles. He had turned to dancing in nightclubs and revues, and became famous overnight for teaching the young Prince of Wales to do the Charleston. From there, it was on to Broadway and Hollywood. His friend Benny Siegel, though, had kind of a wild streak in him. Most Jewish and Italian street toughs eschewed knives and guns, but Siegel was always armed with one weapon or another, and would brandish these at the slightest provocation. For this behavior, and other bizarre habits — it was said that Siegel invented the game called Russian roulette — he was labeled "crazy as a bedbug," which earned him the nickname "Bugsy," though this was an appellation his friends were careful never to use to his face. Bugsy Siegel, as we shall see, eventually did get to Hollywood, though not in the manner he had originally planned.

Into this loosely organized but very effective fraternity came other Lower East Side Jews: Abe "Kid Twist" Reles, whose nickname derived from the fact that even as a kid he was adept at the "twist" of extortion; Arnold "the Brain" Rothstein, much admired for his ability to conceive and carry out grand schemes, and who came up with the notion of fixing the 1919 [baseball] World Series between the Chicago White Sox and the Cincinnati Reds. Then there was Jacob "Greasy Thumb" Guzik, whose thumb, it was said, was stained green from collecting bribes and blackmail; and Abner "Longie" Zwillman, whose nickname referred to the uncommon length of a certain anatomical endowment; and Louis "Lepke" Buchalter, whose doting mother called him "Lepkele," or "little Louis," and whose early career had involved picking pockets and robbing pushcarts. But from the very beginning of the organization, there was only one man who was its acknowledged leader — the little Caesar who planned the battles, deployed the troops, settled internal arguments, and, with his mathematical genius, kept the books — and that was Meyer Lansky. If much of the brawn of the group was supplied by others, it was Lansky who supplied the brains.

Lansky never liked to think of his chosen means of livelihood as anything other than a business. It might not be a legitimate business, but it was still a business, and Lansky tried to keep it on as businesslike a level — no tampering with the books — as possible. It was a business, as he saw it, that was designed to cater to certain basic human needs — a service business. Human beings liked to gamble, and would gamble whether gambling was legal or not, and so Lansky and his associates would put themselves at the service of gamblers. At the same time, Lansky had his own strict moral code. He would not, for example, involve himself in prostitution. Prostitution could also be rationalized as fulfilling a human need, but Lansky would have none of it. Some of his partners called him a prude for this, and in a way he was. But he was also something of a snob. He considered prostitution dehumanizing, but it also got one mixed up with all the wrong sort of people. As a boy, he had seen a beautiful Jewish prostitute named Rachel, to whom he had taken a fancy, beaten to death in a back alley by her Jewish pimp. The grisly, sordid scene remained etched in his mind.

He felt the same way about trafficking in narcotics. Again, the people who were in the drug trade struck him as lowlifes whom he wouldn't want to be seen with, and the addicts they served were the dregs of humanity. Lansky had his standards. In many ways, if you overlooked his source of income, Meyer Lansky was a young gentleman of the old school. As he began to prosper from his gambling operations, he remained a conservative fellow. His friend Bugsy Siegel might favor loud neckties and flashy sport coats, but Lansky always dressed quietly in well-cut three-button suits — which, with his slight figure, he usually bought in the boys' department of Macy's. He did not look like a "gangster," nor did he act like one. In manner, he was genial, soft-spoken — except, of course, when crossed. He was also a devoutly pious Jew and faithfully kept the Sabbath.

Still, Lansky and Company's business might have remained a relatively small one had it not been for an event that, for an organization dedicated to serving human needs, amounted to nothing less than a windfall. On January 16, 1919, the Eighteenth Amendment to the Constitution of the United States was ratified, to become law one year later. The amendment banned the manufacture, sale, and transportation of liquor, wine, beer, or other intoxicating substances. Nine months later, over President Wilson's veto, the Volstead Act was passed by Congress, toughening the Prohibition laws and setting up the machinery for their enforcement. The Women's Christian Temperance Union had been triumphant; the "noble experiment" had begun.

Perhaps never in the history of government folly had an experiment so doomed to failure been undertaken, and certainly never had a scheme so outwardly drenched in piety and righteousness been embarked upon with so much cynicism. America had been a drinking nation since pre-Colonial times, and there was nothing to indicate that Prohibition could change this. Instead, Prohibition was an open invitation to break the law, and to break it in the most daring, glamorous, and exciting ways. Drinking in America had always been associated with parties and good times, and now Prohibition offered Americans a chance to go on a prolonged, illegal binge. Even as Prohibition was being enacted into law, the very legislators who had voted for it were planning ways of obtaining their own personal supplies of liquor. The "year of grace" allowed wealthy hoarders plenty of time to stock their cellars for years to come. Furthermore, it gave legitimate bars and restaurants time to convert to illicit speakeasies, so that by the early 1920s, there were thousands in the city of New York alone. It also allowed men like Meyer Lansky and his friends the time to develop an elaborate game plan for buying and marketing alcoholic beverages, so that when the Volstead Act finally went into effect, they had a virtually foolproof strategy for working around the law. On the very eve of Prohibition, nightclub comics joked about the various ways of obtaining liquor that would become available the following day. Had it not been for Prohibition, men like Lansky, Luciano, and Siegel might have continued as operators of small-time gambling parlors, living in a series of cold-water tenement flats. But Prohibition offered a golden door to riches — for Lansky, what would become one of the larger personal fortunes in America — all for helping Americans defy an unpopular law. The profits, as Lansky saw them, would be far greater than those from gambling operations; the penalties were far less; and the chance of those penalties being enforced was infinitesimal. Once again, he was in a service business. And he was not yet twenty.

There were two kinds of bootleggers, from the beginning. One dealt in cheap, watered-down liquor and in homemade brews from basement stills. The other dealt in the real thing. Lansky counseled his associates to join the latter group. Partly, it was his snobbish nature. But also, he reasoned, dealing in cut, ersatz liquor — in which a bottle labeled "Scotch" might actually be only colored water, raw alcohol, and a splash of real Scotch for flavor — meant that one's clientele would consist mostly of skid-row bums and the sleaziest bars; there would be little repeat business. If, on the other hand, one could offer good, uncut, imported Scotches and gins that had not been tampered with, one would be dealing with the well-heeled — along with the most expensive bars and clubs — who would pay anything for top quality and who, once they had learned to trust their bootlegger, would come back for more of the same. Lansky had also read a book called *Making Profits*, written a few years earlier by a Harvard professor of economics named William Taussig. In it, Professor Taussig had outlined the law of supply and demand. What it meant, Lansky explained to his less literate associates, was, "If you have a lot of what people want and can't get, then you can supply the demand and shovel in the dough." Among his friends, this quickly became known as "Lansky's Law," and it would become the basic precept by which organized crime would live from that point onward, just as legitimate capitalist society lived by it, and had been living by it, all along.

But there was more to it than that. As Prohibition began to lift the underworld from what had been a loosely organized group of friends, relatives, and acquaintances into the stratosphere of Big Business, the many ramifications of the Volstead Act became quickly clear. For the average consumer, Prohibition meant essentially one thing: the cost of liquor went up, to cover the costs of the risks involved. But times were prosperous, and the average consumer understood the situation, and cheerfully paid the price. There was money to be made in all directions. Foreign distillers could raise their prices for the illicit American market. The speakeasies that instantly sprang up across the countryside became instantly prosperous, since they could charge their "member" customers more for drinks by the glass than had previously been charged in legal bars. Soon it was estimated that there were at least twenty-two thousand speakeasies on the island of Manhattan alone — far more than there had ever been legitimate bars. (One popular speakeasy on West Fifty-second Street, Jack and Charlie's 21 Club, operated by two brothers named Kriendler, was the forerunner of today's posh and elegant "21" Restaurant as well as the prestigious "21"-brand liquors.) The makers of fruit juices, mixers, and sweeteners also made money, since the flavors of inferior liquors could be disguised by colas and syrups. (The mixed "cocktail" was a Prohibition invention of necessity.) Bootleggers in the smallest towns could make money. Even poor Italians on the Lower East Side, who had been brewing their own wines and spirits in their homes for years, found themselves proprietors of profitable neighborhood liquor stores. Into all these sources of money Meyer Lansky plunged. As his network of connections in other American cities grew, where local gamblers knew as well as he that their patrons spent more at the gaming tables when their inhibitions had been loosened by alcohol, it was natural that his group should extend its operations into the illegal import of liquor.

Some of the earliest attempts to smuggle liquor into the United States were clumsy and naive. The term "bootlegging," for example, derived from stuffing bottles of liquor into the tops of oversized boots to foil customs inspectors at American borders. Some carried in liquor strapped to their persons under bulky coats.*

For American bootleggers, the handiest source of liquor was Canada, with its long and relatively unguarded border, much of which was wilderness, and as bootlegging grew more profitable, its methods became more sophisticated. Before crossing the border, for example, a truck driver with a load of contraband would select a dirt road, and then attach heavy chains to his rear bumper. He would then charge across the border, refusing to stop for the customs inspector, while his dragging chains kicked up so much dust that he was impossible to follow.

Liquor made its way into Canada from England, Ireland, Scotland, and Europe by way of two tiny French islands (actually a *département* of France) off the Newfoundland coast that most people had never heard of, Saint Pierre and Miquelon. Here the shipments were uncrated for redistribution to the American bootleg market, and most of the wooden houses on the principal, virtually treeless island of Saint Pierre were built with lumber obtained from cast-off liquor crates. From Canada, a particularly popular route of shipment was by boat across Lake Erie, where long stretches of shoreline on both the American and Canadian sides were unpopulated, but where old logging roads led inland from the shore to connect with main arteries. One of Meyer Lansky's first assignments to his underlings was to have maps drawn of these uncharted roads. In his youth, he had worked briefly as an automobile mechanic, and had learned quite a lot about cars. A side operation was organized to service, repair, and camouflage stolen trucks and other vehicles that were used to transport liquor to the marketplace.

Meanwhile, bootlegging had suddenly become a glamorous occupation, and the bootlegger a glamorous figure. Bootleggers in the early 1920s were like cowboy heroes out of the Old West who

---

*This author's own mother, returning from Europe, made her way safely, if clinking slightly and looking somewhat overweight, with bottles plunged into her girdle and a bottle in each cup of her brassiere.

took the law into their own hands, and women chattered about their favorite bootleggers as they might about their favorite hairdressers ("We've found the most wonderful new bootlegger . . ."). In small towns, the bootlegger gained almost the same respect and social status as the local doctor, lawyer, or undertaker. In the cities, bootleggers were invited to all the best parties, and had their pick of the most desirable women. The term "gangster" was used almost reverentially, and Hollywood gangster movies achieved great popularity. A number of silent film stars of the era — Pola Negri, Gloria Swanson, Renée Adorée — were said to have taken gangster lovers. In the best hotels and restaurants, men reputed to be gangsters were given the best tables. When gangsters were recognized, children asked for their autographs.

There were dangers involved in bootlegging, of course, but they were relatively slight. Despite the desperate efforts of American lawmen to police the Canadian border, it was estimated that only five percent of the smuggled booty was ever successfully stopped or confiscated — and any legitimate salesman who succeeded in getting ninety-five percent of his merchandise sold would have considered himself more than fortunate. Occasionally, there were unsettling incidents. In 1927, a convoy of trucks carrying liquor from Ireland was ambushed outside of Boston. The Irish guards who were in charge of the shipment opened fire on the ambushers, and before the shooting was over eleven men lay dead.

The ambushers, who were working for the Lansky organization, were able to make off with the whiskey, but Lansky himself was furious. Whiskey, he roared, was replaceable, but human lives were not. Besides, eleven bodies strewn along the roadside meant that there would be police and federal investigations — the last things he wanted. His men had been instructed that, whenever any actual shooting started, they should run for their lives, and no doubt the Lansky employee who returned the Irish fire would have been disciplined, were it not for the fact that he was already dead.

Later, Lansky learned that the "importer" of the Irish whiskey whom he had robbed was the son of a Boston bartender, Joseph P. Kennedy. For the rest of his life, Lansky would claim that Joseph Kennedy had passed on his vendetta to his sons, Bobby and John, and that Bobby Kennedy's efforts, as United States attorney general, to root out organized crime were in fact a personal attempt to "get even" with Lansky for that long-ago hijacking.*

Meanwhile, to the north of Lake Erie, another gentleman was emerging who was becoming very important to Meyer Lansky and his flourishing American bootleg business. His name was Samuel Bronfman, and it was not long before Lansky and Bronfman had entered into an arrangement that would be enormously profitable to both.

Sam Bronfman was also the son of Russian-Jewish immigrants, but there the similarity ended. Unlike Lansky's parents, Sam Bronfman's father, Yechiel, had been reasonably well-to-do in the old country. Yechiel Bronfman had owned a gristmill and a good-sized tobacco plantation in Bessarabia, in southwestern Russia, and had thought himself on good terms with the czarist government. All that ended, however, in the face of the Alexandrine pogroms, and in 1889 Yechiel decided to emigrate, leaving the plantation and gristmill behind him. Nonetheless, when the Bronfman family set out for North America, they could afford to bring with them a personal maid, a manservant, and even their own personal rabbi — plus the rabbi's wife and two children. Nor was theirs a piecemeal emigration; the Bronfmans traveled as a family. With Yechiel came his nearly nine-months-pregnant wife, Minnie, their two sons, Abe and Harry, and a daughter, Laura. On shipboard, their third son, Sam, was born. (Later, like Sam Goldwyn, Sam Bronfman would take a couple of years off his age and claim to have been born in 1891, not 1889, and give his birthplace as Brandon, Manitoba, rather than the mid-Atlantic.)

The family's initial destination was the little Canadian village of Wapella, in southwestern Saskatchewan, where the Canadian government was offering homesteading sites to immigrants. In the next few years, Wapella — the neighboring towns bore such names as Red Jacket, Uno, Beulah, Birtle, and Moosomin — would become one of the first all-Jewish settlements in North America.

But the ocean crossing, or perhaps the trauma of resettling his

---

*Conspiracy theories of the two Kennedy assassinations have noted the long-standing Kennedy-Lansky feud, suggesting that organized crime was behind both murders. Adding to this is the fact that Jack Ruby was a Jewish barkeep who may, or may not, have had Lansky connections. Many Jewish barkeeps did.

family, seemed to take some of the enterprising spirit out of Yechiel Bronfman, who soon simplified his name to Ekiel. He was unprepared for the rigorous climate of the Saskatchewan prairie, and it was soon clear that the sacks of tobacco seed he had brought with him from Russia, intending to start a new plantation, would be of no use to him here. The first summer, he tried wheat, but his crop was killed by frost, and presently he was forced to abandon farming and was reduced to going into the bush, where he cut logs to sell for firewood. With a sleigh and a yoke of oxen, he hauled his wood into town, some twenty miles away. The family's first home was a drafty lean-to, and their diet consisted mainly of potatoes, dried apples, and prunes. To further straiten the family's circumstances, four more children were born in fairly rapid succession — Jean, Bessie, Allen, and Rose — giving Ekiel Bronfman eight children's mouths to feed. Times were hard.

But by the mid-1890s, when the two oldest boys, Harry and Abe, were old enough to help their father, there was improvement. From hauling and selling firewood, the Bronfmans were able to branch out into selling frozen whitefish to their Jewish neighbors. The sleigh and oxen were replaced by a horse and wagon, and the Bronfmans, father and sons, would transport anything that their neighbors needed carted. The drayage business led them naturally into a bit of horse-trading. Most of these trades took place in the bar of a local hotel called the Langham, the town's only watering place, and for some of these transactions Ekiel brought along his next-youngest son, Sam. Sam would be seated on a barstool, told to keep his mouth shut and his ears open and learn the business. One thing young Sam apparently noticed during these long horse-trading afternoons at the Langham bar was that a great deal of liquor was being consumed there, and with relish.

One day, according to a family story, Sam Bronfman, age eleven, was on his way to the Langham with his father to close a deal over drinks, and said, "The Langham's bar makes more profit than we do, Father. Instead of selling horses, we should be selling drinks."

If the story is true, it was a shrewd observation. In the early 1900s, the hotel and bar business was a lucrative one in Canada. The railroads were rapidly opening up the western part of the country, and hotel space was at a premium. A hotel could not survive without a bar, which was where it made most of its money.

Ekiel Bronfman seems to have sparked to his son's suggestion. There was, after all, a curious coincidence. The name "Bronfman," in Yiddish, means "brandy man." Though no known Bronfman ancestor had been in the liquor business, they had dealt in grain — an ingredient of whiskey.

Financing a hotel venture, it turned out, was no great problem. Eager to promote more bars, distillers and liquor-store owners were willing to lend money to promising hotel operators. This was how, in 1902, Ekiel Bronfman was able to scrape together the money to buy his first hotel — the Anglo American in Emerson, Manitoba.

The Anglo American, as expected, prospered. Ekiel was able to repay his loan, and presently the Bronfmans could expand their interests again, this time investing in a series of modest apartment houses. Soon there were three more hotels, in Winnipeg.

The quality of the hotel clientele in western Canada in those pioneering days was, of course, not uniformly high, and later it would be claimed that the Bronfman caravansaries were little more than brothels in disguise. To this, Sam Bronfman liked to reply, "If they were, then they were the best in the West!" But what is certain is that from the beginning it was Sam who was the guiding spirit of the hotel business, and whose chief bailiwick was the bar receipts.

By 1916, these receipts had mounted to the point where Sam was able to purchase his first retail liquor outlet, the Bonaventure Liquor Store Company in Montreal, which was then Canada's largest city. The store was small, but it was well located, near the railroad station, where travelers leaving for the western provinces — many of which were going dry — could get in their supplies. Also, it enabled Sam Bronfman to be his own supplier, eliminating the cost of a middleman.

Meanwhile, south of the border, the advocates of Prohibition were gathering their forces. Everywhere the Carrie Nations of America were taking to the lecture platform, proclaiming that alcohol was undermining American industry, the home, the family, the teachings of Jesus, the will of God. The Anti-Saloon League of New York even claimed that drink had been behind the Russian revolution. "Bolshevism flourishes in wet soil," one of its leaflets warned. "Failure to enforce Prohibition in Russia was followed by

Bolshevism. Failure to enforce Prohibition here will encourage disrespect for [the] law and invite Industrial Disaster. Radical and Bolshevist outbreaks are practically unknown in states where Prohibition has been in effect for years. BOLSHEVISM LIVES ON BOOZE."

From such rumblings in the United States, and the fact that the passage of the Eighteenth Amendment began to seem assured, it occurred to Sam Bronfman that this might well be the moment to move from bartending and liquor retailing into manufacturing. Yet another middleman would be eliminated.

"Distilling" would be too polite a word to use for Sam's initial efforts. It was more like simple mixology. From the United States, he was able to buy several hundred thousand gallons of raw, overproof alcohol at bargain prices in the panicky pre-Prohibition sell-offs. This he simply thinned with an equal amount of water, added about half as much again real whiskey, and tossed in a bit of caramel for color, plus a dash of sulfuric acid. The purpose of the sulfuric acid was to speed the aging process. While real Scotch whiskey might be aged for two to twelve years, Bronfman Scotch could be aged in about two days. To be sure, there were some mishaps in the beginning. One batch of "Scotch" came out of the vat an alarming purple color. But with more thinning with real Scotch, and some more caramel, the right color was finally achieved and the batch was thereby saved. Next, all Sam had to do was bottle the results and slap on labels. A printer was found who promised that he could produce convincing counterfeits. To be sure, some of his work was either amateurish or deliberately misleading. Johnnie Walker came out as Johnny Walker, Glenlivet was Glen Levitt, and Haig and Haig was Hague and Hague. But few of the customers seemed to notice.

What no one noticed, either — not even Sam Bronfman himself — was that with this haphazard mixing of alcohol, real whiskey, and other ingredients, Bronfman was in the process of inventing a whole new category of alcoholic beverage: blended whiskey. Could he have possibly known, as early as 1920, that one day the most popular and largest-selling whiskeys on the North American continent would be blends? Or that he himself would one day elevate blending to an art form with the declaration, "Distilling is a science; blending is an art"? But what Sam Bronfman surely noticed — as came to light in 1922, when the Canadian government began wondering why none of the Bronfmans had filed any income tax returns — was that a mixture that cost only $5.25 a gallon to produce could be bottled and sold for $25 a gallon. And that, when the distillery was running well, it could process five thousand gallons a week, which put sales figures at half a million dollars a month, or an annual profit of more than $4,500,000.

With Prohibition in effect, Meyer Lansky, who was now very much aware of Sam Bronfman's operation, at first dismissed him as an amateur; his product simply was not good enough for the kind of customers Lansky wanted to serve. But Sam, putting his brother Harry in charge of the distilling operations, had been busily running about the countryside and dashing off to Britain to line up Canadian and Scottish distillers and persuading them to let him be their distributor. He had also, with his profit sheets, been able to make a convincing case for himself with Canadian banks, and to obtain loans, which gave him added capital with which to perfect his blending process — so that every bottle of whiskey produced under the same label would taste the same as every other. And once the Saint Pierre–Miquelon connection had been established, with Sam able to import bona fide brands, Lansky became interested. Sam Bronfman came down from Canada and wooed Lansky with lavish dinners. Lansky responded by getting Bronfman tickets to the heavyweight "prizefight of the century," between Jack Dempsey and Luis Angel Firpo in 1923. A deal was struck, and the two men became partners, a relationship that lasted through Repeal and after.

What impressed Lansky the most was that what Bronfman was doing was all perfectly legal — in Canada, that is. Bronfman had no trouble with customs or police on the Canadian side of the border. In fact, the Ottawa government actually encouraged the export of liquor to the United States by refunding the nine-dollar-a-gallon tax that it imposed on all liquor sold for consumption within Canada.* What was good for Canadian distillers, Ottawa argued, was good for Canada, and in the first year after the passage of the Volstead Act, export sales shot up to a record twenty-three million dollars — a considerable boost to the Canadian economy.

*For the Bronfmans, an "incentive" bonus of $180,000 a month. Not bad.

As the Canadian *Financial Post* editorialized, "Rum running has provided a tidy bit towards Canada's favourable balance of trade."

Sam Bronfman and Meyer Lansky made an odd pair. Like Lansky, Bronfman was short of stature and, at five feet five inches, stood only an inch taller than his American dealer. But whereas Lansky was thin, and never weighed more than 135 pounds at any point in his life, Bronfman tended to plumpness, and his round, pink face often shone with a deceptively cherubic twinkle Also, whereas Lansky was basically only interested in making money, Sam Bronfman had begun to entertain far greater ambitions. The Canadian social establishment was, and to an extent still is, a tight-knit one of old, Anglo-Saxon, Church of England families, who regarded themselves as a smaller and, if anything, more select aristocracy than the British nobility, on whom they modeled their behavior and attitudes. Their ranks were guarded by such exclusive men's clubs as Montreal's Mount Royal and Saint James's. Sam Bronfman, now in his thirties and a rich man, had begun to court the members of this hidebound Canadian inner circle, with an eye to one day being included in its membership. In the process, he would feign elaborate disinterest in the source of his new wealth, and would bridle at the suggestion that he himself was a "bootlegger." In his bespoke suits from Savile Row and his hand-benched English shoes from Lobb of London, he affected the appearance of an English country squire in the city for a few days on a bit of business. He even added a few Briticisms to his speech with an occasional "I say!" or "Fancy that!" He professed indifference to the ultimate destination of his whiskey during Prohibition — that was in the hands of men like Meyer Lansky. Never, he insisted, had he ever transported a single drop illegally across the border, nor, he would add with a wink, had he ever counted the empty bottles of his brands on the other side of Lake Erie. Instead, he concentrated on building an imposing turreted mansion at the summit of Westmount, Montreal's most fashionable suburb, and began filling it with "ancestral" trappings — suits of armor, "family portraits" of no known origin — all with the aim of creating an effect of instant Old Money. The name he gave to the Westmount residence said it all: Belvedere Palace.

He did, however, contribute a few ideas to Meyer Lansky's operation, and came up with at least one "invention" that the

American bootleggers found useful. One of the things that the revenuers looked for along the lakeshore was the telltale sign of heavy tire-tread marks along the muddy bank, indicating that a truck had backed to the water's edge to receive a load of liquor from a boat. To eliminate clues like this, Sam Bronfman proposed that a series of sturdy boards be lashed together with wire or rope. One side of this flexible platform would be sodded with grass. When a boat was ready to unload, the grassy side of the contraption could be flipped over to produce a wooden ramp, down which trucks could be backed. When the operation was completed, the ramp was reversed again so that a customs inspector, looking for tire tracks, would see only a pristine grassy sward. It was a device that was as simple as it was cheap to make. Each reversible ramp lasted a week or so, until the grass died. Then it was resodded.

In 1922, Sam Bronfman was thirty-three and very rich, but a dynast without a dynasty. He had already begun to think of himself as a latter-day Rothschild, but the House of Bronfman was not yet a House. It was time, he decided, for him to marry and start producing heirs, or Heirs; and, since "Mr. Sam," as he was now being addressed, was the unquestioned kingpin of his family, he decided that some of his brothers and sisters should marry as well. For his bride, Sam chose a Manitoba girl named Saidye Rosner, whose father, Samuel, had also emigrated to Canada from Bessarabia, and had achieved a certain distinction for having briefly served as mayor of the little town of Plum Coulee. Sam and Saidye were married on June 20, and two days later Sam's sister Rose married Maxwell Rady, a Winnipeg doctor. Then both newlywed couples boarded a train to Ottawa, where Sam's brother Allan married Lucy Bilsky on June 28. From there, Sam and Allan and their respective brides left for Vancouver, where Sam wanted to look over a distillery.

That Sam and Saidye's marriage was not a particularly romantic one is clear from the fact that Sam rarely spent more than two or three nights a month at home in Montreal. Keeping track of his growing business kept him dashing back and forth across the face of Canada. Also, since his principal source of revenue was coming from the United States, he was required to be in New York so often that he leased a Pullman compartment on the Montreal–New York Express on a permanent basis so that he didn't have to bother with reservations. He was spending so much time in New York, in fact — living in a series of increasingly opulent hotel suites — that a number of American friends suggested to him that he might consider becoming a citizen of the country to which he owed such an expansive style of living. But at this suggestion he balked. Partly it was out of an innate provincialism; Canada had been lucky for him, and he was unwilling and unready to tamper with that luck in a larger, richer country. Also, in the United States it would be difficult to escape the label "bootlegger," whereas in Canada, where what he was selling was perfectly legal, there remained a chance that he might one day achieve the thing he wanted most — acceptance by the social establishment — even though it still eluded him.

There was an even more important reason. The United States did not confer ennobling titles upon its citizens. In Britain, the great distillers had become viscounts, barons, and baronets. There were Lord Dewar, Sir Alexander Walker (of Johnnie Walker), Lord Woolavington, Lord Forteviot, Sir James Charles Calder, and Field Marshal Earl Haig. Canada didn't often confer knighthoods on its citizens, but it sometimes did. Ottawa had already expressed its gratitude to Sam Bronfman's industry in various ways. Then why, someday, should there not be a Sir Samuel Bronfman, and a Lady Saidye Bronfman? It did not seem an impossibility. And it would have a nice ironic twist — the family that had fled Russia to escape the persecution of the nobility, elevated to a nobility all its own in a single generation's time.

Meanwhile, Sam's profitable connection with Meyer Lansky and his growing organization continued apace. Sam Bronfman might not consider himself a bootlegger, but Lansky and Company certainly did. As Lansky's chief confederate, Lucky Luciano, put it, Sam Bronfman "was bootleggin' enough whiskey across the Canadian border to double the size of Lake Erie."

It was no wonder that wags in the liquor trade were beginning to refer to Lake Erie as "the Jewish lake."

7

FITTING IN

Not all Eastern European Jews emigrated to America to escape persecution and pogroms. In White Russia, for example — that section of western Russia known as Byelorussia — the situation was somewhat different. Though anti-Semitism was rife, the notorious pogroms of the 1880s and 1890s did not spread there. The province was, however, easily the most socially and economically backward in the land, and most of the White Russian Jews who, along with many of their Christian neighbors, emigrated in the years before the revolution did so simply to escape grinding poverty, in search of the financial promises that beckoned from the west. Many found what they were seeking, including William Fisher — born Velvil Fisch — who arrived in New York in 1906 and headed westward, working briefly in a mattress factory. Fisher in time laid the groundwork for what today is the Aurora Gasoline Company of Detroit, and his son, Max M. Fisher, adviser on economics to United States Presidents, is known as "the richest Jew in Detroit," and enjoys giving the following directions to his office: "Take the Fisher Freeway to Fisher Boulevard, to the Fisher Building . . ."*

In Hungary, an altogether different set of circumstances prevailed, and in the late nineteenth century the status of the Jews in Hungary was probably higher than in any other European country. After nearly a century of rebellion against the Austrian emperor, the lords of upper Hungary were defeated early in the

---

*Max Fisher is no kin to the (Christian) Fishers of Fisher Body, after whom the freeway, street, and building are named. But he doesn't mind the coincidence.

eighteenth century, and the heads of the Hungarian noble houses
fled to Turkey and Poland. Their estates were confiscated by the
Austrian Crown, and were parceled out to pro-Austrian adher-
ents — thus creating a whole new Hungarian aristocracy. This
instant gentry not only owned large sections of towns, villages,
and cities; they also controlled the government, the army, and the
universities. On their vast agrarian estates, they controlled the
peasant population that toiled for them, and it was here that
the Jews had made themselves useful.

The new archdukes and barons much preferred their city palaces
to their country estates, and the Jews, meanwhile, had for many
years handled the trade in grain and cattle between the country
demesnes and the cities, as well as in foreign markets. It was
convenient, then, for the absentee landlords to lease their estates
to Jews, who saw to it that the rents were paid and collected, and
delivered to the city lords. With such leases went all the privileges
of the country squire, including occupancy of the manor house
and keeping a leash on the peasants, who were required to work
a number of days each week in payment for their tenant hold. The
Jews, then, lived at a level just below that of a landed aristocracy.
During the Hungarian revolution of 1848, they had been given
full citizenship rights, and thereafter became ardent Magyar pa-
triots. The landed Jews went in for sports, politics, and patronage
of the arts. It was not uncommon to see these privileged Jews
driving their snappy four-in-hands into town with uniformed hus-
sars seated on top of their boxes. Such Jews, who still considered
themselves Jews, had nonetheless abandoned most of the trappings
of Orthodoxy and, indeed, by lower-class Jews were scornfully —
if enviously — called "pork-eaters."

It was from this sort of, though not quite, upper-crust background that a Hungarian-Jewish youngster named Emery Roth grew
up in a part of Hungary that is now Slovakia, at the foot of the
Carpathian Mountains where they slope to meet the Hungarian
plain. His family owned the local hotel, the only two-story structure
in town and very much the nerve center, where all important
meetings and civic events took place. As an indication of his
family's social status, he was one of the few local children deemed
worthy of being invited to play with the children of the local baron
and baroness. He was well educated in the local academy, and

showed considerable talent as an artist. But then, in his early teens, bad luck struck the family. His father died, his mother was forced to take an older son out of school to help her run the hotel, and Emery was just one mouth too many to feed. His choice: emigration. At the time, he was deeply embarrassed by this, and invented a story, which he told his friends and schoolmates, that he was going to Munich to study art. "I was ashamed to tell them that I was going to America," he wrote, "because the need to emigrate is a confession of poverty, a disgrace no one — at any rate, any boy, will confess to." He left home in the winter of 1884, and arrived at Castle Garden five weeks later.

Outwardly, the circumstances of his emigration seemed propitious. His principal language was Magyar, which was the language of the Hungarian educated classes, but he was also fluent in Slovene, knew quite a bit of German, and had studied Latin. Surely, he presumed, language would present no problem to him, a linguist, in the United States. He also felt that, for a youth of fifteen, he had had quite a sophisticated upbringing. As a hotel-keeper's son, he wrote, "I attended balls, theatrical performances, town meetings, saw carousing and fights and heard the careless talk of all sorts of men. Before I was six years old I had a chance to listen and gape at the varied strata of our population, drunk and sober, from the Field Marshal and high officers that stopped at the hotel when the maneuvers were held in the Carpathians, through the gentry which we housed during the autumn week of the hare drive and the winter boar hunts, on down to the travelling salesmen and the easygoing public officials and townspeople and finally to the soldiers and peasants who frequented that portion of the establishment known as the inn. Magyar, Slovak, Pole, German, Jew, rich and poor, all were guests at our house."

Then, too, a visiting American from Chicago had promised to take young Roth under his wing during the journey over, and to see that the young immigrant found suitable employment when he arrived. This American, who had returned to Hungary to visit his parents, was Aladar V. Kiss, and it was obvious that Mr. Kiss had become a very rich and important person. His calling card and letterhead said so. They proclaimed him to be a "Real Estate Agent," which Mlle Clothilde — the baron's children's governess — helpfully translated for the Roths. The words, she ex-

plained, stood for "Veritable State Administrator," which certainly
sounded imposing. The calling card also proclaimed that Mr. Kiss
was involved in "Management, Mortgages and Appraisals." In
addition, it announced that he was a "Notary Public." In Hungary,
a notary was a very high government official.

Young Roth did not see much of Mr. Kiss during the ocean
crossing, since Roth discovered that he had been placed in steerage, while Mr. Kiss luxuriated above decks in cabin class. He
did, however, see Kiss agan briefly in New York. Kiss directed
him to an immigrant shelter on the Battery, handed him seven
dollars and change, and a ticket on an immigrant train to Chicago,
worth an additional dollar. Then Kiss scribbled an address on a
piece of paper, told Roth to look him up when he got to Chicago
and he would find him a job.

The trip on the immigrant train to Chicago, at that time, took
two days and two nights, since the train was constantly being
shunted off onto sidings to make way for more important carriers.
During the course of this journey, living on a diet of overripe
bananas — a fruit he had never seen before, but which cost only
five cents a dozen — Roth discovered that he had somehow lost
Mr. Kiss's address. No matter, he thought. Surely everyone in
Chicago would know the whereabouts of someone as important as
Aladar V. Kiss. Imagine his dismay, therefore, upon detraining
at Union Station, when no one he spoke to had ever heard of the
great Mr. Kiss. No one, furthermore, seemed to speak any of Roth's
four languages. "I was rather surprised how few people understood
me," he wrote. "I assumed, knowing what a horde of Europeans
had emigrated, that most people in America would understand
some one of the languages I knew, but it seemed that they were
all what I called English."

He spent the next few hours wandering disconsolately about
Union Station, with a little more than four dollars left, wondering
what to do next. With him in the station was a group of soldiers
from Company C of the Grand Army of the Republic who had a
few hours to kill while waiting for a train that would take them
back to their detachment at Fairplains, Illinois. Most were killing
the time bibulously, and it was inevitable that a few of them should
notice the plight of the luckless youth, and take pity on him. At
the height of their jollity, one cheery soldier announced that he

had a splendid idea. Why not take young Roth back to camp with them as Company C's mascot? That was how Roth found himself on another train, heading for an American military base, where, he discovered the next day, a mascot's job was polishing the boots of servicemen.

Still, he did learn one important lesson early on. He began making sketches of his new protectors. The men who posed for him offered to pay him for their likenesses, and at first Roth refused to accept money from them. But he was taken aside by one soldier, and it was carefully explained to him through gestures and Pidgin English: This was America. In America, one should expect to be paid for services rendered. He could not allow himself to produce these clever sketches for nothing; if he did, he would be thought a fool. He must charge, furthermore, whatever he thought the market would bear.

And America, as we know, is the land of miracles. Was it possible that this luckless youth would in not too many years' time become the founder and president of one of New York City's great architectural firms, Emery Roth and Sons? It was. If there is one street corner in New York that is perhaps the most prestigious, it is the corner of Park Avenue and Fifty-seventh Street — a great commercial-residential nexus, where the commerce of lower Manhattan meets the residential grandeur of upper Park Avenue. The building on the northeast corner of this intersection, the Ritz Tower Hotel, was designed by Emery Roth himself. The skyscraper on the northwest corner was designed by his son Richard. The tower on the southwest corner is by his grandson, Richard Roth, Jr. A fourth-generation Roth, waiting in the wings, has already stated his intention of designing a building for the fourth, and only remaining non-Roth, corner.

In the larger cities of Eastern Europe — Moscow, Saint Petersburg, Krakow, Warsaw — it was also easier for the Jew to survive the pogroms that savaged the smaller settlements of the Pale. For one thing, in an urban milieu, the Jew was less conspicuous. In manner and dress and language he did not stand out as different from the rest of the city's population as he did in the *shtetl*. The Jew was also in a better position in a city environment if he had made himself needed — as a merchant, banker, hotelier, or impresario, say, of a metropolitan opera or ballet company. The urban Jew might hate and dread the czar as much as his more rural brethren, but if he kept his politics to himself, kept a low profile, conformed with regulations and didn't break any laws, he was tolerated. Czars and revolutions could come and go, and the Jew could get by.

If one was a clever young Jewish woman, too, there was not much to worry about. Young women, after all, were not conscripted into the czarist armies, and if a young woman did not immediately marry but had other plans, there were avenues out of obscurity to great success. By 1920, one such clever young woman had begun to make her presence felt in New York. Her name was Helena Rubinstein.

Her personal hegira had been an unusual one. She had been born in Krakow, Poland, around 1878, but it may have been 1873, since Madame Rubinstein was always purposely vague about dates, particularly those dates that would pinpoint her age. In 1898, when she was either twenty or twenty-five, she emigrated from Poland, but not for any of the usual reasons; in fact, the rest of her large family remained behind, without undue difficulties, for a number of years. Her reason for leaving — and here again, we have only her word to go on — was an unhappy romance. She had fallen in love with a young medical student of whom her father disapproved. She was sent to Australia to forget the young man. Why Australia — on the other side of the globe? Because the family had relatives there, she would reply. How had she made the journey? "By boat. . . ." How had her family, who she admitted had been poor, been able to afford the price of the ticket? "Mother sold a trinket!" In her ghostwritten autobiography, *My Life for Beauty*, she typically glossed over all these details, leaving perplexing questions unanswered, but Patrick O'Higgins, who worked for and with her for fourteen years, and wrote an engaging memoir, *Madame*, about the experience, was able to sift out a few of the facts from the fictional version Madame Rubinstein preferred.

She first landed at Melbourne, and then traveled to a sheep-ranching community some eighty miles distant called Coleraine, where she had an uncle. The uncle's name was Louis Silberfeld, or Silberfield, as he preferred to spell it, and in her own book Madame Rubinstein describes him variously as a "sheepfarmer," a "merchant," and a "landowner." In fact, O'Higgins discovered, Mr. Silberfield was an oculist, but, assuming that there was not much business for an oculist in a community as small as Coleraine, O'Higgins concludes that he probably ran a general store where he also ground glasses, and, on the side, maintained a flock of sheep, just as most others in the area did. What had brought Mr. Silberfield to Australia is unknown, but it is known that the young Helena Rubinstein disliked him intensely. He, as she put it, "took liberties."

She disliked Coleraine even more, and in her own book described it: "the sun was strong, the wind violent. The never-ending sweep of pasture, broken here and there by a blue gum tree, presented a very different picture from the one I had imagined." She terribly missed big-city life. But, in Coleraine, she did spend a few months in an elementary school and learned rudimentary English. She also, it would seem, made an immediate impression on the local populace, just as the local populace made a strong first impression on her.

She remarked that the Australian women — being from a nation of outdoorspeople and sun worshipers — looked decidedly weather-beaten. Their skin was cracked, wrinkled, dry, and sunburned. (Throughout her days Helena Rubinstein would be outspokenly opposed to exposure to the sun.) By contrast, the beauty of her own skin drew comment. Of her first Australian days, she wrote, "My new friends could not get over the milky texture of my skin. It was, in fact, no better than the average girl's in my home town in Poland, but to the ladies of Victoria, with their sun-scorched, wind-burned cheeks, its city-bred alabaster quality seemed remarkable." Indeed, early photographs of Miss Rubinstein bear her out. She was tiny, only a shade over five feet tall, and her skin, in contrast to her jet-black hair and eyes, did seem to be unusually pale and smooth. Though not technically beautiful, she was certainly a handsome young woman.

The secret of her complexion, she explained, was what she called "Mother's cream," implying that it was a facial cream her mother had concocted from an ancient family recipe. It was called "Crème Valaze," and she had foresightedly packed twelve jars of this splendid lotion in her luggage before leaving Poland. Where did the name "Valaze" come from? The word means nothing in

Polish, nor does it — though it sounds as if it might — in French. But admittedly *Valaze* has a velvety, soothing sound, and any clever copywriter might be proud to have thought it up. Helena shared her miraculous cream with certain friends, and they were immediately pleased with the results. There followed a final quarrel with lecherous Uncle Louis, and, more or less simultaneously, as she told it, she had "a vision!" She would leave the sunbaked reaches of Coleraine, head for the big city of Melbourne, and market her Crème Valaze to the women of Australia. Overnight success!

Actually, there are at least six Australian years left unaccounted for in her memoir, between the time she left Uncle Louis and when her first Maison de Beauté Valaze appeared in Melbourne's Collins Street. There is evidence that, during some of this time, she worked as a waitress in a Melbourne boardinghouse. But she did send home for more jars of Crème Valaze, which, it turned out, was not her mother's recipe at all but was based on a formula developed by a certain Dr. Lykusky in Poland. And she was also able some-how, between 1898 and 1904, to borrow two hundred pounds, from a woman named Helen Macdonald whom she had met on shipboard, to open her first shop. Her first advertisement, pub-lished in Australia in 1904, read, "Mlle. Helena Rubinstein of 274 Collins Street announces the launching of Valaze Russian Skin Food by Doctor Lykusky, the celebrated skin specialist." Within a few months, over nine thousand pounds' worth of orders poured in. Dr. Lykusky was summoned from Poland, along with two of Helena Rubinstein's younger sisters, Manka and Ceska, to help her handle the business. She was on her way, and it was not long before stories headlined POLISH GIRL MAKES GOOD IN AUS-TRALIA were hitting the newspapers.

Within two years, her advertising copy had changed somewhat. Dr. Lykusky was no longer credited as the inventor of the skin cream, nor was there any mention made of its being Russian. Instead, the implication was that Crème Valaze had been created by Mlle Rubinstein. (Dr. Lykusky had either died or been suffi-ciently paid off.) An advertisement from this period was headlined, WHAT WOMEN WANT! A FEW REMARKS BY HELENA RUBINSTEIN. The copy went on to say, in part, "The healthy woman with an unhealthy or ill-nourished skin is not doing her duty to herself or those nearest her. . . . We cannot all be ladies of Milo, but we can all be the best possible in our individual cases." The advertisement also included a bit of uplifting doggerel:

> *Little blots of blemish*
> *In a visage glad*
> *Make the lover thoughtful*
> *And the husband mad.*

Meanwhile, her Maison de Beauté Valaze had become Maison de Beauté Helena Rubinstein.

This would be her method of operation as her business expanded its marketing from a single cream to a long line of creams, cosmetics, and other beauty products. Though she liked to be photographed in a long white laboratory technician's gown, mixing together unguents with a mortar and pestle in what she called her kitchen," she had a genius for creating cosmetic collages. Instead, the "First Lady of Beauty Science," as she later liked to bill herself, often took the creations of others — offering, if they insisted, a small royalty — and marketed them under her own label. As Patrick O'Higgins points out, she was "a masterful adapter" — and merchant — of other people's ideas.

Which is not to say that she was not responsible for some masterful merchandising innovations. She was the first to decide, for example, that skins could be divided into "types" — "dry," "oily," "combination," and "normal." That meant four different kinds of creams right there. She also decided that each skin type required at least three different kinds of creams — one for morning, one for daytime (and as a base for makeup), and one for wearing at night. (Crème Valaze became her morning, or "Wake-Up," cream.) She also began to see her "vision" expanding on a worldwide scale.

By 1905, she was ready to extend her operations to London, dogged by a man named Edward Titus, who had fallen in love with her, but whom she had not decided to marry. A year later, another Maison de Beauté Helena Rubinstein opened in Paris, was an immediate success, and the bright young businesswoman was swept into the glittering prewar world of Misia Sert, Marcel Proust, Jean Cocteau, Gertrude Stein, André Gide, James Joyce, and the painters Pierre Bonnard, Jean Edouard Vuillard, Raoul

Dufy, Paul Helleu, and Pablo Picasso, while Poiret and Chanel made dresses for her.

By 1914, worried about the approaching war in Europe — and by now married to Titus, who was an American citizen, and also having somehow managed to give birth to two sons — she was ready to move on to New York, where she was advised that some of the city's best apartment houses had been built along Central Park West, West End Avenue, and Riverside Drive. She sized up these neighborhoods immediately — "too Jewish" — and settled instead for a brownstone on West Forty-ninth Street. Her family took the top floor, and on the lower two floors she established the first Maison de Beauté Helena Rubinstein in the United States.

Following America's brief experience in World War I, the country was certainly ready for someone with the entrepreneurial skills of a Helena Rubinstein. Prohibition had sparked the country with a sense of gaiety and mischief. Women who would never have dreamed of doing so five years earlier were now sipping cocktails in public. They were also screwing cigarettes into long lacquered holders and lighting up. Everyone was talking about Sigmund Freud, and sex had come out of the bedroom into the drawing room and speakeasy bar. The dizzy decade of the 1920s, the Era of Wonderful Nonsense, was about to begin, and hemlines were shooting up while necklines were plunging down. Before the war, only "fast" women wore cosmetics, but now every woman under the age of fifty wanted to be thought of as a little bit fast, and women were painting their lips and eyebrows, rouging their cheeks as well as their knees, glossing their fingernails and toenails, and thanks to Seventh Avenue a woman no longer needed to be rich to be a la mode.

Helena Rubinstein's first appraisal of American women had been every bit as harsh as that of the Australians. "The first thing I noticed," she wrote, "was the whiteness of the women's faces and the oddly grayish color of their lips. Only their noses, mauve with cold, seemed to stand out." That, of course, was on a January day in 1915 when no New Yorker could have been looking her best, but by the war's end Helena Rubinstein was ready with a full line of lipsticks, rouges, and powders to relieve the whiteness and the grayness, and the rest of the fashion industry — indeed, the whole entertainment industry, from Broadway to Hollywood — was ready to go along with her.

From the beginning, too — though Helena Rubinstein didn't care to admit it — her American clientele consisted largely of Jewish women who had made it out of the cocoon of East Side poverty into a new world of fun, freedom, and affluence. Here she was, after all, one of them — a successful Jewish woman proudly waving her unmistakably Jewish name like a banner. Helena Rubinstein had made it out of the ghetto, too. She remembered what it was like. She cared. In her very personal style of advertising — "I, Helena Rubinstein . . ." — she told women so. Beauty-conscious Christian women, who shopped at Best's, De Pinna, and Lord and Taylor, might remain loyal to Elizabeth Arden, who would become Helena Rubinstein's chief competitor, and whose Blue Grass line suggested horsiness and tweeds. But upscale Jewish women, who shopped at Saks and Bergdorf-Goodman, would for the next generation become devotees of Helena Rubinstein and her mysterious Crème Valaze.* It was because her products sounded so — well, so wonderfully European.

Many of the signposts along the avenue leading out of the ghetto of the Lower East Side into American middle-class prosperity were, of course, addresses. But by the early 1920s, addresses had been codified to the extent that, from one's address, you could almost pinpoint his station in life. In New York, for example, the Upper East Side, from the East Sixties through the low Seventies, was pretty much the domain of Christian rich. Farther north belonged to wealthy German-Jewish bankers: Felix Warburg's Renaissance castle stood at the corner of Fifth Avenue and Ninety-second Street, Otto Kahn's mansion was a block farther down, a few more blocks down lived Adolf Lewisohn and Jacob Schiff, and so on.

The West Side had become heavily Russian Jewish, but of a rather special sort. The big apartments along Central Park West

*Patrick O'Higgins once asked Madame Rubinstein what went into her Crème Valaze. She waxed rhapsodic and replied, "It's made of a wonderful mixture of rare herbs, the essence of Oriental almonds, extracts from the bark of an evergreen tree . . ." Later, he stumbled on the formula, but could not find any of these exotic ingredients listed. Instead, there were commonplace materials such as ceresin wax (a petroleum derivative used as a substitute for beeswax), mineral oil, and sesame.

and West End Avenue were expensive and luxurious, but they
attracted a somewhat ostentatious group of families — new-rich
kings of the garment industry, for example, and a number of
underworld kingpins, including Meyer Lansky. These neighborhoods were also favored by show-business people — Broadway
producers, agents, theater owners; Jewish performers, composers,
writers, set designers, musicians, singers (including Sophie Tucker),
and comedians (including Fanny Brice, Eddie Cantor, and Al
Jolson). These were all successful people, but they were high
rollers, and led the upside-down lives of theater folk. For solid,
middle-class respectability and probity, meanwhile, there was no
place quite like the Bronx.

It is hard today to imagine that the Bronx was once considered
a very proper Jewish address. But, for a Russian-Jewish family in
1920 to have made it all the way to the Bronx — with, perhaps,
a way stop in between of a few years in the Brownsville section
of Brooklyn, which was more working class — was a symbol of
having arrived in more ways than one. As early as 1903, a Yiddish
writer visiting the Bronx had described it as "a beautiful area . . . a
suburb that could have sun and air and cheaper rents. . . . Go
take a look," he urged his readers; "the Bronx is becoming our
new ghetto." A few years later, in 1912, the British novelist Arnold
Bennett visited both the East Side and the Bronx, and caught the
difference: "In certain strata and streaks of society on the East
Side things artistic and intellectual are comprehended with an
intensity of emotion impossible to Anglo Saxons. . . . The Bronx
is different. The Bronx is beginning again, at a stage earlier than
art, and beginning better. It is a place for those who have learnt
that physical righteousness has got to be the basis for all future
progress. It is a place to which the fit will be attracted, and where
the fit will survive."

In other words, the Bronx was a neighborhood for a whole *second*
fresh start for the immigrant, and a place to forget, if possible,
the hardship of that first fresh start on Hester Street — not a place
in which to muster rent strikes and demonstrations, or to haggle
with a vendor over the price of whitefish on his cart, but a place
to be "righteous," fit, and seemly, another step toward Americanization, assimilation. And there was another point about the Bronx
that Bennett may have missed, which was emotional and psycho-

logical: the Bronx is the only borough of New York City's five that is not situated on an island. In the Russian Jews' trek to freedom they had been hopping from island to island — from the insularity of the European ghetto, to England, to Ellis Island, to lower Manhattan. But when they had made it to the Bronx, they were setting their feet firmly on the soil of the American mainland, for the first time.

Of course, the Bronx comprised a large amount of real estate, and it was not all equally desirable. Moving from east to west, you went from Tiffany Street poverty through neighborhoods that got progressively better until you reached Independence Avenue, and wealth, in Riverdale, where the mayor's mansion was, and where Toscanini lived. Meanwhile, roughly in the center of the borough, the Speedway Boulevard and Concourse had been renamed Grand Concourse. This splendid eight-lane north-south thoroughfare, completed in 1914, had been laid out by the city planner Louis Risse, whose inspiration the Avenue Champs-Élysées in Paris had been. By the 1920s, the Fordham Road–Grand Concourse intersection had become a great transportation nexus, and the business and social center of the Bronx, with stores, banks, restaurants, and the RKO Fordham Theatre. Farther along Grand Concourse, great apartment houses had gone up, and alongside it lay Joyce Kilmer Park, where mothers could take their children out in strollers and sit on park benches and gossip under the big shade trees.

But the climax of the Grand Concourse was the completion, in 1923, of the Concourse Plaza Hotel, the first hotel in the Bronx and designed as a showplace. Governor Alfred E. Smith spoke at the dedication ceremony, and a borough newspaper called the *Bronx Tabloid* declared that the hotel would "enable the social life of the borough to assemble amid luxurious surroundings, in keeping with its prestige as the sixth greatest city in the country." All the important county political dinners were given there, in the glittering ballroom with its gilded balcony railings and huge crystal chandeliers suspended from ceilings twenty-eight feet high. In the dining room, the French chef was partial to elaborate menus that included tournedos Rossini and — daringly, for a Jewish neighborhood — lobster thermidor, though most of the residents of the Grand Concourse were second-generation Jews who had abandoned the strictures of their parents' Orthodoxy.

The hotel's lobby and public rooms were favorite gathering places for stars of the New York Yankees, from Yankee Stadium just three blocks away, as well as for Bronx politicians and businessmen and their wives. Every Bronx Jewish girl dreamed of being married at the Concourse Plaza with the best wedding that money could buy, and Jewish mothers promised their little boys that, if they were good, that was where their bar mitzvah parties would take place. By the 1920s, the Jewish families who lived along the Grand Concourse had nothing in common with West End Avenue families in the fashion and entertainment industries, who led more here-today-gone-tomorrow lives. Instead, these were solid, white-collar Jewish professionals — doctors, lawyers, dentists, accountants, educators, druggists, and civil servants: a new Russian-Jewish American bourgeoisie.

Many of these men were graduates of New York's City College. During the early 1900s, City College had provided another avenue of escape from the Lower East Side — but that it had done so was a matter involving many contradictions and anomalies. For one thing, City College was not located anywhere near what could be called a "Jewish neighborhood." It was not in Brooklyn or the Bronx, or on the West Side. It was at the corner of Lexington Avenue and Twenty-third Street, near fashionable Gramercy Park, and, even on the new subways, it was not exactly an easy commute uptown from Rivington or Grand streets. City College had not set out to be a Jewish college. Nor had its original intent been to Americanize or homogenize the foreign-born. Two successive presidents, Horace Webster and Alexander Webb, were not only Christians but ex–West Pointers, from a day when West Point was not at all hospitable to Jews. Webster and Webb, furthermore, had established a tradition of running the school in a paramilitary manner, a fact that young immigrants from police-run states should have found repellent.

In many ways, City College took a hostile stance toward Jewish students. For example, Jews were originally barred from its fraternities, a fact that would forever incense Bernard Baruch, a City College alumnus of 1889. And so it is hard to say why or how City College managed to earn the deep affection, the almost passionate loyalty of Jewish immigrants. Yet, it did. For a Jewish mother, to be able to say that her son was studying at City College was to wear a badge of tremendous pride. To young immigrants themselves, by the early 1900s, City College had become a shining symbol — as one alumnus put it, "a passport to a higher and ennobled life." The passions that City College stirred in the breasts of its alumni were almost like a parent's devotion to a seriously handicapped child.

Its teachers were, for the most part, mediocre. Its physical plant was in no way beautiful or inspiring. Its exterior was shabby, its interiors dark and grim, its plumbing primitive, its desks and chairs rickety and splayed, its library ill kept and out-of-date. On top of everything else, City College was not even a real college, but more like a combination of high school and college. If, for instance, a boy had completed grammar school, he could take a City College entrance examination, and if he achieved a passing grade of 70, he could be admitted as a "sub-freshman." Then, during his sub-freshman year, he was expected to cram four years' worth of high school study into a single year. Similarly, if he had completed one year of high school, he could also apply for sub-freshmanship, and if his exam grades were good enough, he might actually be admitted to a freshman class. Naturally, this system meant a high degree of turnover among the student body, and whereas hundreds of young men had started City College as freshmen and sub-freshmen, only two or three dozen remained in the graduating class four or five years later. The graduating class of 1906 was typical. One hundred and forty men graduated that year. Over a thousand had entered as freshmen and sub-freshmen four or five years earlier. This steep rate of attrition also meant that competition to succeed was particularly fierce. City College was a survival course. Perhaps that was why the school stirred such fervent loyalties among those relatively few youths who actually made it through, and why it conferred upon its graduates the almost mystical belief that they were members of a privileged and special Elect. It was not the school or its teaching staff that inspired its Jewish students. It was the students who inspired themselves.

In the 1880s and 1890s, only a tiny handful of Russian-Jewish boys joined the few German-Jewish students enrolled at City College. But as the new century progressed, the word of the challenge of City College began to spread. By 1903, more than seventy-five percent of the students at City College were Jewish, most of them the sons of Russian immigrants, and in the graduating class of 1910, of the 112 graduates, at least 90 were Jewish. Finally, after the First World War, with Jewish soldiers who had seen a bit of the world returning home determined to make more of their lives than their parents had, and with tuition loans available, City College became a virtually all-Jewish school. By then, of course, the restrictive clauses against Jews in fraternities had become meaningless.

By then, too, the academic standards of City College, and the quality of education it delivered, had improved dramatically. It was not quite Harvard or Columbia, perhaps, but it was close. And it was all thanks, probably, not so much to the efforts of its administration or its faculty as to the zeal and ardor of its students themselves, and their determination to educate themselves into the mainstream of America.

8

MINSTRELS AND MINSTRELSY

IN 1919, Irving Berlin had made a decision that would make him a millionaire, even though, at thirty-one, he was already a very prosperous young man. He had walked out the door of the music-publishing house that employed him, and for which he had been composing popular songs at an alarming rate — and being paid a small royalty based on sales of the sheet music — never to come back. Instead, he intended to form his own music-publishing firm, Irving Berlin, Inc., to market his own songs.

The lore of songwriting is full of bitter tales of composers who wrote enormously popular songs — even minor classics — but who, having sold their rights to them for a pittance, died poor and were buried in potter's field. John Philip Sousa, for example, was supposedly paid only ninety dollars for "Stars and Stripes Forever." For "When You Were Sweet Sixteen," Jimmy Thornton was paid thirty-five dollars. And such old favorites as "The Stories That Mother Told Me" came from the days when Harry Von Tilzer and Andy Sterling were peddling their songs around Union Square for two to five dollars apiece.

But the music world also has more inspiring stories, such as that of Mrs. Carrie Jacobs Bond, a plucky Chicago housewife, whose husband's sudden death left her a widow with a young son to support. Her son got a job selling newspapers, and Mrs. Bond, who had always considered herself vaguely musical, thought she'd try her hand at writing songs. She wrote song after song, submitted her compositions to publisher after publisher, and they were all uniformly rejected. Finally, she decided to publish them herself, and with two hundred dollars borrowed from a friend and three hundred dollars scraped together from her own savings, she set about to do the job from her kitchen table. As it happened, one of the songs she was working on at the time was a wistful, sentimental ballad called "The End of a Perfect Day." While trying to get that song into the marketplace, she ran short of cash to pay her printer, but was able to borrow an additional fifteen hundred dollars from her doctor, who lived down the street, promising to pay him a share of the profits, if any. "The End of a Perfect Day" became one of the best-selling songs of all time, and in its first fifteen years sold an unprecedented five million copies, by which time her doctor alone had made more than a hundred thousand dollars on his investment. The song has been sung at weddings and at funerals, by church choirs and on the concert stage, has been translated and recorded in every language, including Urdu. It still sells briskly, and earns its composer's estate a tidy annual sum. It was the Carrie Jacobs Bond route that Irving Berlin decided to follow.

He had been born Isidore Baline in 1888 in a Russian village called Temum, which no longer exists, the youngest of eight children. Since he was only four when his family emigrated to America, he had no clear memories of the old country except one: lying on a blanket beside a road and watching his house, along with the rest of the town, burn to the ground. Of the family exodus to America that followed, he retained no memory at all.

Perhaps because he was the youngest of such a large brood, he was a rather solitary, introspective child. Rather than being the most babied of the family, he seems to have been the one most overlooked by his busy mother. He was desultory in his schoolwork, and not even City College held out any lure for him. He did, however, learn to swim the traditional way — by being tossed into the East River by some older Irish youths — and actually became so adept at it that he perfected a little trick. In the impromptu swimming pools that had been created out of disused East Side docks, children were allowed to swim in groups of fifty or so for fifteen minutes. Then a lifeguard blew his whistle, whereupon all swimmers had to get out of the pool to make room for the next group. Isidore Baline, however, developed a tactic whereby, at the sound of the whistle, he would submerge himself and remain underwater until the next group had entered the pool — a matter of three or four minutes. Then he would surface and continue his swim undetected. He became such a good swimmer that he once swam all the way to Brooklyn and back. His only other talent, as a boy, seemed to be singing: he possessed a sweet soprano voice, and he liked to sing. His idol became George M. Cohan, whom every Jewish boy of the era simply assumed was a Jewish composer and performer.

At the age of fourteen, and for no particular reason, Izzy Baline ran away from home. He was apparently not very much missed, because he did not run far — only a few blocks away, to the Bowery. The Bowery, in those days, did not have the skid-row aura it emanates today. In fact, it was almost glamorous. It was the Broadway of the Lower East Side, crammed with bars, restaurants, and nightclubs that offered vaudeville-style entertainment. It was an era when "slumming" was a popular diversion for uptowners, when debutantes and their escorts dressed in their shabbiest clothes and came down to the Bowery for a taste of how the other half lived, and for the thrill of rubbing shoulders with gamblers, gangsters, and other East Side lowlifes. From the slummers and from their regular neighborhood customers, the bars of the Bowery did a thriving business. Izzy Baline decided he could earn a living as a "busker" in the Bowery bars.

Buskers were free-lance entertainers who cruised from bar to bar, singing songs, or dancing, or performing comedy routines, then passing the hat for pennies among the customers. On a good night, a busker could earn as much as a dollar, which, in a neighborhood where a steak pie cost a nickel and a room in a boardinghouse cost a quarter a night, was enough to provide him with food and shelter and even a bit of pin money. For a while, Baline worked as a kind of Seeing Eye dog for a blind busker known as Blind Sol. He led Blind Sol on his singing rounds of the bars, sometimes joining him in a duet, and was paid with a share of Blind Sol's take. For a brief period, too, he sang — for five dollars a week — with an itinerant vaudeville troupe that billed itself as THREE — KEATONS — THREE. There was Ma Keaton, who played the saxophone. Pa Keaton did a comedy routine, and their baby, Buster Keaton, was a comic prop who got laughs by being tossed back and forth across the stage by his parents.

In terms of his later career, however, Izzy Baline's most important employment occurred when he was hired as a singing waiter in a bar called the Pelham Café on Pell Street, in the heart of Chinatown. The Pelham Café had a perfectly dreadful reputation. To begin with, Chinatown, full of "sinister Oriental types," opium dens, and tong wars, was considered one of the most dangerous areas in the city, where police were always breaking up dope rings and trying to solve the periodic clueless throat-slittings. At the center of all this unlovely activity stood the Pelham Café, which was known far and wide not by its official name but by the even unlovelier sobriquet of Nigger Mike's. Nigger Mike's was said to be the favored hangout of all the most notorious criminals and the most flamboyant and popular prostitutes. In Nigger Mike's back room, it was said, illegal gambling, opium smoking, and Lord knew what else went on. It was the unsavory reputation of Nigger Mike's, and of its alleged "back room" (which, in fact, did not exist), that had made it one of the most sought-after slumming places in town. Naturally, "Nigger Mike" Salter, who ran the place, did nothing to discourage his establishment's expanding ill repute. And Mike Salter, meanwhile, was not a black at all, but a Russian Jew whose swarthy complexion had earned him the nickname — one he didn't mind at all. If anything, it enhanced his saloon's shady image, which was its chief drawing card.

The songs that Izzy Baline sang while working as a singing waiter at Nigger Mike's were a pastiche. Like Helena Rubinstein, he was proving himself to be a masterful adapter. Some were simply the popular songs of the day — "Dear Old Girl," "Ida, Sweet as Apple Cider," and "Sweet Adeline." But then, for variety, he sometimes added new and slightly off-color lyrics to well-known favorites, and he also offered a few tunes that he had simply composed in his head. At Nigger Mike's there was a battered upright piano, and in his off hours, he laboriously picked out these new songs on the keyboard, though, unable to read or write music, he had no idea how to transcribe his tunes to make musical manuscripts. In fact, he never really did master the piano. Years later, after Irving Berlin had become one of the most popular composers in America, it was something of a shock to strangers to discover that he could play in only one key — F sharp — and had never learned to read music, or to transcribe it.

It was while singing at Nigger Mike's, meanwhile, that Izzy Baline had his first brush with fame. Prince Louis of Battenberg was visiting New York and, it seemed, the notoriety of Nigger Mike's saloon had traveled as far as Europe. One of the sights the prince wanted to see in the city was the famous Chinatown café. Nigger Mike himself was not at all sure how to deal with such an illustrious customer, and when the prince and his party arrived he announced that drinks would be on the house. When the prince was ready to leave, he thanked his host, and then offered a tip to his singing waiter. Baline, thinking that he too must appear as hospitable as his boss, politely refused the tip. A reporter named Herbert Bayard Swope — later to become the editor of the New York *World* — who was covering Prince Louis's visit, decided that here was an amusing story: an immigrant Jewish waiter who would refuse a tip from a visiting German prince. Thus the name of Izzy Baline found itself in the papers the following morning.

This bit of extra publicity for his establishment, however, did nothing to endear Izzy Baline to Nigger Mike, who, when he was drunk, had a terrible temper. Some nights later, when Baline's job was to watch the cash register, he nodded off over the half-opened drawer. Nigger Mike found him that way, and summarily fired him.

But he had no trouble finding another job, and he was presently doing his song and parody routines at another bar, called Jimmy Kelly's, on Union Square. In appearance, it was not much different from Nigger Mike's, but it was at a slightly better address and attracted a slightly higher-class clientele. It was here, with a pianist friend named Nick Nicholson, who knew someone who could put notes on music paper, that Izzy Baline wrote a song called "Marie from Sunny Italy," which the two decided was good enough to try to get published. They took their composition to the music publisher Joseph Stern, who promptly accepted it. The song became mildly popular in the music halls of 1907. The lyric writer's revenue from it was thirty-seven cents, and when the sheet music first appeared it bore the legend "Words by I. Berlin."

Just how Baline became transformed into Berlin would always be something of a mystery, even to the composer himself. It may have been the careless publisher's error. Or it may have been Baline's own fault, since, as he would admit, in the Yiddish-accented speech of the Lower East Side his name came out sounding like "Berlin." Later, when the modest "I. Berlin" became Irving Berlin, it was Berlin's own doing. He decided that both Isidore and Israel, his Hebrew name, sounded "too foreign." Irving sounded "more American." In any case, Joseph Stern capitalized on the new name, touting Berlin's first song as "about an Italian girl, written by a Russian boy, named after a German city."

Two more not very distinguished songs followed "Marie" — "Queenie, My Own," written with an itinerant pianist at Jimmy Kelly's, and "The Best of Friends Must Part," which Berlin wrote alone. But it was with a humorous bit of verse called "Dorando" that Irving Berlin came — almost accidentally — uptown to Tin Pan Alley, as the neighborhood around West Thirty-ninth Street and Broadway was known, where the big-time music publishers had their offices. "Dorando" had been commissioned — for ten dollars — by a song-and-dance man at Kelly's who wanted to do a comic routine, in an Italian accent, about an Italian marathon runner named Dorando, who had just lost to an American Indian named Longboat. Berlin's verse was about an Italian barber who had wagered his life's savings on Dorando and, of course, had lost. But the song-and-dance man defaulted on the deal and refused to pay for the routine, whereupon Berlin took his words uptown to the offices of the then legendary publisher Ted Snyder.

For some reason, he was admitted immediately into the great man's office, though he did not even have an appointment, and recited his verse. "Well," Snyder said, after hearing it, "I suppose you've got a tune to this." In fact, Berlin did not, but he quickly lied, and said, "Yes." Snyder then waved him down the hall to his music-arranger's office, with instructions that Berlin was to sing his tune for the arranger. Somehow, between Snyder's office and the arranger's, Berlin managed to compose some notes in his head to go with the words, and a full-scale song was born.

For the next three years, most of Irving Berlin's output was in collaboration with Snyder or one of his stable of composers. Although some forty-five new Berlin songs appeared during this period, none is particularly memorable today, even though many — such as "Yiddisha Eyes" — were popular music hall favorites of the day. For his work with the Snyder office, Berlin was paid a comfortable — for 1910 — salary of twenty-five dollars a week, plus a royalty on sheet-music sales of each new title. But it was not until 1911, when he began writing his own music and lyrics without resorting to collaborators, that he began to come into his own. His first big hit that year was "Alexander's Ragtime Band," a song that would remain popular for years and that seemed to provide a glorious overture to the Jazz Age that was to follow. He was only twenty-three.

Irving Berlin songs began to appear that are still sung in college dormitories, nightclubs, beer halls, and on concert stages all over the country — "I Want to Go Back to Michigan," "Oh, How I Hate to Get Up in the Morning," "He's a Rag Picker," "A Pretty Girl Is Like a Melody" — now mandatory background music for every Miss America Pageant — and on and on. Which came first, the lyric or the tune? It could happen either way. The genesis of "I Want to Go Back to Michigan" was simply that Berlin had been playing around, in his head, with the couplet "Oh, how I wish again / That I was in Michigan." It was a place, incidentally, that he had never visited when he wrote the song in 1917.

Music theorists and historians have tried to parse and analyze the music of Irving Berlin, searching for forms and early influences that might have shaped his talent. This is not an easy chore because, in addition to his prodigious output, the variety of Berlin's modes and moods is remarkable. He wrote simple love songs ("What'll I Do"), and he wrote ragtime romps ("Everybody's Doin' It"). He wrote sentimental ballads ("I Lost My Heart at the Stagedoor Canteen") and patriotic marches ("This Is the Army, Mr. Jones"). He wrote sad songs, funny songs, high-stepping jazz songs, and romantic waltzes. Theorists have claimed to hear strains of other cultures in Berlin's music — echoes of Negro spirituals, for instance, which is interesting, since Berlin had almost no familiarity with the genre. Others have sensed a relationship between Berlin's music and old Yiddish folk songs, Hasidic chants, and even ancient Sephardic liturgical music from the synagogues of fourteenth-century Spain — all unlikely sources of his inspirations.

Perhaps, again, the best way to see Irving Berlin's music is as pastiche — a piecing together of this and that, of everything that went into the experience of the American melting pot. Many of his songs had Jewish themes, but he also wrote songs with Italian themes, French themes, German themes, Irish themes, Spanish themes, and blackface and American Indian themes. One could not label as a "Jewish" composer the man who celebrated America's principal Christian holidays with "White Christmas" and "Easter Parade," and who celebrated America itself with "God Bless America," a hymn so popular that it has become virtually a second national anthem — to the point where many Americans believe it *is* the national anthem. Just as America itself has become, if not a melting pot exactly, a tossed salad of ethnic influences and traditions, so is the collective oeuvre of Irving Berlin a tossed salad. And so deeply entrenched in the American idiom are his songs that they don't translate well into foreign tongues. Even in England, audiences have had difficulty understanding Berlin's songs — "What'll I Do," for instance, puzzled the British, who wondered at the meaning of the word "whattle." As for Berlin's style, "American" is the best adjective for it. His contemporary and chief competitor in the songwriting field, George Gershwin, called him "America's Franz Schubert," but that falls somewhat wide of the mark. Harold Arlen once said that Berlin's songs "sound as though they were born that way — God Almighty! — not written!" And asked to define Irving Berlin's place in American music, Jerome Kern replied, "Irving Berlin has *no* place in American music. He *is* American music." And the wonder of it all is that he was born in Russia.

When he left Ted Snyder's firm to form his own Irving Berlin, Inc., he was not only making a move that would make him a very rich man; he was also moving into the mainstream of the American free-enterprise system, and fulfilling every American's dream of becoming his own boss.

Meanwhile, throughout the 1920s, new Russian-Jewish names and faces were emerging by the score in the American entertainment business — singers, actors, comics, composers, lyricists, and dancers. Their names are legion — Theda Bara (Theodosia Goodman), Jack Benny (Benjamin Kubelsky), Fanny Brice (Fanny Borach), Harry Houdini (Ehrich Weiss), Al Jolson (Asa Yoelson), Sophie Tucker (Sonia Kalish), George Burns (Nathan Birnbaum), Eddie Cantor (Isidor Iskowitch), and Libby Holman (Catherine Holzman) are only the beginning of a long, imposing list of folk who turned their talents, in one form or another, to the performing arts. Why this headlong rush of Eastern European Jews into show business? It is a little difficult to explain.

To begin with — considering the craving of most Jewish immigrants for solid American "respectability," for the Grand Concourse via City College — was the fact that show business was considered in no way a respectable American calling. Performers and other theater folk occupied a position on the status ladder just a short step above prostitutes and pimps. Furthermore, if the entertainment business was looked on as a low calling by most self-respecting Americans, it was regarded as an even lower calling by most right-thinking and pious Jews. Rabbis inveighed against the theater as a form of idol worship, and the Hebrew phrase *moshav letzim*, meaning "the seat of the scornful," was often used in Russia as a synonym for the theater, while the first Psalm warned, "Blessed is the man that walketh not in the counsel of the ungodly, nor standeth in the way of sinners, nor sitteth in the seat of the scornful." The word *letz*, or "scorner," was often used to describe an actor.

To be sure, there was the tradition of the Yiddish theater to be considered. At the same time, while the Yiddish theater was enjoyed as spectacle, those connected with its performances were held in low esteem, and though Yiddish theater was transported to the Lower East Side, it can in no way account for the enormous outpouring of show-business talent that emerged from Jewish immigrants in the United States. In Russia, there had also been the tradition of the *badchen*, or street jester, juggler, or fiddle player — but the *badchen* was also a figure of scorn and ridicule, little better than a beggar, an organ-grinder with his monkey, a blind man with his cup. And yet, as a singing waiter, Irving Berlin had been an American *badchen*, just as Eddie Cantor — singing and telling jokes and doing imitations at weddings and bar mitzvahs — had thereby launched himself as a comedian.

Still, this does not satisfactorily explain the phenomenon of American Jews in show business. One can, of course, assume that part of the explanation was the fact that, once the Jews were freed from the shackles of poverty and discrimination, great wells of talent that had been forced into hiding in the old country became uncapped in the new, and that with this came a longing for more than respectability — for achievement, recognition, and fame; the name in lights on Broadway, the cheers and applause of an audience. But sheer ambition does not invariably lead to fame, nor is it necessarily an accompaniment to theatrical talent.

It is true, however, that by the 1920s much of the business end of show business was in Jewish hands. Many of the legendary producers and impresarios on Broadway, such as Billy Rose (William Rosenberg) and Florenz Ziegfeld, were Jewish. So were many of the theatrical agents. The theaters themselves, meanwhile, were in the hands of the formidable brothers Shubert — Sam, Lee, and Jacob — the sons of an immigrant Syracuse peddler, who by the 1920s were to Broadway showplaces what the Rockefellers were to Standard Oil. All this helped Jewish performers find employment without fear of anti-Semitism, and among the careers launched by Flo Ziegfeld were those of Al Jolson, Eddie Cantor, and Fanny Brice. Then there was the fact that, by 1920, much of the Prohibition liquor trade was in Jewish hands, and a good number of the speakeasies and nightclubs where would-be stars could do their turns were also Jewish-owned. But still, where did so much *talent* come from? How to account for the wonderful songs — that seemed not to be written, but simply to "happen" — from the musically untutored Irving Berlin?

Much of the answer may lie in the streets of the Lower East Side themselves, where a bit of theatrical talent — or a plucky stab at it — could be a means of survival. More than gumption and street wisdom were required of a Jewish child to make it through the average day of taunting and bullying, and an ability to improvise was often helpful. If a Jewish youth were slightly built and not particularly athletic (like Irving Berlin), a potential tormentor could often be as diverted by a soft-shoe shuffle, a bit of clever mimicry, a comedy routine, or a song as by the use of fists. Once diverted by the young performer, the tormentor found himself disarmed and going along with the joke. The explosion of talent that erupted from the Lower East Side in the 1920s very likely grew out of the art of self-defense.

Having found that he could hold an audience, the young performer discovered that he could sell his ability for pennies in the street, or in the shabby saloons along the Bowery, or in the speakeasies of Brooklyn and Harlem. From there, the next step might be an engagement at one of the increasingly lavish resort hotels, such as Grossinger's and the Concord in the Borscht Belt of the Catskills. Here, vacationing Jewish families demanded entertainment of all varieties when not sunning themselves in lawn chairs, eating sumptuous meals, and admiring mountain scenery. Here, Meyer Lansky would establish several pleasant, and illegal, gambling parlors, and here budding comics, singers, and actors would hone their techniques and develop new routines. At one of these hotels, a young comedian named David Daniel Kominski, the son of a Russian-born Brooklyn tailor, later to be known as Danny Kaye, was hired to do zany acts in the lobby on rainy days to prevent guests from checking out. These Jewish performers, furthermore, were playing for Jewish audiences and were delighting them with a kind of Jewish self-parody that a generation later might have raised eyebrows. Fanny Brice, for example, did her acts in a heavy Yiddish accent — full of "oys!" and "Oy vehs!" — which she actually had to teach herself, since hers had not been a Yiddish-speaking family. Danny Kaye's comedy relied heavily on mocking Russian-Jewish mannerisms and shibboleths and speech patterns — a takeoff on a newly rich Jewish businessman with an unpronounceable name was a particular favorite — and the Marx Brothers had a routine called "Misfit Sam the Tailor." Sophie Tucker, meanwhile, could always bring the house down by closing her act with a rendition of "My Yiddishe Mama." It was at the Catskill resorts that producers and agents were scouting for fresh talent, and, for the performer, the next step might be the vaudeville circuit, or Broadway, or Hollywood.

In Hollywood, however, the situation for the Jewish performer was somewhat different from what it was in the Catskills or even in New York. Though the motion picture business — led by men like Goldwyn, Louis B. Mayer, William Fox, Adolph Zukor, Marcus Loew, and the brothers Warner — had become a heavily Jewish industry, its national audience was not. Jewish jokes and Jewish themes might be popular in the Borscht Belt or even on Broadway, but Hollywood, with its eye ever on the largest possible box-office receipts, made carefully de-Semitized films for the Christian majority. During the 1920s and even into the 1930s, it was unlikely that a Jewish actor would be cast as a romantic lead unless, like John Garfield (Julius Garfinkle), he happened not to "look Jewish."

Part of this had to do with Hollywood's preoccupation, during this period, with turning out Westerns, and it was assumed that a Jewish face or physique would appear incongruous dressed in a cowboy outfit. But there was also genuine business fear that Christian audiences would not react kindly to Jewish stars. Theda Bara's Jewishness was a closely guarded secret, as was the fact that Douglas Fairbanks's mother had been Jewish. There was a great deal of elaborate name-changing, in the course of which Irving Lahrheim became Bert Lahr, Emmanuel Goldberg became Edward G. Robinson, Pauline Levee became Paulette Goddard, and so on. One of the most ingenious of these changes was made when an actor named Lee Jacob became Lee J. Cobb. The euphemism used in studio casting offices was "Mediterranean type," and if an actor was branded a Mediterranean type he usually found good roles in the movies hard to come by. Both Rudolph Valentino and Clark Gable had, in the early stages of their careers, difficulty getting parts because they "looked Mediterranean," though neither was Jewish.

The one area of films where an actor could get away with being Jewish, or looking Jewish, or where one could pretend to be Jewish even if one was not — where it was even an advantage to be Jewish — was comedy, and so it is no coincidence that some of the greatest comedians in the world — Eddie Cantor, Jack Benny, Fanny Brice, the Marx Brothers — have been Jews nourished to prominence by Hollywood. For years, it was assumed that the greatest movie comedian of them all, Charlie Chaplin, was Jewish. He had to be, because he was so funny. He went to his grave, however, heatedly denying the rumors.

But it is an interesting comment on the timidity and insecurity of Hollywood's Jewish moguls who, by the 1920s, had become the most powerful purveyors of mass culture in America — a comment, perhaps, on their own ethnic embarrassment or even downright shame — that the only way a Jew could be a Jew on the screen was to play a tramp, a clown, a grifter, or a *nebbish*.

And yet, it had to be admitted, playing the *nebbish* had helped many a bright young Jew make it through the Lower East Side, out of it, and onto a theater marquee.

9

HIGH ROLLERS

ONE of Sam Goldwyn's gifts as a filmmaker was his genius at generating publicity. Though he personally oversaw every detail of the movies he produced — from the writing and editing to the actresses' hairstyles and makeup — the part of his job he relished most was getting his name, his studio's name, his stars' names, and his pictures' names in the papers. One of the great social events of the Prohibition era was the wedding, in 1927, of one of Goldwyn's stars, Vilma Banky, and Rod La Rocque, an actor under contract to Cecil B. DeMille. The affair was almost entirely staged — and was completely paid for — by Goldwyn. He had discovered Miss Banky on a trip to Budapest, and after getting her to trim down by some twenty pounds and having her teeth capped, Goldwyn brought her to Hollywood to make her a star. (It mattered not, in those days of silents, that she spoke not a word of English.) In the process, Goldwyn had created the myth that she was a "Hungarian countess" — though in fact he had met her getting off a streetcar.

There were many prenuptial showers for the bogus countess, all paid for by Goldwyn, and he had hired the pastor to perform the rites and had selected the Church of the Good Shepherd, the most fashionable Catholic church in Los Angeles. He paid for a fifty-voice choir to sing at the church, selected and paid for the bride's wedding gown, and offered her a veil borrowed from his studio's wardrobe department (Miss Banky had worn it in *The Dark Angel*). Goldwyn had chosen the bridesmaids for their newsworthiness, and they included Mildred Lloyd, Norma and Constance Talmadge,

Norma Shearer, Marion Davies, and Dolores Del Rio. Louella Parsons, Hollywood's most powerful press figure, was matron of honor. Tom Mix arrived at the wedding wearing a purple cowboy costume and purple ten-gallon hat, driven in a purple coach-and-four with footmen in purple livery, and nearly stole the show. When everyone had settled in the church, and the Wedding March was struck up, there was no bride. She finally appeared, fifteen minutes late, as Goldwyn had instructed her to be, for added suspense and drama.

Following the ceremony, Goldwyn put on a huge wedding breakfast and reception, and, throughout it, kept nervously asking everyone in sight, "Is Sunday a legal day? Is Sunday a legal day?" No one knew what he was talking about, but Goldwyn did have some reason for concern, though it had nothing to do with the legality of Miss Banky's marriage to La Rocque. It seemed that La Rocque was involved in an ugly lawsuit over his contract with DeMille, though Goldwyn had chosen DeMille to be La Rocque's best man. It had occurred to Goldwyn that this somewhat unusual arrangement might have been seen, by lawyers, as some sort of collusion between the two parties to the lawsuit. He need not have worried because, as it turned out, Sunday was *not* a legal day.

Much champagne was consumed at the reception, and only when the guests felt it was time to turn to the food — huge hams, turkeys, and standing rib roasts of beef had been spread out on a long table — did they discover that all the viands were plaster of paris imitations, borrowed from the Goldwyn prop department. Not a morsel of the nuptial repast was edible. When it was time for the bride and groom to depart, and the new Mrs. La Rocque tossed her bridal bouquet, it was caught, by prearrangement, by Norma Shearer. This was because she was to be married later that year in another wedding that would be much publicized — to Irving Thalberg, production head of Metro-Goldwyn-Mayer.

During its early years, Goldwyn's company had prospered from a number of now almost forgotten hit films. Goldwyn had hired the beautiful opera star Geraldine Farrar to make *The Turn of the Wheel*, and she had gone on to make a series of lightweight romances for him. From Oklahoma, Goldwyn had brought an offbeat, crooked-grinned comedian named Will Rogers, and introduced him in a movie called *Laughing Bill Hyde*. When the pretty daughter of an Alabama congressman won a beauty contest, Goldwyn put her under contract and starred her in something called *Thirty a Week*. Her uncommon name was Tallulah Bankhead. For writers, Goldwyn hired such big names of the day as Mary Roberts Rinehart, Rex Beach, Gertrude Atherton, and Rupert Hughes.

In the beginning, financing his films had been a problem, as it was with other Jewish producers, and each new film was paid for out of the earnings of the last, which meant that each film was another roll of the dice. The big commercial banks in the East had little interest in the fledgling motion picture business. It was considered much too risk-ridden and, too, there was an element of snobbishness and anti-Semitism here. Nearly all the eastern banks were controlled by wealthy Protestants, bound together into a fraternity with old-school Ivy League college ties. By unspoken gentlemanly agreement, they refrained from involving themselves with Jewish enterprises. In California, however, Sam Goldwyn had found an exception in the person of an Italian Catholic banker named Amadeo Peter Giannini. Mr. Giannini had formed his Bank of Italy — later the Bank of America — in 1904 with the express purpose of offering loans to small farmers and businessmen, particularly Italian immigrants, who had similar difficulty borrowing money from such older established California banks as the Crocker, Anglo, and Wells Fargo. Giannini had flown in the face of banking tradition and orthodoxy by actively soliciting loan customers, instead of the other way around, and his bank had become the popular bank "of the little man." With A. P. Giannini, Sam Goldwyn found a sympathetic reception, and soon Goldwyn's pictures were being produced in financial partnership with Giannini's bank.

Shortly after the war, however, the film industry went into what would be one of its periodic slumps, and Goldwyn's company got into serious trouble. He had temporarily exhausted his borrowing power at the Bank of Italy, and a new source of working capital had to be found. This was why, when Goldwyn's friends Lee and J. J. Shubert, the Broadway theater owners, told him of a man the Shuberts claimed had an uncanny knack for making money, Sam was immediately interested, and asked that the fellow be brought around. The name of this alleged financial genius was Frank Joseph Godsol, and upon meeting him, Goldwyn immediately brought Godsol in as a partner. Uncharacteristically — so pressing was

his need for ready cash — Goldwyn made no attempt to investigate
Mr. Godsol's background. In view of what was to happen, one
cannot help wondering if Sam had been taken in by a Shubert
brothers scheme to ruin him, even though he considered the brothers his friends. The Shuberts were not his competitors, exactly,
but at the same time the popularity of movies was having its effect
on the box-office receipts at legitimate Broadway theaters, on which
the Shuberts had a virtual monopoly. What interest could the
Shuberts possibly have had in helping out a financially troubled
movie producer? And if Frank Joseph Godsol was such a financial
wizard, why hadn't the wily Shuberts snapped him up for their
own organization? Beyond the vague claim that Godsol had a talent
for making money grow on trees, the Shuberts appeared not to
have looked into Godsol's credentials, either.

Joe Godsol was tall, dark-haired, suavely handsome, and athletic. He had a courtly continental manner and style of speech
acquired, he claimed, from having swum in the perfumed waters
of the highest society in Europe. He casually dropped the names
of dukes and countesses of his acquaintance. He appeared to be,
in other words, exactly the kind of grand seigneur that Goldwyn
himself aspired to be. In fact, he seemed almost too good to be
true, but Hollywood and Goldwyn quickly clasped Joe Godsol to
their respective bosoms.

Actually, if Goldwyn had checked into Mr. Godsol's past a bit,
he would have uncovered a somewhat different story. Godsol was
not a European at all, but had been born in Cleveland, Ohio, the
son of a tailor. He had made his way to Europe, where he had
enjoyed a career as an elegant swindler and con man. His first
major brush with the law had occurred in 1905, when he had been
brought up before the Paris Commercial Tribunal for selling cheap
imitation pearls as the real thing. At the time, the press had labeled
Godsol "the most colossal fake in the history of jewelry." From
then on, he was in and out of trouble and in and out of jail. During
the war, as a French army officer, he was arrested for embezzling
funds from the French government by tinkering with military payroll records. He had been discharged, and ordered to leave France.
Still, shortly after the war, Joe Godsol found himself vice-president
of the Goldwyn Pictures Corporation.

It was perhaps not surprising, then, that the money Godsol had promised to bring into the company did not immediately materialize. Godsol, however, had connections from his colorful international days who were not aware of his shady past, and among these were members of Wilmington's wealthy du Pont clan. With Godsol providing the entrée, Sam Goldwyn was introduced to two of the multitudinous du Pont cousins, Henry F. and Eugene E. du Pont. Together, Goldwyn and Godsol were able to convince the du Ponts that movies were making everyone connected with them rich, that to invest in a motion picture company meant the possibility of hobnobbing with beautiful actresses and famous writers and artists, and that filmmaking was more glamorous than munitions-making. The result was an infusion of three million dollars of du Pont money into the Goldwyn company. With their investment, both du Ponts, along with Mr. E. V. R. Thayer of the Chase National Bank, moved onto Sam Goldwyn's board of directors. Soon they were joined by yet another member of the Delaware family, T. Coleman du Pont. All seemed well. It seemed, furthermore, that the film industry was at last moving up in the world. No longer associated with immigrant furriers and glove salesmen, it had apparently been given the imprimatur of the eastern business establishment.

Within months, however, disaster again loomed on the horizon. The industry itself remained depressed, and Goldwyn pictures were doing particularly poor business at the box office. The du Ponts were now having a taste of the less glamorous side of the movie business, and were nervously wondering what had become of their three-million-dollar investment, on which no return seemed to be forthcoming. Meetings were called in New York and Wilmington, and there were demands for a financial reorganization and overhaul of the company. Testily, Sam Goldwyn resisted this, and when the du Ponts continued to apply pressure, Sam presented the board with another of his angry resignations. It was accepted.

Now, for a while, Coleman du Pont, with no movie experience whatever, served as president of Goldwyn Pictures, but when things failed to get better without the founder at the helm and, indeed, got worse, a repentant board of directors went with hat in hand and asked Sam Goldwyn to return. Graciously, he accepted the invitation. Eighteen more months now passed, but without improvement.

As Goldwyn saw it, the trouble was that, during his brief absence from the company, Joe Godsol had been working to strengthen his position with the du Ponts. Godsol may have seen a more secure future for himself in an alliance with one of the largest private fortunes in America than with the seesawing fate of a young California motion picture company. In any case, in a series of even stormier quarrels within the board, Godsol increasingly sided with the du Ponts against Goldwyn. Clearly, another Goldwyn resignation scene — which Goldwyn seemed to enjoy more and more as each new chance for one appeared — was building, and in March, 1922, it occurred. Goldwyn stood up in front of his board and announced that he was quitting, "And this time for good!" Then he added, for good measure, "And don't try coming back to me on bended elbows."

With him he took his block of Goldwyn Pictures stock, and this meant that the quarreling between Sam Goldwyn and Goldwyn Pictures was far from over. Though Sam owned the stock, he no longer owned the corporate name. As an independent producer, Sam Goldwyn saw no reason why he could not present movies under the banner SAMUEL GOLDWYN PRESENTS. Goldwyn Pictures, however, objected that this interfered with their right to produce under GOLDWYN PICTURES PRESENTS. Both names now had a certain appeal at the box office, and audiences would inevitably confuse one product with the other. In the court battle that followed, it was ruled that in all Samuel Goldwyn productions, wherever his name appeared on the screen, it had to be followed by the disclaimer NOT NOW CONNECTED WITH GOLDWYN PICTURES. Furthermore, these words had to appear in the same size type as the rest of the legend. This was galling to Sam Goldwyn. It seemed like providing free advertising for his former company on his own pictures. It was a situation, however, that he would not have to endure for long.

At Goldwyn Pictures, meanwhile, the irony of it all was that Joe Godsol, who had started all the trouble to begin with, had moved into a commanding position.

In 1924, rumors were circulating through the show-business worlds of both New York and Hollywood that a giant motion picture merger — the first of its size and importance — was about to take place. Marcus Loew of Metro Pictures Corporation had absorbed

the six-year-old Louis B. Mayer Pictures Corporation. Now Loew
was eager to acquire Goldwyn Pictures. Secret meetings were being
held between Godsol, Mayer, Loew and his other partners, Joseph
and Nicholas Schenck and Robert Rubin, and, on April 17, 1924,
a merger was announced, resulting in a new company to be called
Metro-Goldwyn-Mayer. Needless to say, the only Goldwyn stockholder who voted against the merger was the irascible Sam Goldwyn
himself. He distrusted Loew and the Schencks, and had had run-
ins with Mayer, whom he considered his archrival. But his voting
shares were not enough to block the merger. For the new company
to be formed, Sam Goldwyn had to be bought out for cash. Thus
it was that when Metro-Goldwyn-Mayer was formed, Sam Goldwyn
did not own a single share in the big company that bore his name.

Which suited him just fine. Sam Goldwyn had already demonstrated himself to be a man who was not emotionally cut out for
partnerships. The long list of his shattered relationships with partners — Lasky, DeMille, Loew, Zukor, the Selwyns, Godsol, the
du Ponts — attested to that. From now on, independence would
mark his style, and at the time he outlined his producing philosophy. "A producer," he declared, should not be hampered by the
opinions and rulings of a board of directors." And he added, "This
business is dog eat dog and nobody's gonna eat me."

What was not announced when the formation of MGM was made
public was that an unusual agreement had been secretly drawn
under which three men at the top of the company were given the
privilege of dividing one-fifth of the company's annual profits among
themselves, before any other profits were passed along to other
stockholders. This juicy piece off the top of the profit pie was to
be sliced as follows: fifty-three percent to Louis B. Mayer, a clear
indication of his production dominance; twenty percent to Irving
Thalberg, Mayer's youthful protégé and creative right-hand man;
and twenty-seven percent to Robert Rubin, who was considered
the company's financial brain. And where, one might wonder, had
Joe Godsol come out in this fast shuffle? Asked what Godsol's title
would be in the new company, Louis B. Mayer merely smiled and
said, "Mr. Godsol is no longer with us." Just as mysteriously as
he had materialized, Godsol had disappeared.

That same year, another formidable competitor to both MGM
and Sam Goldwyn would appear on the Hollywood scene in the

person of thirty-three-year-old Harry Cohn. Just six years earlier, Cohn had joined Carl Laemmle's Universal Pictures as Laemmle's secretary. Now Cohn announced the formation of his own Columbia Pictures Corporation.

With the founding of Metro-Goldwyn-Mayer, of course, Sam Goldwyn was no longer required to add the irksome NOT NOW CONNECTED WITH . . . line to the credits on his pictures. And privately he was pleased and flattered that the new corporation had decided to include his copyrighted name on its masthead. Even though he had nothing to do with Metro-Goldwyn-Mayer, most people just naturally assumed that he did. Now every MGM production was advertising him. He particularly liked the fact that his name got higher billing on the letterhead than that of his rival L. B. Mayer, and could even rationalize that his was the top name of all, "because Metro isn't anybody's real name." He was delighted that the company would keep his roaring "Leo the Lion" as its corporate logo and trademark. He saw this as another nod in the direction of his greatness, his immortality. Goldwyn, whose birthday was August 27, liked to point out, "After all, Leo is *my* birth sign."*

By 1925, Goldwyn and the former Blanche Lasky had been divorced for ten years, and no one in the Lasky family was on speaking terms with Sam. As bitter as the divorce had been — with the tug-of-war over the couple's small daughter, Ruth, whose mother had finally been granted custody; with the prolonged fight over money; and with accusations of infidelity and other malfeasance flying back and forth between the divorcing couple — Sam Goldwyn still professed to be in love with Blanche. Long after Blanche had moved back to New Jersey and resumed her maiden name (she was raising their daughter as Ruth Lasky, with the rest of the family forbidden to tell Ruth who her father was), Sam was still referring to Blanche as "my fairy princess." After the divorce, Sam had been dating the actress Mabel Normand. But then, early in 1925, he met a twenty-one-year-old blond actress named Frances Howard.

Frances Howard had been born in Omaha in 1903, and shortly

*Astrology was not his strong suit. In fact, he was a Virgo.

after that her father had moved the family to southern California, where Frances grew up in a tiny bungalow outside San Diego. The Howards were English-descended, and Roman Catholics, and Frances Howard's upbringing had been strict, Spartan, and mass-going. As a teenager, however, she had become stagestruck, and had been allowed to go to New York to try her luck in the theater. She had managed to obtain parts in two mildly successful Broadway plays, *The Swan*, and *Too Many Kisses* with Richard Dix. Among the various interesting men the pretty young ingenue had managed to meet had been Coudert Nast, the son of Condé Nast. One evening she was invited to dinner at Condé Nast's Manhattan apartment, which by then had become something of a salon where everybody in New York who was young and talented and doing things gathered to meet people from out of town who were young and talented and doing things. For the occasion, she bought a $310 dress that she could ill afford. At the party, she was introduced to Samuel Goldwyn, who had just come in from Hollywood and who had arrived at the Nasts' with a beautiful woman on his arm.

Their opening words were not auspicious. Goldwyn, who had seen Frances in *The Swan*, approached her and said, "You're an awful actress." Frances replied coolly, "I'm sorry you think so," and was about to turn away to seek more congenial company when Goldwyn touched her arm and asked her if she would like to join him at an after-dinner party that was being given for Gloria Swanson and her new husband, the Marquis de la Falaise. Miss Howard was about to say no when her host, Mr. Nast, said, "I'll take you there, so you'll be escorted." At the Swanson party, Sam Goldwyn said to Frances, "I'd like to see you again." This time she thanked him and said no very firmly. Later, she commented to her friend Anita Loos, "Guess who wants to take me out. That awful Sam Goldwyn!"

And yet there was obviously something about the man that fascinated her — his brusqueness of manner, his cocky self-assurance, his obvious need to dominate every scene in which, and every woman with whom, he found himself — even though he was more than twenty years older than she. When he telephoned a few days later and asked her to have dinner with him, she found herself saying yes. At the time, she was living in a small apartment at Eighty-first Street and West End Avenue. When she gave him the address, he said, "I can't be seen in that part of town. Take a taxi to my hotel, the Ambassador, on Park Avenue." Even with that, she went. They dined at the Colony Restaurant and, on what was their first real date, Sam Goldwyn asked her to marry him.

Frances had been talking with Paramount about the possibility of doing a film on the West Coast, and so her reply to his proposal was an airy, "Well, perhaps I'll see you in California." But, less than four months later, when she arrived in Hollywood, Frances Howard was the second Mrs. Samuel Goldwyn. "It wasn't that he was a bit nice," she said later. "He had the most appalling manners. And it wasn't because I wanted to marry a movie producer to get into the movies. He'd made it very clear that the only career I was going to have was as his wife. And it certainly wasn't because he was rich because, at the time, I knew he was up to his ears in debt to the Bank of America. But there was something about him that was different from any man I'd ever known. He seemed so lonely — the loneliest man I'd ever known. Maybe it was because he brought out the mothering instinct in me."

Her family was appalled. There was the difference in their ages, and the difference in their religions. Still, Frances Goldwyn was to prove herself a stubborn woman who knew what she wanted and who, when she had it, was determined to keep it. She had made Sam promise that any children would be raised as Catholics. She knew of Sam's reputation as a flirt and a womanizer, and knew only too well of his long-standing relationship with Mabel Normand, but had decided wisely to overlook such matters. She knew of Sam's reputation as a high-stakes gambler, and decided that, if she could not change that, she would live as best she could with it. She knew of Sam's love of ostentation and display — he operated on the theory that the more money he owed the more he must therefore spend, lest the competition suspect he was in difficulties of any sort — and in an effort to trim his budget got him to dispose of his "show-off Locomobile." She understood Sam's ghetto-bred fear of tying up money in real estate, but she was also determined that they would live in a house and not spend their lives, as Sam had been doing, in a series of hotel suites. Her wedding gift to him was typically understated and commonsensical: a dozen neckties from Macy's.

Frances Goldwyn was both thrilled and horrified by the Hollywood of the mid-1920s that she discovered when she arrived. She and Sam had no sooner stepped off the Santa Fe Chief than he advised her that they were invited to a dinner party that evening. Hastily, she selected a pink chiffon dress embroidered with tiny imitation shells, but she was totally unprepared for what she saw when she arrived at the party. There was Pola Negri in a silver lamé turban, a dress covered with sequins, and most of the upper part of her body cascaded in diamonds. There was Constance Talmadge in white satin with a waterfall of orchids in dozens of different colors pinned to her shoulder and hanging to the floor so that she had to kick the corsage out of the way with her feet as she walked. Her sister, Norma, was also in orchids and in a long dress stitched with opals and moonstones. There was Ernst Lubitsch, King Vidor, the almost-too-handsome John Gilbert, and — most exciting of all to Frances — Earl Williams, the Robert Redford of his day. Frances Goldwyn had had a desperate girlhood crush on Earl Williams and had kept a Huyler's candy box full of photographs of him clipped out of *Photoplay* magazine. Dizzily, she discovered that she had been seated next to him at the dinner table. But, once seated, she discovered something else about her idol. Earl Williams was totally without conversation. Desperately, she tried one topic after another — politics, the theater, the stock market, recent books, even the weather. Earl Williams responded by munching on celery sticks. At last she decided to try bringing up her Huyler's candy box. Immediately he was transfixed, and wanted to hear more. Which photographs had she liked best? Which profile did she prefer? Did she think his eyes were too small? Did she prefer him smiling or looking serious? She had discovered a fact that would stand her in good stead with every Hollywood actor: Earl Williams was interested only in Earl Williams. On the subject of his photographs he became voluble, and monopolized her for the rest of the evening. When he said good night to her, he told her, "You are the most fascinating woman I've ever met!"

At that first Hollywood party Frances Goldwyn learned other things less pleasant. She noticed, for example, the prodigious consumption of bootleg liquor. She noticed that, even in 1925, there were certain other chemicals involved in the Hollywood social scene. "There was something they sniffed, and something they smoked," she would recall. She also learned, to her dismay, what the position of a woman was in the movie capital. Across and around the table, where she tried to catch as much of the conversation as she could when Williams was not going on about himself, she heard the men talking, and the men were doing most of the talking. The women smiled and preened and nodded, and studied their reflections in the mirrors of their compacts. The men spoke of this gathering or that, and of who was there, and it was all first names — "Jack," and "Joe," and "Nick," and "Cecil," and "Sam," and "Charlie," and "Darryl," and "David," and "Lew," and "Doug." Then someone would add, almost as an afterthought, "And the usual wives, of course." At that dinner party Frances Goldwyn decided that, whatever happened, she would not let herself become just another of Hollywood's "usual wives."

Because, like the Polish crown prince he had observed as a youth in the streets of Warsaw, Sam Goldwyn now absolutely refused to carry money, Frances did that for him (even when they were engaged, she had had to pay for everything where cash was required). Now, she began handling his accounts, writing out his checks, balancing books that no bookkeeper had looked at for fifteen years. Though he did his best to keep his gambling debts a secret from her, she usually managed to find out about them anyway, and quietly see that they were settled — a cardinal Hollywood rule said that a man's gambling debts must be paid before all others. She had a series of meetings with Mr. Giannini at his bank. When one of Sam's girl friends threatened to cause trouble, Frances just as quietly bought the lady off with a diamond bracelet from Cartier — "Not too expensive. I wanted to save our money." Sam began bringing home movie scripts for her to read, and when she criticized them, he criticized her criticisms. They argued, but the more they argued, the more Frances Goldwyn was learning about the motion picture business.

At the studio, she began noticing examples of extravagance and waste, and proposed cost-cutting methods. Lights that had theretofore been left burning all night long were ordered turned off at the end of a working day. Lavish stars' dressing rooms were divided to make a more thrifty use of space. Budgets for films were trimmed, salaries were held in rein. She also kept an eye on studio maintenance. When she discovered faulty plumbing in the men's room, she had it repaired. When a roof leaked, she had it patched. In short, she was doing things that no other Hollywood wife had ever dreamed of doing.

Most important, in the inevitable intra- and interstudio fights and skirmishes that were forever erupting, when horns locked and heads knocked together, it was Frances who coolly took on the job of patching the cracked skulls. One fact about Sam Goldwyn had become quite clear by that point in his producing career: he had a certain difficulty getting along with the people he worked with. When frictions arose, and Sam seemed on the point of exploding, it was Frances Goldwyn who stepped in to smooth things out with tact and diplomacy. Whether he realized it or not, Frances Goldwyn was running Sam Goldwyn. And, whether he knew it or not, he had acquired his most important business asset when he married her. Though she would always modestly deny it, it is quite possible that Sam Goldwyn would have failed utterly as a producer if it had not been for her. He was in a business for which he was temperamentally unsuited because it was one that required cooperation and coordination. These he could never manage. But she could. Never, after marrying Frances, would Sam Goldwyn stalk angrily out of a meeting or boardroom again. When he wanted to pay her a particular compliment, he would tell her that she reminded him of his first wife, his fairy princess. She shrugged it off, knowing that it wasn't true.

Meanwhile, Frances Goldwyn still wanted them to have a house, and when she was not at the studio, she shopped for a piece of property. As usual with Sam Goldwyn, there was a shortage of ready cash; but Frances had managed to scrape a sum together, and within a few months had located a hilltop plot overlooking Laurel Canyon in Beverly Hills. The view was spectacular; visible across the valley, through tapering cypresses, was Pickfair, the home of Hollywood's royal family, Douglas Fairbanks and Mary Pickford. A flat space of ground would allow for the mandatory croquet court. The seller of the property wanted seventy-five thousand dollars for the lot. But Frances — "I Gentiled him down" — got it for fifty-two thousand. She supervised the design and building of the house, and then the furnishing and decorating of it. Sam had bought what he had been told was a "fake Picasso." Frances researched the painting and discovered, to her delight, that it was a *real* Picasso. It went on a living room wall.

Throughout the construction of the house, Sam showed little interest in the project, and busied himself making movies. In fact, by the time the house was finished — on their first wedding anniversary — and was ready for the Goldwyns to move into, Sam had not even visited the building site. Now the house was done, down to the last decorative detail, including the ashtrays, and Frances took her husband to tour their new home. He walked through the large and airy rooms, looking bemused, saying nothing. He walked up the curved staircase to the second floor, where Frances had provided one whimsical touch that she thought might amuse him: on each of the white Porthault towels in the bathrooms she had ordered embroidered a small yellow goldfish, to remind him of his earlier name. She waited downstairs for his reaction. There was suddenly an explosion from above. "Frances!" he bellowed. "There's no soap in my bathroom!"

"It was absolutely typical of him," Frances Goldwyn said later. "His first wife must have been terribly bored with him. He was a terrible man. But I loved that terrible man."

Goldwyn liked to say that he was only interested in producing "quality" films. "Quality" and "good, clean family entertainment" were two of his principal watchwords. And, to a large extent, he was true to his word, turning out such cinematic milestones as *The Eternal City, Stella Dallas* — first, in 1925, as a silent, and later, in 1937, with sound — *Dodsworth, Arrowsmith,* and *Wuthering Heights.* He liked to say that one of his goals in life was to prove "that fine things, clean things can be done" in films.

Meyer Lansky was also interested in quality. Just as, with his snobbish streak, he preferred to operate "high-class" gambling casinos in the back rooms of posh Catskill resorts, and chose to offer his bootlegged products to the tonier speakeasies and nightclubs rather than to skid-row saloons, he was also concerned that his liquor customers should receive high-quality goods. Before Prohibition, the liquor business in the United States consisted of small, family-owned distilleries and tradesmen, a number of them Jewish, who turned out spirits and bottled them with no attempt at consistency or quality control, and no two bottles of liquor under the same label tasted quite the same. But since the American drinking public didn't seem to care, it didn't seem to matter. Some pre-Prohibition whiskey was bottled as it came out of the aging barrel. More often, it was cut with new whiskey, raw alcohol, and water. In 1899, the Distilling Company of America had been organized — the ill-famed Whiskey Trust — by a group of Jewish distillers who for a while managed to control most of the whiskey-manufacturing business in Kentucky. The trust failed fourteen years later when it could not compete with the lower prices asked by regional distillers in their local areas. Also, Kentucky whiskeys were supposed to be aged three or four years, but the cost of keeping an inventory of three or four years' production had become prohibitive. To ease its cash-flow problem, the trust sold whiskey, unaged, to distributors as it came out of the still, with the suggestion that the distributors take care of the aging themselves. The distributors, who bottled the whiskey under their own labels, either aged it or not, as they saw fit. Most did not. The result was poor — or, at best, uneven — quality. In view of the number of Jews involved in these somewhat unscrupulous liquor dealings, it would not be unfair to say that one of the unspoken motives behind the Prohibition movement was anti-Semitism, just as, in a later year, there would be a successful movement on the part of the United States to wrest the motion picture business from "Jewish control" by forcing film companies to divest themselves of their theaters. Hints that Prohibition was in part an anti-Jewish reaction lie in the Drys' arguments that drinking was responsible for bolshevism. Bolshevism meant Russia, and to most Americans, Russia meant Russian Jews.

But the law that went into effect in January, 1920, would have the paradoxical result of *improving*, in the long run, the liquor Americans drank. Prohibition quickly made bootleggers much more careful and choosy about what they were selling to their customers. To be sure, a few unprincipled sellers might offer poisonous wood alcohol disguised with flavorings, and call the result sloe gin, but this was not a very good way to encourage repeat business. Meyer Lansky and his friends figured, quite sensibly, that it would be unwise for word to get around that Lansky offered anything but the real thing. Similarly, men like Samuel Bronfman began to be much more careful about what they sold to men like Meyer Lansky. A bad batch of whiskey could have a distressing domino effect, with repercussions bouncing from the unhappy customer to the local bootlegger, to his supplier, and finally to the manufacturer. Lives — and money — could be heavily at stake along the way. And so "quality control" — a notion unheard-of before 1920 — came willy-nilly to the liquor business, forced on it by Prohibition.

Of course, there were little games that could be played. Scotch, for example, when Lansky first entered the bootleg trade, cost him about $25 a case, including overhead — the cost of bribing border guards, hiring boats to transport the contraband across the Jewish lake and stevedores to do the loading and unloading, and warehousing. The going price for bootleg Scotch was about $30 a fifth, which gave Lansky a profit of about $330 a case, or 1500 percent. Soon, however, he was able to devise a system that tripled his profits, to $1,000 a case, or 4500 percent.

One of the yawning loopholes in the Volstead Act was that, although alcohol could not be sold, it could be prescribed by doctors for patients who required it for medical reasons. Therefore, medicinal alcohol continued to be manufactured perfectly legally in the United States, and all at once a great many doctors seemed to have a great many cases where daily dosages of alcohol were required to keep patients in the full bloom of health. In every major American city there was at least one government-licensed manufacturer of medicinal spirits, and what Lansky and his group began to do was to buy up these companies. Later, Lansky would admit that it was occasionally necessary to apply strong-arm tactics, with "offers that couldn't be refused," but for the most part licensed manufacturers were more than willing to take in new partners when they were apprised of the spectacular extra profits they could expect to earn.

The system worked like this: Every quart of illegally imported Scotch whiskey was mixed with approximately two quarts of inexpensive, legal, and cheap raw alcohol. Then coloring agents were added to make sure that the resulting mixture had the right hue. Lansky hired professional chemists and tasters to make sure that the final flavor was indistinguishable from that of real Scotch. Obviously, the mixture had to be sold in Scotch-looking bottles with Scotch-looking labels, and so Lansky bought bottle manufacturers and printing companies to turn out the distinctive bottle shapes and labels of Johnnie Walker, Haig and Haig Pinch, Dewar's, and so on, which were near-perfect facsimiles. In the process of turning one bottle of authentic Scotch whiskey into three bottles of counterfeit Scotch-alcohol blend, Lansky soon found himself in the real estate business, since it was also necessary to buy warehouses in which to store his vast stocks. At the height of Prohibition it was estimated that sixteen million gallons of legally produced alcohol were being used to make forty-eight million gallons of Scotch a la Meyer Lansky.

It has often been said of Lansky that, had he chosen a more legitimate enterprise, he could, with his business genius, have run General Motors. In 1925, Lansky himself boasted that his business was probably bigger than Henry Ford's, and he may have been right.

His profits, by the mid-1920s, were enormous, but then so were his expenses. Approximately a hundred thousand dollars a week — or over five million dollars a year — went for bribes and "grease" for city officials and for other forms of protection. In New York City alone, the payoffs to police ran ten thousand dollars a week, paid all the way down the line from precinct captains to patrolmen on the beat. Still, Lansky and his partners were dividing a net income of over four million dollars a year, while enforcement of Prohibition by law went out the window. During the decade and a half that Prohibition was in effect, federal agents arrested 577,000 suspected offenders, confiscated over a billion gallons of bootleg liquor, seized 45,000 automobiles and 1,300 boats assumed to be involved in the illicit trade. And yet the assistant secretary of the U.S. Treasury, Lincoln C. Andrews, who was in charge of enforcing the Volstead Act, estimated that less than five percent of the liquor traffic was being stemmed. Looked at another way, bootlegging had become the most cost-efficient business in the world.

In 1925, Lansky had another money-making idea. He was always being drawn back to his first love, gambling, and now, though he had always preferred doing business with well-heeled customers, he had a notion for making money from the poor. The idea occurred to him at the posh Beverly Hills Supper Club outside Newport, Kentucky — a wide-open little city across the Ohio River from Cincinnati. Newport, favored by a laissez-faire and bribable city government, had turned Cincinnati into something of a tourist attraction, so close was it to a place where illegal gambling parlors operated openly, while prim and proper Cincinnati looked the other way. Watching the white-coated waiters and black-tied croupiers of the Beverly Hills serve their well-turned-out clientele, Lansky wondered aloud if the same kind of gaming pleasure could not be offered to those at the other end of the economic scale. Italy, he pointed out, and other Latin countries had their national lotteries. The Irish had the sweepstakes. In all these games, for a few pennies a day a workingman could take a chance at winning a huge pot. At first, when Lansky explained that he was talking about betting pennies, his associates were skeptical. But the more he explained his idea, the more their ears pricked up. He and Lucky Luciano sat up all night working out the details.

The idea was simple. Every day, the customer would buy a three-digit number — from 000 to 999. The winning number would come from a supposedly unriggable source that would be published in every newspaper — the last three figures of the total sales on the New York Stock Exchange, for instance, or the betting totals at a particular racetrack. This way, no bettor who lost could claim to have been cheated. The winning number would pay at odds of six hundred to one, which would make it attractive, and since the actual chance of winning was less than one in a thousand the profits could be enormous. Thus the numbers game, or policy game, was invented. Lansky suggested that the game be introduced in Harlem, where a great many poor southern blacks had migrated after the war in search of better jobs. It was immediately a hit in Harlem, as it remains to this day, and the numbers game was quickly introduced in other urban ghettos — Cleveland, Detroit, Chicago, and on and on.

As though such schemes as this were not enough, Lansky would also develop what he wryly called "my laundry business." Again, it was brilliantly simple. Funds were skimmed off the profits from the illicit operations and shipped to Switzerland, where they were deposited anonymously in numbered accounts. Then Lansky would arrange for some of his legitimate businesses — real estate, ware-housing, and so on — to borrow that money. The interest on these perfectly legal loans was then paid right back into the pockets of Lansky and Company. These interest payments, furthermore, were a tax-deductible business expense. As Lucky Luciano explained, "It was like we had a printin' press for money."

Up in Canada, meanwhile, Sam Bronfman seemed to have discovered a similar printing press. And as his comings and goings between the United States and Canada accelerated with his expanding business, he had to keep careful track of his whereabouts, because if he had spent as much as six months' time in the United States in any given calendar year he would have been subject to American income taxes. He was also becoming an expert on, and outspoken advocate of, American and Canadian blended whiskeys. He had developed an interesting theory: that the congeners, or chemical aldehydes or esters, that were retained in blended whiskeys were of such a nature that they made blended whiskey not only a smoother but also a "safer" drink. That is, if a drinker sipped a blend all evening he would enjoy the pleasant euphoria that drink induces, but was less apt to get drunk. Also, he was less apt to suffer the unpleasant hangover effect on the morning after.

A finding by the Pease Laboratory seemed to bear Bronfman out, and the Pease Report suggested that blended whiskeys, being lower in congeners, were better for you than straight whiskeys. Excitedly, Sam Bronfman hired a psychologist to conduct a series of tests on drinkers in upstate New York. The tests lasted several weeks, and responses were measured between men drinking straights and men drinking blends. Not surprisingly, perhaps, considering who was paying him, the psychologist's conclusions confirmed the boss's hunch. Blends were more reliable. A "doctor" had proved it!

Blends, Sam was convinced, could be made more palatable to women. The very word *blend* had a softer, cozier, more reassuring sound than the harsh *straight*. Gin, he was convinced, turned a drinker mean and quarrelsome, and he argued that gin "stayed in the system longer," thereby increasing the chance of a hangover. Brandy was "an alcoholic's drink," and whenever he encountered a man who drank nothing but brandy, Bronfman was convinced that skid row lay right around the corner. His personal drink was always blended Canadian whiskey, taken in a tall glass topped with water or soda, and to demonstrate the superiority of blends —

that they could be "trusted" — Mr. Sam, as he was now universally called, sipped on his whiskey throughout his business day and on into the evening, and it had to be admitted that no one ever saw him drunk. His own personal tastes, of course, did not deter him from also dealing in gins and brandies.

By 1925, Sam Bronfman was one of the richest men in Canada, but the one thing he could not seem to buy was *yikhes* — status, respectability, legitimacy. In Montreal, status was conferred by membership in the Mount Royal Club, by a directorship of the Bank of Montreal, by being named a governor of McGill University. But all these honors somehow managed to elude him. In fact, after he was taken to lunch at the Mount Royal Club by one of its members, the member was requested not to invite Sam Bronfman to the club again. It was not just that he was Jewish, exactly, and that made the snubs all the more galling. Sir Mortimer Davis, another Montreal Jew, not only belonged to all the best clubs — the Mount Royal, the Saint James's, the Montreal Hunt, the Montreal Jockey, the Royal Montreal Golf, and the Forest and Stream — but was on the board of the Royal Bank of Canada and had been knighted by George V in 1917. Sir Mortimer was in the tobacco business. Was tobacco more respectable than liquor? In prim and proper Canada, yes, and for all he might protest that he was just another honest businessman, Sam Bronfman could not shake the "bootlegger" and "rumrunner" labels that had been attached to him.

Part of the problem, too, was Mr. Sam's personality. He could be charming and congenial, but he often had trouble concealing his rough underside. He was known to have a violent temper, and when crossed, he would explode with four-letter epithets that would make even a Montreal stevedore blush. With underlings, he was as autocratic as the Bourbons of old, while with higher-ups or those he wanted to impress he was fawning and obsequious. The man whose staff lived in terror of their boss's displeasure was also a man who, in a gathering of people over whom he had no personal control, seemed uncertain, shy, frightened, unable to think of a word to say. The best that could be said for Sam and Saidye Bronfman, socially, was that they tried — giving lavish entertainments at their Westmount castle — but that they tried too hard, too defensively. They let their hands show too much — always a fatal error in the art of social climbing. Their insecurity was too apparent. At a party, the short, plump, balding figure of Mr. Sam Bronfman would be seen standing at a little distance from the center of things, frowning, shoulders hunched as though to ward off real or imagined snubs that were bound to come.

Worst of all, Sam Bronfman had arrived in smart and civilized Montreal — a city that liked to think it combined the best attributes of Paris and London — from the wilds of western Canada, and with very little history, not to mention education. Furthermore, what was known of his family's history had its untidy chapters. In 1920, his brother Allan had been arrested for trying to bribe a Canadian customs official who had stopped three improperly registered cars heading for the border filled with Bronfman liquor. Then, in 1922, Sam's brother-in-law Paul Matoff, who was married to Sam's sister Jean, was murdered with a sawed-off shotgun in a Canadian railroad station while paying for a shipment of liquor. The family immediately declared that the motive was simple robbery, and Mr. Matoff's murder was never solved, leaving the distinct impression that the family wanted it that way, with no further questions asked.

But in 1928 an event occurred that would supply Sam Bronfman with the history he needed, even though it would be a borrowed one. That was the year he acquired the firm of Joseph E. Seagram and Sons, Ltd. Seagram's was a fine old Canadian distilling firm, and bore a fine old Christian name. Now that the Bronfman distilling business could use the name of Seagram, Sam Bronfman could incorporate Seagram's respected history into his own, and soon, in a very much laundered corporate history, Sam would be able to declare, "Our company had its origin in 1857 in Canada, when Joe Seagram built a small distillery on his farm and sold its products in the surrounding area."

The familiarity with which Mr. Sam would treat "Joe" Seagram, or "old Joe" — as in "old Joe would be proud of us today"— made it sound as though old Joe had been Sam Bronfman's grandfather. But in fact even the "old Joe" story was not quite correct. It was true that the Seagram business could be traced back to 1857, when a small distillery had been built on the banks of the

Grand River in Waterloo, Ontario. But the builders had been two men named William Hespeler and George Randall; in 1857, Joseph Emm Seagram was still a sixteen-year-old Ontario farm boy with no connection to the Hespeler-Randall distillery. That connection did not occur until 1869, when Seagram married William Hespeler's niece, Stephanie, and went to work for his wife's uncle. A year later, he bought out Hespeler's interest in the company, and changed its name.

In acquiring the Seagram name, Sam Bronfman, as the saying goes, "tried to become instant Old Money." But still the invitations to join the clubs and to adorn the boards of the banks did not come.

The timing of the Seagram acquisition, however, could not have been better. The noble experiment of Prohibition — doomed to failure from the beginning — was coming to an end. Everyone knew it, and it was only a matter of time before the Eighteenth Amendment would be repealed. Seagram's gins and whiskeys were well known and popular in the United States. The interim between the Seagram-Bronfman marriage and Repeal would give Mr. Sam just time enough to gear up Seagram's for its reentry — legitimately at last — into the American market.

Yikhes — it was something all the immigrants from Eastern Europe wanted. But, confronted abruptly with a different culture and set of values in the capitalist democracies of North America, each Russian Jew, in trying to adapt to and assimilate in the New World, interpreted *yikhes* differently. Though Sam Bronfman saw *yikhes* as being attained through memberships in the right clubs and corporate boards, in the old country his aspirations would have been sneered at as trivializing a very complicated concept.

In Russia, the word *yikhes* had carried connotations of "pedigree," "genealogy," or "family prestige," but it went even farther than that, for *yikhes* must be rightfully earned, honestly deserved, as well as inherited from one's ancestors. *Yikhes* has nothing to do with wealth, fame, or even personal achievement, though it does have a good deal to do with what an aristocracy consists of — an aristocracy of learning, rather than (as Americans have) an aristocracy of money. In Russia, there were levels of *yikhes*. The highest degree of *yikhes* was awarded to the scholar of the Talmud, the man of God, and a *shadchen*, or matchmaker, would carefully cite the list of scholars, teachers, or rabbis in the family pedigree of the marriage candidate, whether male or female. The longer the list, the loftier the *yikhes*. A rich Jewish family would far prefer that its daughters marry rabbis, however poor, than merely rich men. Similarly, it would seek out rabbis' daughters as its sons' wives.

From godly learning, next down on the *yikhes* scale came virtue, or conformity to moral rectitude as to a divine law. Next came philanthropy, then service to the community through good works. But having generations of *yikhes* in one's family tree was no guarantee of *yikhes*. He who failed to live up to his family's standard and record was quickly stripped of his *yikhes*.

Rose Stokes, among others, strove for *yikhes*. Having failed to achieve it through her marriage, she sought it through work for her Communist workers' cause. But the trouble was, in the gloriously prosperous 1920s, nobody much wanted to hear about the woes of downtrodden workers, about exploitation of the poor. Her audience had shrunk, and her cause had gone out of date. The passions of Jewish radicalism that had first moved Rose to action had died down, had been channeled elsewhere, and Rose herself had been nearly forgotten, though her passions still burned as fierily as ever.

In 1925, her name appeared briefly in the papers again when James Graham Phelps Stokes sued his wife for divorce. The Jewish Cinderella tale was over; the glass slipper had not fitted. Graham Stokes was charging his wife with "misconduct," which was usually interpreted as a euphemism for adultery, but which was the only available grounds for divorce in New York State at that time. Rose immediately issued an angry statement denying any wrongdoing on her part, denouncing New York's divorce laws, and saying that she and her husband had been agreeably disagreeing on many matters, political and otherwise, for years. Her bitter statement served no clear purpose, except that it brought all the old business of the Kansas City sedition trial out into the newspapers again. It was, however, an attempt to preserve some last shred of *yikhes*. Graham Stokes was granted his divorce later that year.

Not long afterward, he married Lettice Sands, a member of a socially prominent New York fam'ly that was related, through marriage, to the Pirie family of Chicago, who had founded Carson, Pirie, Scott. The new Mr. and Mrs. Stokes moved into an apartment at 88 Grove Street in Greenwich Village, not far from the University Settlement House, where he still maintained an active interest, and Hartley House, which he had founded. For some time afterward, Rose kept an apartment on Christopher Street, just across from the tiny park that separates Grove and Christopher streets, within full view of the Stokeses' new apartment. It was as though she had stationed herself there to keep an eye on her former husband and his new wife. The new Mrs. Stokes, however, was unaware of this situation, and if her husband knew, he never spoke of it. But the Stokeses' cook, Anna, who had also worked for Rose, and who liked her, was very much aware of it. In fact, it made Anna very nervous. Only when, after a few years, Rose finally gave up her lonely, angry vigil on Christopher Street, and moved elsewhere in the city, did Anna confess to Lettice Stokes that she had had a recurring nightmare about the two women living in such close proximity. She had been terrified that when Lettice walked her dog, which had also previously belonged to Rose, the dog might recognize Rose on the street, run to her, and there would be an unpleasant confrontation. But in the anonymity of the New York City streets this never happened, and the wife and ex-wife never met.

Throughout the late 1920s, Rose continued to appear as a participant in strikes, demonstrations, and labor rallies in the city — marching, shouting, wielding placards, ever the voluble and fiery militant. In 1929, she was arrested again in a garment workers' strike, and at the time it was revealed that she had been secretly remarried — to an Eastern European Jew named Isaac Romaine, who was described as a "language instructor."* That same year, a demonstration against the repression of the people of Haiti erupted into violence, and Rose was hospitalized for multiple bruises and contusions. At the time, she and her new husband were living at

---

*This, at least, was how the *New York Times* described him. Perhaps because Rose herself was by then slipping into obscurity, there is some confusion about the identity of her shadowy second husband. The *Universal Jewish Encyclopedia* (1943) gives his name as V. J. Jerome, and describes him as a "Marxist writer and editor."

215 Second Avenue, a dingy area near Fourteenth Street, where, it was said, poverty became her. She looked even more proud and beautiful than when she had married a rich man two dozen years earlier. She had, however, continued to use the name Rose Pastor Stokes, the name that had made her famous, even though the *Social Register* had long since stopped sending her its little annual questionnaire, and had dropped her from its pages.

10

LITTLE CAESARS

WHY, one might wonder, did so many Russian-Jewish businessmen — and -women — once they had become successful, become more despotic and fearsome than the czars they had fled Russia to escape, the czars who took as their titles the Slavic form of "Caesar"? Was it because they had been too busy building their businesses to learn the subtle nuances of American speaking patterns, manners, and body language that mark the conventional, diplomatic, soft-spoken wealthy WASP? Was it because their success had come with such amazing speed that they had not had time to adjust to it? Was it because they were, for the most part, short in stature (their children and grandchildren, thanks to better nutrition, would tower over them), and had developed the so-called Napoleon complex of short men? Or was it because they had prospered in businesses — liquor, fashion, cosmetics, entertainment — that seemed, au fond, frivolous; that lacked the solid Protestant respectability of commercial banking, insurance, stockbrokerage, automobile manufacturing; that they were secretly ashamed of, and therefore defensive about? All these possibilities have been offered to explain the rough-diamond qualities of the people who made these first-generation fortunes, and some or all may apply, but the real answer may lie deeper than that, in the kind of terrible compromise the Jew in America had to make between his new situation and his past. It was a compromise that was both psychological and sociological. For centuries, as W. H. Auden has pointed out, the Jews of Eastern Europe had lived under a system where an individual's identity and worth were defined by his lifetime membership in a class. Which particular class was not important, but it was a class from which neither success nor failure — except on an unlikely spectacular scale — could remove him. In the volatile, competitive spirit of America, however, any class or status was viewed as temporary, reversible. Any change in an individual's achievement altered it, and an individual's sense of personal value depended upon the continuous ups and downs of achievement. In this new Diaspora, where the values and desires of the poor were expected to be transformed in the twinkling of an eye to the values and desires of the rich and would-be rich, the result could be severe anxiety. Though the quick-success stories of the Eastern European Jews in the United States might read like fairy tales, they could seem like personal nightmares in real life.

What else but anxiety explains the apparent double identity of a man like, say, Samuel Bronfman — out of his immediate business element a shy, introverted, lost-looking, and uneasy little fellow, but hell on wheels in his office? If Meyer Lansky was the Little Caesar of the Underworld, Bronfman was the Little Caesar of Distilled Spirits. His fits of temper were legendary. A specially reinforced telephone had to be installed for him, because of his habit — whenever he heard something he disliked or disbelieved — of first holding the receiver away from his ear, snarling at it like an enraged wildcat, and then slamming it into its cradle with such force that a number of ordinary instruments had been shattered. He also not infrequently threw the entire telephone across the room, or at a visitor, yanking the cord out of the wall as he did so. Once he hurled a heavy paperweight at an employee, who managed to duck, and only a metal sash prevented the object from flying through a window and out into a busy street below. Trying to make light of this incident, his staff prepared a plaque to mark the point of the paperweight's impact, in the wistful hope that such an outburst might not occur again.

He had a habit of pouncing into his employees' offices unexpectedly, with questions for which he demanded immediate answers. Woe betided the person who didn't know the answer or, even worse, who pretended that he did, and tried to fake it. Mr. Sam had an impressive vocabulary of abuse, and when aroused to fury, he would string his epithets together so that a son of a bitch would become "that lousy, no-good son of a son of a son of a bitch." One Seagram executive likened his nature to a tiger's, but a more apt analogy would have been to a man-eating shark. After one particularly blistering outburst, at a dinner meeting, Sam had started throwing his food, and eventually his plate and all the crockery in sight, at a beleaguered associate, and then fired everyone in the room. Later, he was asked if he oughtn't to worry lest his tantrums brought on an ulcer. He growled in reply, "I don't *get* ulcers. I *give* them." He had a point.

No foe to nepotism, he employed a number of members of his family in his company. Yet there was no question but that Sam was in absolute charge. A nephew might address Sam's brother as "Uncle Allan," but Mr. Sam was always "Mr. Sam." And relatives were fired with the same furious abandon as nonrelatives when, in Mr. Sam's opinion, they failed to measure up to his own rigorous standards. He was a notorious penny pincher, and the salaries he paid were among the lowest in the liquor business, yet when anyone complained, he lost his job. Sam was equally reluctant to pass out titles as rewards for loyal service, and a number of valued associates who, in another situation, might have expected to have been made vice-presidents never achieved such rank in the Bronfman organization. Occasionally, however, he begrudgingly conferred a title, if it meant an alternative to a raise — as happened with one man who asked if he didn't deserve the title of general manager. Sam agreed with a wave of his hand, but a few months later the man was fired. "The damn fool . . . started to *act* like a general manager," Sam explained. "*I* am the general manager."

His attitude toward money was peculiar, to say the least. Once, when he was fixing his first drink of the day, which was around ten in the morning, a visitor commented that the Schweppes soda water he was using had probably cost more than the whiskey. Horrified, Sam buzzed for his secretary and told her not to buy any more Schweppes. "It's expensive!" he bellowed. "Thirty-five cents a bottle!" And yet, hard by his office, there was a fully equipped kitchen staffed with a full-time chef, whose chief duty was to prepare lunch for the boss. Much of the early portion of Mr. Sam's working day was spent planning his midday meal, and he would go over menu selections at length with his secretary, discussing seasonings, sauces, entrées, desserts. For some reason, he called his stomach "Mary," and when he had settled on a combination of dishes that pleased him, he would rub this part of his anatomy and say, "Mary, you're going to be well fed today!"

He was an inveterate clipper of money-saving coupons from newspapers and magazines, and was forever entering contests that offered cash prizes, though he never won anything to anyone's knowledge. The last few minutes of every business day were spent turning out all the office lights to save on electricity costs, though he tipped Pullman porters with hundred-dollar bills. Once, on a shopping trip to New York with his wife and one of his sisters, Saidye Bronfman admired a hat in a millinery shop. The hat cost fifty-five dollars, and Sam told Saidye that she couldn't buy it. Later, back at their hotel suite, Sam told Saidye to telephone the shop and order the hat. When Saidye asked him why he had changed his mind, he said, "I don't want my sister to know I'd let you spend that much for a hat."

And yet, for all his crotchets and tyrannical ways, Mr. Sam occasionally revealed a gentler side. He was fond, for example, of Tennyson's poetry, and could quote it at astonishing length from memory. He also had a pungent sense of humor. Asked once what he considered mankind's greatest invention, he snapped back, "Interest!" And asked what he felt was the secret of his success, he said, "Never fire the office boy!" It was true that, particularly among the lower echelons of his organization, he had built up a cadre of employees who would lay down their lives for him.

No less a despot was Helena Rubinstein, who, having made her first fortune, almost by accident, in Australia, having added to it substantially with Maisons de Beauté in London and Paris, had now made New York her headquarters for a cosmetics empire that would expand throughout the 1920s until it included a hundred countries. Throughout the 1920s, too, her feud with the older, established beauty queen, Elizabeth Arden, would escalate. At one point, Miss Arden hired the entire Helena Rubinstein sales staff away from her. Madame Rubinstein quickly retaliated, and hired Miss Arden's ex-husband, Thomas J. Lewis, as *her* sales manager, crowing at the time, "Imagine the secrets he must know!" (It turned out that he didn't know many, and Lewis was let go not long afterward.) After divorcing her first husband, Helena Rubinstein married a Georgian prince, Archil Gourielli-Tchkonia, for whom she created her House of Gourielli line of men's toiletries. (Rumored to have been a former Parisian taxi driver, Gourielli nonetheless played a mean game of backgammon, which had helped him climb in French society. And, some twenty years Helena Rubinstein's junior — no one knew exactly, since her age was as closely kept a secret as Miss Arden's and their respective beauty formulas — he was still a prince.) Miss Arden retaliated by marrying a prince of her own, Prince Michael Evlanoff. Though the two women were never formally introduced, they had frequent glaring contests across the rooms of fashionable New York restaurants, where maître d's were careful never to seat them too close together. Refusing to dignify her competitor by name, Madame Rubinstein always referred to Arden as "the Other One."

Madame Rubinstein's rages were as famous as Sam Bronfman's, and she was always shouting "Dumkopf!" "Nebbish!" "No-good bum!" "Liar!" "Cheat!" and "Thief!" at cowering employees in her loud, whiskey-tenor, heavily accented voice, which could be heard from one end of her offices to the other. New employees were advised by old-timers, "Try not to let her notice you." Once, a new secretary — all the secretaries were imperiously addressed as "Little Girl" by their employer — was looking for the ladies' room and actually opened, by accident, the door to the facility that was Madame Rubinstein's private toilet. There was a raucous scream, and the luckless girl was fired on the spot.

Even her own two sons never learned how to deal with her, so violently did her opinions of them swing from day to day. Her relationship with her son Horace was particularly explosive. "Horace is a genius!" she would exclaim one day. "Horace is gaga!" she would announce the next. But there was no doubt that she was as shrewd as she was tough. When a thirty-room triplex penthouse at 625 Park Avenue, one of the avenue's most luxurious buildings, became available, she wanted to buy it, offering cash. She was advised that the cooperative building's board of directors did not want Jewish tenants. So Helena Rubinstein simply bought the building.

Meanwhile, her policy on salaries was becoming notorious. She would demand to know what a prospective employee wanted to be paid, and when he or she mentioned a figure, Madame Rubinstein would offer exactly half. When cleverer job seekers tried asking double what they expected to get, Madame somehow sensed this and offered a quarter of the figure. The Rubinstein payroll structure thus became somewhat surreal. Like Sam Bronfman, Madame was a demon about keeping down office expenses, and about twice a month she took unannounced after-hours inspection tours of her offices, turning out unnecessary lights and poring through the contents of wastebaskets, fuming at evidence that office time had been used for personal business, or at staff members who had failed to use up both sides of a scrap of paper. At the same time, employees discovered working late at their desks were given grunts and clucks of approval.

A great many members of her large family were on her payroll in one capacity or another, but even kinship did not protect her relatives from the vagaries of the boss's quixotic personality or high-handed business tactics. When her sister Stella, who was in charge of Rubinstein's French operations, was about to be married, Madame Rubinstein asked for a thousand dollars of company funds to buy Stella's wedding present. When asked to whose account these funds should be charged, she replied, "Stella's, of course!"

She was a woman who, seeing an ad for manufacturer's seconds of hosiery at Bloomingdale's, would send her secretary out to snap up as many pairs of stockings as she could carry at ninety cents a pair. At the same time, she was amassing a million-dollar collection of paintings (a number of them portraits of Madame herself), and another spectacular collection of African art. She claimed to care little about her personal appearance, and indeed her mascara was often smeared and her lipstick streaked. But she spent another fortune on clothes and other personal adornments — diamonds, rubies, sapphires, ropes of emeralds, and yards of pearls. She scavenged wastebaskets for reusable paper clips while, at the same time, buying houses and estates all over the world and filling them with antiques. Soon, in addition to the Park Avenue triplex, there was a town house in Paris on the Île Saint-Louis, a country place at Combe-la-Ville, a town house in London, and an estate in Greenwich, Connecticut. She often held business meetings in her bedroom while she sat in bed, munching on a chicken leg.

One of her most brilliant business coups occurred in 1929. Had she somehow foreseen the great stock market crash that would occur later that year? In some uncanny way she may have, because early in 1929 she arranged to sell her American business to the banking house of Lehman Brothers for eight million dollars. She then repaired to Paris, where she planned to concentrate on her European operations. Then came the Crash, and Helena Rubinstein stock tumbled along with everything else. Meanwhile, she expressed dissatisfaction with the way Lehman Brothers was running her American company. They were taking her products "mass market" — into small groceries and drugstores, whereas previously they had been sold only through prestigious department and specialty stores. She decided to buy her American company back. She did this by writing thousands of personal letters to small Rubinstein stockholders, most of whom were women, asking them if "as one woman to another" they thought that a bunch of Wall Street bankers could run a woman's cosmetic business as well as a woman could. If they agreed with her, would they please give her their voting proxies? Meanwhile, she bought back as much Rubinstein stock as she could at bargain-basement prices. Thus, within a year, she had enough stock and votes to force Lehman Brothers to sell the company back to her at her price, which was somewhat under two million dollars. Her profit: over six million dollars. "All it took," she would shrug, "was a little chutzpa."

"I make a rule for you," Sam Goldwyn would say — it was one of his favorite expressions, and he was always "making a rule," usually jabbing a stubby forefinger into the chest of an opponent as he made it. When asked why the sets of his motion pictures were always the scene of so much strife, turmoil, and dissension, he replied, "I make a rule for you. A happy company makes a bad picture." He may have had a point because a number of good and profitable pictures did emerge from production companies that were famously unhappy.

He was unquestionably a most difficult man to work for. He had a theory, for example, that writers and directors were not good for one another, and that on any picture they should be kept as far apart as possible. This meant that any writer-director collaboration that took place had to be done on the sly. Goldwyn insisted on having a hand in every phase of his studio's operation, and was forever interfering with other people's jobs. King Vidor, at one point, refused to direct a Sam Goldwyn picture unless it was stipulated in his contract that Goldwyn remain off the set throughout the shooting of the film.

But Goldwyn paid very little attention to contracts. In the paramilitary structure of the early studios, the producer was the supreme commander in chief, and at the very bottom of the pecking order were the writers, the privates. When Sam Goldwyn at one point wanted Anita Loos to write a picture for him, he called Miss Loos in and offered her a year's contract at five thousand dollars a week, which she quickly accepted. Later, an associate gasped, "My God, Sam! That's two hundred and sixty thousand dollars a year!" Goldwyn replied, "Don't worry. I can get out of the contract when I'm through with her." And, to be sure, he did.

His running feud with Louis B. Mayer at MGM became legendary. Once, during an altercation in the locker room at the Hillcrest Country Club, Mayer, who was much smaller in size than Goldwyn, managed to back the larger man into a corner and then pushed him into a laundry hamper full of wet towels. By the time Goldwyn had clambered out of the hamper, Mayer had disappeared. The feud occasioned one of Goldwyn's choicest Goldwynisms. When a friend chided him about the amount of bickering and fighting that went on between the two men, Goldwyn looked shocked and surprised. "*What?*" he cried. "We're like friends, we're like brothers. We love each other. We'd do anything for each other. We'd even cut each other's throats for each other!"

In the office, Sam Goldwyn was given the code name "Panama" — for the large white Panama hats he often wore — and he was referred to as "Panama" in secret little interoffice memos that circulated about the studio. "Panama's on the warpath!" a scribbled note might say, and that inevitably meant that he *was* on the warpath, and when on the warpath he was abusive to his staff as well as to his household servants. Dinners at the Goldwyns' were often punctuated with explosions from the head of the table, at the butler, the maid, or the cook. "Take back these peaches!" he would roar, and Frances Goldwyn, in her role as peacemaker, would quietly explain to the cook, "These canned peaches aren't Mr. Goldwyn's brand."

At the studio, invitations to Mr. Goldwyn's table in the executive dining room were naturally command performances. Once, when Goldwyn had invited an associate named Reeves Espy to join him for lunch, Goldwyn startled Espy by appearing at Espy's office door to pick him up. It was usually done the other way around. At the time, Goldwyn had been feuding with an art director named Richard Day, and Mr. Day, who had had his fill of Goldwyn, was threatening to quit. Now Goldwyn further startled Espy by saying, "Call Dick Day and ask him to come along for lunch." Espy was quite sure what Day would think of the invitation. The problem was that interoffice communication was by intercom, and if Espy got Day on the intercom, Sam Goldwyn would be able to hear everything Day had to say. But Espy did as he was told, rang for Day's station on the intercom, and to the voice that answered said quickly, "Dick, Sam Goldwyn wants you to join us for lunch. *Dick, Mr. Goldwyn's standing right here!*"

At Goldwyn Pictures, it became a tradition that every departing employee was given a farewell lunch by the boss, and at Goldwyn Pictures people came and went with some frequency. At these lunches, most of the hour was consumed with speeches extolling Sam Goldwyn, and at one of them, producer Fred Kohlmar said, "Sam, this is the fifth of these lunches we've had in a month. Can we have one when *you* leave?"

He was redeemed, perhaps, by the famous Goldwynisms. Each new example of fractured English was passed around Hollywood, chuckled at, and embellished. As a result, a few of the celebrated utterances are apocryphal, but most are true. He really did say, "Let me sum it up for you in two words — im possible!" And he did say, on a number of occasions, "Let me pinpoint for you the approximate date." But though a number of his people took the Goldwynisms to mean that the boss was a little soft in the head, there was always a certain germ of truth and sense in most of them. When he said, "Include me out," it meant that he wished to be included among those who were out. When he said, "A verbal contract isn't worth the paper it's written on," he was absolutely right — it isn't. When he said, "I took the whole thing with a dose of salts," one had to admit that a dose was as good as a grain. And when, proposing a toast to the visiting Field Marshal Montgomery, he rose, lifted his glass, and said, "A long life to Marshal Field Montgomery Ward!" one could understand his confusion. When he said, "Every Tom, Dick, and Harry is named John," he had a point. And a touch of sarcasm could not be ruled out when Edna Ferber mentioned that she was writing her autobiography, and he asked her, "What's it about?"

Even Hollywood's favorite Goldwynism turned out to be laced with truth. The occasion was when Sam and Frances were about to embark on a cruise to Hawaii, and his studio staff came down to the dock to see the Goldwyns off. While the staff stood waving at him from the pier, Sam stood at the ship's railing, waving back, and calling, "Bon voyage! Bon voyage! Bon voyage to you all!" Sure enough, a few days after his return from his holiday, most of those same well-wishers were sent voyaging off into the choppy seas of unemployment.

Everyone knew, furthermore, that Goldwyn never paid any attention to the three-hour time difference between New York and Los Angeles. Therefore, when Goldwyn telephoned Marcus Loew's son Arthur in New York, and woke him at two o'clock in the morning, and when Loew said, "My God, Sam, do you know what time it is?" no one should have been surprised to hear that Sam turned to his wife and said, "Frances, Arthur wants to know what time it is."

Even more famous than the Goldwynisms, within the movie industry, was Goldwyn's ability to assume the offensive in any business deal, and to immediately get his opponent on the run. At MGM, David Selznick was in charge of loan-outs of performers, and a typical phone call from Goldwyn would begin, "David, you and I have a very big problem." Asked what the problem was, Goldwyn would reply, "You have an actor under contract, and I need him for a picture." Another tactic was to completely befuddle a competitor, to throw him off his guard by making him think he was losing his mind. Goldwyn once telephoned Darryl Zanuck to get him to part with a director whom Zanuck had under contract. He was told that Zanuck was in a meeting. Goldwyn told Zanuck's secretary that Zanuck must be got out of his meeting, that the business was urgent, an emergency, a matter of life and death. When, after a long delay, Zanuck finally came on the phone, Goldwyn said pleasantly, "Yes, Darryl. What can I do for you today?" He used the same technique on Lillian Hellman to get her to write the screenplay for *Porgy and Bess*. After spending several days trying to locate her, and leaving urgent messages for her in a variety of locations, he finally found Miss Hellman at her summer home on Martha's Vineyard. He opened the conversation with, "Hello, Lillian. How nice of you to call. What can I do to help you?"

Though he relied heavily on the talent, it irked him whenever an actor, director, or writer tried to take credit for the success of a movie that he, Sam Goldwyn, had produced. When Eddie Cantor, already a radio star, came to Hollywood to do *Kid from Spain,* he was nothing but trouble. He refused to accept the dressing room assigned to him because it had once been Al Jolson's, and Jolson's career had petered out, and Cantor was superstitious. Cantor also tried to get his wife, Ida, into the publicity buildup for the film, thus diluting Goldwyn's own publicity campaign. He gave an interview to reporters in which he complained about Goldwyn's studio policies, and about the low salary Goldwyn was paying him. Yet, when the film was finished, Goldwyn was pleased with it, and at a private screening he instructed his staff, "Don't anybody tell Cantor how good he is. I want to use him for another picture." Then, when *Kid from Spain* became a hit, Eddie Cantor had the temerity to announce that it was all thanks to him, and to the popularity of his radio show. Goldwyn was furious. "Are you kidding *me?*" he roared at Cantor. "A little radio show made a big motion picture? Why don't you do a little motion picture, and get a big radio show?"

"I make a rule for you," he said to his story editor, Sam Marx, when Marx proposed buying a novel called *Graustark* that was set in a mythical kingdom. "I make a rule for you — never bring me a story about mythical kingdoms." Then, from rival MGM, along came *The Prisoner of Zenda,* set in a mythical kingdom, and a big hit. Immediately Goldwyn wanted to buy and produce *Graustark.* When the negotiations for *Graustark* were completed, Goldwyn said to Marx, "Look — who thought of *Graustark?* I did! Why didn't *you* think of *Graustark?*" Marx reminded him of the recent rule. "I didn't mean classics," replied Goldwyn. He had to have the last word.

Occasionally, Goldwyn's last words betrayed his essential innocence. When the filming of *Romeo and Juliet* was proposed to him, Goldwyn liked the story, but wondered if it couldn't have a happy ending. Jokingly, an associate said, "I don't think Bill Shakespeare would like that, Sam." Goldwyn replied, "Pay him off!" And, long after the rule against mythical kingdoms had been discarded, Goldwyn conceived the idea of making a movie of *The Wizard of Oz*, and ordered his secretary to send out for a copy of the book. The only copy that could be found was a child's edition, in large print and with pop-up illustrations. Seeing Goldwyn poring studiously over this volume, an aide said, "Don't bother reading it, Sam. MGM has already bought the book." Furious, Goldwyn picked up the telephone and called L. B. Mayer. "L.B.," he said, "I am sorry to report some very bad news to you. You have bought a book that I want."

When Norman Taurog was directing *They Shall Have Music* for Goldwyn, Goldwyn asked to see a set of daily "rushes." After watching them, he announced that he couldn't understand the story. Taurog, protesting that the story seemed perfectly clear to him, finally brought in a six-year-old singer from the children's choir that was performing in the film, and ran the rushes through for him. The child said that *he* understood the picture. "So?" said Goldwyn in triumph. "I'm making a picture for six-year-olds?" And somehow Goldwyn's critical hunch about the film was correct. *They Shall Have Music* was both a critical and a box-office flop, with the critics complaining that the plot was difficult to follow. As a result, Goldwyn would never again hire anyone who had been associated with the picture.

One director whom Goldwyn held in considerable awe was the legendary John Ford. In fact, Ford's reputation for genius and temperament actually frightened Goldwyn. Like King Vidor, Ford had stipulated in his contract that Goldwyn not interfere with his filming in any way. When Ford was directing *Hurricane* for Goldwyn, which starred John Hall and Dorothy Lamour, Goldwyn secretly managed to see a "rough cut" version of the movie, and became concerned that Ford was not using enough close-ups of the actors' faces. He fussed privately over this for several days, and then said to an aide, "Let's take a walk over and see John Ford." When he approached Ford on the set, Goldwyn was very nervous, and Ford's look, when he saw Goldwyn coming, was not welcoming. Shifting his weight from one foot to the other, Goldwyn touched on a variety of subjects — the weather, Ford's health,

Ford's wife's health, and so on. Finally, Ford grew impatient with the interruption and said, "What's on your mind, Sam? Spit it out!" Shyly, Goldwyn mentioned what he considered to be the shortage of close-ups. "Listen," said Ford, "when I want to, I'll shoot an actor from *here* up," and he jabbed Goldwyn in the stomach, "or from *here* up," and he poked him in the chest, "or from *here* up," and he flipped his finger in the producer's nose. Walking away from the meeting, Goldwyn said, "Well, at least I put the idea in his mind." It wasn't the last word, exactly, but it was close.

By the 1920s, David Sarnoff was not yet in a position to be a despot, benevolent or otherwise. He was still cautiously working his way up a corporate ladder. Not long after his *Titanic* triumph, while continuing to work in the Marconi station atop Wanamaker's, Sarnoff had written a long memorandum to his employers that began, "I have in mind a plan of development which would make radio a 'household utility' in the same sense as the piano or phonograph. The idea is to bring music into the home by wireless." The memo went on to describe what Sarnoff called the "Radio Music Box," what its range could be, how it might be installed, what kind of antenna it would require, and how much it might cost — Sarnoff estimated that home radios might be made to sell for about seventy-five dollars apiece, and that as many as a hundred thousand Americans might buy radio music boxes. The prophetic memorandum was duly read, filed away, and nothing was done about it.

Then, in 1919, the American Marconi Company was reorganized as the Radio Corporation of America under the financial sponsorship of General Electric, which had been doing some research of its own into the field of radiotelephony at its laboratories in Schenectady. Owen D. Young was named as head of the new company, and Sarnoff was given the title of commercial manager, though he was not put on the board. Mr. Young, a lawyer, knew next to nothing about radio, but fortunately his twenty-eight-year-old commercial manager knew quite a bit. From the outset, Young found himself turning to Sarnoff for technical advice and suggestions.

Sarnoff, meanwhile, was busily casting about for new ways to popularize radio as an entertainment medium, and to sell radio to the general public. What he needed was another *Titanic*, but preferably not a grim disaster — something that would be lively, entertaining, fun, and popular. In 1921, he believed he had found just what he was looking for.

On July 2 of that year — a Saturday night in the middle of a long Fourth of July weekend — the heavyweight champion of the world, America's own Jack Dempsey, was to fight a foreign challenger named Georges Carpentier, known as "the orchid man of France." The country was whipping itself into a patriotic frenzy over the event. Millions of dollars' worth of wagers — many of them being handled by Meyer Lansky and his men — rode on the outcome. Seats in the Jersey City arena where the match was to be fought had been sold out months in advance, and scalpers were hawking tickets for as much as a thousand dollars each. David Sarnoff proposed that RCA broadcast the fight, live, blow by blow, from ringside.

A number of his RCA higher-ups were dubious. For one thing, RCA had no radio station in the vicinity of Jersey City, and so how could the broadcast be transmitted? Also, since there were only a relative handful of crystal radio receivers in the country, belonging to amateur radio buffs, how would a general public be able to receive the broadcast? David Sarnoff set about solving these problems, and he had very little time to do so. General Electric, it seemed, had just completed the construction of what was then the world's largest radio transmitter, and Sarnoff proposed that RCA "borrow" it for the fight. But there was a hitch. GE's transmitter had been built under contract for the United States Navy, which owned it, and the navy brass were unwilling to lend their costly new apparatus for a prizefight. A New Yorker named Franklin D. Roosevelt, however, who had been secretary of the navy under Woodrow Wilson, was presumed to still wield some power with his former naval colleagues. Roosevelt was approached, and he turned out also to be a Dempsey fan. He was able to persuade the Navy Department to part with their transmitter for the fight and "the glory of America."

Meanwhile, Sarnoff knew from some earlier experiments with radio communication between moving trains that a tall transmitting tower stood, unused, over the Hoboken railroad station, just two and a half miles from the Jersey City arena. The navy's equipment was shipped to Hoboken, hooked up to the tower, and the Pullman porters' changing room at the Hoboken railroad station became a radio station. The telephone company was then persuaded to run a line between the station and the scene of the fight.

The only remaining problem was how the public was going to hear the broadcast, but to Sarnoff the answer seemed simple enough — in movie theaters. Marcus Loew of MGM, who was in charge of his company's theater operations, was contacted, and was quicker than most to see the commercial possibilities of the undertaking. For a share of the box-office take, Loew turned over his chain of New York theaters and installed extra loudspeakers and amplifiers for the event.

The live broadcast was a complete sellout throughout the metropolitan area as families from outlying areas flocked to New York to snap up the precious tickets. Even more happily, Jack Dempsey won, as everyone had hoped he would, knocking out the handsome French challenger in the fourth round. America's honor had been defended. Boxing had its first million-dollar gate, when more than 90,000 spectators paid $1,700,000 for tickets at the arena. Dempsey himself took home $300,000. Carpentier's consolation prize was $215,000. RCA and MGM made hundreds of thousands more from the largest radio listening audience in history. The genius of young David Sarnoff was once again a topic at dinner tables everywhere. So was the sudden demand for radio receivers. Virtually overnight, RCA found itself in the radio manufacturing business. Sarnoff was given a raise, and a new title — general manager of RCA.

Of course, this new burst of fame and public acclaim for David Sarnoff did not assure him of instant popularity within the corporate framework of the company. On the contrary, corporate jealousies being what they are, he was heartily disliked in some quarters, and resented in others. For one thing, there was his obvious youth, his obvious brains, and the obvious fact that he had the ear of the company's chief executive officer. Then there was the fact that he did not even possess a high school diploma, and that he was Jewish. Also, though he was carefully deferential and polite to those in positions higher up than he, he had adopted a rather offhand manner — a bit brash and cocky, if not actually condescending — to those a notch or two below. He was not exactly a handsome young fellow, but he had large, bright eyes and he always seemed to be grinning over some inner joke. He had a look, in other words, of being rather pleased with himself — as indeed he had every right to be — but to say that this sat well with his fellow employees would be far from the truth. In fact, whenever possible, they rode him unmercifully. Jobs that were patently impossible somehow found their way to his desk. The most difficult, as well as the most boring, salesmen were referred to his office. If a way, however petty, could be found to make David Sarnoff look ridiculous — or, even better, wrong — it was tried. But — and this was the most irritating thing about the man — despite all this, he seemed impossible to ruffle. Nothing seemed capable of erasing the grin, the look of self-confidence, the look of success.

If anything, David Sarnoff's air of self-confidence seemed to grow maddeningly more pronounced. He had already begun to think of himself in nautical terms — as the man "on the bridge," the skipper of some great ship, the pilot plotting the course of radio communications through the stormy seas of the future. He would draw a parallel between the date of his own birth, in 1891, and "the birth of the electron," as though some cosmic destiny awaited him as the result of these coincidental dates — overlooking the fact that it was newspaper work, not electronics, that he had originally chosen for a career.

But there was no doubt that, at age thirty, David Sarnoff was already a tycoon in the making.

In a famous novel, Budd Schulberg addressed the question "what makes Sammy run?" But in the case of many of these Eastern European success stories, the question could be asked: were they running *for* something, or away from something? Unlike the stolid German Jews who had come to America intent on bettering their lot, because America was "the land of golden opportunity," because there were nineteenth-century fortunes to be made and they fully expected to make them, the Russians had come for an entirely different set of reasons. They had come to save their lives, and their children's lives. Success had been the last thing on their minds, much less success on the scale of a Sam Goldwyn, a Sam Bronfman, a David Sarnoff, or even a Meyer Lansky. Yet success had happened anyway, and so quickly, and almost as if by crazy luck or accident. Was this what they had wanted? Not in the beginning, surely, and now it was more than they had ever dreamed of, more than they felt psychologically comfortable with.

They came from a Russian-Jewish culture, furthermore, that for centuries had taught that there was high honor in poverty. Poverty itself was holy. The poor man was more blessed than the rich man — the Talmud taught this, and the rabbis preached it. God and Mammon could not both be worshiped. To be a Jew *was* to be poor, and to suffer. Perhaps this helps explain the curious double personalities of these early Eastern European tycoons, why they could be loving husbands and fathers at home, but hellions at the office. Sam Goldwyn also had his tender, generous side. When distant cousins in Poland heard of their relative's success, they wrote to him, telling him their problems. He was soon sending regular gifts of money and clothing to people across the ocean whom he had never met. And yet he was a man who really believed that a "happy company" could not make a good product. Perhaps it was because America had handed men like Goldwyn more than they had asked for — more than they had been taught it was right to accept — and they were embarrassed, even ashamed, to be caught accepting it by the shades and memories of their proud, poor ancestors.

Nowhere was this Jewish dilemma more poignantly apparent than in the story of Anzia Yezierska. Touched by the golden wand of Hollywood, handed a check for ten thousand dollars — more money than she had ever seen in her life — taken to a private lunch with Goldwyn, offered a stunning contract by William Fox, she had behaved, some might say, quite foolishly. At lunch with Goldwyn, she had babbled almost incoherently about "art." And, offered the Fox contract, she had simply run away. After the Hollywood experience, in fact, whatever talent she may have had seemed to dry up, and it was years before she was able to write again. But Hollywood was not entirely to blame.

In 1950, sixty-five years old and virtually forgotten, she wrote a memoir, *Red Ribbon on a White Horse*, in which she tried to come to grips with what had happened all those long years ago. Flushed with excitement over her movie sale, her ten-thousand-dollar check from Goldwyn for the sale of her first novel in her hand, she had run eagerly to tell her father, expecting from him some word of praise, pride, or congratulation. She was disappointed. Her father, an Old World Jeremiah of Hester Street, spent his days at the *shul* or in his tenement flat poring over his phylacteries and holy books. Faced with his daughter's accomplishment, he berated her mercilessly for her preoccupation with money and earthly success. A woman's only earthly concern, he told her, was to marry and bear children. She had done neither. She might as well be dead or, worse, never have been born. As she remembered the dreadful scene:

"Woe to America!" he wailed. "Only in America could it happen — an ignorant thing like you — a writer! What do you know of life? Of history, philosophy? What do you know of the Bible, the foundation of all knowledge?"

He stood up, an ancient patriarch condemning unrighteousness. His black skullcap set off his white hair and beard. "If you only knew how deep is your ignorance —"

"What have you ever done with all your knowledge?" I demanded. "While you prayed and gloried in your Torah, your children were in the factory, slaving for bread."

His God-kindled face towered over me. "What? Should I have sold my religion? God is not for sale. God comes before my own flesh and blood. . . .

"You're not human!" he went on. "Can the Ethiopian change his skin, or the leopard his spots? Neither can good come from your evil worship of Mammon. Woe! Woe! Your barren heart looks out from your eyes."

His words were salt on my wounds. In desperation, I picked up my purse and gloves and turned toward the door.

"I see you're in a hurry, all ready to run away. Run! Where? For what? To get a higher place in the Tower of Babel? To make more money out of your ignorance?

"Poverty becomes a Jew like a red ribbon on a white horse. But you're no longer a Jew. You're a *meshumeides*, an apostate, an enemy of your own people. And even the Christians will hate you."

I fled from him in anger and resentment. But it was no use. I could never escape him. He was the conscience that condemned me. . . .

What this scene illustrates is more than a clash of cultures. It is more a clash of faiths, a clash of consciences. In America, a whole history and system of beliefs was being turned upside down, and a people who had been taught to believe in an aristocracy of the poor were trying to adapt to a society that accepted an aristocracy of the rich. Anzia Yezierska was not tough enough, not cynical enough, not heartless enough to escape her Jewish father's "condemning conscience." Trapped between two powerful forces, she struggled briefly, then gave up the fight.

So perhaps one of the things that made Sammy run was the searing inner doubt — a guilt that wouldn't go away — about the worthiness of success, a very real fear that success was evil, ungodly. Assimilation was not free. One of its prices was constant inner conflict, a crisis of conscience, a divided soul.

11

DEALS

BY 1928, it was clear to everyone that repeal of Prohibition was only a matter of time. It had never worked and, it seemed, could never be made to work. Though five more years would pass before Utah became the thirty-sixth state to ratify the Repeal amendment in December of 1933, those five years gave Sam Bronfman all the time he needed to draw up his plans to enter — legitimately at last — the lucrative American liquor market. In 1928, he made a decision that would transform him from a millionaire into, literally, a billionaire.

As long as Prohibition was in force, he figured, Americans would put up with "rotgut" liquor from questionable sources. But, with Repeal, he suspected that drinking tastes would demand fully aged, mellowed, and ripened whiskeys, and that Americans would willingly pay the price for these. On this theory, Bronfman began maturing huge stocks of whiskey in his Canadian warehouses. It was a gamble, of course, and there was considerable risk. It meant withholding his liquor from a lively and thirsty marketplace, and it meant that Seagram's shareholders would have to endure some belt tightening during this uncertain period. Mr. Sam's hunch could have been wrong. American tastes could have become so jaded during nearly fifteen years of Prohibition that the average drinker no longer cared what was in his glass. But Mr. Sam, as usual, was certain that he was not wrong. And, as a result, when liquor sales became legal in the United States once more, Seagram's was in control of the largest stock of fully aged rye and bourbon whiskeys in the world.

Meanwhile, other preparatory steps had been taken. Office space had been rented in New York's prestigious new Chrysler Building, then the world's tallest skyscraper. Learning that the Rossville Union Distillery in Lawrenceburg, Indiana, was for sale, Mr. Sam bought it for $2,399,000 in cash. And in 1930, Mr. Sam imported a bright young Scotsman named Calman Levine, and conferred upon him an Old World title Bronfman had never previously employed in his company — that of master blender.

Calman Levine had been born in Russia in 1884, and had emigrated at an early age with his family to Scotland. He was mild-mannered, well-spoken — with a British accent, which Mr. Sam admired — a man whose bearing suggested that of a university don rather than a whiskey expert. Indeed, Levine had made a long, scholarly study of liquors — not only of their physical attributes, such as taste, aroma, color, texture, and "feel," but also of the almost spiritual associations of certain flavors, since, in the end, a blender's "nose" and palate are based on intuition more than anything else. Levine had grown up in the Scotch business. With a brother-in-law, he had worked as a blender for Ambassador Scotch, and for a while had operated his own small distillery in Glasgow, called Calman Levine and Company, which produced an elegant Scotch called Lochbroom. As the master blender for Lochbroom — most Scotch whiskeys are blends — Levine's job had been to sample, and spit out, literally thousands of different combinations a day from a huge library of little bottles before coming up with the formulas that he felt, intuitively, would be satisfactory. Mr. Sam had often talked about the "art" of blending, but he really knew very little about it. Now Calman Levine was to be his artist-in-residence. He was introduced to the Seagram staff as its prize corporate showpiece, and he certainly looked the part — a gentleman and a scholar, of all things, in the often deadly North American liquor trade. His assignment was, in a sense, twofold. His presence and his title were to be used to provide prestige and luster for the Seagram name when it made its first respectable debut in the American marketplace. And he was to create, in the process, a flagship blend to carry the Seagram banner proudly to the United States.

It took Levine nearly four years to come up with what he considered a winning formula, but there was no hurry. A master blender's art cannot be exercised under a deadline. Millions of combinations were tried in what might seem an endlessly boring routine of sniffing, sipping, rolling whiskeys on the tongue, spitting them out, making notes. But, to carry the artistic metaphor farther, there was always the artist's reward waiting tantalizingly at the end of the search for the right arrangement of colors on the canvas. By early 1934, Levine and his staff had narrowed their choices down to some two dozen different samples, which were numbered consecutively, and long hours of comparisons began, often lasting well into the night. Finally, a decision was reached. Sample number seven was declared the winner. Now all that was left was to give the new whiskey a name. "We can't just call it Number Seven," someone said, to which Mr. Sam replied with a single word: "Crown." Thus was Seagram's Seven Crown born.

Adding the word *Crown* was characteristic of Mr. Sam. He was awed by royalty, and still harbored the fierce hope that the British Crown might one day make him a knight. "Seagram" and "Seven" were of course already alliterative, and by adding the word *Crown*, Seagram's would be saying that this whiskey was their crowning achievement. In the process, Seagram's would be doffing its corporate hat to the royal family. It was one of many such gestures. Earlier, Mr. Sam had bought the Chivas distillery in Aberdeen primarily because Chivas also operated a fancy-foods division that supplied groceries to the royals during their annual summer visits to Balmoral Castle. Chivas foods had thus earned the royal warrant: "Purveyors of Provisions and Victuals to H. M. the King." Unfortunately, though he would dearly have loved to have it emblazoned on his label, Mr. Sam was never able to get a royal warrant conferred upon his Chivas Regal Scotch, though he did his best with "Regal." Other Seagram products would similarly evoke the English aristocracy — Lord Calvert, for example, and Crown Royal, and Royal Salute.

But Seagram's Seven Crown was a clever name for other reasons. There were, for instance, the mystical and magical connotations of the number seven — the seven seas, the seven hills of Rome, the seven arts, the seventh seal in Revelation, the seven deadly sins, and the seven trumpets signifying the consummation of God's plan. But seven was also a popular — though for no particular reason — number of years for aging a whiskey. Seagram's Seven

Crown was not a whiskey that had been aged for seven years, nor would its advertising ever make such a claim directly.* On the other hand, if the customer chose to infer that the number was the whiskey's age, that was all right with Seagram's and with Mr. Sam. Mr. Sam's next move, after having named Seven Crown, was equally adroit. He proposed that Seagram's Seven Crown be introduced along with a second brand — Seagram's Five Crown, which would sell at a lower price. Thus the customer might harmlessly be misled into supposing that, if Seven Crown were aged for seven years, Five Crown must be aged for five. "Besides," Mr. Sam added, "I always like to have money on two horses in every race."

But when Seagram's Seven Crown and Five Crown joined the other Seagram brands — Seagram's 83, Seagram's gin, Seagram's rye, Seagram's bourbon, and Seagram's V.O.† — in the marketplace, Seven Crown was such a clear winner that there didn't seem to be any need for a second horse. Within two months, Seagram's whiskeys were outselling all others in the United States and within a decade Seagram's Seven Crown had become the best-selling whiskey in the world. Five Crown was quietly discontinued, but Calman Levine had done his job well.

In setting up his distributorships and sales force in the United States, Mr. Sam naturally turned to the men who knew the territory best. These, not surprisingly, turned out to be found among the ranks of the recently unemployed bootleggers — men who, for the previous fifteen years, had been full- or part-time criminals. Still, though the reputation of everyone in the liquor business was more than a little tainted, a facade of respectability had to be maintained. One way was through public relations and advertising, and Seagram's earliest U.S. ads were replete with Sam Bronfman's favorite themes — jeweled crowns, orbs, scepters, fancy Olde English lettering, and the slogan "Say Seagram's and Be Sure," which left the impression that other brands were not to be trusted. In Sea-

---

*There were ways to make the claim subliminally, however. In 1941, an advertising campaign was headlined "Seven Years." In smaller print, the copy revealed it meant seven years "since Repeal."

†Another somewhat misleading brand name. A number of European liquors, particularly brandies and cognacs, used initials following their names — "V.S.O.P.," for example, which stands for Very Special Old Pale. Most people not in the know assumed that "V.O." stood for "Very Old." In fact, Sam Bronfman had inherited the label from old Joe Seagram's days in the nineteenth century, and he was said to have used the initials to stand for "Very Own."

gram's "Men of Distinction" series for its Calvert line, Seagram's traded on the reputations of prominent Americans to give its products class and tone and snob appeal.* Its Men of Distinction, the company announced, were paid for their endorsements, but in the form of contributions to their favorite charities, which all true blue bloods had. (The fact that, in a deepening economic depression, a number of Men of Distinction chose themselves as their favorite charity was no concern of Seagram's.)

Still, projecting an upper-crust image was a little hard at first. Soon after Repeal, the United States secretary of the Treasury, Henry Morgenthau, Jr. — who happened to be a German Jew — claimed that Canadian distillers such as Bronfman owed the United States some sixty-nine million dollars in duties and excise taxes on the liquor they had illegally shipped into the country during the dry years. An angry argument between the two countries resulted, and at one point, Morgenthau threatened to impose an embargo on *all* goods imported from Canada until the alleged debt — which many thought a modest estimate of the taxes that had been evaded — was paid. At length, Ottawa agreed to pay a twentieth of the figure, or three million dollars, and Sam Bronfman agreed to pay half of that, and wrote out a check for 1.5 million. With that, he announced, he had paid his debt, even though his Seagram profits during the Prohibition years had amounted to close to eight hundred million dollars.

Throughout Prohibition, meanwhile, Mr. Sam had been fascinated with an American-born Jew named Lewis Rosenstiel. Seemingly above the law, Lew Rosenstiel had spent the Prohibition years boldly transshipping contraband liquor from England, Europe, and Canada via Saint Pierre and then, by truck, right into Cincinnati, Rosenstiel's hometown and center of operations. In the process, he was building what would become his giant Schenley Distillers Corporation. Bronfman and Rosenstiel had met often, during the latter's trips to Canada, and had become gin-rummy-playing friends.

Lew Rosenstiel, meanwhile, had a personality even more despotic and erratic than Mr. Sam's. In fact, he may have been a certifiable sociopath. Convinced that everyone in his organization

*Interestingly, there was never a Jewish Man of Distinction.

was conspiring against him, he had all of his executives' telephone lines tapped, and his house was a veritable spy center. At one point during his long reign of terror, he decided to test his employees' loyalty in an ultimate fashion. He had his secretary phone his top men to tell them that the liquor baron was dying. The men gathered solemnly in their boss's drawing room. Presently the secretary appeared and murmured, "He's gone." Rosenstiel, meanwhile, was in the bedroom with his listening devices. He tuned in to what was being said about him, and had the satisfaction of having all his suspicions confirmed as he heard his executives cheering and congratulating one another over the fact that the Grim Reaper had finally done what each of them had always wanted to do. Still in his pajamas, he marched down the stairs and fired the lot of them.

He had survived one stormy marriage, but his second was even stormier. He had married the former Leonore Cohn, a palely beautiful woman considerably younger than he, who had been traumatized early in life, first, by her mother's death in an auto accident when she was a child; second, by being raised by a California uncle who happened to be the legendary despot of Columbia Pictures, Harry Cohn; and, third, by an ill-advised youthful marriage to a rich Las Vegas businessman named Belden Kattleman.

Soon she was being traumatized again by Lew Rosenstiel. Though he provided her with every conceivable kind of luxury, she was made to pay for it in humiliating ways. When she became pregnant with her second child — her first, a daughter, had been by Mr. Kattleman — Rosenstiel promised to settle a million dollars on the baby when it was born. Then, furious because it was another girl, he reneged on the promise. When she caught the eye of another very rich man, who happened to be Walter Annenberg, she asked Rosenstiel for a divorce. He refused, and instead had both his wife and Annenberg tailed by detectives in an attempt to dig up scurrilous details about the publisher's private life. Finally, Lee asked for a divorce. Enraged, Rosenstiel confiscated every article of clothing, fur, or jewelry that he had given her during the marriage. When she finally walked out of his house for good to marry Annenberg, she had to undergo the ordeal of being frisked and having her purse searched by Rosenstiel's bodyguards.

Rosenstiel and Bronfman had often discussed the possibility of joining forces, and in the early 1930s, with Repeal on the horizon, the two liquor lords had a series of meetings on the subject of a merger that, with any luck, would give them supreme control of the world's liquor market. Rosenstiel would bring to the partnership his knowledge of the U.S. trade, and Bronfman would bring to it his prestigious connections with the great distillers of Scotland. It was to be a fifty-fifty partnership, and, to this end, Seagram's began buying Schenley stock in 1933.

But negotiations began to break down when it suddenly turned out that each man wanted fifty-*one* percent of the proposed merger, and, naturally, neither was the sort of man who would accept a mere forty-nine percent. And things came to a screaming finish when Mr. Sam visited one of Schenley's plants and discovered that at least one Schenley brand, Golden Wedding, was being bottled "hot" — right out of the stills, without aging. Sam had done this, too, of course, in the old days, but now he was going legitimate, respectable, and this sort of practice did not at all fit in with the aristocratic image he wanted Seagram to project. Bronfman accused Rosenstiel of lying to him, of trying to cheat him, of selling cheap rotgut, and Rosenstiel countered by calling Mr. Sam a number of unprintable names. In a final meeting on the subject of a merger, the two hurled curses and insults at each other, each man accused the other of having carnal knowledge of his mother, and each man vowed to destroy the other for all time.

Afterward, whenever Rosenstiel spoke of Mr. Sam it was as "Sam the Bronf." Bronfman's name for Rosenstiel was "Rosenschlemiel," or, simply, "My enemy." The result of the falling out was furious competition between the two giants for a larger share of the market, and a conviction on the part of both Seagram's and Schenley's that spies from the enemy were infiltrating their respective organizations, that certain employees were possibly "double agents." Valuable employees were forever being lured from one house to the other with offers of money on the theory that they would share their secrets.

But it was a curious kind of enmity in that it lasted only during business hours. Like Sam Goldwyn and L. B. Mayer, who fought furiously all day long and yet spent many pleasant evenings together playing cards, Mr. Sam and Lew Rosenstiel remained — on a purely social level — backslapping pals. Neither man had anything but abuse for the other from nine to five. But evenings and weekends they still played gin rummy.

And of course it was part of the nature of the liquor business that there *were* many secrets, many mysteries, many skeletons in closets. Prohibition had made it a business of bribes, payoffs, secret deals, possibilities for blackmail. Whenever he traveled, for example, Mr. Sam insisted that Seagram brands be placed prominently front and center, their labels facing squarely outward, on bartenders' shelves and in the window displays of liquor stores. This meant that advance men had to be sent on ahead of Mr. Sam's visits, and that cash had to be passed under retailers' and bartenders' counters. Mr. Sam, furthermore, refused to believe — or pretended to refuse to believe — that such bribes were necessary, and refused to reimburse his men for these outlays, which meant that his men, to stay in his good graces, were required to make these payments out of their own pockets.

Then there was the curious matter of Mr. Julius Kessler — a mysterious case that is still occasionally pondered by old-timers at Seagram's, along with the question of who murdered Paul Matoff, and why. Kessler was a spendthrift, devil-may-care fellow who came out of the old Whiskey Trust, much loved for his habit of cheerfully giving away money to almost anyone who asked. Then the brief economic depression of 1921 plunged his already shaky liquor business into bankruptcy. For a while, he tried other fields, including selling corsets, but with little success, and finally he announced his intention to retire to Budapest, where food and wine and women were cheap. Whatever funds he had left he put in the care of a longtime secretary, one Miss Bohmer, in New York. Whenever Julius Kessler needed money, Miss Bohmer cabled it to him.

One day in 1930 a mysterious visitor, identified only as "a Hungarian," appeared at Miss Bohmer's office and asked to borrow two hundred thousand dollars of Julius Kessler's money. Miss Bohmer cabled Kessler for instructions. Rather testily, Kessler cabled back that the Hungarian was his friend, and that she should give the man whatever he wanted. Miss Bohmer wrote out the two-hundred-thousand-dollar check, and then wired Kessler to tell him that that was the end of his American money supply. Kessler replied that he was aware of this, and Miss Bohmer then wanted to know how her salary was to be paid. It wasn't, Kessler informed her in his cabled response. He had no further need for a secretary. She was fired. Miss Bohmer, a spinster who had spent many years in Kessler's service, went home that night and, apparently despondent, swallowed a bottle of poison, and died.

Over the next two or three years, Kessler made occasional visits to the United States to look up old friends in the liquor business and to offer his services as a "consultant" for as little as two hundred dollars a month. He was by then almost eighty, and most of his old friends, embarrassed for him, pushed checks across their desks for him while declining his services. Proudly, Kessler tore up the checks and returned to Budapest, and poverty.

Then, in 1934, a mutual friend of Kessler's and Sam Bronfman's named Emil Schwartzhaupt (the mysterious "Hungarian," perhaps?) came to Mr. Sam with a suggestion that something be done to help out the aging, ne'er-do-well Kessler. Surprisingly — since Mr. Sam barely knew Kessler — Mr. Sam immediately agreed, saying that "to do this good deed would redound to the credit of the Industry." He then announced the creation, as a subsidiary of the Seagram Corporation, of the Kessler Distilling Corporation, with Julius Kessler as its president and chairman of the board. Master Blender Calman Levine was assigned the job of creating a new blend, to be called Kessler's Special, which was to be of high quality but to sell in the medium-price range. It was a difficult assignment, but Levine eventually came up with a formula that satisfied all the requirements — a superior blend that would be affordable by the workingman.

Levine even stepped outside his normal field of expertise and designed a special bottle and a special label for Kessler's Special, with Mr. Sam kibitzing over his shoulder, saying, "Make the name 'Kessler' bigger — bigger." Together, they planned an elaborate advertising and promotion campaign, and a national marketing strategy for Kessler's Special. In fact, no one at Seagram's could recall Mr. Sam's working so hard over, and giving so much of his personal time to, the launching of a new brand since the Crown brands had been introduced. Even more unusual was the use of the Kessler name on the label. No Seagram brands had ever been given names that sounded remotely Jewish. There was no whiskey called "Bronfman's Special," nor did the Bronfman name appear, even in the tiniest print, on any Seagram label. Why was Mr. Sam so intent on immortalizing this elderly gentleman?

Mr. Sam even announced that, from now on, Kessler's Special was going to be his personal drink. When the new brand, amid much publicity and hoopla, appeared on the shelves, it was an immediate and huge success. Julius Kessler, in his eighties, became a millionaire. He also became an instant old friend, despite the disparity in their ages — Mr. Sam was then in his lusty early forties — of Sam and Saidye Bronfman, and became a frequent houseguest at Belvedere Palace in Montreal. In fact, Julius Kessler became a part of a frequently told Bronfman family story — told to illustrate the early signs of business acumen on the part of Mr. Sam's elder son Edgar, even as a little boy. Little Edgar, then about six, admired a musical watch that Julius Kessler wore on a watch chain. Kessler said that, if Edgar liked the watch, he would give it to him as a bar mitzvah gift. Said Edgar, "But you're an old man now, and you may not be here for my bar mitzvah." With that, Kessler removed the watch and presented it to Edgar Bronfman on the spot.

Along the corridors of Seagram's, of course, there were many jokes about Kessler's Special. "Kessler certainly *is* special," they said, "special to Mr. Sam." That the boss should have made such a Herculean effort, at such great expense, just to help out an octogenarian whom everyone else had written off as a loser seemed inexplicable. Good deeds on such a scale were not at all Mr. Sam's style. Unless, of course, there was blackmail involved, and Kessler "had something" on Mr. Sam from Prohibition days, when, it was assumed, there had been much dirty work at the crossroads that Kessler could have known about.

There were a number of intriguing pieces to the puzzle, but no clear solution. Who, for instance, was the mysterious Hungarian? Was he part of the scheme, and was the two hundred thousand dollars his fee for helping Mr. Kessler bring it off? But four years had elapsed between the Hungarian's loan and Mr. Sam's magnanimous gesture. Or was this time merely allowed for the scent to cool? And what was to be made of Miss Bohmer's sudden suicide? True, it was 1930, the Great Depression was settling in, her longtime boss had treated her very shabbily, and she may have felt at the end of her rope. Or was it not really a suicide at all?

Did Miss Bohmer, in underworld terms, "know too much," and need to be got rid of?

Then there was the ambiguous role of Emil Schwartzhaupt, the first to suggest the good deed to Mr. Sam. That same year, 1934, Mr. Sam concluded a — for him — rather unusual business deal with Mr. Schwartzhaupt. Schwartzhaupt owned the Calvert distillery at Relay, Maryland, and Mr. Sam wanted to buy it. Instead of making Schwartzhaupt an offer, which would have been customary, and waiting for Schwartzhaupt to come back with a higher price, then agreeing on a figure in the middle, Mr. Sam told Schwartzhaupt to name his figure. Whatever it was, Mr. Sam would pay it. There would be none of the usual haggling. Schwartzhaupt named his price, and was paid. Later, Schwartzhaupt would grumble that he had probably named too low an amount.

Mr. Schwartzhaupt, however, had done all right. He had already become the second-largest shareholder in Schenley's, having sold his Bernheim Distilling Company in Louisville to Lew Rosenstiel, Mr. Sam's bitter rival.

The year 1934, the first full year of Repeal, was a hectic one throughout the revived American liquor industry, a year of fast deals, scrambling for markets, price wars, hastily patched together new laws and regulations, and sudden changes. Many facts that might have come to light were irretrievably lost in the shuffle of that uncertain year, and all the principals in the Kessler affair are now dead. The Seagram Corporation, in response to queries, remains officially unaware of any underhanded dealings that may or may not have gone on, but is also unwilling to forward such queries to the Distilled Spirits Institute, of which Seagram's is a member. Seagram's offers only one explanation for Mr. Sam's beneficence to Julius Kessler: it was a "good deed."

If so, Mr. Sam was certainly consistent. Even after Julius Kessler's death, Mr. Sam remained loyal to Kessler's Special whiskey, and devoted special attention to the way the brand was marketed and promoted, loudly announcing, "A Kessler's and soda, please!" whenever he ordered a drink in a public bar or restaurant. But then, after all, Kessler's whiskey had become a money-maker for Seagram's. It still is.

But Mr. Sam himself may have had the last word on the whole subject. Looking over the galley proofs of his company's carefully

laundered official history that was to be included in one of Seagram's annual reports to its stockholders, Mr. Sam slammed the
pages down and said, "This is so much bullshit. If I only told the
truth, I'd sell ten million copies!"

As the dark years of the 1930s marched forward in Europe, and
as Nazi Germany grew in power, more and more American Jews
were becoming aware of the increasingly institutionalized anti-
Semitism that would lead to Hitler's Final Solution for the Jews
of Europe. By 1933, it was apparent that Hitler's rantings were
more than political rhetoric, and Americans were warily eyeing
the deteriorating situation in central Europe. That was the year
when Rose Pastor Stokes became ill, and her malady was diagnosed
as cancer of the breast. A physician in Germany had announced
great strides in the treatment of cancer — the doctors of Germany
were still considered the finest in the world — and her husband
and friends decided that she should be sent to Germany for medical
care. There was no small amount of risk, to be sure, because of
the Nazis, and there was also the problem that neither Rose nor
her husband had any money.

In April of that year some five hundred of her old friends and
admirers held a meeting at New York's Webster Hall to try to raise
funds for the trip abroad. The chairman of the gathering, Alexander
Trachtenberg, claimed that Rose's cancer had been caused by the
brutal kicking and beating she had received from a policeman
during the garment strike in 1917. Her new husband confirmed
the incident, but said that it was probably just a contributing factor.
Enough money was raised to send Rose to the German doctor.

Though she was only fifty-three, she now looked much older.
Her famous mane of Titian hair had turned mousy and was streaked
with gray, and she wore it carelessly, pulled back with pins and
combs. She seemed to have lost all interest in her once-lovely
appearance, and the wonderfully delicate and slender figure that
Harper's Bazar had written so admiringly about in 1905 had gone
heavy. Her face — she wore no makeup — was lined, and there
were dark circles under her eyes. The face, though fuller, coarser,
also seemed saddened and sunken from the weight of lost causes.
She seemed to have been defeated by both love and time.

Though she had been called a traitoress and a seditionist, Rose was at heart a patriotic woman. Her patriotism — and that of her fellow founders of the American Communist party — was perhaps idealized, unrealistic, impractical. She saw American society as flawed, but the remedies she fought for were for all Americans, not just Jewish Americans. She had foreseen a social revolution in America, and of course her vision was faulty. In 1933, with fifteen million Americans out of work, the country was probably closer to a revolution than at any other point in its history. But it would not happen.

Once in Germany, her whereabouts were kept secret to protect her from harassment. But it was announced that she was sending home two trunkfuls of papers — an autobiography that she was writing. If the papers were sent, they never arrived. She died in Germany on June 20, 1933, and her crusade — which she herself may not have altogether understood — was ended.

On July 24, about four hundred of her fellow Communists met in a drab old hall called the New Star Casino on 107th Street and Park Avenue, at the seedy fringes of Harlem, for a memorial service. Though no note was made of it, it was just a few days past what would have been her twenty-eighth wedding anniversary to James Graham Phelps Stokes, whose Old New York name she had continued to wear so proudly, and her own fifty-fourth birthday. It was noticed that most of those in attendance were women. Rose's ashes had been flown home from Germany, and her urn was carried in a procession by a special escort and placed on a red-draped card table on a platform. Two prominent members of the Party, Clara Zitkin and Sergei Gussev, made short speeches. A chorus sang revolutionary songs — "Meadowlands," and "The Peat-Bog Soldiers."

Then the audience stood at attention, in silence, for one full minute. The Romance of the Century, and the Cinderella Story of the Lower East Side, was over.

Later, it was announced that the writing of a biography of Rose Pastor Stokes was "in the hands" of a man named Cedric Belfrage, who was the author of a book called *South of God*. The biography has never appeared.

12

WAR

As the news from Hitler's Germany grew more alarming, a number of American Jews wondered why no voices of protest had been raised from a number of important places. President Roosevelt had said nothing, and neither had Stalin, nor the Pope. It seemed to many people that a cry of outrage from at least one major world power might give Hitler pause, and persuade him to change his course, but the world powers remained strangely silent, pursuing some sort of policy of wait and see. Hitler, the Jews pointed out, was a man who had shown he could be cowed by much lesser men. Generalissimo Franco had stopped Hitler's army at the Spanish border with what amounted to no more than a lot of double-talk. And when the Germans had told the king of little Denmark that they could "cleanse" Denmark of its Jews, the king had replied firmly that the Danes would never stand for such a crime against humanity, nor would he. He himself had put on the identifying Jewish yellow armband, and urged his subjects to do the same. They did, and the Danish Jews were allowed to live. Why couldn't President Roosevelt take such a stand? If he wouldn't, it behooved wealthy Jews in North America to do what they could on their own.

For the Jewish fraternity of motion picture producers in Hollywood, however, this was a very ticklish subject. They had so convinced themselves that the success of their movies depended on the movies' non-Jewish character that they were reluctant, no matter how it might trouble the conscience, to step forward and identify themselves with Jewish causes, no matter how urgent.

Furthermore, their attitude was reinforced by none other than the man whom Roosevelt had appointed as ambassador to the Court of St. James's in 1937 — Joseph P. Kennedy. Just back from London, Kennedy had called a secret meeting with some fifty of Hollywood's leading motion picture men, including Goldwyn, Mayer, the Schencks, the Warners, Fox, and Zukor. In firm tones, Kennedy had told them that, as Jews, they must not protest what was going on in Germany, and must keep their Jewish fury out of print and off the screen. Any Jewish protests, Kennedy insisted, would make a victory over the Germans impossible. It would make the world — and the United States public in particular — feel that what was going on in Europe was "a Jewish war," and a Jewish war would not be a popular idea, would actually increase anti-Semitic feeling in the United States. Kennedy delivered the same argument to a group of New York's Jewish businessmen in the banking and fashion industries. In New York and Hollywood, the leading Jews quietly agreed to Kennedy's plea for silence, and to keep any Jewish feelings, along with their Jewishness, under wraps. Whatever Kennedy's intentions may have been, it was curious, even chilling, advice.

But it was advice that many Hollywood men were probably somewhat relieved to hear. It eased them of some guilt they might have felt, and after all, it came from a very highly placed source. Not only was Kennedy very rich, but he was also a high government official. Furthermore, he was a power on Wall Street, where he had headed the Securities and Exchange Commission, and much in Hollywood rode on what Wall Street said. He was also a considerable force in the motion picture business, thanks to, of all people, David Sarnoff.

Back in the 1920s, Sarnoff had predicted that the radio and the phonograph would be combined, and that a national network — or "chain," as he called it — of radio stations would be created, whereby a program originating in, say, New York, could be transmitted simultaneously from a series of high-wattage towers across the country. With the advent of sound in motion pictures, Sarnoff saw that talking pictures meant business for RCA, too, since all the components that went into sound for movies were actually by-products of radio science. Sarnoff had proposed that RCA get a foothold in the movie business, and with that in mind he approached Joe Kennedy in 1927.

Kennedy owned a substantial piece of a small production company called Film Booking Office, which had a friendly relationship with the large Keith-Albee-Orpheum chain of theaters. Kennedy also had an interest in another film company, called Pathé Pictures. At the time, however, Kennedy's interest in films seemed mostly to be based on his relationship with Gloria Swanson, and his desire to promote her career. David Sarnoff proposed to Kennedy that, with half a million dollars of RCA's money thrown into the pot to sweeten the deal, Film Booking Office, Pathé, and Keith-Albee-Orpheum might be merged to form a new studio that would rival the existing Big Five. Kennedy liked the idea, and the result of the merger was RKO Pictures (Radio-Keith-Orpheum). It was certainly a nice thing for Kennedy, who saw his RKO stock climb from twenty-one to fifty dollars a share just before the Crash, when he sold out at the top.

Later, Kennedy would claim that the idea for forming RKO was his own, but his biographer, Richard J. Whalen, in *The Founding Father*, refuted this, and called the creation of the new company "Sarnoff's grand design." For such coups as this, Sarnoff was rewarded with the presidency of RCA in 1930. And in Hollywood, where Kennedy made himself president of RKO, there was awe. Adolph Zukor had asked, "A banker? A banker in this business? I thought this was a business for furriers."

Kennedy, when not telling Hollywood producers what they should or shouldn't do, could also be very useful to his movie friends. As ambassador, he had made high-level connections in London, and England at the time was the second most important market for American-made films. In a confidential memo to Sam Goldwyn, Joseph M. Schenck in MGM's New York office was able to report that, working through State Department channels — and in coded telegrams that Kennedy had let Schenck see — Kennedy was developing a formula whereby the film industry could withdraw, and transfer out of England, much more money than had been allowed by law. A five-million-dollar ceiling had been in force for such withdrawals, but Kennedy had assured Schenck that this ceiling could be raised to between twenty and thirty million. Furthermore, the money would come out of England in dollars, not English pounds, which was important since the pound was in a weakened, war-frightened state. Schenck warned Goldwyn not to try to interfere with Kennedy's plans since, as Schenck put it, Kennedy was a "tough customer and resents anyone who tries to go over his head or that of the State Department." In his ambassadorial role, Kennedy would deal directly with the British chancellor of the Exchequer, Sir John Simon. Was any of this legal? Who knew? But it did seem an odd bit of extracurricular activity for our American ambassador. And it showed that Hollywood was more than a little frightened of Mr. Joseph P. Kennedy.

Kennedy would prove helpful to his Hollywood colleagues in still other ways. Following Repeal, like others in the liquor trade, Kennedy had become a legitimate importer, and an important new source of Kennedy wealth became the importation of a Scotch whiskey called Black Tartan. When Britain declared war on Germany in 1939, Scotch became a very difficult commodity to obtain in the United States. While other American distillers experimented with something called "Scotch-type whiskey," a very poor imitation, those who had connections with Ambassador Kennedy never had any trouble getting the real thing. It was said that the Beverly Hills Hotel was one of the few places in the country where, throughout the war, good Scotch was always available, and it was always Black Tartan. How it arrived, other than by diplomatic pouch, has never been made clear.

Hollywood's Jews reacted to Kennedy's edict of silence on the subject of Hitler's treatment of the Jews in different ways. Sam Goldwyn, for example, rationalized that reports of concentration camps and mass murders were "probably exaggerated," and others took this comforting view. But at least one man decided not to be daunted by Kennedy and to be vocal on the subject — the volatile screenwriter Ben Hecht. Born in New York of Russian immigrant parents, Hecht had become something of a Hollywood maverick and gadfly. In various articles for newspapers and in the *Reader's Digest*, Hecht had begun to complain about the process of "de-Semitization" he was observing in the popular arts, and "the almost complete disappearance of the Jew from American fiction, stage, and movies." It was a process, he claimed, that was designed to stifle any outrage over Hitler's Jewish policies, and to minimize, as much as possible, the human connotations of the word *Jew*. In Hollywood, however, Ben Hecht was considered a little crazy, as, indeed, all writers were. ("No writers at story conferences!" had been one of Sam Goldwyn's famous rules.)

But Hecht's protestations had brought him to the attention of a young Jewish activist named Peter Bergson. Bergson, a Palestinian, was a member of the Irgun Tzevai Leumi, the armed, anti-British organization that had been founded by Menachem Begin to aid Israel's struggle for freedom. Members of the Bergson group had come to the United States to raise money for the Jewish forces in Palestine. Bergson himself had been a disciple of a militant Zionist named Vladimir Jabotinsky, who had been born in Odessa but grew up in Italy, where he had been strongly influenced by the risorgimento. In Palestine, Jabotinsky had organized a Jewish legion, which had done a great deal to bolster Jewish morale, but which had come on the scene too late to do much damage to the Turks or to dislodge the British presence. Jabotinsky was convinced that Jewish armed forces were essential to the creation of a Jewish state, much to the displeasure of more conservative Zionists, such as Chaim Weizmann and Louis Brandeis. The trouble was that Zionists were divided as to priorities. Some felt that the creation of the State of Israel should come first, in order to give Europe's Jews a place to which to emigrate. Others felt that the more pressing task was saving Jewish lives at any cost.

Early in 1940, Jabotinsky came to the United States, and before a cheering audience of thousands of Jews at Madison Square Garden, urged that the only solution to the plight of Europe's Jews was the creation of a Jewish army to fight alongside the Allies as an independent unit, like the Free French. Such an army, Jabotinsky asserted, would put the lie forever to the claim that Jews made poor soldiers. Though Jabotinsky thrilled his audience in New York, the British Foreign Office was less pleased with his crusade. In London, it was feared — with some justification, as it turned out — that what Jabotinsky really had in mind was a Jewish brigade formed, trained, paid for, and equipped by Britain, which would later be used to seize Palestine from British guardianship. Already, in Palestine, the British had enacted a number of anti-Semitic laws. For one thing, it had been stipulated that only one Jew could volunteer for His Majesty's army for each Arab who enlisted. Since no Arabs were joining, this meant that no Jews could, either. In London, Jabotinsky had been labeled a "Jewish Fascist." A few months after his Madison Square Garden appearance, however, Jabotinsky died of a heart attack. The banner for a Jewish army was taken up by Peter Bergson.

Sparked by Ben Hecht's articles, Bergson contacted Hecht and met with him in New York, and immediately asked him to be the American leader of the great cause. Funds were needed, not only for the Jewish army but also to mount an extensive campaign of demonstrations and newspaper advertisements to alert the American public to the plight of Europe's Jews. Some of the richest Jews in America, Bergson pointed out, were in Hollywood, and Hecht, with all his "powerful connections" in the movie capital, could surely and with ease extract "millions" from the Jewish moguls there. Bergson, of course, had a rather unrealistic grasp of Hecht's standing in the Hollywood community. Hecht was a mere writer, which fact alone placed him close to the bottom of the Hollywood pecking order. Furthermore, in 1940, Hecht was struggling with a reputation for "unreliability," and was then seriously on the outs with at least two important producers, for allegedly having botched a rewrite job on a film called *Lullaby*. Also, Bergson was probably overestimating the wealth of the studio heads. Though they paid themselves huge salaries and lived like kings, most, like Sam Goldwyn, were at the same time heavily in debt to New York and California banks.

Still, flattery has always been an important means of persuasion, and no doubt Hecht was delighted to hear from Bergson that he was a figure of such importance. Without hesitation, Hecht accepted the chairmanship of the Jewish army cause and, early in 1941, headed for the West Coast to press his cause with the producers.

The initial response was far from encouraging. In fact, it was loud and angry. Harry Warner, for one, ordered Hecht out of his office and threatened to call the police. The general reaction was: was Ben Hecht out of his mind? Jews fighting as Jews? If Jews wanted to fight, they could fight as Americans or Englishmen. If the British weren't allowing the Palestinian Jews to fight, should American Jews tell a great nation like Britain how to run a war? If the Hollywood studio heads criticized the British, with whose ordeal everyone in America sympathized, the Jews would be hated even more. Not mentioned was the matter of Joe Kennedy, whose covert operations with London promised a means of drawing more movie receipts out of British escrow, and who had made it perfectly clear that Hollywood's Jews should maintain as low an anti-Hitler profile as possible. It was practically a matter of United States foreign policy. Yes, Hecht found, Jews were always willing to help other Jews in trouble, but not to help Jews *make* trouble. He called on twenty different studio heads, including Mayer and Goldwyn, but the response to his campaign was uniformly and resoundingly negative.

Wearily, Hecht took up the matter with his friend, the director Ernst Lubitsch, the only Hollywood Jew who seemed remotely supportive of Hecht's position. After Hecht recited his litany of failures with one powerful man after another, Lubitsch expressed surprise that Hecht had not contacted David O. Selznick, who was by then one of the mightiest men in town. Selznick was still riding on the crest of his 1939 hit, *Gone with the Wind*, which was threatening to become one of the biggest grossers in film history. Himself the son of a pioneer producer, Lewis Selznick, David Selznick had also made the closest thing to a Hollywood dynastic marriage, to Louis B. Mayer's daughter Irene. Now, in the wake of such successes, David Selznick might be the one man with the courage of his convictions; might be willing to stand up and be counted as a Jew. If, Lubitsch pointed out, someone of David Selznick's stature could be persuaded to sign a telegram as co-sponsor, with Hecht, of a rally for the cause of a Jewish army, then everyone in Hollywood — stars, directors, studio heads, the press — would turn out for it. In Hollywood, an invitation from Selznick was a command. Ben Hecht related what happened in his memoirs:

I called on David the next day and was happy to find there was no cringing stowaway in my friend. Nevertheless, he was full of arguments. They were not the arguments of a Jew, but of a non-Jew.

"I don't want anything to do with your cause," said David, "for the simple reason that it's a Jewish political cause. And I am not interested in Jewish political problems. I'm an American and not a Jew. I'm interested in this war as an American. It would be silly of me to pretend suddenly that I'm a Jew, with some sort of full-blown Jewish psychology."

"If I can prove you are a Jew, David," I said, "will you sign the telegram as cosponsor with me?"

"How are you going to prove it?" he asked.

"I'll call up any three people you name," I said, "and ask them the following question — What would you call David O. Selznick, an American or a Jew? If any of the three answers that he'd call you an American, you win. Otherwise, you sign the telegram."

David agreed to the test and picked out three names. I called them with David eavesdropping on an extension.

Martin Quigley, publisher of the *Motion Picture Exhibitors' Herald*, answered my question promptly.

"I'd say David Selznick was a Jew," he said.

Nunnally Johnson hemmed a few moments but finally offered the same reply. Leland Hayward answered, "For God's sake, what's the matter with David? He's a Jew and he knows it."

As Lubitsch had predicted, with David Selznick's name at the bottom of the telegram along with Hecht's, acceptances to the Jewish army rally poured in from all over town. Sam Goldwyn wired back immediately to "accept with pleasure this worthy cause," and then spent several hours with his wife, fussing over what she should wear to the event — whether she should "dress rich," or "dress poor." The Hecht-Selznick telegram seemed to find even Harry Warner in a more receptive mood, and even though he had ordered Hecht ejected from his office a few weeks earlier when the same subject had been broached, he now replied that he would be absolutely delighted to attend. So did Charlie Chaplin, which was an even greater surprise. Chaplin had always avoided attending anything that smacked of being a "Jewish affair," lest he give credence to the rumor, which had persisted for years, that he was a crypto-Jew. The magical name of Selznick had done the trick.

The rally was held in the commissary of Twentieth Century–Fox on a balmy spring night in 1941. The first speaker was Senator Claude Pepper of Florida, who had dined earlier at the Lakeview Country Club while his California hosts for the evening waited outside — in accordance with the restricted club's policy that no Jews could be admitted to the dining room. Pepper, in silver tones, spoke warmly of the virtues and culture of Jews and their role in history but, to the disappointment of Hecht and Peter Bergson, failed to touch on the subject of a Jewish army. Next on the dais was Colonel John H. Patterson, DSO, of the British army, who, during World War I, had commanded the Jewish Legion when it crossed the Red Sea and entered Palestine. Colonel Patterson, in full uniform and emblazoned with medals and decorations, was an imposing figure, and as he rose to speak, he was given a standing ovation as befitted a true British hero on a night when the well-being of Britain was foremost in every American's thoughts.

As the colonel began developing his remarks, however, there were looks of confusion and distress among his audience. He began by extolling the bravery of the Jewish Legion and of Vladimir Jabotinsky. He then turned to a detailed account of how Jabotinsky had been mistreated by the British. The British, the good colonel went on to say, were basically anti-Semites, and after the Jewish Legion had bravely entered Palestine, Britain had tried to degrade the legion to a mere labor battalion. He went on to cite instance after instance of British foul play and anti-Semitism, and from there he moved to the subject of the British pledge to the Jews to make Palestine their homeland. The British were actually intending to do nothing of the kind, the colonel asserted. Instead, under the guise of policing and protecting the land, they were preparing to take over Palestine and drive the Jews out. On and on went Colonel Patterson, denouncing the treacherous, duplicitous, perfidious British — his own countrymen and country! — and the British hatred of the Jews.

Of course there was more than a little truth in what the colonel was saying, and he may have supposed that his obvious philo-Semitism would win him a sympathetic audience. But his timing could not have been worse. Though America had not yet entered the war, there was no question of which side Americans would fight for, if and when it did. Earlier in the year, President Roosevelt had proposed the Lend-Lease program to aid Britain and its allies in the struggle against the Axis powers. Colonel Patterson's audience could not believe its ears. No one had been remotely prepared for anything like this. It was all right for the colonel to love and admire the Jews — but at the expense of America's best friend? It was unthinkable, particularly tonight, while the British were undergoing what Churchill would call their finest hour. Now was the time to forgive Britain for its sins of commission and omission in the past. Suddenly there were boos and catcalls from the audience. Sam Goldwyn rose to his feet and commanded the speaker to "sit down! Sit down!" A number of people headed for the door — at least one to place a telephone call to the FBI to report the outrageous goings-on at the Fox commissary — but still the speaker continued, laying bare more and more examples of the blackness of the British soul. When he finally concluded, there was a stunned silence among what remained of the audience, and no applause. Hecht and Bergson fidgeted in their seats, and David Selznick threw his cohost a murderous look. He had been right. It was a time when Jews wished to be Americans first, Jews second.

There were more speakers on the program, including Burgess Meredith, Peter Bergson, and Hecht, each of whom did his best to salvage what was left of the evening. When the speeches were over, there was general confusion in the commissary until one clear voice rose above the audience. It belonged to, of all people, Hedda Hopper, the gossip columnist, who said crisply, "We're here to contribute to a cause. I'll start the contributions with a check for three hundred dollars." And Miss Hopper was not even Jewish. Immediately the remaining movie moguls, not to be outdone by a woman and a *goy* at that, began pledging contributions. These ranged from a hundred dollars up to five thousand dollars — though Hecht was somewhat sorry to notice that among the five-thousand-dollar pledgers were men like Gregory Ratoff, Sam Spiegel, and one or two others who were known at the time to be in a state of questionable solvency. Nonetheless, in the space of an hour, $130,000 had been pledged.

It was not the "millions" Bergson had hoped for, of course, nor was it sufficient to finance an army. But it did seem sufficient to make the evening a moderate success. In the weeks that followed, however, when Hecht and his committee attempted to get the movie men to make good on their pledges, the true state of affairs was revealed. Many reneged. In the end, only nine thousand dollars was collected in cash, not enough for a full-page ad in the *New York Times*.

In Yiddish, the expression is *sha-sha*, which can be loosely translated as hush-hush, don't say it. In the early months of 1941 America was whipping itself into a near-hysterical frenzy of patri-

otism, and any sentiments that were not profoundly and resoundingly pro-American came across as disloyal or even treasonous.
Just a few months earlier, the America First Committee had formally announced its existence — a curious mixture of people who
traditionally feared "foreign entanglements," along with political
radicals and pacifists, and some who were probably secretly, if
not openly, pro-German. The most celebrated America Firster was
the all-American-boy hero from America's heartland, Charles A.
Lindbergh, who on September 14 of that year would make a speech
in Des Moines, Iowa, that certainly *sounded* like anti-Semitism.
So this was not the time to stir up Jewish political causes. It was
sha-sha time, not for Jews themselves, but for Jewish*ness*.

In Hollywood, there was particular reason for fear. Whether as
a direct result of the meeting at the Fox commissary or not, a few
months later, in August, and three thousand miles away, in Washington, the United States Senate was pushing through Senate Resolution Number 152, authorizing "an investigation of propaganda
disseminated by the motion picture industry tending to influence
participation of the United States in the present European war."
The resolution was spearheaded by Senator Bennett Champ Clark
of Missouri, an America Firster, who said, "What I am protesting
about is the control of a great agency of propaganda in the hands
of a small monopolistic group undertaking to plunge this country
into war." Though Senator Clark seemed not to have understood
Hollywood's attitude toward the war very well, and though he made
no specific mention of Jews, his comments also had anti-Semitic
overtones, as he spoke darkly of "propaganda that reaches weekly
the eyes and ears of one hundred million people . . . in the hands
of groups interested in involving the United States in war," and
of "Powers . . . real or potential, partial or whole, economic, political, or social, and trade practices, organizations of motion picture producers," and so on, which made the movie men sound
like part of an evil conspiracy, or at the very least a cabal.

Within four months, of course, the Japanese attacked Pearl
Harbor, and America was in the war without the moviemakers'
help. The America First Committee, stranded without a cause,
disbanded, and the Senate investigation, much to Senator Clark's
disappointment, was called off. In Hollywood, the movie people

turned their talents to making a long stream of patriotic wartime films.

Nor did the Jewish army in World War II ever come to be. Peter Bergson would claim that the movement had been effectively and finally killed by the American Zionists, led by Rabbi Stephen Wise, who had tried to link the rescue of Europe's Jews with the Jewish emigration to Palestine, thereby distracting attention from the mounting Holocaust. "The Zionists," Bergson said, "fought the project not because they are against it, but because they are against us. Stephen Wise will not tolerate any other Jewish organization working for Palestine and stealing honors and publicity from him." If true, this would constitute a sad irony. And yet, that there was an American government effort to save the Jews at all — that there was, for example, a War Refugee Board that sponsored the Raul Wallenberg mission to rescue the Hungarian Jews — was largely due to the efforts of Peter Bergson's group. But, Bergson has added, "If the Jewish leadership [in America] would have acted, the number of survivors would have been double, triple, fourfold." And, in his most chilling indictment, Bergson has said that if he were an American Jewish leader during the wartime period, "I would be turning in my grave."

This was a harsh judgment, perhaps too harsh. Bergson, after all, was an outsider, not an American, and, given hindsight, any judgment is possible. It was a curious and sinister confluence of forces — some logical and necessary, some mad — that was coming together in 1941. It was triangular, and could almost be diagramed. Britain was at war with Germany; Germany had embarked upon its systematic program to annihilate the Jews of Europe; in Palestine, Jewish guerrillas were fighting the British to establish a homeland for the Jews. The three forces seemed unconnected, except by time, yet disaster seemed inevitable somewhere along the way. It was small wonder that American Jews were faced with an almost numbing dilemma of choices, of priorities, of loyalties. And compounding the dilemma was the longing of the American Jews to be assimilated into the American culture, to be considered loyal Americans, and to forget the past.

In California, one symbol of assimilation — or the extent of it — was the Hillcrest Country Club of Los Angeles. Prosperous

Americans, the Eastern European Jews had discovered, enjoyed
a country club society, and the East Europeans had eagerly taken
up the popular American country club sports — golf, tennis,
swimming, riding. In Hollywood, the joke was that the movie
tycoons had gone "from Poland to polo in one generation." But in
Los Angeles, as in other cities, the leading Christian club, the
Los Angeles Country Club, would not accept Jews, not even as
guests of members, and an unwritten rule excluded anyone in the
movie business (though an exception was made in the case of Walt
Disney). So the Jews of Hollywood had formed Hillcrest, a country
club of their own.

Hillcrest, like other Jewish country clubs formed in the 1920s
and 1930s, was not only designed to make the best of a poor
situation. It was built out of Jews' deep inner convictions that any
attempts to join the Christian community, on a social level, were
probably doomed to failure. And it was also built out of the belief
that, since this was America, the prosperous Jew was entitled to
his own separate but equal country club facility, where Jews could
enjoy American pastimes in an American setting while not ob-
truding upon the established ways of the Christian majority.

In the process, Hillcrest became far more separate from than
equal to the Los Angeles Country Club. Since it was newer, its
facilities were far more modern and luxurious than the Los Angeles
Country Club's, and its kitchens produced some of the finest food
in southern California. It was just as exclusive as the Los Angeles
Club and membership was rigidly closed to Christians, though
many, including Joseph P. Kennedy, tried to join. Its initiation
fee of twenty-two thousand dollars was the highest in the country,
and when oil was discovered on Hillcrest property, it became
America's richest country club, with each member becoming a
stockholder in the private oil company.

Hillcrest gave the Jews of Hollywood something very American
to be proud of; it confirmed their conformity to the American mode.
At the same time, it became one of the few centers of Jewish
identity in Hollywood, more important to the Jews of the movie
industry than any synagogue or charity or political cause, or even
the romantic legends of their own movies. It was the closest thing
they had to a Hollywood Jewish community center. A great deal

of business was conducted at Hillcrest, along with the golf and tennis and high-stakes games of poker, bridge, and gin rummy. Jokes and insults were swapped in Yiddish, a language never used in the office or on the set. Here, in fact, was one place in Hollywood where it was permissible to celebrate Judaism, and where Judaism was not treated as a guilty secret.

Outside the club, and to the world at large, the facade the movie men projected was that of non-Jews. Once, at MGM, a disgruntled director muttered that Louis B. Mayer was a "Jewish son of a bitch." He was sternly reminded by an associate that "in this business, there's no such thing as a Jew, so there's no such thing as a Jewish son of a bitch." Hollywood's films were laundered of Jewish themes, as well as of themes having to do with any form of racial or religious prejudice. The whole idea of "message movies" was anathema, on the theory that audiences went to films to get away from their troubles and not to be lectured on what was wrong with the world. "If you want to send a message, go to Western Union," Sam Goldwyn had said. But of course Goldwyn often broke his own rules, and the closest thing to a Jewish movie prior to World War II was his *Earth and High Heaven,* based on a novel by Gwendolyn Graham. Even so, the film's underlying theme of religious intolerance was so muted as to be nearly imperceptible.

Just as Samuel Bronfman preferred to hide his company's ethnic identity under the mantle of the Seagram name, and David Sarnoff preferred the grandly chauvinistic name of Radio Corporation of America even after he himself had moved to the head of it, so the motion picture companies gave themselves names that were either patriotic (Columbia, Republic) or ethnically innocent but portentous (Twentieth Century, Paramount, Universal, United Artists, RKO). Only Metro-Goldwyn-Mayer contained a recognizably Jewish name (who remembered Sam Goldfish, much less Gelbfisz?). And only Warner Brothers announced its founders' names in its corporate title. Though the four brothers were Polish Jews, the name Warner sounded properly American.

But none of this is to say that Hollywood's Jews in the early 1940s were too preoccupied with matters of style and status and American assimilation to be philanthropic. In Los Angeles, the movie men contributed millions to create the magnificent Wilshire Boulevard Temple, the second-largest Jewish house of worship in the world. They gave generously to Mount Sinai and Cedars of Lebanon hospitals. They sent large checks to United Jewish Appeal and, less enthusiastically, to B'nai B'rith, which they thought of as "too militant." They also gave to non-Jewish causes like the Boy Scouts of America.

Russian-born Louis B. Mayer had his own idiosyncratic ways of giving. For one thing, he said that he preferred to give to Catholic charities rather than to Jewish ones, explaining that the Jewish philanthropies always published the size of his gifts, whereas the Catholic ones did not. (This is not true; one can give as quietly and anonymously to a Jewish cause as to any other.) Was Mayer flirting with conversion to Catholicism? Some people thought so. One of his good friends and frequent traveling companions was Francis Cardinal Spellman. But a more practical explanation was that the Catholic Legion of Decency had been coming down harder than ever on the issue of "morality" in Hollywood films. The word *God* could not be uttered in a movie, nor could the word *breast;* a pregnant woman could not be shown, and even when a man and woman were married in a film story, they could not be shown on the same bed, even if they were merely sitting side by side, fully clothed. To Mayer, it was simply good business to have friends among the princes of the church. Mayer had also been criticized for publicly wining and dining the openly anti-Semitic Henry Ford, Sr., and for posing for a photo with him on a bicycle built for two. On the other hand, Mayer wanted to film *Young Edison*, and the Edison Museum, which he wanted for a set, was on Mr. Ford's property.

Mayer liked to boast that he was a one-hundred-percent patriotic American, and claimed that he had been born on the Fourth of July. (True or not, no one knew.) And he could produce a rationale to demonstrate that he was one of the principal benefactors of the American public at large. By the early 1940s, Mayer's salary was the largest of any individual in the United States. And a high official of the Internal Revenue Service, so he claimed, had congratulated him on his generosity to himself. After all, this unnamed IRS man had said, if he paid himself a lower salary he would pay less in taxes. And those big taxes of his, Mayer said proudly, were caring for widows and orphans all over America, and were helping American soldiers fight the war against the Nazis.

Sam Goldwyn's philanthropies were sporadic, and of course he never forgave a personal slight. He presented a gruff, hardhearted exterior, and was never able to forgive his first wife for divorcing him. When their only daughter, Ruth, long estranged, wrote to him many years after the divorce — as a married housewife living in New Jersey — saying, "You will probably think it strange to hear from me," she went on to tell him that she was going to have a baby, his first grandchild. In the margin of Ruth's letter, Goldwyn scribbled angrily, "Ignore this letter!" At the same time, however, he continued to send regular checks to relatives in Europe. An uncle in Warsaw got a hundred dollars a month, and a distant unmarried cousin named Lily Linder got the same monthly stipend. Even more distant relatives got annual gifts for Hanukkah. To be sure, he often scolded these people in the letters that accompanied their checks. One sister, Nettie, was a particular problem. Nettie suffered from "nerves," and from a husband who couldn't seem to hold a job. "Please stop crying!" he wrote to Nettie. "I didn't marry your husband — you did!" Still, over the years, he had raised Nettie's allowance from fifty dollars a month to sixty-five, and eventually to one hundred. After Hitler's invasion of Poland in 1939, Nettie's letters became less frequent. Then they stopped altogether. What became of her can only be imagined. Sam Goldwyn refused to speak of her.

Of course, not all wealthy American Jews turned a deaf ear to the cries for help from Jews across the Atlantic. In 1939, for example, on a visit to Cuba to oversee his extensive gambling operations there, Meyer Lansky learned that a boatload of Jewish refugees had entered Havana harbor. The Cuban government had refused to let them ashore, had ordered them deported, and a number had been so desperate that they had jumped overboard and swum to shore. Lansky, who had no shortage of influence with the Cuban government (his casinos and hotels were among the island's principal employers, and the Cuban president collected a share of the casinos' take), simply went to the immigration inspector and demanded a change of policy. He also promised to pay five hundred dollars for each refugee admitted, and offered his guarantee that if any refugee became a burden on the Cuban state he himself would be responsible.

And in Montreal, increasingly wearied by continued rebuffs from the Canadian establishment, Sam Bronfman had begun shifting more and more of his philanthropic energies to Jewish causes. If the Christians did not want to accept him among their leaders, then he would work for the Jews. He and his brother Allan headed a fund-raising drive to build Montreal's Jewish General Hospital. Their initial goal had been to raise eight hundred thousand dollars. Before they finished, they had raised twice that amount. Mr. Sam had then been elected to head the Canadian Jewish Congress, a post he would hold for twenty-three years. And, in 1940, in response to what was happening in Europe, Mr. Sam created the congress's Refugee Committee. One of his committee's accomplishments was persuading the Canadian government to pass an act permitting twelve hundred Jewish "orphans" to enter Canada from Germany, Austria, and Czechoslovakia. Then, with a certain amount of élan, Mr. Sam and his committee demanded — and got — permission from Ottawa to accept the Jewish orphans' parents and grandparents as well. All told, Mr. Sam's efforts saved some seven thousand lives.

Still, sad to say, impressive as these individual accomplishments were, they were not enough; although the Jews saved numbered in the thousands, those who perished numbered in the millions. And as the war with Germany progressed, and as the ultimate ends of Hitler's anti-Semitism became ever more nightmarishly clear, a disturbing phenomenon was taking place in the United States. The process of de-Semitization that had been noticeable primarily in the film industry in the 1920s and 1930s, where it had been treated as something of a joking matter, now appeared to be spreading inexorably into every area of American life. It was as though Jews were going underground, or were being forgotten or overlooked, or were being written off by — and out of — history, and it was no longer funny. In the Catskill resorts, Jewish comics were dropping their Jewish peddler and Jewish tailor routines. Sophie Tucker no longer closed her act with "My Yiddishe Mama," but with Irving Berlin's stirringly patriotic "God Bless America."

Back in 1939, Danny Kaye had met his wife-to-be, the composer-lyricist Sylvia Fine, at an "adult summer camp" on the Borscht Circuit called Tamiment. Together, they wrote and performed a number of Jewish-parody songs like "Stanislavsky" and "Pavlova" at Tamiment, and that year Kaye got his first Broadway role in *The Straw Hat Revue,* with Imogene Coca. In 1940, he opened at a New York nightclub called La Martinique, and became an overnight sensation using much of the Tamiment material. But by 1942, when Sam Goldwyn hired him for his first film role in *Up in Arms,* the mood had already begun to change, and *Up in Arms* was not going to contain any Jewish-parody material, nor was Kaye to play a Jewish character.

Goldwyn, furthermore, who had made a special trip to New York for just one night simply to catch Danny Kaye's act at La Martinique, had been so entranced with the comic's performance that he had signed him to a starring contract without the usual precaution of having him screen-tested.

It was not until several months later, when the script for *Up in Arms* was finished and a number of sequences around Kaye had already been committed to celluloid, that Danny Kaye actually arrived in Hollywood to do his scenes — and to be screen-tested. When Goldwyn looked at the first test, he was horrified. "Danny's face was all angles," Frances Goldwyn recalled, "and his nose was so long and thin it looked like Pinocchio's."

"He looks too — too —" Goldwyn muttered, unable to bring himself to say "Jewish."

"Well," his wife reminded him, "he *is* Jewish."

"But let's face it," Goldwyn said, "Jews are funny-looking."

Goldwyn then summoned Kaye to his office. "Do something about your nose," Goldwyn ordered. But Kaye declined. If Goldwyn wanted him, he would have to take him nose and all.

More tests were made, and still more. In each of them, new lighting was tried, and new makeup. But none of the takes seemed to draw the focus of Kaye's face away from the nose, and Goldwyn continued to be dissatisfied with his star's appearance. Meanwhile, the rest of the *Up in Arms* company stood idle, waiting for its star, and a number of the people at his studio whom Goldwyn most trusted and respected began — at first hesitantly, then with increasing insistence — urging Goldwyn to accept the loss in pride and money and call the picture off, to forget about doing anything with Danny Kaye, to buy out his contract, and cast someone else in the part. Danny Kaye would never "look right" for movies. He might be fine for Broadway and nightclub acts, but he would never be a film star.

Goldwyn could accept, albeit with difficulty, the loss of money. But swallowing his pride was impossible. He had "discovered" Danny Kaye. He had brought him to Hollywood. To lose face in the eyes of his peers, to admit a mistake, was not in Sam Goldwyn's nature. "In dealing with my husband," Frances Goldwyn would recall later, "there was one thing you had to remember. *You* could be right. But he *could not be wrong*." One night late in 1942 Sam and Frances Goldwyn sat up until dawn; Goldwyn paced the floor of the Laurel Canyon house, arguing with himself, and with his wife, about ways in which it might be possible to make Danny Kaye photographable. In the morning, having had no sleep, the Goldwyns drove down to the studio to run through, in the projection room, the long series of Danny Kaye screen tests one more time. After perhaps the third test, Goldwyn suddenly yelped, jumped to his feet, and cried, "I've got it! I've got it!" He seized the studio telephone and asked for the hairdressing department. "Expect Danny Kaye in ten minutes," he shouted. "He'll be having his hair dyed blond." It was done. And Danny Kaye's wavy mane of blond hair — it had been a dark, reddish brown — became his most enduring trademark, the one caricaturists would focus on for years. The blond hair drew the camera's, and the audience's, eye away from the telltale nose. It gave him a Nordic look. He looked like a jaunty Dane. He went on to such fame and popularity that, when he was at his peak, his daughter Dena recalls, and fan letters from abroad, addressed simply "Danny Kaye, U.S.A.," arrived in the United States, the post office delivered them to his door.

The hard-to-please film critic Pauline Kael has named *Up in Arms*, the musical that almost didn't get made because of a Jewish nose, as one of the dozen or so best movie musicals ever made. Sam Goldwyn's brainstorm about the hair has been cited, in Hollywood, as an example of Goldwyn's production genius.

But in the process Danny Kaye, the Jew, had disappeared.

In an article for *Commentary* called "The Vanishing Jew of Our Popular Culture," Henry Popkin wrote of this strange trend, observable during the war and immediately afterward. The Jew in popular culture, he noted, had become "the little man who isn't there," and he offered a few very trenchant examples. In Irving Shulman's best-selling novel *The Amboy Dukes*, two characters had been named Goldfarb and Semmel; for the paperback reprint, they became Abbot and Saunders. Similarly, in the reprint of Jerome Weidman's *I Can Get It for You Wholesale*, the character Meyer Babushkin became transformed into Michael Babbin, and one Mr. Pulvermacher became Mr. Pulsifer. When Ben Hecht's own play *The Front Page* — co-written with Charles MacArthur — had been first produced on Broadway in 1928, and made into a film in 1931, a comic character had been named Irving Pincus. In a second movie version, called *His Girl Friday*, in 1940, Pincus was renamed Joe Pettibone. In George S. Kaufman's *Butter and Egg Man*, another comedy character had been named Lehman. He was still named Lehman in the first film version, under its original Broadway title, in 1928, and also in a second movie version in 1934 called *The Tenderfoot*. But by 1937, when the Kaufman story was resurrected in film for the third time as *Dance, Charlie, Dance*, Lehman, which was the name of a prominent Jewish banking family, had become Morgan, the name of a great Christian banker. And in yet a fourth incarnation of the same story in 1940, *An Angel from Texas*, Morgan became Allen. Prior to the war, the popular columnist Walter Winchell had been having periodic fun with a comic Jewish-dialect character he called Mefoofsky. Mefoofsky had disappeared from Winchell's columns by 1940, and Winchell had begun piously inveighing against the poor taste of dialect humor. Popkin went on to cite many more examples of ethnic revisionism, or ethnic evasiveness.

America seemed to have reentered an era of Victorian nicety, when mild expressions were substituted for disagreeable truths; an era of euphemism, when to *die* became to *pass away*; when *toilet* became *rest room* or *convenience* or *powder room*; when *poverty stricken* became *underprivileged* or *disadvantaged*; when *crippled* became *handicapped*, a *garbage collector* became a *sanitation engineer*, and a *defeat* became a *strategic withdrawal of troops*. Of course even *anti-Semite* is a euphemism for *anti-Jew*, since a true anti-Semite would be one opposed to all Semitic peoples, including Arabs. And even the term "Jewish" could be construed as evasive or defensive, since there are no equivalent terms, such as "Christianish" or "Moslemish." Hitler was himself fond of euphemisms, and instead of *murder* spoke of a *final solution*.

Mr. Popkin did not note that euphemism is a characteristic form of expression in totalitarian countries, where *assassination* becomes *liquidation*, where an *invasion* is a *liberation*, and where a *military takeover* is an *appropriate action*. But he did conclude that the gradual elimination of the Jew from the American public consciousness was not a matter of anti-Semitism, exactly. "This," he wrote, "originates not in hate, but in a misguided benevolence — or fear . . . [and the source of it] is Hitler. When Hitler forced Americans to take anti-Semitism seriously, it was apparently felt that the most eloquent reply that could be made was a dead silence."

13

AT LAST, A HOMELAND

IN 1937, Benny Siegel — whom everybody called Bugsy, though never to his face — had left the East for Hollywood with the idea of becoming a movie star. After all, he was a friend of George Raft, and Benny knew that he was handsome and bore more than a passing resemblance to Errol Flynn. Nothing much had come of the acting ambition, but he had also been given an assignment by his old friend Meyer Lansky, which was to set up the organization's own racing wire to the West Coast, to supervise bookmaking operations there, and to introduce Lansky's numbers game to the Mexican-American population of Los Angeles. At all three of these tasks he had succeeded.

He had also, on his own, made a number of trips to investigate a dusty little desert crossroads called Las Vegas. Gambling had been made legal in Nevada in 1931, and its capital had become Reno, in the north, where gambling operations were pretty much under the control of two or three Christian families. But when the federal government started work on the Hoover Dam in the early 1930s, the nearest town of any size where the construction workers could come to gamble was Las Vegas. And when the dam was finished, Siegel figured, Las Vegas would have something that it desperately needed if it was to sustain any growth at all — a water supply. Siegel began to dream of turning Las Vegas into a huge, luxury resort dedicated to gambling. Las Vegas was only a little over five hours' drive from Los Angeles, and it would attract the high rollers from the movie crowd. These glamorous types, furthermore, would attract tourists. Siegel shared his idea with Lan-

sky, and Lansky liked it. There was little likelihood that he and
his group could invade the claims that other casino operators had
already staked out in Reno, but there was no reason why they
couldn't have the southern part of the state to themselves.

Lansky carried the idea of Las Vegas one step farther. The
resort should offer the most luxurious accommodations, the most
elegant restaurants and bars, topflight entertainment in its nightclubs — the proximity to Hollywood made that feasible — all at
rock-bottom prices, affordable to almost anyone. The money, after
all, would be made at the gaming tables. Plans to develop Las
Vegas would probably have got off the drawing boards in the late
1930s if the war and wartime shortages had not intervened.

Meanwhile, Benny Siegel cut quite a swath in Hollywood. He
was impeccably tailored, favoring cashmere sport jackets, mono-
grammed silk shirts from Sulka, snappy ascots, and hand-benched
English shoes. He was swept up by the movie crowd, invited to
all the best parties, seated at the best tables at Romanoff's and
the Brown Derby, and dated the likes of Ava Gardner, Lana Turner,
and Betty Grable. Meyer Lansky had also supplied him with a
plump little sidekick, assistant, and bodyguard named Mickey
Cohen.

Cohen was by no means as dashing and debonair as his boss.
Short and round, a chewed-up cigar usually stuck between his
teeth, he looked like a character Damon Runyan might have invented, and talked like one, too. But there was something about
Mickey Cohen that struck people — women, particularly — as
cute. He was teddy-bear cuddly, and he was fun to be around.
Mickey Cohen, too, had no trouble making friends in the movie
capital, and no trouble dating movie stars. He brought out their
mothering instincts. Among his celebrated friends he counted Judy
Garland, Betty Grable, Alice Faye, and Don Ameche. As a criminal, Mickey Cohen was something of a joke, but he was an affable
joke. He had a neurotic obsession about cleanliness and would
wash his hands hundreds of times a day. Even in prison — through
a miscalculation, Cohen had spent some time in the penitentiary —
his daily consumption of Kleenex and toilet paper was monumental.

But, like his superiors, Lansky and Siegel, Cohen insisted that
he didn't think of himself as a criminal, but as a man in a service
type of business. Crime, as Cohen defined it, was when a father

and his ten-year-old son got off a plane at the Los Angeles airport after a holiday in Hawaii, and were held up at gunpoint by a band of young hoodlums. The father and son turned over their money, their watches, their rings. The gunmen then shot them both, killing the boy and paralyzing the father for life. This had actually happened and that, to Cohen's mind, was crime — pointless murder. To speak of that sort of thing in the same breath with what Mickey Cohen did for a living gave his livelihood a bad name. That sort of criminal, as he put it, was "not good for anyone's image."

In Hollywood, Mickey Cohen was a good friend to have, in more ways than just helping place a bet at an out-of-town track. If one was hoping for a particular movie role, or was having difficulty negotiating a contract, or was having union problems at one of the studios, Mickey would make a phone call or two and work it out. He was Hollywood's Mr. Fixit. As an example of the kind of power he wielded, a young and ambitious California politician named Richard M. Nixon had sought Cohen's support. But Cohen hadn't liked Nixon, who reminded him, he wrote, of "a three-card Monte dealer . . . a rough hustler of some kind."

Mickey Cohen had what he called his "code of ethics," as his story of how he became Betty Grable's friend illustrates. Early in his career, on orders from Lansky and Siegel, Cohen had organized a holdup at a Los Angeles nightclub operated by one Eddie Neales, who had not been "cooperating" with his protection payoffs. Cohen had been "at the stick," meaning he had a shotgun trained on the room while the others carried pistols. The patrons were instructed to put their wallets and jewelry on the tables, where they were collected. One of the jeweled ladies at the club was Miss Grable. Later, when Cohen had been promoted to less menial chores in the organization, he met Miss Grable socially, and, like the gentleman he was, apologized to her for the incident at Eddie Neales's place. Miss Grable giggled and confessed that she and her friends had found the whole thing pretty exciting. Then she whispered in Cohen's ear, "We were insured anyway."

Mickey Cohen also became a good friend of, and did favors for, Ben Hecht. But of how they became friends, and of what the favors were, each man would tell a different story.

In his 1954 autobiography, *A Child of the Century,* Hecht wrote that Mickey Cohen had first approached him in 1941, not long after the disappointing fund-raising rally at the Fox studio commissary for Peter Bergson's Jewish Brigade. According to Hecht, Cohen also had the notion that "millions" could be raised from the studio heads for the Bergson cause, though presumably Cohen had somewhat different fund-raising tactics in mind. According to Hecht, when he explained to Cohen that this had already been tried, and had failed miserably, Cohen had said, "Knockin' their own proposition, huh?"

But in his own 1975 autobiography, Mickey Cohen gave this version of their meeting and its purpose: First of all, said Cohen, Ben Hecht approached him, and not the other way around. And the year was not 1941, but 1947, an important difference considering the fact that a whole world war had begun and ended in the interval. At that point, Cohen said, he had never heard of Hecht, and learning that the writer wanted to see him, had asked, "Who the hell is Ben Hecht?" Finally, Cohen recalled an entirely different reason for the meeting. It had nothing to do with Bergson's Jewish Brigade — by then a dead issue, anyway — but had been to enlist Cohen's support for Israel in its bitter war of independence. This would seem to make sense, because by 1947 Hecht had become a militant Zionist.

In the United States at the time, there were almost as many kinds of Zionists as there were Jews. There were religious Zionists, labor Zionists, Zionist moderates, Zionist militants. The splinter groups of Zionism operated with as much internecine conflict as with cooperation. Jewish Socialists tended to see the Zionist movement as competitive with their own — a distraction that would draw the attention and energies of American Jewry away from what the Socialists saw as a more important goal, the improving of living and working conditions of the masses. The Socialists saw the creation of the State of Israel as an essentially bourgeois, capitalist enterprise.

In 1947, Palestine was in a state of siege as the days of the British mandate drew to a close, and it became clear that Britain had no intention of implementing the Balfour Declaration of thirty years earlier, which had stated that London and His Majesty's government would "view with favour the establishment in Palestine of a national home for the Jewish people." A civil war was raging between Palestine's Arabs and Jews, and there were terrorist incidents by both Arab and Jewish guerrillas against the British forces. One of the Jewish guerrilla groups, the Haganah ("Defense"), had been organized by David Ben-Gurion, and contained men who had been trained by the British in commando tactics during the war for missions behind enemy lines. Now this British training was being used as the British had feared it would be — in raids and forays against British troops, to attack and blow up bridges, railroads, and radar installations. The Haganah had been formed completely illegally; nonetheless, it considered itself the "legitimate" Jewish army.

Less legitimate guerrilla contingents were the so-called Stern Gang, and Menachem Begin's violent Irgun Tzevai Leumi. Between 1943 and 1947, Begin's Irgun had waged relentless war against the British rule, and Begin had begun to be seen — and perhaps to see himself — as a kind of personification of Jewish bravery, stamina, and military ruthlessness, a Jewish Attila or Genghis Khan. Ben Hecht, wrote Mickey Cohen, had come to see him to ask his help in raising funds for Begin and the Irgun terrorists.

At the time, Cohen admitted, he had not been paying too much attention to international affairs or to what was going on in Palestine. But Cohen considered himself a good Jew, and when he met with Hecht — and when Hecht explained to him in dramatic terms the Irgun's aims and considerable successes — Cohen quickly became excited and volunteered his services to the Irgun's cause. The violent nature of the Irgun's activities obviously appealed to the gangster in Cohen. As he wrote, "This guy got me so goddamn excited. He started telling me how these guys actually fight like racket guys would. They didn't ask for a quarter and they gave no quarter. And I got pretty well enthused with them."

Cohen could also understand why some of Hollywood's higher-ups showed less enthusiasm over the possibility of an independent Israel. "Jewish people," he wrote, "are very complacent, particularly when they become high in their society walk of life, high in their field of endeavor." It was true. The more the Russians moved upward socially and economically, the more they seemed to think and behave like the Old Guard, anti-Zionist Germans. (Though even the Germans had a Zionist concept of sorts. While they dismissed the idea of a Jewish state as an unrealistic fantasy, and though a resolution had been passed by American Reform rabbis declaring themselves "unalterably" opposed to such an idea, they had characteristically added, "America is our Zion.")

By the 1940s, more and more prosperous Russians were abandoning the Orthodoxy, and joining the Germans' "more American" Reform temples. Orthodoxy had become synonymous with poverty, with lack of progress — the party line that the Germans had adopted more than a generation earlier. The writer Doris Lilly has put this phenomenon another way: "When one has ten million dollars, one is no longer Jewish." This de-Semitization process, noticeable in the acquisition of wealth and status, has also been described as the Law of Diminishing Concerns.

But Cohen still saw himself as a member of the fighting Jewish underclass, and promised Hecht that he himself would toss a fund-raising affair for the Irgun. This was held at Slapsie Maxie's restaurant in Hollywood, of which Cohen happened to own a share. As a matter of course, the major studio heads like Goldwyn and Mayer were invited but, as Cohen had guessed they would, they declined, though Cohen's lawyer did come to him with a message to the effect that Goldwyn and the others might be more receptive if Cohen would switch his allegiance to the more moderate, less terrorist Haganah. But Cohen would have none of that. As a result, the gathering at Slapsie Maxie's was not of the elite that had met at the Fox commissary six years earlier. But there was a respectable contingent of film stars, including Betty Grable and Harry James, along with every important gambler in the area, plus a number of prominent judges, for in Mickey Cohen's line of work it was important to have friends among the judiciary. (Though gambling was illegal in nearby Burbank, Lansky-run gambling parlors flourished openly, and no wonder — the Burbank sheriff's office, the police department, and even some state officials in Sacramento shared in the take.) One judge, who was not even Jewish, came all the way from Galveston to deliver his personal check for five thousand dollars. Unlike the Fox affair, at this gathering no pledges were accepted — only cash. And unlike the Fox affair, Cohen's evening was a resounding success, with more than half a million dollars collected for the Irgun fighters before it was over.

Soon Mickey Cohen was spending so much time and energy on behalf of the Irgun and Israeli independence that he was having to curtail his regular activities. But that was all right with Meyer

Lansky, who was also throwing his weight behind the Israeli cause. Lansky's bailiwick was the East Coast, and in particular the docks of New York and New Jersey, where he wielded more than a little power. With the war in Europe over, shiploads of military hardware — machine guns, grenades, mines, explosives, and other matériel — were arriving in East Coast harbors from the European theater of operations to be put into mothballs. Some of this equipment had seen action in the war, but much of it was brand-new and had never been used. There were machine guns that had never been assembled, and were still packed in oil and straw. Lansky, with his influence on the docks, had no trouble seeing to it that these shipments got diverted from their intended destinations and sent directly to the Israeli fighters. Helping him were Albert Anastasia, who was in charge of the New York docks, and Charlie "the Jew" Yulnowski, who handled New Jersey.

It was a remarkably streamlined operation. At one point, for example, a large shipment of dynamite was smoothly rerouted from Newark to Haifa. Then word came back from Palestine that the Jewish guerrillas were not using the dynamite properly. Mickey Cohen had a solution. He had a friend known simply as "Chopsie," whose specialty was blowing up things. Chopsie was immediately dispatched to Palestine, where he spent eleven months giving lessons to the Israeli troops on the fine art of handling explosives.

Meyer Lansky learned through his grapevine of informants that, while scattered Israeli armies were battling Egyptian forces in the Gaza Strip and in the Sinai, certain American armaments dealers were somehow managing to smuggle arms to Egypt. This was illegal, since there was an embargo against shipping arms from anywhere in the United States to the Middle East, supposedly to be fair to all sides in the conflict. But the law wasn't working. In fact, the Arab states had succeeded in buying more than fourteen million dollars' worth of surplus American arms. The British were also selling arms to the Arabs, and making a lucrative business of it, and the Arabs were able to buy arms from other European countries as well.

To correct this situation, Lansky, as usual, took the law into his own hands. One munitions firm in Pittsburgh was found to be the chief smuggling culprit, and, with the cheerful help of the New York and New Jersey longshoremen, a number of baffling accidents began to happen to this firm's Egypt-bound consignments when they reached the East Coast ports. Some shipments fell overboard as they were being loaded. Others mysteriously vanished. Still others got loaded on the wrong ships, and somehow those ships were usually bound for Haifa.

Meanwhile, Mickey Cohen, who loved anything to do with a party, was in charge of American fund-raising, and was tossing more affairs in New York, Philadelphia, Boston, Cleveland, Detroit, and Miami, traveling with Ben Hecht as his principal speaker.*

But sometimes Cohen had to turn his attention to less festive matters. When, in one incident, three young Irgun guerrillas were killed by British soldiers and strung up in a public square in Palestine, Cohen decreed immediate vengeance. Contacting his Irgun friends, Cohen ordered that the same number of British officers be killed and hung in the same square. It was done.

Just how aware, in 1947, American Jews were of the role of organized crime in the fight for an independent Israel is unclear. Probably most were not aware. Those who were, numbed by reports of the Holocaust that were at last appearing in the American media, preferred to look the other way, or to take the attitude that the end justified the means. But Meyer Lansky and Mickey Cohen would always insist that all their activities of this period had the tacit blessing of President Harry S Truman. Truman, both men believed, had to have been aware of what was going on. Of course, he could not publicly condone or endorse it. But he sympathized with the Israeli cause. And, by simply doing nothing, he managed to lend his silent support to both the Israeli fighters and the work of the American men who were already being called the Kosher Nostra. "To me, he was the greatest man in the world, Harry Truman," Mickey Cohen wrote in his hard-boiled English, "because of what he done for Israel and because he made it available for us to do."

When, on May 14, 1948, Israel officially became a nation, and Britain withdrew its troops, there was cause for great celebration in that part of the Middle East. After nearly two thousand years

---

*For Hecht's activities on behalf of the Irgun, his books would be banned in Great Britain for a number of years.

of statelessness and dispersion, and a half-century after the first
Zionist congress in Basel, Switzerland, the image of the Jews as
a "rootless" group of "lost" tribes seemed erased from history
forever. The preceding ten years had been the most tragic decade
in Jewish history. On the continent of Europe, out of a Jewish
population of 8,255,000, an estimated 5,957,000 had been murdered by the Nazis. Now those dark years were ending on a note
of triumph. The price had been enormous, but now the score
seemed to have been settled. The old arguments between Zionists
and anti-Zionists seemed now to be both behind the times and
beside the point. So did the endless discussions as to whether the
Jews constituted a race, a religion, a nation, or a loosely defined
"people." They were now a *nationality*, and would carry passports
to prove it.

Throughout the new country there were parties, dancing in the
streets, the waving of flags and the tooting of automobile horns.
One sabra — a Jewish native of Palestine — now living in America recalls the first long evening of revelry, which, for her and her
young friends, ended up on a beach outside Tel Aviv while the
sun came up over the Caesarean hills and lighted up the Mediterranean on what would be the first full day of the State of Israel.
"We had been talking about our new country as though it was
going to be a new paradise on earth," she said later, "a kind of
magical Land of Oz, a new Eden, where there would be peace and
freedom and happiness for Jews forever. But then we began to
pinch ourselves, and to remind each other that we had to face
reality. We had to remember that now that we had a country of
our own, it would be a country like any other, with all the problems
any country faces. There would be Israeli heroes, yes, but there
would also be Israeli burglars, Israeli rapists, Israeli muggers,
Israeli pimps and Israeli prostitutes, Israeli policemen to chase
Israeli purse snatchers, and Israeli soldiers to fight, kill, and be
killed in — probably more Israeli wars. . . ."

Meanwhile, from the new State of Israel, its first premier, David
Ben-Gurion, was throwing open his nation's arms to Jews of all
nationalities, urging, beseeching them to "return home" to Israel.
To make the return easier, no bureaucratic paperwork was required. All who considered themselves Jews were welcome. But

to most American Jews the idea of going "home" to Israel had little appeal. Home was not there, but here, and it was difficult to envision Israel except in a very abstract way.

There was also some confusion — a complicated panorama of mixed emotions. For the Jewish socialist movement, for example, the fact of Israel took much of the wind out of its sails. What was the point, now, in complaining about the unfairness of the American capitalist system? If the Jewish socialists were unhappy with the state of affairs in America, they now had their own country to go home to, where they could ply their political wares.

For the affluent, the emigration from Eastern Europe to the United States had turned out to be the most golden of all diasporas — and the luckiest. The journey from the tumbledown *shtetls* and ghettos of Russia and Poland to two-car garages and Saks Fifth Avenue charge accounts had been almost miraculously brief. Whose babushka-wearing grandmother, or even whose unlettered mother, would believe the sight of her offspring driving Cadillacs and walking poodles in Central Park? Dogs as *pets?* The idea would have been unthinkable just one generation earlier, when the dog had been the ferocious sidekick of the *pogromchik*. And yet it had happened. Somehow, the Eastern Europeans had arrived in America at the precise moment when their particular talents and energies — in the garment industry, the film industry, broadcasting, publishing, the liquor business — had been most needed. Success, for even the halfway enterprising, had been downright inevitable, and this seemed more wondrous than the creation, in another part of the world, of a state called Israel.

For most American Jews, yes, it was nice to know that Israel was *there*, for those who needed it, and as an alternative to assimilation, a place to retreat to should life in America ever for some reason become intolerable. But most Jews felt that they had assimilated fairly well, and that America had been good to them. What more, exactly, did Israel have to offer them? They had no need for a refuge now, even though that refuge was there, beckoning and demanding their attention and support. Most would be interested in visiting Israel, out of curiosity, as tourists. And, as a concession to old and almost-forgotten loyalties, most would be willing to buy Mr. Ben-Gurion's bonds. But that was about the extent of it; most would not feel so deeply about Israel as to pull up their now firm American roots to go there to live.

Even the most recent American arrivals — those who had narrowly managed to escape from Hitler — felt this way. Anna Apfelbaum Potok, for example, had arrived in the United States in 1940, barely eight years before the creation of the State of Israel. Born in Warsaw in 1897, she was in the third generation of prominent Polish furriers. As a little girl, she had often visited her grandfather's shop, where he had let her play with the silky skins, and where she had learned to love the touch, of sables particularly, and even the pungent, gamy smell of raw and untreated pelts. There was no question but that Anna and her older brother Maximilian would both join the family's fur business, and after their father's death in 1921, they took it over. The Apfelbaum family had survived the czarist pogroms with no inconvenience whatsoever, because the Apfelbaums supplied fur coats to the Polish nobility and all the high officials of the country. The mayor of Warsaw and the president of Poland were their customers. After the Russian revolution, they felt no pressure because leaders of the Communist hierarchy traveled from as far away as Moscow and Leningrad to be fitted with coats of Apfelbaum sable, lynx, and karakul. Even after the partition of Poland in 1939, and Warsaw's surrender to the Germans, the Apfelbaums continued to feel secure, and though acknowledged as Jews, were permitted to travel freely about Europe — to the fur market in Leipzig, for example — as non-Jews.

By 1940, however, with the fall of France, Belgium, the Netherlands, Luxembourg, Denmark, Norway, and Rumania to the Germans, and with Hitler's Final Solution grimly under way, things were very different. It was essential that the Apfelbaums get out of Europe or perish. There was a hasty family conference, and they discussed escape routes. But for several weeks no rail tickets were available out of Warsaw. Then two tickets were obtained to Switzerland, and the plan was for Anna and brother Max to use these, go to Zurich, get funds from Swiss banks, and send for the rest of the family, which included Anna's husband, Leon Potok, their son, her brother's wife and their daughter.

From Zurich, Anna and her brother went to Paris, where they

planned to send for the others, only to find that Paris had just been occupied by the Germans. Then, in a terrifying decision, Anna and Max decided to return to Warsaw and personally collect the rest of the family. Somehow — aided by the fact that they both spoke perfect German — they managed this, and the clan regrouped in Warsaw. In the end, five people — Anna, her husband, her brother, and the two children — set off in a small car with a single suitcase, headed they knew not where. Max's wife had agreed to stay behind. There was no room for her in the car, and it was important that the party look like ordinary travelers and not like refugees; she would be sent for later. Max never saw his wife again.

At first, the little car headed south, toward Rumania and the possibility of some Black Sea port, such as Odessa, where passage to some neutral country, such as Spain, might be found. They were stopped at the Rumanian border by Nazi soldiers. Then, in a quick decision, they turned north again, to make a dash for Lithuania, where they were able to make it across the frontier. From there, the little group managed to book passage across the Baltic Sea to Sweden, where, through the intervention of the American consulate in Stockholm, they were able to obtain visas to the United States, by way of Montreal. The consulate stayed open all night to handle the paperwork.

Anna Potok and her brother Max had often talked of introducing haute couture into their fur business, and Max Apfelbaum, who had read about glamorous American movie stars and their luxurious tastes, thought it might be a good idea to try that approach in New York. He was tired of designing cold-weather furs for Polish and Russian bureaucrats and their plump little wives, and so Anna, who had studied art in Poland, went to her sketch pad. Their first salon, on West Fifty-seventh Street, was small, but their first showing of luxury furs was a huge success. Their original clientele didn't consist of movie stars, exactly, but it did include the likes of Mrs. William S. Paley, Thelma Chrysler Foy, Marjorie Merriweather Post, Mrs. Loel Guinness, and the Duchess of Windsor, who became regular customers for furs with the "Maximilian" label. The choice of the label was an accidental stroke of genius, carrying as it did connotations of grand, expensive, European imperial splendor. One wonders if the brother-sister team of fur designers would have had the same success with "Furs by Apfelbaum."

Had "Madame" Anna Apfelbaum Potok, as the dowager octogenarian head of Maximilian Furs is now called, ever — after that frantic, frightening, zigzag journey across the face of Europe — ever considered emigrating to Israel, where the Jews had at last found a homeland? "Oh, never," she replies. "We loved it here, we were happy here, we were lucky here, and we were successful here, from almost the first moment we arrived." With a twinkle, she adds, "This was where we found our ladies," and she points to the autographed photographs of the American First Ladies she has outfitted with furs, including Jacqueline Kennedy — whose inaugural wraps she designed — Lady Bird Johnson, and Nancy Reagan.

And so, for the majority of American Jews who saw themselves as part of a whole American success story, the new State of Israel had mostly a symbolic meaning. It was not *their* homeland. It did, on the other hand, provide a useful refuge for the persecuted, the misfit, the zealot, the radical, or the malcontent, a place for less fortunate Jews or, rather, those who had been more fortunate than the truly unfortunate who had lost their lives to Hitler — a place for the survivors of the Holocaust. And for Americans who had lost relatives and friends in the Holocaust, there was a certain amount of bitterness, too, and the feeling that Israel had been offered as a homeland too late.

14

TOUCHES OF CLASS

"If there was one good thing that came out of the war, it was the fact that it united the American Jewish community. The old social dividing line between the German Jews and the Russian Jews simply melted away."

This platitude, phrased in various ways, became something of a commonplace in the years immediately following World War II, but was, alas, merely a platitude. The social line between the Germans and the Russians remained as firmly drawn as ever. When it became apparent that the Christian community, in terms of social clubs, did not wish to mingle with Jews as a class, the Jews had simply created social clubs on their own. But now, in nearly every American city of any size, there were at least two Jewish country clubs — the "good" one (German), and the less good (Russian). In New York, the best Jewish country club was the Germans' Century Country Club in suburban White Plains. The second-best was the Russians' Sunningdale Golf Club in Scarsdale. There was even a third-best, also Russian — the Old Oaks Country Club. In the city, the elite Jewish men's club was the Harmonie (German).

Even Jewish houses of worship remained divided along the same lines. New York's splendid Temple Emanu-El on Fifth Avenue, one of the largest Jewish houses of worship in the world and certainly the costliest, had been founded early in another century by German Jews whose fortunes had come out of the Civil War. Of course, Temple Emanu-El could not bar any Jew — or non-Jew, for that matter — from attending services there. But, with its board of trustees consisting of members of the German-Jewish Old Guard families, it could create the distinct impression of not welcoming Russian-Jewish congregants. For one thing, all the best pews belonged to German families. The dividing line went even deeper. At such German-Jewish-founded hospitals as New York's Mount Sinai, Russian-Jewish doctors were not welcome on the staff. It was a situation that was galling to all but the most insensitive. If Jewish Americans as a whole were treated, socially, as second-class, then the Russians were third-class citizens.

All this simply added to the Russians' ambivalence about their Jewishness. If, the feeling seemed to be, they were not — even with all their money — considered good enough to rub shoulders with the *goy* elite, perhaps there was a reason. After all, they had not been considered good enough in the old country, either.

Perhaps, to be sure, it had something to do with the lines of work the Russians had gone into. The garment industry was, after all, even when it was creating hundred-thousand-dollar sable coats by Maximilian, still known as the *shmattes* business, or "rag trade"; Maximilian was just a glorified tailor. The entertainment industry was, after all, just "show biz," and even such a "great lady of the screen" as Joan Crawford had started her career as a prostitute and making pornographic films. The liquor business remained seriously tainted by Prohibition, and so on. No Jew could say, "I am the president of the Manufacturers Trust Company," or "I am chairman of the Aetna Life Insurance Company," or "I am a senior partner at Sullivan and Cromwell." Instead, a Jew was forced to identify himself to the outside world with a little shrug and a little grin that was almost an apology. Even Frances Goldwyn, when explaining what her husband did for a living, would say, "Oh, he's just a little old movie producer."

To fight these feelings of social and professional inferiority, the new Russian-Jewish millionaires used various tactics. Helena Rubinstein, on her way by 1947 to becoming one of the richest women in the world, was always "Madame" Rubinstein in the office. But, outside it, going to meet people she didn't know, she would always remind her escort, "Don't forget — introduce me by my *good* name," which was Princess Archil Gourielli. In the Samuel Bronfman household, there were several taboos. The word *booze* could not be used, nor could the expressions "bootlegger" or "rum-runner." Banished from the family vocabulary, too, was the word *Prohibition*. And Bronfman's children, who were too young to remember it — the oldest was born in 1925 — were brought up as though Prohibition had never existed, and though they eventually learned that it had, were never told that it had had any effect on the family's fortunes. (This rewriting of family history for the children evidently worked. In 1969, at the age of forty, Sam's son Edgar would write in the *Columbia Journal of World Business* that until Repeal, the family had done no business outside of Canada, and write this with such sincerity that it would be apparent he believed it.) Similarly, the Bronfman children grew up believing that Joseph E. Seagram was some distant Canadian ancestor, and since it had been explained to them in a vague sort of way that they were Jewish, the children assumed that Joseph E. Seagram was also Jewish.

Still, in very private moments, and with very old and trusted friends, Mr. Sam's eyes would get a faraway look, his brow would furrow, and he would say, "How long do you think it'll be before they stop calling me a goddamn bootlegger?"

In Hollywood, the movie moguls were particularly sensitive to gossip that portrayed them as illiterates or boors. And yet, when they tried to be genteel and refined, the results were often somewhat less than subtle. One of Louis B. Mayer's favorite words, for example, was *class*. He recognized it in others, and longed to acquire it himself. One of the pet actresses in his stable was Greer Garson, who, with her gently demure good looks and polished English accent, seemed to him the personification of class. But when Mayer, the former junk dealer who had been born in a village outside Minsk, tried to be classy himself it just came out awkward and inept. Someone had told him that golf was a classy American sport, and so he immediately took up golf. But he never quite understood that golf is scored in strokes, and seemed to see it, instead, as a kind of footrace across the golf course. To increase his speed from the first hole to the last, he played with two caddies. When he hit a ball, one caddy was posted down the fairway in order to locate the ball immediately. Meanwhile, the second caddy ran ahead to station himself for the next shot, with Mayer running behind. At the end of the game, Mayer would check his watch and exclaim, "We made it in one hour and seven minutes! Three minutes better than yesterday!"

He had noticed that most upper-crust Americans voted Republican, and so Mayer became an enthusiastic supporter of Republican causes, both in California and nationally. Convinced that after Roosevelt's long presidency, Americans would put a Republican in the White House, Mayer contributed large sums to promote the candidacy of Thomas E. Dewey. Like Sam Bronfman, who secretly dreamed of being knighted, Mayer had a secret ambition — to be posted as American ambassador to some important foreign country. He would then be entitled to the designation "Honorable." There is evidence that Dewey had discussed such an appointment with him but, alas, Dewey never made it to the White House.

Mayer had also heard that the breeding of thoroughbred racehorses was an occupation of true aristocrats — the Sport of Kings. And the show-biz aspect of the racing world also appealed to him. He had known nothing at all about horses until a writer-producer friend named Leon Gordon invited him to a race in which Gordon happened to have a horse running. Gordon's horse won, and down went Gordon into the winner's circle to great applause and cheers, to be awarded encomiums and presented with wreaths of flowers. That, Mr. Mayer decided, was where he himself would like to be — at the center of the stage and the cynosure of all eyes.

He immediately sent out for all the books that could be found on the care, feeding, and breeding of racehorses. There turned out to be quite a number. Of course, he had no time to read all these lengthy volumes, so he ordered his story department to reduce each book to a one- or two-page synopsis, just as he did with novels that he was thinking of buying for the screen. With no more information than this, Mayer proceeded to buy a thoroughbred named Busher. Busher had the distinction of becoming the first western horse to be entered in the Kentucky Derby. Unfortunately, Busher did not win. Mayer then decided to concentrate on breeding, and purchased Beau Père, a famous Australian stud.

Breeding racehorses, he liked to say, was a gamble very similar to that of show business. You could breed a prize stallion to a prize mare, but you still had no guarantee that the result would be a winner. It could just as easily turn out to be a dud. It was like putting William Powell in a picture with Myrna Loy, pairing Tracy with Hepburn, or Ginger Rogers with Fred Astaire. If the chemistry of the combination was right, you had a hit — and from then on a string of hits, with luck. It was no wonder Mayer referred to his MGM contract players as his "stable."

Sam Goldwyn was also touchy on the subject of his own lack of formal elegance and formal education. When each new Goldwynism made the rounds, instead of laughing it off, he vociferously denied he had said any such thing, which only added fuel to the story and made more people chuckle over it. He was, at best, an indifferent speller, but his secretarial staff had learned that it was unwise ever to correct the boss, and so, in his handwritten memos that went out, "research" became "researsh," "immediately" became "immediantly," and so on. He often had difficulty reading the scripts that his writers placed on his desk, and once, in a screenplay about pharaohs in ancient Egypt, Goldwyn protested that a slave would not respond to his master with "Yessiree!" Politely, the writer explained that the line of dialogue read, "Yes, sire." He just as often mispronounced the names of his actors, but did not like to be corrected on that score, either. He always called Loretta Young "Lorella," and Joel MacRae was "Joe MacRail." Once, in a meeting, MacRae said quietly, "It's Joel MacRae, Mr. Goldwyn." Goldwyn cried, "Look! He's telling me how to pronounce his name, and I've got him under contract!"

He was always convinced that his rival L. B. Mayer was up to dirty tricks. When, in the 1940s, Metro-Goldwyn-Mayer began using the slogan "More Stars Than There Are in Heaven," it was too much. "Frances!" Goldwyn bellowed at his wife, "Find out how many stars there are in heaven. L.B. says he's got more." When Frances replied that the answer was probably billions, if not trillions, Goldwyn telephoned his lawyer to see if MGM could be sued for using false and misleading advertising. When his lawyer informed him that MGM was just using "hyperbole," and that nothing much could be done to stop it, Goldwyn shot back, "That's all Mayer is — a goddamned hyper bully!" He fumed over this for weeks.

In Hollywood, Louella Parsons was the closest thing to a society columnist, and though her own command of the King's English was limited, she wielded great power through her nationally syndicated column.* Sam Goldwyn feuded with Miss Parsons on and off for years, alternately flinging abuse at her and showering her with praise. When she wrote disparaging things about him, his movies, or his stars, he would dash off an angry letter to her. And yet, when she once was taken to a hospital for minor surgery, he filled her room with flowers. And when she appeared on a Goldwyn set to view the filming of an important sequence, Goldwyn hovered over her, murmuring, "How long have you and I known each other, Louella? . . . How long have you and I been friends?"

When Sam Goldwyn's film *The Best Years of Our Lives* was released in 1946, it won more Academy Awards than any previous film in motion picture history. As for the fifty-four- (or fifty-seven-) year-old producer, this was treated as the crowning achievement of his career, and it was certainly a source of great pride for him. The film bestowed upon him, personally, large helpings of class. Also, though L. B. Mayer might claim more stars than there were in heaven, Goldwyn's picture had collected more Oscars than any other, ever. Though Goldwyn would always claim that his personal favorite of all his films was *Wuthering Heights* — a classy English classic written by an English gentlewoman — there was no doubt that all the critical and audience praise for *The Best Years* bolstered his ego enormously.

Coming as it did at the war's end, and telling the story of the homecoming of a soldier mutilated by the war, *The Best Years* found itself described, by certain critics, as an antiwar film — a picture with that element Sam Goldwyn claimed to disdain the most, a *message*. Goldwyn didn't see it that way at all. To him, it was a tribute to the selflessness and bravery of America's fighting men, and a testament to the values that made America great: the fabric of the American family, its tragedies and its triumphs, particularly in small communities across the country — its strengths, its resilience, and most of all, its durability — "a kind of love song to this country of ours," he once said, "in war or out of it, it doesn't matter. The war theme is strictly coincidental." (He probably meant "incidental.")

While basking euphorically in the critical praise for — and the

---

*Once, in her column, she evoked the poet Robert Browning, and quoted him as saying, "Oh, to be in England, now that it's May." The next day, she cheerfully acknowledged her error, and wrote that the line should be, "Oh, to be in England now that May is here."

box-office receipts of — *The Best Years*, Goldwyn received a letter
with a postmark he had not thought about in years: Gloversville,
New York. The letter was from Gloversville's mayor. The mayor
had heard that the great motion picture producer of the great new
patriotic film classic was going to be on the East Coast. Would
Mr. Goldwyn possibly be able to come up to Gloversville to attend
a banquet that the town wanted to give in his honor? Gloversville
wanted to name Sam Goldwyn its favorite son.

Its favorite son! It was astonishing. Sam Goldwyn had certainly
not forgotten Gloversville, but it seemed inconceivable that Gloversville remembered him. And now none other than the mayor of
the little upstate city had remembered him, and wished to make
the poor immigrant youth from Poland an honorary native. He was
overwhelmed.

Sam and Frances Goldwyn had by then dined at the Roosevelt
White House a number of times. In their own house at 1200 Laurel
Lane they had entertained for the likes of the Duke and Duchess
of Windsor and Queen Marie of Rumania. One would have assumed
that Goldwyn could have taken an invitation to visit Gloversville
(pop. 19,677) in his stride. Not at all. He reacted to the mayor's
letter as though he had been placed on the king of England's
Birthday Honours List. It was almost too much for him. He struggled over the wording of his response to the mayor's invitation for
several days before he was satisfied that he had it right, then
humbly wrote to the mayor, accepting the high honor.

The next few weeks were spent in furious preparation for the
trip, and the event. For days beforehand, he fretted over what
Frances ought to wear — should it be a dress or a suit? Rummaging
through her closets, he finally settled on a dark blue suit. When
that was decided — which coat? Since it was fall, and it could
be chilly in the Adirondack foothills, Frances suggested her mink.
"Too showy," said Sam, though the mink had not been new for
some time. Frances then proposed a somewhat older nutria. In the
end, her husband decreed that it be the mink after all — but
without any jewelry. Though that meant merely removing her wrist-
watch, she did as she was told. Then Sam could not decide which
suit, shirt, and necktie he himself should wear.

The Goldwyns had arranged to travel from New York City to

Saratoga Springs by Pullman, and from there to Gloversville in a hired chauffeur-driven car. On the train, Sam was tense and fidgety, and said hardly a word. When Frances suggested a snack in the dining car, he could not eat. By the time they reached Saratoga, he was so pale that Frances worried that he might be ill.

In the car, he tied and retied his necktie a number of times, and fussed with the points of his handkerchief in his breast pocket. Several times he had to ask the driver to pull off to the side of the road so that he could empty his nervous bladder. As the Goldwyn limousine approached the outskirts of the little factory town, Sam Goldwyn suddenly began to scream, "Turn back! Turn back! I can't go on!" Gently, his wife reminded him that it was too late to turn back now. The whole town would be waiting for him.

For years, Sam Goldwyn had regaled his wife with tales of Gloversville — of his boss, Mr. Aronson, of the rooming house where he had lived, and particularly of the splendors of Gloversville's proudest hotel, the Kingsborough. Sam had never stayed at the Kingsborough, nor had he ever eaten a meal there — that would have cost a whole dollar — but he had got to know its magnificent lobby intimately, and had described it to Frances in lavish detail: The floors were of marble, the walls of carved mahogany. There were potted palms, polished brass spittoons, enormous leather armchairs and sofas, and tall plate-glass windows through which, standing outside on a Saturday night, the young Sam Goldwyn had watched the elite of Gloversville disporting themselves in their evening finery. The dinner in Sam's honor would of course be held at the Kingsborough.

Though, when they arrived, Frances Goldwyn did not find the Kingsborough Hotel to be quite the palatial establishment of her husband's memory, it was very crowded. There were little ceremonies. Frances Goldwyn was presented with a box containing a pair of Gloversville gloves, which she quickly put on. Sam's old boss, Mr. Aronson, was there, and Sam was presented to a Mr. Libglid, who asked if Sam remembered him. At first, Sam could not recall Mr. Libglid, but then they fell into each other's arms. Mr. Libglid had been the benefactor in Hamburg who had taken up a collection for Sam in the ghetto in order to pay for his passage to England. Mr. Libglid had emigrated to America, and Gloversville, during the Hitler period. It was all very emotional.

During dinner, Sam reminisced with his old friends and former fellow employees about the old days, how he had started as an errand boy, become a glove cutter, and eventually a salesman in the Hudson Valley territory. There was also some more serious talk about the current state of the glove business — of market and fashion trends, of the quality of skins, cutting, and so on. From the way Sam Goldwyn joined in on the business talk, Frances got the distinct impression that her husband could still manage to do rather well in the glove business, should necessity ever force him to return to it.

Finally it was time for Sam to make his speech. He was introduced by the mayor and started up the aisle, carrying his hat. Halfway up the aisle, he dropped the hat, and had to stoop to pick it up. Then he stood for a moment, uncertain whether to walk back and place the hat on his chair or to continue up to the stage with it. He decided on the latter course, and carried the hat to the speaker's platform, where he placed it, and where it looked somewhat awkward and conspicuous. He then tried to place the hat underneath the lectern, and it fell to the floor again. He left it there. Then he faced the audience, stood there for a moment, and began, "I've always been honest —"

Then he burst into tears.

The war had shot a large hole through the gambling business. Gambling, as Meyer Lansky saw it, was an outgrowth of the tourist industry, and tourism had understandably languished during the war years. The capital of Lansky's gambling empire had been the gaily glittering resort capital of prewar Havana, where the Lansky group had controlling interest in a number of casinos, including the largest at the Hotel Nacional. There were also other casinos — both legal and illegal — in the Caribbean, in the Catskills and the Adirondacks, in New Jersey, in Kentucky, in California, and in gambling boats anchored off the coast of Florida. All these could, and would, be revived from the wartime doldrums. But there was another, more pressing, business problem.

During the war years, while Lansky, Mickey Cohen, and their friends — now beginning to be known as the "syndicate" — had been devoting much energy and money to the cause of Israel's independence, huge reserves of capital had been lying, untouched, in Swiss bank accounts, quietly accruing interest. In Lansky's personal accounts reposed something in the neighborhood of thirty-six million dollars, most of it from Prohibition profits. All this was fine, though Lansky did not consider earning interest a very exciting way to make money. The problem was that the syndicate was cash poor. It had an excess of venture capital, but no new venture to invest it in. On the drawing boards, in the meantime, lay Benny Siegel's idea for Las Vegas.

It seemed a natural. Not only was gambling legal in Nevada, but so was prostitution. Lansky disapproved of that, but he conceded that prostitutes would provide Las Vegas with an added attraction. And he liked Benny Siegel's concept of Las Vegas providing a luxury resort for the "little man." Las Vegas would not turn away the big-time gambler, but it would appeal primarily to the middle- to lower-income American. To do this, it would not only be inexpensive, but it would at the same time project the kind of classiness that middle- to lower-income Americans associated with the way rich folk lived, which was the way they saw rich folk live in movies — chandeliers, mirrors, swimming pools, hovering servants, sunken bathtubs, gilt, velvet, plush, velour. A new luxury had appeared on the market since the war. It was called air-conditioning. Las Vegas would have that — and, indeed, it would need it.

To Siegel's original concept, Meyer Lansky added a few new wrinkles of his own. The average American's idea of a gambling casino, he argued, again came from movies — the swank casinos of Evian and Monte Carlo, where men wore white ties and tails and monocles, and women sported tiaras and jeweled cigarette holders. A Las Vegas resort, he suggested, should not be so intimidating. There should be no dress code. Should a gambling patron wish, he or she should be able to enter the casino in swimming trunks or a nightie. In the midst of opulence would flourish a mood of libidinous abandon. Lansky also recommended that nowhere in the proposed resort should there be any clocks, since nothing was so distracting to the gambler as an awareness of the passage of time. To this end, the casino should be located at the heart of the hotel, without windows, where night would fall and dawn would come up with no one noticing the difference. This would also mean that no guest could pass from the reception desk to the elevators, from the swimming pool to the tennis court, from the bar to the dining room, without passing through the casino.

No one knew more about gambling than Meyer Lansky. He had other suggestions. Among them, he proposed that slot machines be placed at the arrivals gates of the Las Vegas airport. These would be adjusted to yield a high payoff, so that the arriving visitor, dropping a dime into the machine, would usually be rewarded with a handful of shiny coins. Flushed with the possibilities of winning big, he would then head immediately for the casino, where, of course, the odds of winning would be much less favorable. All these details were worked out at a meeting of the syndicate in 1945, and Benny Siegel was placed in charge of the Las Vegas project, with a budget of a million dollars.

Siegel and Lansky, meanwhile, had often watched the dancing and precision marching of the trained flamingos in the infield of the Hialeah racetrack. Not only was the flamingo a beautiful and exotic bird, but, it was said, the Seminole Indians believed the flamingo was a symbol of good luck, and that to kill a flamingo was to invite misfortune. What better name for the ultimate gambling palace? It was settled that Siegel's Las Vegas resort would be called the Flamingo.

Benny Siegel was the obvious choice to head the Flamingo project. Las Vegas had been his brainchild from the beginning, and he had served Lansky and the syndicate well during his years in southern California. There was no reason not to trust him completely with a million dollars of the syndicate's money. There was, on the other hand, something going on in Siegel's private life in 1945 that Lansky and his partners were aware of but chose to overlook. Benny Siegel had always been a notorious womanizer, and had taken out, at one time or another, nearly every star in Hollywood. He also had a nice Jewish wife, the former Esther Krakower, whom everybody liked, and two lovely daughters. Since Esther Siegel must have been aware of her husband's well-publicized philanderings, and since she seemed to accept them, and since after each fling Benny always came home to Esther, no one saw fit to criticize Benny's behavior.

Recently, however, Benny had embarked upon an affair that seemed far more serious than anything he had been involved in before. He was then forty, and may have been undergoing some sort of midlife crisis, but at any rate he fell head over heels in love. The lady's name was Virginia Hill, and she was not even a movie star. She was an empty-headed blonde who had been a sometime model, sometime showgirl, and all-time plaything who liked gangsters. Most of the members of the mob had bedded down with Virginia at one time or another, and no one had any use for her, nor could anyone understand how Benny Siegel could have become so smitten by her. Still, an Old World code, observed by the Russians as well as the Italians in the organization, decreed that a man's sex and domestic lives were his own business, and no one would have dreamed of criticizing Benny's choice of girl friends. Among other things, there was Benny's hot temper to contend with — he had killed people in arguments over matters much more trifling than this. Still, behind his back, Benny's side-kick Mickey Cohen referred to Virginia as "that tart."

Meyer Lansky knew that things were serious between Benny and Virginia when, that year, Esther Siegel came to him and asked him if there was anything he could do to break up the romance. Sadly, Lansky replied that there was nothing, but he did offer a suggestion. If Esther threatened Benny with a divorce, and demanded custody of the two girls, that might bring Benny to his senses. Esther followed Lansky's advice, and to her dismay, Benny agreed to a divorce on whatever terms Esther wanted.

Meanwhile, construction of the Flamingo proceeded. As promised, the hotel would be the ultimate in luxury. The finest woods, the costliest marbles, the most sumptuous fixtures and appointments were going into it. Each bathroom would have not only its sunken tub, but its own individual plumbing system and — that naughtiest of imports from the European hotel scene — its own porcelain bidet. No cost was being spared, and suppliers from as far away as Denver, San Francisco, and Salt Lake City were shipping their wares to the Flamingo. While other builders were still experiencing postwar shortages and delays, Lansky's and Siegel's friends in the Teamsters union had a way of facilitating shipments. There was alarm, however, when Benny Siegel announced that Virginia Hill had been placed in charge of the hotel's interior decor, and was being given a free rein.

Early in 1946, a meeting was called of the hotel's backers — with Benny Siegel not invited to attend — to discuss what was now no longer called "the project" but "the situation." A grim-faced Meyer Lansky opened the proceedings to report that the Flamingo was now five million dollars over budget, and the end appeared not yet in sight. In fact, the hotel was not even half completed. Another fact had to be noted. Virginia Hill had been making a number of trips to Europe. Her excuse was that she was purchasing furniture and fabrics for the hotel, but there was also the possibility that she and Benny had been skimming off some of the construction costs, and that Virginia had been depositing the skim in Swiss banks. These suspicions had been confirmed when a Lansky informant in Switzerland advised that Virginia had deposited some five hundred thousand dollars in a numbered Zurich account.

The situation was now very serious. At the 1946 meeting, one of the investors — it is not clear who — suggested that the solution might be that Benny Siegel be "hit."

Lansky, however, cautioned patience. He had never liked the idea of killing people, and certainly did not like the idea of killing Benny Siegel — a fellow Jew, one of his oldest friends. He had been best man at Benny's wedding. The thing to do, he said, was to get the hotel open and get it making money. Then, if it turned out that Benny had been cheating his partners, Lansky could deal with that, and would get Benny to give the money back.

The logical thought, of course, is that someone might have suggested "hitting" Virginia Hill. But killing a woman was beneath the syndicate's dignity. The thought, on the other hand, that a mere woman could wield enough power over her lover to cause him to betray and steal from his associates was an intolerable insult to the male sex.

From that meeting on, Lansky knew that his friend Benny was in deep trouble, for not all the others who had money in the Flamingo venture were as moderate-minded as he. He immediately warned Siegel to do everything in his power to get the hotel finished, opened, and producing income as quickly as possible. No further delays or overruns would be tolerated.

Siegel got the point, and his activities toward completing the Flamingo became feverish and frantic. He went so far as to move out of the house at 810 North Linden Drive in Beverly Hills that he had rented for his sweetheart, and to the construction site, where he could oversee matters personally. Workers were now paid overtime and double time, and offered special work-incentive bonuses to make sure that the hotel would be ready for occupancy, and gambling, by the scheduled date of Christmas, 1946. The new urgency to get the Flamingo open, of course, made costs soar even higher. And back in the offices of syndicate members, faces grew longer and darker, while Lansky implored his partners to at least give Benny the chance to open his hotel.

Siegel had announced the gala opening of the Flamingo for the week between Christmas and New Year's, and he worked desperately to meet that deadline. Later, it would be claimed that his timing was wrong, and that for the entertainment business the days between the two holidays had always been considered the deadest period in the entire year. Siegel, if he was still thinking clearly, may have felt that the opening of a spectacular new hotel might serve as a remedy for that deadness. But as the date of the opening approached, it was clear that much else was wrong.

By mid-December, the hotel was far from finished or ready for occupancy. Only a handful of guest rooms were completely furnished. Then bad luck made matters worse. Siegel had hired a small fleet of Constellations to fly in celebrity guests from Hollywood for the gala opening party on December 26. On the afternoon of departure, bad weather in Los Angeles caused the flights to be canceled. A few movie notables made it — among them Charles Coburn, George Sanders, and Siegel's old friend George Raft —only to be received in a lobby that was still festooned with painters' drop cloths and noisy with carpenters' hammering, and guest rooms that were half finished and, in some cases, had no sheets or towels. Some bathrooms had bidets, others just had open spaces in their floors. The air-conditioning worked fitfully, and guests sweltered in the desert heat. The green and untrained staff had not mastered the hotel's layout, or their own routines and duties, and service ranged from slow to nonexistent.

Back in the East, Lansky and the other partners received the grim news: Benny Siegel's opening had been an unmitigated disaster. As usual, "the genius," as Lansky was called, had a stopgap solution. The hotel should immediately close, and the corporation go into receivership. Then the original investors could buy back their shares at ten cents on the dollar, and needed capital would be raised to complete the hotel. But not all the partners were happy, and Lansky contacted Mickey Cohen and alerted him never to leave Benny Siegel's side. His life, Lansky warned, was in danger.

By February, 1947, the Flamingo was still not furnished, and things were not much better in March, when the hotel reopened, and guests checked out complaining of construction noise, room service orders that never came, burned food from the kitchen, telephones that didn't work, and toilets that would not flush. By April, however, things had improved somewhat, and income began to exceed outgo. But the partnership was still heavily in the red, the hotel seemed far from capable of producing the profits Siegel and Lansky had predicted for it, and it was still suffering from the poor word-of-mouth reviews it had received during its first months.

That spring, Benny Siegel and Virginia Hill flew down to Mexico and were married. He had made an honest woman of her at last. But now the pair seemed doomed by the Fates. In Mexico, Virginia supposedly begged Benny to fly with her to Paris. Realizing that her new husband was a marked man in the United States, she suggested that they could live out their lives in Europe on the money she had squirreled away in Swiss banks. If indeed this happened, something — perhaps macho bravado, perhaps fatalism — made Benny insist that they return to Los Angeles, to face whatever was coming to him. Possibly he felt that in a final show of courage he could demonstrate to his partners that he could, after all, behave like a man and not like a sex-ridden adolescent.

For several weeks after their return, there was a period of relative calm for the newlyweds. At the Flamingo things continued to look up. The month of May was better than April, both in quality of the hotel's service and in the profit picture, as the last square of thick carpet was laid, the last glittering chandelier hung, and the last bits of gilt paint and antique mirroring were applied. Siegel may have had good reason to believe that the crisis had at last passed. By mid-June, he was in an expansive mood. The Flamingo's ledger sheet was showing more black ink. Esther Siegel had consented to let Benny's two daughters spend the summer with him. On the afternoon of June 20, Benny had his regular weekly manicure at Harry Drucker's barbershop in Beverly Hills, and talked enthusiastically of how well the Flamingo was doing, and of how the pieces of his life seemed finally to be falling into place. That evening, in the big house on North Linden Drive, Benny Siegel was relaxing with Allen Smiley, an old friend, in the living room. Upstairs, Virginia's brother, "Chick" Hill, was with a girl friend in one of the bedrooms. Virginia was off on one of her trips to Europe, but was due home in a few days. Mickey Cohen, instructed by Lansky never to leave Benny's side, was mysteriously absent. At a few minutes after ten o'clock, the barrel of a .30-30 carbine crashed through a living room windowpane, and eight shots rang out. One tore through Benny's skull, ripping out an eye, and four others plunged into his upper body, through his heart and lungs. Three more bullets went astray, and Allen Smiley was unhurt. That evening, employees of the Flamingo were informed that the hotel was under new management, appointed by Lansky and Company.

The murder of Benny Siegel was never solved. In the investigation that followed, one assumption was that Lansky had ordered the killing. He was the mob's linchpin, the reasoning went, and no one else would have dared to do it. Bitterly, Lansky would always deny that he had ever done such a thing. He had loved Benny Siegel, he insisted, as much as he loved his own sons, his own brothers, his own father. He had done everything in his power to warn Siegel that some members of the syndicate were not happy with his performance, that his murder had been proposed. He had also done everything in his power to persuade his partners to give Siegel time to turn the hotel into a success and that, in fact, the hotel had already rounded the corner. Esther Siegel, when questioned, also defended Lansky as the last person who would want to see her ex-husband dead.

Another possibility was that Lucky Luciano had ordered the killing. From his exile in Italy, Luciano pooh-poohed the notion. How could he have engineered such a thing from seven thousand miles away? Nonetheless, Luciano still wielded enormous power, personal and financial, in the organization, and he was one of the important silent partners in the Flamingo venture. Only Luciano, it was argued, had sufficient clout to arrange for Mickey Cohen, in defiance of Lansky's orders, to be elsewhere on the night of the murder. As for Cohen, he simply shrugged and said he hadn't been hovering over Siegel because he and Siegel had both assumed the heat was off.

But the heat hadn't been off. And there were any number of disgruntled Flamingo investors who might have decided, acting on their own without consulting anyone, that Benny Siegel had to be eliminated. Not everyone in the syndicate was as fond of Benny as Meyer Lansky was. And Benny had committed the cardinal sin of violating the code of honor among thieves. He had stolen from his brethren. In any case, the 1947 murder gave Benny Siegel a certain distinction: he was the first member of the syndicate's board of directors to be gunned down by one of his own.

The murder left Virginia Hill Siegel alone and unprotected, presumably a very frightened lady. But Lansky knew how to handle her. Once the dust had settled, he quietly approached Virginia and asked her to return whatever money Siegel had passed to her from the hotel's construction budget. Virginia, who knew which side her bread was buttered on, immediately complied. It was as simple as that.

Following Siegel's death, Virginia, insisting that Benny had been the only man she had ever really loved, went into a deep depression and tried, unsuccessfully, to kill herself. There followed years of alcohol and drugs, in which she returned to her old profession in a desultory way. She didn't need to work very hard. A Chicago mobster who had been a long-ago flame still kept her on a regular monthly allowance. In 1966, she finally killed herself with an overdose of barbiturates.

By then, of course, the Flamingo in Las Vegas had become the enormous financial bonanza that Benny Siegel, and Meyer Lansky, had said it would be all along, and all the investors were very happy. The Flamingo had also become the prototypal Las Vegas hotel, the very cornerstone of the Strip — that garish stretch of outlandish hotels that extends for four miles west of town into the Clark County desert. From the Flamingo outward, hotel followed hotel and casino followed casino, each trying to outdo and out-gimmick the last in extravagance and overstatement and Las Vegas "high class." From the first days of the Flamingo onward, Las Vegas has grown from a dusty crossroads of sand and sagebrush to a glittering Oz-like metropolis, with a permanent population of well over half a million; an entire city supported by, and devoted to, a single pastime: gambling. It is Benny Siegel's city.

In Las Vegas today, his name is spoken with reverence and awe. He is to Las Vegas what Benjamin Franklin is to Philadelphia. Las Vegas was Benny Siegel's vision, his grand design. Had it not been for his dream, there might be nothing there at all.

15

ALL THAT MONEY CAN BUY

B Y the late 1940s, the social and economic dominance of the German Jews in the American Jewish community had all but disappeared, but few of the old German-Jewish upper crust were willing to admit that this had happened. Within the tight and interrelated circle of German-Jewish families, where dynasty had interlocked with dynasty for a hundred years or more, the myth was maintained that the Germans were the "best" Jews, and that the Russians were "riffraff." All the Germans would concede was that the Russians now outnumbered them, as they did by several millions; what was harder to swallow was the fact that the Russian Jews also outpowered them in nearly every area, from the marketplace to philanthropy.

Some people would trace the demise of German-Jewish overlordship to as far back as 1920, and the death of the patriarchal Jacob H. Schiff, who had been called the conscience of the American Jewish community. Schiff's mission had been to remind the Jews periodically that they were indeed Jews, with Jewish responsibilities, and it had been he who had headed most of the Jewish social welfare programs that had aided the turn-of-the-century Russian immigrants. Schiff had passed his mantle of Jewish leadership to another German Jew, Louis Marshall, a prominent New York lawyer, but Mr. Marshall had not had the commanding authority or personal charisma of Jacob Schiff. It had been under Marshall's leadership, however, that the elite German congregation of Temple Emanu-El had begun its plans to move its house of worship from Forty-fifth Street and Fifth Avenue to an even grander address uptown, at Fifth Avenue and Sixty-fifth Street, facing Central Park.

The ostensible reason at the time for the move was noise. Fifth Avenue and Forty-fifth Street had become one of the city's busiest commercial corners. The noise of commerce, Marshall explained, did not bother Christian churches in the neighborhood, since they held their services on Sundays. But Saturdays were heavy shopping days, and members of Temple Emanu-El claimed to find the street sounds disturbing on the day of worship. Not stated was the fact that the move uptown was also an attempt to disassociate themselves, socially, from the continuing uptown movement of former Lower East Siders, from the onslaught of the parvenus, or "the newer element," as the Russians were sometimes called. At the time, upper Fifth Avenue was pretty much the exclusive domain of wealthy Christian families and Old Guard German Jews. The width of Central Park would separate Temple Emanu-El from the "Russian side" on Central Park West, or so the reasoning went.

The real problem seemed to be that Reform Judaism had become *too* popular, *too* successful — so successful that it was difficult for Emanu-El to maintain its traditional German-Jewish exclusivity. When the congregation had first been formed in 1845, its treasury had contained exactly $28.25, and its first services had been held in a Lower East Side tenement at the corner of Grand and Clinton streets. But the congregation had quickly been able to move to better and better addresses until, by 1868, the temple had been able to build — for six hundred thousand dollars — an entire building of its own, on Fifth Avenue, New York's premiere street, where all the most fashionable Christian churches were.

By 1930, however, when the grand new building, which had cost seven million dollars, opened its doors, the possibility of exclusivity had gone out the window. The upward and outward mobility of the Eastern Europeans had been so rapid that Russian Jews were able to afford the higher rents and taxes of the fashionable Upper East Side now, and were moving there in goodly numbers. Ironically, the new temple's first service was for the funeral of Louis Marshall, and the eulogy was delivered by its first Russian-Jewish head rabbi.

The Old Guard had given way to the new, who had overcome by sheer numbers.

Throughout the 1930s and 1940s, Temple Emanu-El drew Eastern European worshipers like a magnet until, by the late 1940s, Russians outnumbered Germans by a ratio of something like five to one. The reasons for this dramatic switch from the little Orthodox synagogues of the Lower East Side to this stronghold of the American Reform movement were several. For one thing, there was the physical magnificence of the new Temple Emanu-El itself, with its glorious rose window and its altar framed and valanced with carved woods and glittering handworked mosaics. In size, it ranked behind only the Cathedral of Saint John the Divine and Saint Patrick's Cathedral in New York City, and could seat twenty-five hundred in its main sanctuary, and accommodate at least thirty-five hundred more in an adjacent chapel and auditorium for the High Holidays. Architecturally, it radiated self-confidence and importance.

Then, too, Emanu-El had long been considered New York's most *fashionable* Jewish congregation, and the appeal of fashionability to families moving upward on the economic scale could not be ruled out. All the heads of important Jewish philanthropies had traditionally been Temple Emanu-El members — the presidents of the Federation of Jewish Philanthropies, Bonds for Israel, the United Jewish Appeal, the American Jewish Committee, the Friends of Hebrew University, and the boards of directors of Hebrew Union College, Montefiore and Mount Sinai hospitals, and the American Jewish Historical Society. Rubbing shoulders with the leaders of the community also had its appeal.

But the most important appeal of Emanu-El and the Reform movement was that they represented a step in the assimilation process, part of the Russians' drive to adapt to the prevailing mode and environment. Reform was more "modern," more "enlightened," more "American." While many of the first-generation immigrants liked to keep a toehold in the Old World — out of habit, out of fear, out of nostalgia — through their Orthodoxy, the second generation wanted to blend in, to move with the times. "My parents were Orthodox, but I'm Reform," became the phrase. Reform meant up-to-date. Everyone knew, for example, that the Jewish dietary laws had become, by the twentieth century, anachronisms and, in the United States, a nuisance. Reform Jews had come right out and said so, and by the 1940s, any Jew who still kept a kosher household was, in the eyes of Reform, either a sentimentalist or a zealot. The reaction of a Midwest housewife is typical: "I used to cook kosher meals when my in-laws came to dinner, but after they died I stopped." To be able to serve what one liked and eat in restaurants where one wished was part of entering the American mainstream.

Meanwhile, signs that the Russian Jews had become Temple Emanu-El's dominant group were apparent at the temple itself. Some changes were cosmetic. In the old days of German-Jewish leadership, for example, the temple's board of trustees had dressed in black tie for their meetings in the paneled, portrait-hung boardroom. This practice was abandoned by the Russians as stuffy and old hat. The Russians also proposed that the facade of the building be floodlit at night. The German minority cringed at this notion, considering it "too showy." But, the Russians countered, bathing the Fifth Avenue face of the building with floodlights would result in a lovely light being cast through the stained-glass rose window for evening services. In the end, the building's architecture defeated this project. The designer of the rose window, it seemed, had made it of the heaviest glass to withstand the rays of the afternoon sun. Only a floodlight with the intensity of the sun would penetrate the glass at night.

Other changes were liturgical. The new Eastern European leadership decided that it would also be a nice idea to broadcast the temple's Friday evening services over New York's WQXR radio station every week. Once more, the Germans were opposed, calling the idea "publicity-seeking," and "evangelizing through the media." But the proposal was passed, and the Russians could boast of their new, much larger, "radio congregation." (When the radio congregation began sending in checks to the temple, the Germans' mutterings diminished somewhat.) In 1872, the then all-German temple had abandoned the practice of conducting bar mitzvahs as "barbaric." But the Russians, it seemed, liked bar mitzvahs, and so the practice was resumed under the new leadership.

Faced with such changes, some old German families withdrew their support from Temple Emanu-El. Alas, that didn't seem to matter much. Their support was no longer needed. Others merely

carped and complained, calling the Russian newcomers "the Emanu-
Elbowers — they've elbowed their way in." True or not, they were
in to stay.

Bastions of German-Jewish supremacy were falling on all sides
by the 1940s. Down on Wall Street, the staid old investment
banking firm of Goldman, Sachs was feeling it. (The interrelated
Goldman and Sachs families were among America's pioneering
German Jews.) For years, all the partners in the firm had been
either Goldmans or Sachses, but then, fresh out of P.S. 13 in
Brooklyn, came a bright youngster named Sidney Weinberg. The
Russian-born lad had spent some time looking across the harbor
at the towering financial district of lower Manhattan, and decided
that that was where the money was. He had gone, by his own
account, "to the top of the tallest building" in the district, and
started working his way down, floor by floor, asking for jobs at
each elevator stop. He had made it all the way down to the second
floor before he found Goldman, Sachs, where he was hired as an
office boy. By 1947, Sidney Weinberg was the firm's senior partner,
and was the principal architect of a high-financial plan by which
the heirs of Henry Ford, Sr., were saved hundreds of millions of
dollars in inheritance taxes. In Weinberg's design, Ford's heirs
were left in control of the Ford Motor Company, while the bulk of
the $625,000,000 estate was placed tax-free in the Ford Foun-
dation, making it the richest philanthropic organization in the
history of the world. The Ford heirs' federal tax bill amounted to
only $21,000,000 on a taxable estate of $70,000,000. Sidney
Weinberg's bill for this service? A little over $2,000,000.*

Social barriers against Russian Jews were also tumbling. At the
Century Country Club, which considered itself not only the best
Jewish club in New York but the best Jewish country club on
earth, and where the anti-Russian bias had been all but written
into the bylaws for generations, a few Russians were now being
cautiously taken in as members, and one of the first of these, in
1948, was the Flatbush-born Dr. Herman Tarnower, the son of
Russian immigrants. At the time, the club's variance from standard
practice was explained by the fact that Tarnower was "a nice
doctor," many of whose patients were Century members. But the

---

*That the automobile pioneer's estate should have hired Weinberg to shelter it from taxes was
in itself remarkable, considering the senior Ford's unabashed anti-Semitism.

hard facts were economic — as German Jews died out, or slipped quietly across the border into Christianity, the Century needed new members to support it. The only candidates were Russians.

The same thing was happening at the equally exclusive men's club, the Harmonie, in Manhattan. Founded by German Jews in 1852, the Harmonie Club's minutes and records had all been kept in German until America's entry into the First World War, and a portrait of the German kaiser had hung prominently in the entrance lobby. The lavish club, with such athletic facilities as squash courts and a swimming pool, sat on a costly piece of real estate on East Sixtieth Street, just off Fifth Avenue, and, if anything, was even more expensive than the Century to staff and maintain. An infusion of new blood, and money, was needed. This could be achieved only by taking in Russian members. It would not be long before a member of the Harmonie's board, addressing a meeting in a heavy Russian accent, would want to know why, if the Harmonie was originally a German-Jewish club, and was now a Russian-Jewish club, the menus in the dining room were printed in French and not in Yiddish that everyone could understand.

In 1937, the Radio Corporation of America had raised its president's salary to a hundred thousand dollars a year, making David Sarnoff one of a small handful of Americans with a six-figure income in that Depression year. His salary was more than that of the President of the United States. That same year, Sarnoff and his wife, Lizette, had also purchased their first Manhattan town house at 44 East Seventy-first Street, a block from Fifth Avenue and Central Park and a few blocks from Temple Emanu-El, where Sarnoff had also been made a trustee.

The house, in the heart of WASP country, though a few German-Jewish Loebs, Lehmans, Lewisohns, and Warburgs lived nearby, was one of the finest in the city. It contained over thirty rooms on six stories, connected by a private elevator. Its ceilings were high, its scale grand. On the ground floor was a large paneled formal dining room, from which French doors led out into a capacious private city garden landscaped with boxwood, evergreens, and fruit trees. On the second floor was the principal sitting room, which was decorated in an Oriental motif, taking its theme from a series of ancient Chinese murals that had been set into the walls. On this floor, too, there was a screening room, where the Sarnoffs could entertain their guests with previews of the latest RKO films, shipped to him from Hollywood. Adjoining this was David Sarnoff's "radio center," powered and equipped so that he could pick up almost any radio station in the world — as well as tune in and monitor the goings-on at his National Broadcasting Company rehearsal studios.

The third floor was the family floor, and contained the Sarnoffs' bedrooms, dressing rooms, and baths, as well as the bedrooms and baths of their three sons, Bobby, Eddie, and Tommy. The fourth floor, however, was entirely David Sarnoff's, and was the most extraordinary collection of rooms in the house — his private sheikhdom. It was part office, part library, part club, and part shrine to Sarnoff's personal achievement. A long central gallery was filled with testimonials and memorabilia — the awards, citations, plaques, medals, and honorary university degrees with which he had been presented, even though he had never earned a high school diploma. Mounted, lighted, displayed on shelves and in illuminated cases, arrayed for inspection, were also the silver and bronze cups, bowls, beakers, and figurines he had been awarded. On shelves, in thick leather covers, lay bound copies of all his speeches, and other leather albums were filled with newspaper clippings chronicling his career. Everywhere, in silver and leather frames, were autographed photographs of David Sarnoff smiling and shaking hands with important people — Woodrow Wilson, Warren G. Harding, Calvin Coolidge, Herbert Hoover, Franklin Roosevelt, Albert Einstein, Guglielmo Marconi, Arturo Toscanini, as well as all the NBC radio stars.

Off the museumlike gallery, or "memory room," as Sarnoff called it, was a clublike lounge, with a fully equipped bar (though Sarnoff was a teetotaler), card tables (though he never played cards), many deep leather chairs and sofas, and a temperature-controlled humidor for the oversize cigars that he puffed on constantly. From this part of the house, it was also possible to get the impression that the unathletic Sarnoff was an outdoorsman and big-game hunter. Heads and tusks and horns of wild beasts adorned the walls — lion, panther, impala, dik-dik, leopard, wild boar. An elephant's foot had been fashioned into a wastebasket. A giant marlin arched, stuffed and mounted, above the bar, and mummified game birds posed inside bell jars. The taxidermic menagerie in this trophy room was, however, misleading. Sarnoff, if pressed, would admit that he had never pulled a trigger or baited a fishhook in his life, and that all the carnage had been done by others.

The fifth floor contained servants' rooms, and on the top floor of the house guest bedrooms opened out onto a huge trellis-shaded roof garden, with a spectacular view of the midtown skyline, including the new RCA Building. And on this level, too, David Sarnoff had given himself a particular indulgence — his private barbershop.

Throughout the house, meanwhile, on every level and in virtually every room, were television sets. Some were concealed behind sliding doors, and others were treated as pieces of furniture. There was never a clear-cut way of counting the sets, since they were changed and rearranged and replaced with such frequency, but there were usually at least three dozen in the Sarnoff house at any given time. To most Americans, of course, television came as a post–World War II phenomenon, but Sarnoff had been trying out various television receivers since the early 1930s, and television had been more than a glimmer in his eye as far back as 1923, when, in a memorandum to his company, he had pondered the future of the medium as he saw it then:

I believe that television, which is the technical name for seeing instead of hearing by radio, will come to pass in due course.

Already, pictures have been sent across the Atlantic by radio. Experimental, of course, but it points the way to future possibilities. . . .

I also believe that transmission and reception of motion pictures by radio will be worked out in the next decade. This would result in important events or interesting dramatic presentations being literally broadcast by radio and, thereafter, received in individual homes or auditoriums where the original scene will be re-enacted on a screen, with much the appearance of present day motion pictures. . . .

The problem is technically similar to that of radio telephony though of more complicated nature — but within the range of technical achievement. Therefore it may be that every broadcast receiver for home use in the future will also be equipped with a television adjunct by which the instrument will make it possible to see as well as to hear what is going on in the broadcast station.

If that description of television sounds a little loose and imprecise, Sarnoff had a better grasp on the idea a year later when he told an audience at the University of Missouri in 1924: "Think of your family, sitting down of an evening in the comfort of your own home, not only listening to the dialogue but seeing the action of a play given on a stage hundreds of miles away; not only listening to a sermon but watching every play of emotion on the preacher's face as he exhorts the congregation to the path of religion." And, by 1927, he had expanded the idea even farther and said, "If we let our imagination plunge ahead, we may also dream of television in faithful colors."

David Sarnoff was neither a scientist nor an inventor, and so it is not possible to say that either he or the scientists and engineers who worked for RCA actually *invented* television. As early as 1880, Alexander Graham Bell, the inventor of the telephone, had taken out patents for television devices, and in the mid-1920s both General Electric and the American Telephone Company had succeeded in beaming moving pictures across considerable distances. Sarnoff's genius lay, not in inventing things, but in seeing the commercial possibilities of other people's inventions. Like so many other Eastern European entrepreneurs, he was a skillful adapter of the ideas of others. As such, he made his company the first to put serious time and money into the development of television broadcasting, and Sarnoff himself became the country's most ardent spokesman for the new medium. RCA scientists and technicians worked on perfecting television transmission and reception throughout the 1930s, and, with typical showmanship, Sarnoff was able to unveil the company's device at the RCA Pavilion at the 1939 New York World's Fair.

The RCA Pavilion became one of the fair's biggest attractions, and long lines of people formed to watch the astonishing new gadgets called television sets. (Cameras had been arranged so that fair visitors could actually see themselves passing across the tiny screens.) As a result of the pavilion's popularity, several hundred people purchased the rather costly RCA sets — for about six hundred dollars apiece — and so, though further development of commercial television was halted by the war, a few Americans were able to watch a very limited program schedule during the war years.

There were problems to be faced, of course. NBC's rival network, the Columbia Broadcasting System, did not manufacture television sets. Sarnoff's company, on the other hand, did, and once the war was over, planned to manufacture and market them in a big way. Thus, as the two networks lined up to do battle over television programming, wartime viewers were treated daily to this curious announcement from CBS television stations:

Good evening. We hope you will enjoy our programs. The Columbia Broadcasting System, however, is not engaged in the manufacture of television receiving sets and does not want you to consider these broadcasts as inducements to purchase television sets at this time. Because of a number of conditions which are not within our control, we cannot foresee how long this television broadcasting schedule will continue.

Viewers might not have had any idea what CBS was trying to say, but to RCA it was gallingly clear — don't buy television sets, there are many bugs to be worked out still, and we are not at all sure that television is here to stay. Sarnoff, of course, was stumping the country with the opposite message, trying to whip up Americans into a frenzy of excitement and anticipation for the Age of Television that would dawn as soon as the war was over. At the same time, RCA and Sarnoff could see competition building from other electronics manufacturers — General Electric (which was no longer associated with RCA), Philco, Dumont, and a number of smaller companies. Sarnoff, however, was determined to make RCA synonymous with television. He almost succeeded.

One of the biggest hurdles that the whole television industry would have to surmount, meanwhile, was the vociferous opposition of privately owned American radio stations. Most station owners did not agree with Sarnoff's views that television and radio could share the airwaves and coexist compatibly. Most were convinced that television would destroy the radio industry. In radio editorials across the country, David Sarnoff was denounced as a "televisionary," and listeners were confidently told that television would never work. In at least one national advertisement by an association of radio broadcasters, David Sarnoff was caricatured as King Kong crushing poor little radio beneath his simian heel. Unfazed by these outcries, Sarnoff and RCA marched on with the development of television.

In 1944, the Television Broadcasters Association bestowed another of the long series of awards and honors on Sarnoff, and it was perhaps the one that would please him the most. At the association's annual dinner, Sarnoff was named "Father of American Television." The award went straight to the wall of his fourth-floor gallery on East Seventy-first Street.

By the late 1940s, he had been proved right about radio as well. Radio and television could coexist, and RCA's new sets contained radio dials as well as television screens. To be sure, television would change radio programming drastically; there would be a period of readjustment as the radio soap operas and big comedy shows flew off to the television screen, and radio settled down to music, news, and talk. And now that television had finally come of age, Sarnoff did not mind at all that much of the general public — remembering the thrill of seeing it for the first time at the RCA Pavilion — assumed that television was an RCA invention, nor did he protest being labeled the "father" of it. His contribution had been, if anything, more important. He had learned about television just as he had learned about radio, had had a hunch that it could be made to work somehow or other, and had kept his company persistently at it until it did.

Throughout all those years, Hollywood — mysteriously — had been much less foresighted. In the late 1930s, Sam Goldwyn had said, "I don't think this television thing is going to work. But what the hell — if it turns out that it does, we'll just buy it."

By 1950, however, the Radio Corporation of America was not for sale.

A television set and a home in the suburbs — these were the two things Americans seemed to want the most in the years immediately following the war, and a forest of television antennas would become one of the symbols of suburbia. Historically, after a war, real estate values become depressed, and a number of economists had predicted that this would happen after World War II. But — helped in part by GI loans — the real estate market boomed, particularly in the suburbs of large cities, and new houses went up by the hundreds of thousands.

The war had also changed the demography of such cities as New York. As had happened following the first war, a new influx of poor blacks was moving up from the rural South, and another wave of immigrants was arriving from the island of Puerto Rico. The pale, pinched faces of New Yorkers that Helena Rubinstein had noticed a number of years earlier were now less in evidence, and the city had taken on a decidedly swarthy cast. The new metropolitan black population had expanded the traditional boundaries of Harlem — to the north, south, and west — and now practically all the Manhattan real estate north of Ninety-sixth Street, between the East River and Washington Heights, fell under the designation of "Harlem." Harlem now even extended into the South and East Bronx, and the once-proud Grand Concourse and its crowning jewel, the Concourse Plaza Hotel, wore a sad and seedy look as middle-class Jews moved out in the face of the advancing black population. It was a pattern that would be observed in a number of American cities, as a neighborhood first "went Jewish," and then, making way for the next ethnic group that was struggling up from poverty, "went black." And since Jews frequently retained their properties in their former neighborhoods, becoming absentee landlords, a social problem between blacks and Jews would be created that is evident to this day.

From the South and central Bronx, some Jewish families moved westward, to the bosky and pleasant reaches of the West Bronx and Riverdale, overlooking the Hudson River. Still more moved northward, into suburban Westchester County, and owning a house in Westchester would become the newest Jewish status symbol. In Westchester, moneyed Christian families had already taken dibs on the most desirable waterfront properties, along the Hudson and Long Island Sound, but pleasantly rural stretches in the interior of the county, in Scarsdale, Harrison, Purchase, and White Plains, were still available for development. To be sure, some inland communities — most notably Bronxville — remained restricted against Jews by gentlemen's agreements. (Bronxville's Jewish merchants could not live in Bronxville.) And longtime Christian residents of Westchester County would complain that the postwar movement into the county was responsible for a "Bronxification" of Westchester, as more suburban shopping centers, restaurants, bars, motels, and high-rise apartment houses went up.

Still, Westchester was a country club place. Most of its social life revolved around its clubs, and golf and tennis were its symbols — the first golf course in America had been laid out there. Though there were many clubs that would not take Jewish members, there were nearly as many Jewish clubs, many of them quite luxurious. Even the huge, glossy Westchester Country Club, where the tone was predominantly Roman Catholic, had, during the hard financial times of the Depression, taken in a few Jewish families, and once the barrier had gone down, it was difficult to put it back up again. One of the appeals of Westchester was the fact that it appeared to be an area where Jews and Christians could live pleasantly and comfortably side by side. The town of Scarsdale, for example, by the early 1950s had a population that was roughly evenly divided between Jews and Christians, and Scarsdale was considered the prototype upscale New York suburb.

Another appeal of Westchester was its reputation for an excellent public school system. Scarsdale High School boasted of an academic record equal to such top New England boarding schools as Exeter and Andover, and regularly sent its graduates to the leading Ivy League and Seven Sisters colleges.

There was also a postwar Jewish movement to the near suburbs of Long Island. Here again, the North Shore "Gold Coast" of Nassau County, with its high bluffs commanding views of Long Island Sound, had been preempted by the Christian rich (though Otto Kahn, a German Jew, had a large estate at Cold Spring Harbor). But attractive real estate was available on the flatter land of the South Shore, particularly around Hewlett Harbor. Here the Five Towns — Hewlett, Cedarhurst, Woodmere, Lawrence, and Inwood — became a snug enclave of new-made Jewish money. Lives that had begun on the Lower East Side and had passed through the Grand Concourse tended to continue a northward trek into Westchester County. Others from the Lower East Side, who had graduated to Brooklyn, gravitated farther east on the island to the Five Towns.

Many American Jews today, who have since moved on to even more prestigious addresses, recall the cozy postwar days of the Five Towns with bittersweet nostalgia. For children, growing up in the Five Towns was a rather special experience. Everyone, it seemed, knew almost everyone else, and children's parents all visited one another. The neighborliness and closeness was like that of the Lower East Side, but with trees, lawns, gardens, an occasional swimming pool, clean sidewalks, and quiet, well-policed streets. In place of the fire escape there was the backyard patio. Some people in the Five Towns lived in apartments, but every family who could afford one wanted its own home, its own piece of America.

The architectural styles of the Five Towns were all carefully in keeping with those favored by the Christian majority — tidy Colonials, red-brick Georgians, exposed-beam Tudors — a touch of Mount Vernon here, a dash of Nantucket there, and a bit of Olde England for good measure. Little in the Five Towns was built in the Spanish, Italian, or French style, nor was anything Oriental or Moorish or, Lord knew, Russian. And yet there was something about life in the Five Towns that was confining and insular, a sense of physical and emotional separation — of being right in the mainstream of New York life, on a main commuting stem of the Long Island Rail Road, and yet somehow cut off from it. Though the area was not set apart by walls, the invisible barrier of the ghetto could be felt beyond the manicured shrubbery, the well-dressed windows, and the shiny new tricycles. Not on the main line of the Long Island Rail Road, but on the Rockaway Branch, the area was called "the Peninsula," because it was a dead end — not on the way to anywhere, but a destination. The writer Sue Kaufman, who grew up in Lawrence, used to clench her fists in angry frustration whenever she was reminded of the Five Towns. For her, it had been a stifling experience. She called the towns "a golden ghetto."

But others recall the special privacy of the towns. "Be civil, but strange, with the neighbors," one mother advised her children. And there was also the beachfront, Atlantic Ocean closeness to nature, and what were considered the salubrious effects of "good sea air." Not that the Five Towns comprised a completely homogeneous community. On the contrary, there were marked differences among the various villages. In Hewlett, for instance, Jews were in the minority, and at least one area of Lawrence was restricted. In Woodmere, there was a sizable German-Jewish population, and it was difficult for an Eastern European to become a member of such German-Jewish clubs as the Inwood Beach Club. And yet, of the five communities, Woodmere had the most status. In Cedarhurst and Lawrence, the balance between Germans and

Russians was more equal, and, though census figures do not reveal such distinctions, there were probably more Russians in Lawrence than Germans — at least those who recall the situation felt that way. And yet both the Lawrence Beach Club and the Atlantic Beach Club were restricted against Jews.

Inwood had the least social status of the five communities. It was in Inwood, as well as in parts of Cedarhurst and Lawrence — literally on the other side of the Long Island Rail Road tracks — that the *schwartzes*, or blacks, who provided household help for the better-off lived. Also in Inwood lived a number of Italian families and a smattering of Irish — many of whom had originally come to help build the railroad, and who had stayed on to work as domestics, gardeners, construction workers, carpenters, and house painters. There were parts of Inwood that were actually considered dangerous, and Jewish children were warned not to walk through the black "Sugar Hill" section after dark. Still, Inwood was an essential fifth to the other four towns. It was the servants' quarters.

Binding the little clutch of townships together, giving them a sense of specialness and clubbiness, was Woodmere Academy, a private day school. Though the Five Towns boasted excellent public schools, in its academic heyday in the late 1940s, Woodmere Academy was rated equal to the New England prep schools, and its school spirit was considered remarkable. Woodmere graduates went sailing on to Harvard, Princeton, and Columbia, where the sons of tailors-turned–garment manufacturers studied to be lawyers, doctors, and engineers. If the ethnic cast of Woodmere Academy seemed to be more Eastern European than German, it was perhaps because immigrant parents were particularly ambitious for their children, and would not settle for less than an academy education. What City College meant in the 1920s, Woodmere Academy meant in the 1940s. Acceptance at Woodmere carried great cachet, and as a result the school was snobbish and clannish, and added in no small measure to that curiously insular Five Towns feeling. At Woodmere, *they* became *we*, and the others were simply the others.

Best of all, when one moved out of one of the five boroughs of New York City into one of the Five Towns on Long Island, it seemed like the American dream come true — because what symbolized the American dream after the war better than the suburbs? A house of one's own, unheard-of in the old country, with that marvelous capitalist invention, a mortgage; an automobile; a maid; a fine private school; a country club — what was missing? Only, perhaps, a sense of history. The Five Towns businessmen who gathered each morning on the commuter platforms of the Long Island Rail Road worked at various occupations, but the principal endeavor of the Five Towns seemed to be the erasure of memory. The Five Towns were places to forget the pushcart past, and though it might not really be forgotten, the past was diverted as far back into the consciousness as possible. It was the *ordinariness*, the everydayness, of the place that seemed to be in such sharp contrast with the struggle it had taken to get there. Only the old grandparents, living in guest rooms with pretty wallpaper and comfortable chairs and radios, could tell what it had been like and what it all meant, but the children were too busy to listen. Or, when the children asked their grandparents what it had been like growing up on the Lower East Side, or in Russia, the reply would be, "Don't ask!"

Years later, in the 1980s, when the area south of Houston Street in Manhattan called SoHo became actually fashionable, and when young people were converting Lower East Side lofts into roomy studios and apartments, the granddaughter of a Five Towns woman told her grandmother that she was moving into a SoHo loft. The older woman looked at her granddaughter with shocked disbelief. "And your grandfather and I worked so hard to get out of Hester Street!" she cried.

Part Three
HERE WE ARE: 1951-

16

CROWN PRINCES

AN obituary notice in the *New York Times* in the late 1960s told an interesting story to those who make a hobby of reading between the lines. It announced the death of MRS. ROBERT LEVY, CIVIC WORKER, 69. "Mrs. Levy," the account began, "who was active in civic and philanthropic affairs, . . . was born in New York September 27, 1897, the daughter of Jesse Isador Straus and Irma Nathan Straus." The Strauses were a proud old New York German-Jewish family, but Mrs. Levy's mother was descended from even prouder Jewish stock — the Sephardic Nathans, who could trace their ancestry back to the first Jewish settlers in America in 1654, and, according to at least one Nathan family genealogist, even farther, to a union between King Solomon and the Queen of Sheba. For Jesse Isador Straus, therefore, the marriage had represented a social step up. "Her father," the account continued, "was president of R. H. Macy & Company, Inc., and served as United States Ambassador to France from 1933 to 1936." The account did not include the fact that Mrs. Levy's grandfather was the Isidor Straus who had gone down with the *Titanic*, and that Mrs. Levy's father had been one of the privileged few New Yorkers permitted to enter David Sarnoff's radio studio atop Wanamaker's to await word of survivors. The obituary continued with a few words about the career of Beatrice Nathan Straus Levy's husband, a prominent cardiologist, and their surviving children, and concluded with the words, "A memorial service for Mrs. Levy will be held . . . at St. James Episcopal Church, Madison Avenue and 71st Street."

Thus three great Jewish strains had been brought together in
America — the Sephardic Nathans, the German Strauses, and the
humble Russian Levys — only to earn interment from Saint James's,
Manhattan's most fashionable Protestant church. It was a story,
one might say, of total assimilation. And it added a bittersweet
postscript to the assertion *kol Yisrael hem chaverim* — all of Israel
are brethren.

Still, the Christianizing saga of Nathan/Straus/Levy told only a
part of the story of what was happening to Jews in America in the
second half of the twentieth century. Not many years later, in
Cincinnati, young Calman Levine II was bar mitzvaʰᵉd in an
elaborate ceremony in that city's fashionable Plum Street Temple,
the Reform congregation founded by Rabbi Isaac Mayer Wise.
Though young Levine was the only one of five brothers to have
chosen the rite, it, too, represented another form of assimilation —
from the Orthodoxy of his namesake grandfather into the "liberal
enlightenment" of American Reform Judaism. This rite of passage
might, to an older generation, have been seen as a kind of obituary.
And if various Nathans and Strauses — not to mention Levys! —
might have been spinning in their graves at the news of the
Episcopalian memorial, so might the original Calman Levine's
father at the news of his great-grandson's conversion to Reform.

Calman Levine had died a bitter man, the victim, as he would
always see it, of Sam Bronfman's long struggle for respectability,
for admission — assimilation — into the society of rich and cul-
tivated and philanthropic men and women in the United States
and Canada of which he so desperately longed to be a part, to rid
himself of the "goddamn bootlegger" label that seemed to have
attached itself to his name. He had tried high-class advertising.
He had even tried the pious approach of urging Americans to drink
less. Keying this theme to the leading Christian holiday, the Christmas season of tippling and jollity, he had started, as early as 1934,
an annual Seagram's advertising campaign in hundreds of newspapers across the United States that proclaimed, WE WHO MAKE
WHISKEY SAY: DRINK MODERATELY. The high moral tone of these
advertisements and Seagram's stand against drunkenness drew
praise from Wets and Drys alike, from the clergy and from the
judiciary, but they did not get Mr. Sam into the Mount Royal Club.
It began to seem as though nothing would.

Mr. Sam had also tried to polish his tarnished image by hiring prominent Christians, and placing them in high positions in his company. Brigadier General Frank Schwengel of the United States Army Reserve was hired and placed in charge of U.S. sales for Seagram's. Fred Willkie was brought in to oversee Seagram's production at the company's distillery in Louisville. Mr. Willkie's chief qualifications for the post seemed to be that his brother, Wendell L. Willkie, had been a Republican candidate for the United States presidency, and that the Willkies were blue-blooded descendants of the old New York Wendell family, and were in the *Social Register*.

It was Fred Willkie's arrival at Seagram's that spelled the end of Calman Levine's career with the company. The two men did not see eye to eye from the beginning. It was Mr. Willkie's notion, furthermore, to hire scientists to supervise the blending of Seagram's products. Mr. Levine's celebrated nose and palate, he implied, were not enough to assure the blends' scientific uniformity. Mr. Levine, understandably, vociferously defended his ancient master-blender's craft. But Mr. Willkie disagreed, and, despite Mr. Sam's often-repeated maxim that "distilling is a science, but blending is an art," he apparently got Mr. Sam on his side. Mr. Levine wrote a number of memorandums to Mr. Sam, complaining about the new order of things under the Willkie regime in Louisville. Typically, these went unanswered, as did any expressions of disagreement with company policy. (Mr. Sam had explained unequivocally enough what *that* was: "*I* am company policy!") Finally, Levine wrote what amounted to an ultimatum: either he or Fred Willkie would have to go. The response from above was that Mr. Levine would be relieved of his duties in Louisville, and would be sent on a speaking tour around the country to extol the superiority of Seagram's blends.

For the man who had created Seagram's best-selling brand, this situation rankled, and soon the word of Calman Levine's unhappiness reached the ear of one of Lewis Rosenstiel's informants. Rosenstiel responded by making Levine a handsome offer at Schenley's, and Levine decided to accept it. He brought the news of his decision to Mr. Sam.

Mr. Sam sprang from his chair in his Chrysler Building office, screaming, *"You go to my enemy!"* He then proceeded to hurl one of his most explosive strings of curses, threats, imprecations, and verbal abuse at his longtime employee. The tirade lasted fully half an hour, and at the close of it Levine was close to tears. Then Mr. Sam ordered Levine bodily removed from his office.

Though the Schenley job offered a much better salary — Lew Rosenstiel was less miserly than Mr. Sam — Calman Levine never really recovered from the emotional wringer he had been put through that afternoon, and remained resentful about his Seagram experience to the end of his days.

In addition to having developed Seagram's flagship whiskey, Levine had performed many extra services for Mr. Sam far beyond the regular line of duty. Once, when a Polish scientist in Italy had claimed to have invented a liquor that produced a pleasant high, but was not intoxicating — "elation without inebriation," the scientist called it — Mr. Sam asked Levine to check on it. Levine made a special trip to Italy and Vienna to meet with the man, but was not impressed with his concoction, which, among other traits, left an unpleasant film on the inside of a glass. Levine recommended against acquiring the patent. (The scientist was later declared insane.) Levine had also been instrumental in curbing some of Mr. Sam's more harebrained notions. No one at Seagram really knew how the popular vogue of ordering "Seven and Seven" — a jigger of Seven Crown mixed with Seven-Up — began, though the trend seemed to have started in the Midwest. Widespread as this bar order became, it irked Mr. Sam that his whiskey was giving a free word-of-mouth-advertising ride to a soft-drink company. He had asked Calman Levine to look into the feasibility of a sparkling whiskey — a Seven Crown with Seven-Up flavor and sparkle built right into the bottle. Using an ordinary siphon with a carbon dioxide cartridge, Levine was able to demonstrate that the carbonation of whiskey worked havoc on its flavor.

Finally, the split with Seagram saddened Levine because he had considered Mr. Sam his personal friend. Levine and his wife had dined often with the Bronfmans at Belvedere Castle. At holiday times the two families had regularly exchanged gifts of fruit and delicacies. The Bronfman and Levine children had gone to summer camp together at Camp Algonquin in the Adirondacks, and a Levine governess had become a Bronfman governess. But Sam Bronfman never forgave a defection, and from that moment all

communication between the two families ceased. The grudge would
be borne into the next generation. Years later, Calman Levine's
daughter Rita would try to telephone one of her old playmates in
New York, only to be told by a secretary, "This call is not welcome."

Like the pharaohs of old, who caused the names and achieve-
ments of their predecessors to be effaced from their monuments
and temples, the name of Calman Levine, who had perfected
American blended whiskey and revolutionized the drinking tastes
and habits of Americans, was expunged from the corporate history
of Joseph E. Seagram and Sons. In *The Story of Seagram's Seven
Crown*, which the company published in 1972, Levine's name was
not mentioned. Instead, the inventor of the blend had become
Samuel Bronfman.

In the meantime, Sam Bronfman himself may have had good
reason for bitterness. None of the honors he had expected from
Canada had been bestowed upon him. The knighthood, the gov-
ernorship of McGill University, a directorship of the Bank of Montreal (where he was the largest depositor), the club memberships,
the seat on the Canadian Senate he had tried to buy, the ambas-
sadorships — all had eluded him. In 1951, now in his sixties and
perhaps weary of his long and unsuccessful social climb north of
the border, Mr. Sam purchased a large estate in Tarrytown, in
New York's Westchester County. Since it overlooked the Hudson
at Tappan Zee, he renamed this new castle Belvedere too, and,
in a series of elaborate parties, began to woo new American friends.*
Next door to Mr. Sam's new Belvedere stood Lyndhurst, the castle
built by the railroad tycoon Jay Gould. In it lived Gould's daughter
Anna, by then the Duchesse de Tallyrand-Périgord. The duchess,
however, did not invite her new neighbors to her entertainments.

Then, in 1953, there were two events that buoyed Sam Bronfman's spirits somewhat. The first was the marriage of his elder
daughter, Minda, to the French banker Baron Alain de Gunzburg,
whom she had met while he was a student at the Harvard Business
School. In Paris, the Gunzburgs, who were German Jews, were

---

*He never took out American citizenship papers, however, in the faint hope that the Canadian
honors might still someday be forthcoming.

considered bankers almost, if not quite, on the level of the Rothschilds, to whom they were distantly related. (Baron Guy de Rothschild's mother was a first cousin of Alain de Gunzburg's
grandmother.) Now at least someone in the family had a title, even
if it wasn't Mr. Sam, though the new baroness's treatment of her
rank at her wedding seemed a little cruel. When her father went
to kiss the bride, Minda said, "But Father, don't you know that
you should *bow* to a baroness?"

The second, just as startling event of that year was the marriage
of Mr. Sam's elder son, Edgar, to Ann Margaret Loeb, the German-
Jewish daughter of the John L. Loebs of New York, and the granddaughter of the founder of the investment house of C. M. Loeb
Rhoades and Company. Miss Loeb's mother was a Lehman, her
maternal grandmother a Lewisohn, and her paternal grandmother
a Sephardic Moses, whose family had been plantation owners in
the Old South. The Bronfman-Loeb union shocked New York's
German-Jewish Old Guard. "But those Bronfmans," said Mrs.
Arthur Lehman, "have just come down out of the *trees*." It was
confidently predicted that the marriage would not last. Indeed, it
didn't.

Just three years earlier, another intergalactic marriage had equally
unsettled the German-Jewish Old Guard. After marrying and divorcing a popular young — and Roman Catholic — Manhattan
socialite named Esmé O'Brien, David Sarnoff's son Bobby had
married Felicia Schiff Warburg. If anything, Miss Warburg's German lineage was even more distinguished than Miss Loeb's. Her
uncle was the banker-yachtsman-philanthropist Felix Warburg.
Her grandfather was Jacob H. Schiff. One of her great-grandfathers
was Solomon Loeb, the Kuhn, Loeb founding partner, and one of
the "old" Loebs. The John L. Loebs, who had come from Germany
later and were unrelated, were "new" Loebs. Warburg cousins
were Seligmans, Kahns, and Kuhns. At the time of the Warburg-
Sarnoff nuptials, Robert Sarnoff was identified by one of the clannish German-Jewish crowd as "the son of that Russian radio man."
It was predicted that this Russian-German mesalliance also would
not last, and, indeed, it did not.

Of course it wasn't easy being the son of a self-made tycoon.
"Somebody up there likes him" became the private joke at NBC
about Bobby Sarnoff's rapid rise from the sales department, in

1948, to the presidency of the network in 1955, at which point he began climbing the corporate ladder of the parent company. He would be named chairman of the board and chief executive officer of RCA by 1970, when still a youthful fifty-two. All these promotions occurred under the watchful eye, and powerful parental thumb, of the founding father. The relationship between father and son was ambivalent. On the one hand, David Sarnoff was proud of his son's ability to fill his shoes. On the other, he was suspicious, questioning his son's every move and every idea, openly critical of some of Robert Sarnoff's more farfetched "predictions."* It made for a relationship that was uneasy, at best, with each man constantly challenging and testing the other.

One of the problems with the self-made men was that, as their companies grew from virtual one-man operations to giant multi-national corporations, their businesses exceeded their personal grasp. It was no longer possible for the one man at the top to keep a finger in every part of the corporate pie, to keep track of what every scattered department head was doing. By the 1950s, Mr. Sam Bronfman's dictum, "*I* am company policy," no longer made much sense since, with thousands of stockholders to account to, corps of lawyers and scientists and advertising experts whose advice had to be taken into consideration, Seagram's company policy was really out of Mr. Sam's hands altogether. His company had taken on a giant life of its own, and Mr. Sam was little more than a figurehead. Still, men like this had trouble relinquishing their sole and final authority. It was difficult for Mr. Sam to delegate authority to others, and hard for him to accept the fact that there were some decisions that were going to be made without him.

Still, he continued to try to run Seagram's as a one-man show, continually poking his head into offices to make sure that his people were doing the jobs assigned them, asking for reports from regional sales heads and account executives, scrutinizing contracts and merger documents that he no longer fully understood, always certain that the moment his attention wandered, dirty deals would be pulled behind his back. Mr. Sam had often said that one of the secrets of his success was "work, hard work," and it was difficult

*In 1959, for example, Robert Sarnoff predicted that "for home use the 1969 set will replace the present picture tube with a thin, flat screen that can be hung on the wall like a painting."

for him to adjust to the fact that the hardest work was now being done by teams of others, or by sophisticated machines; that much of his company was automated and no longer needed, or wanted, his personal supervision. Still, he would not let go the reins.

Because of the boss's mercurial nature, the personnel of the Seagram executive suite lived in a state of perpetual terror, and in a perpetual revolving door. Not even their weekends were free, for Mr. Sam thought nothing of calling a secretary on a Saturday night or a Sunday morning to fire off his orders and commands. Higher-ups learned that the most effective way of dealing with Mr. Sam was to give him a wide berth. In *Bronfman Dynasty*, the Canadian writer Peter C. Newman tells the tale of Frank Marshall, a director of export sales who so dreaded confrontations with the boss that he arranged to be out of town whenever Mr. Sam was *in* town — an easy thing to do since Marshall's duties carried him all over the world. Marshall even kept a packed suitcase in his office so that, in case Mr. Sam made a surprise visit, he could be out the door and on his way to the airport and to some foreign shore where Seagram's did business before the boss collared him.

After a while, however, Mr. Sam began to realize that it had been a long time since he had seen his export director, and the word went out: "Find Marshall. Mr. Sam wants to see him." Still Marshall managed to be elusive.

In 1951, Seagram's celebrated Mr. Sam's "official" sixtieth birthday, though he was actually sixty-two, with a gala dinner in the ballroom of Montreal's Windsor Hotel. There were the usual windy speeches and presentations extolling the genius and generosity of the company's worthy founder, and recitations of the successes of all the years past. Then the evening turned to what were intended to be more lighthearted matters. An elaborate film had been prepared as a spoof of some of the activities of Seagram's executives. A screen was lowered, the lights were dimmed, the movie began, and, as Peter Newman relates it:

Sam was sitting in the front row . . . enjoying himself hugely, laughing as he watched scenes of slightly tipsy Egyptian army officers toasting one another with Crown Royal on the terrace of Shepheard's Hotel in Cairo. This was followed by a long-shot of a Bedouin riding a camel toward the Pyramids, bottle tucked into his burnoose. The camel approached the camera. Sam suddenly sat up, peering at its swaying rider. The focus was much tighter now, and the "Bedouin," it became clear, was none other than Frank Marshall in long nightshirt with a fez on his head, brandishing a bottle of V.O.

Sam leaped out of his chair. Pointing excitedly toward the image of his errant export manager, he bellowed at the screen, "There's the son of a bitch! That's where he's been spending his time! Riding a goddamn camel!"

It was a while before Sam had calmed down, and the movie could proceed.

Someone in the company had to take on the job of being Mr. Sam's handmaiden and at his constant beck and call. In Hollywood a similar system had evolved for the care and feeding of the movie moguls. Sam Marx, a former story editor at MGM, has recalled how once, on the studio lot, he encountered L. B. Mayer strolling down the sidewalk, an attentive secretary at his side. Mayer and Marx fell into a conversation, and the secretary excused herself. Then the two men parted, and walked off in different directions. Presently the secretary reappeared, running down the sidewalk after Mr. Marx, crying, "Where's L.B.?" Marx replied that he had last seen him walking off in a northerly direction. "My God!" cried the secretary. *"He must never be left alone!"*

It was no different with Mr. Sam. On his travels, an underling had to be assigned to accompany him. For one short airplane trip, during which there would be no meal service, an elaborate airborne picnic had been planned. Once they were in the air, however, and Mr. Sam had announced that he was ready to eat, the luckless aide realized that he had left the picnic basket behind in the trunk of his car. Mr. Sam jumped from his seat and began marching up and down the aisle of the plane, pointing at his cowering assistant and shouting to all the other passengers, "See him, there he is! There's the goddamned fool! I'm surrounded by lunatics!"

Though Peter Newman's book, from its title onward, tries to make the case that Sam Bronfman saw himself as the founder of a family "dynasty," most of the Eastern European tycoons seem to have been rather reluctant dynasts. Unlike the European House of Rothschild, or the interrelated German-Jewish families of New York, where positions of power and trust were doled out to family

322 Here We Are: 1951–

members generation after generation, the Russian Jews, when they practiced nepotism, tended to give their relatives big titles but little authority, and to keep them close to home, where they could be kept out of trouble, and monitor their every move. Sam and Frances Goldwyn's son, Sam Jr., was given the title of producer in the Goldwyn organization, but was given almost nothing of importance to do. Helena Rubinstein, who had at least a dozen relatives on her payroll — sisters, nieces, nephews — never let it be forgotten that she, and only she, made all final decisions. On her two sons, Horace and Roy, she continued to blow hot and cold, praising them as geniuses in one breath, calling them stupid fools in the next. The boys would be handed challenging assignments one day, only to have them taken away the day following. Meanwhile, as her cosmetics empire grew, the command post became Madame Rubinstein's bedroom on the bottom floor of her Park Avenue triplex. Here, on an extraordinary Lucite bed, its head- and footboards eerily illuminated with hidden fluorescent lights, the plump little president pushed telephone buttons, scrawled uncertainly spelled memorandums, ate lunch — wiping her fingers on the coverlet and blowing her nose into the satin sheets — and, as she grew older, worked on her will. This massive document was rewritten almost daily, as relatives who had displeased her temporarily were written out of it and then, if they had managed to redeem themselves, written back into it again. It was a will that, on her death in 1965, would reveal her as one of the richest women in the world. She was either ninety-four or ninety-nine, and her personal fortune was over one hundred million dollars. The bulk of it went not to her sons, but to a foundation for "Women and Children."

At Seagram, Mr. Sam's elder son, Edgar, was assumed to be the crown prince and heir apparent. But, again, Edgar Bronfman was given titles in the company but little in the way of authority, as Mr. Sam continued to test his son's "readiness." Physically, Edgar resembled his pudgy father not at all. Tall, slender, dark, and handsome — even dashing — he looked like a youthful version of the actor Joseph Cotten. He also had a reputation for enjoying high living — nightclubs, fast cars, motorcycles, and the company of film stars. His father often accused him of being a "playboy." But there was a toughness about Edgar that he had inherited from his father, and a quick temper, and employees at Seagram quickly learned to treat Edgar Bronfman with extreme respect. Edgar was shrewd. He had waited until he was old enough — shades of the days of the czars' forced conscriptions of Russian Jews! — to escape being drafted into the United States Army, before he became an American citizen. He and his wife then proceeded to build the first full-scale estate that had been built in Westchester County in over a generation — manor house, tennis court, stables, garages, pool, pool house, helicopter landing pad — hard by what amounted to the family compound of his wife's German-Jewish relatives, the Lehmans, Lewisohns, and Loebs.

In the 1950s, a writer for the old *Holiday* magazine described Edgar's new house as "a huge Georgian pile," and Edgar was not amused. The editor of *Holiday*, Ted Patrick, was summarily summoned to appear, along with the writer of the story, at Edgar's office to apologize for the slight. The threat, if this was not done, was that Seagram's would cancel all its advertising in all Curtis magazines. These, at the time, included not only *Holiday* but the *Saturday Evening Post*. The Bronfman ultimatum was delivered to Ted Patrick while he was on a train between New York and Washington. Patrick's reply was: "Tell Mr. Bronfman to fuck himself."

Later, Patrick would admit that he had taken this stand with some trepidation. The *Saturday Evening Post* was already in shaky financial circumstances, and the loss of Seagram's advertising would amount to several million dollars a year. But, in the end, Patrick's hunch proved right. Seagram did not cancel its Curtis budget — reportedly because Mr. Sam had called his son into his office and reprimanded him for overstepping himself, muttering gruffly, "We advertise in those magazines because we need *them*, not because they need *us*."

But though the episode ended as a tempest in a teapot, it showed that Edgar Bronfman was a man to be reckoned with.

In the summer of 1957, Edgar Bronfman, then twenty-eight, confronted his father and told him that it was time for him to be made president of Joseph E. Seagram and Sons. Mr. Sam disagreed, and took the position that Edgar might be better suited to work in a field other than the liquor business. A stormy scene followed, at the end of which Edgar stood up and said, "If you're saying that the company isn't good enough for me, then I don't want to work for it." It sounded like another ultimatum and Mr. Sam, after consulting with his wife, knuckled under, and gave Edgar what he wanted.

This might never have happened, however, had not Mr. Sam, over the previous few years, made an important marketing mistake for Seagram's — one of the very few mistakes, if not the only one, that he would ever admit to making in his life. He had refused to take seriously the growing popularity of vodka in the Unitied States. He had been repeatedly advised by others in the company, including his son, of the trend toward vodka, and had been urged to get into the vodka business. But Mr. Sam, ever the believer in the supremacy of blended whiskeys, refused to accept the fact that Americans would take up a drink that had absolutely no taste or aroma, and one that was associated with Soviet Russia to boot. By the late 1950s, with competing companies capitalizing on the new vodka craze, Mr. Sam — while stubbornly maintaining that the fad would not last — reluctantly agreed that his judgment had been wrong. His son then had the exquisite pleasure of telling his overbearing father, "I told you so."

A great deal has been written about Italian-American "crime families" in which sons were trained to follow in their fathers' footsteps. But Jewish criminals, with whom the Italians frequently did business, had different notions. Though, like the Italians, they were family men, the Jews did not have dynastic ambitions for their sons to succeed them in lives of crime — the "Godfather" syndrome, as it were. On the contrary, the Jewish gangsters usually saw to it that their children were educated in the finest boarding schools and colleges, and that they were otherwise steered into lives of traditional American upper-class respectability and civic rectitude. Their sons were educated to be doctors, lawyers, scientists, and they guided their daughters into marriages with solid, upstanding young men who had charge accounts at Brooks Brothers. For the most part, the family of the Jewish gangster was kept unaware of what the breadwinner did for a living. ("In real estate," Meyer Lansky's wife would say, which, in a sense, was true.) As Mickey Cohen put it, "We had a code of ethics like the ones among bankers, other people in other walks of life, that one never involved his wife or family in his work." Like the socialists and reformers, the Jewish gangsters saw an American system that was skewed and bent in favor of the rich and well-established, where the cards were stacked against the immigrant and the poor. Gangsterism offered a simple shortcut, outside the system, to money and power and social mobility. Once these had been achieved, the next generation was supposed to give the family "a good name."

At the same time, there was still a kind of begrudging admiration for the Jewish criminal in the Jewish community at large. For one thing, he competed physically, and successfully, with the non-Jewish enemy, showing the hostile and violent anti-Semite that he could be beaten at his own game. When the Jews of Europe were under threat of annihilation, the gangster offered American Jews a secret and vicarious sense of satisfaction and pride.

The fact was that the gangsters provided a real social service to the Jewish community, as protectors and defenders of their own people. At a time when America was awash with anti-Semitism coming from high places — Henry Ford, the Ku Klux Klan, Gerald L. K. Smith, Father Charles Coughlin, the German-American Bund — the Jewish community appreciated anyone who would come to its defense, regardless of the means. Meyer Lansky's men had helped break up Bund rallies in New York and New Jersey. In Detroit, Jewish mobsters had saved Jewish peddlers and store owners from having to pay protection money to Polish and Italian hoodlums. In Chicago, more than five thousand Jews had turned out for the funeral of the Lansky-connected gangster Samuel "Nails" Morton to express their gratitude for his helping to protect poorer neighborhoods against raids by anti-Semitic and Jew-baiting Irish and Italians. In a sense, men like Morton were community servants, and in a sense, they were good Americans. And their children would be even better.

This was certainly the attitude of Meyer Lansky. Lansky liked to recall how, as a boy, he had watched in bewilderment as the older Jews in his Delancey Street neighborhood shuffled past — in their *yarmulkes* and prayer shawls, with beards and side curls — on their daily rounds of worship at the synagogues and yeshivas. "Where are they going, I asked myself? Where were they getting

in the new world? They had simply carried the old world across
the ocean with them. They had gone nowhere. They were going
nowhere. They were at a dead end."

Lansky, who had gone far, was determined that his children
would go much farther. He was devastated when his first son,
Bernard, suffered a birth trauma that resulted in a diagnosis of
cerebral palsy, and Lansky was told that Buddy, as he was called,
would be severely handicapped for the rest of his life. But his
second son, Paul, was born normal and healthy, to Lansky's great
relief, and it was on Paul that he centered his ambitions. He doted,
meanwhile, on his daughter, Sandra, who was called Sally. But
the children were soon a cause of dissension between Lansky and
his wife.

For one thing, Anna Lansky accused her husband of blaming
her for Buddy's pathetic disability. She also accused him of spoil-
ing Sally with too many expensive toys and gifts. And, as for Paul,
Anna Lansky wanted her son to be a rabbi. Lansky had quite a
different plan for Paul. He wanted to send his healthy son to West
Point, and have him become an American army officer. These
disagreements ended, in 1947, with the Lanskys' divorce. The
following year he married Thelma Scheer Schwartz, a pretty blond
divorcée who had been his manicurist in the barbershop of the
Embassy Hotel in Miami Beach. "Teddy" Lansky was five years
younger and several inches taller than her new husband, but these
discrepancies seemed to bother the newlyweds not at all, and theirs
would be a long and singularly happy marriage.

Of his three children, the only one he would permit to work for
his organization was the crippled Buddy, and Lansky saw to it
that Buddy was employed only in licit businesses — in one of the
hotels Lansky operated legally in Florida, Nevada, or Cuba, where
Buddy worked as a switchboard operator. Of course, it would be
darkly suggested that its switchboard was a hotel's nerve center,
and that Buddy's real assignment was to tap and monitor calls
between underworld figures and other important guests. Lansky
himself ridiculed this suggestion, pointing out that a simple, sed-
entary job as a telephone operator was probably the only sort of
work poor Buddy would ever be able to perform in life. Even at
that chore, Buddy was frustratingly slow.

Sally Lansky was sent to the exclusive Pine Crest School in Fort

Lauderdale, where she earned very good grades. After graduating, she delighted Lansky with her marriage to a Jewish boy named Marvin Rappaport. The Rappaports were old family friends from Prohibition days, and were now legitimately and respectably in the liquor business.

Meanwhile, Lansky moved forward with his plan to have Paul appointed to the United States Military Academy.

A gangster's son at West Point! It seemed an idea right out of a Hollywood movie. It seemed an impossible dream. But Lansky wanted Paul to be shaped into a true American, and in the service of his country. (This unswerving patriotism was rather typical of Jewish gangsters, despite the fact that they had gotten rich by bending America's laws.) And the dream came true, as most things in Meyer Lansky's life had a way of doing. Despite a deep undercurrent of anti-Semitism at West Point, Paul Lansky received his appointment. (Like many sons of immigrants, Paul was taller, huskier, and handsomer than his father.) How had Lansky done it? Naturally there were mutterings that he knew and dealt with a number of important Washington politicians, many of whom were bribable. Meyer Lansky would always hotly deny that any bribery or arm-twisting was involved in getting Paul his appointment; he had got it on his own academic and athletic merits — and, indeed, that appeared to be the case.

At West Point, Paul Lansky comported himself admirably. One of his roommates was the son of Colonel Monroe E. Freeman, an aide to General Eisenhower. After graduating in 1954, Paul became a captain in the air force, and an ace pilot in the Korean War. Following that, he toured American college and university campuses as a lecturer and recruiter. In the latter capacity, he was considered one of the finest in the military — a salesman of American ideals in war and in peace.

When Paul had married and Meyer Lansky's first grandson was born, Paul informed his father that the baby was to be named Meyer Lansky II. Lansky was appalled, and begged his son not to do this. So much ill fame had gathered around the name of Meyer Lansky, he argued, that it seemed unfair to ask this child to bear the same burden for the rest of its life. But Paul was adamant. He was proud of his father, and wanted to honor him this way. Lansky was deeply touched.

When Eisenhower was elected President in 1952, Meyer Lansky was rather surprised to receive, through Colonel Freeman, an invitation to the inaugural and ball. Feeling that it would be inappropriate for someone of his tarnished reputation to attend the inauguration ceremonies of a United States President, Lansky demurred. Colonel Freeman wrote back, "Don't you know that in our clubs we play the same slot machines that you've got in your casinos, and that we used to drink your bootleg whiskey?"

Lansky was touched by this sentiment as well. But, ever the gentleman, always the believer in seemliness and propriety, Meyer Lansky nonetheless wired back his regrets.

17

WITCH-HUNTING

THE 1950s were troubled times for the entertainment industry. With the war over, but with wartime energies still at a peak, America once again turned, with superpatriotic zeal, to the task of rooting out enemies, real or imagined, at home. It was the same kind of sentiment that had gripped the country after the first war, and that had brought Rose Pastor Stokes to trial for sedition. Soviet Russia had been America's ally in the second war, but that no longer mattered, and Russia was now America's archenemy again. Communists and Communist sympathizers were suspected of lurking in high places, and the target of the Red hunt became show business, and particularly that "pervasive shaper of American thought," the motion picture industry.

The Communist witch-hunts of the early 1950s were not motivated by anti-Semitism exactly — at least, no one on the House Un-American Activities Committee had the courage to come right out and say so. But, since the movie business was heavily Jewish, and most of HUAC's targets in Hollywood were Jews, the effect was the same. And, though the cause of Russian-Jewish radicalism — in Hollywood and elsewhere — had been quiescent for at least a dozen years, as American Communists had become disillusioned with the party in the wake of news of Stalin's excesses in the 1930s, the phrase "Jewish radical" still had an inflammatory ring. The idea that Jewish radicals pervaded the film industry was an easy one for the committee to sell to the public, which had been whipped into a frenzy of fear that Russia was about to conquer the world. And, of course, Hollywood, with all its connotations of wealth, glamour, and excess, made an obviously tempting target for HUAC. The subpoenaing of movie stars to testify as to their political leanings assured the committee that its abundance of anti-Communist zeal would be well publicized.

Hollywood had foreseen the committee hearings. As early as 1947, a meeting of studio heads had convened at New York's Waldorf-Astoria Hotel. With not at all the best intentions in the world, but hoping to purge itself of leftist undesirables before Washington stepped in to tell it what to do, this group of movie men had compiled a "Hollywood Black List," composed of the names of some three hundred men and women known or suspected to have Communist sympathies. The effects of the blacklist were immediate and dire. The list spread from Hollywood to Broadway, from television studios to Madison Avenue advertising agencies, as those listed were dismissed from their jobs in film, radio, television, and the theater. A chill swept through the entertainment world, as old friends and associates eyed each other cautiously, never certain who would or would not name names of other leftists in order to save a career. The quality of television programming and film content suffered.

Once named, those blacklisted had either to work pseudonymously, to change their names, or to work at a fraction of their former worth. In *Scoundrel Time,* Lillian Hellman wrote that, after she was blacklisted, her annual income plummeted from $140,000 to $10,000 and that, after it dropped even lower, she was forced to work part-time in a department store to make ends meet. One of her un-American "crimes," it seemed, had been to write an anti-Nazi play, *Watch on the Rhine*. In Hollywood, the director Irving Pichel was blacklisted for his "un-American" film *A Medal for Benny,* which depicted Mexican-Americans in a sympathetic light.

Although the number of people implicated amounted to only one-half of one percent of the total number employed in the entertainment industry, the repercussions were enormous. Some people changed their occupations, some emigrated, and a few took their own lives. Even those not blacklisted were affected. The director Lewis Milestone, born in Russia, was not on the blacklist, but had had the temerity to hire Ring Lardner, Jr. — one of the so-called Hollywood Ten who refused to tell the committee whether they were Communists or not — to write one of his films. This created guilt by association, and Hedda Hopper wrote in her column, "Let's take a look at Lardner's new boss. He was born in Russia and came to this country years ago. . . . He has a beautiful home in which he holds leftish rallies, is married to an American and has a fortune here. But still his heart seems to yearn for Russia. Wonder if Joe [Stalin] would take him back?" Milestone was out of a job for the next eleven years.

Looking back, some of the testimony heard soberly at the HUAC hearings seems so absurd that one wonders why it was not laughed out of court. But by then no one was laughing. Dalton Trumbo, who, in fact, had joined the Communist party in 1943, was another of the Hollywood Ten — all of whom would draw prison sentences — and the committee heard Ginger Rogers's tearful mother, Lela Rogers, tell of how her daughter had been forced to utter the "Communist line" in Trumbo's film *Tender Comrade:* "Share and share alike — that's democracy." The fact that the romantic comedy had the word *comrade* in its title did not go unnoted.

During the dark years of the HUAC hearings, it seemed to matter not how one testified. Whether one denied vigorously that he had ever been a Communist; whether one refused to testify; whether one came forward as a "friendly witness"; whether one admitted to having once been a Communist, but had since seen the error of one's ways; whether one confessed that one was still a Communist; or whether one sought the protection of the First and Fifth amendments — the results were the same. The very fact that one had been summoned before the committee at all was enough to make one an unemployable pariah in the entertainment industry.

The case of the actor Howard Da Silva was typical. Born Howard Silverblatt, he had made over forty films between 1939 and 1951, and had worked for every major studio. But when, at the Hollywood HUAC hearings, actor Robert Taylor in the role of a friendly witness testified that Da Silva "always had something to say at the wrong time" at meetings of the Screen Actors Guild, that seemingly petty and innocuous remark was enough to finish Da Silva's career in Hollywood. He had just finished filming *Slaughter Trail* for RKO. After Taylor's testimony, the film's producer announced that Da Silva's part would be cut from the film, and that it would be reshot with another actor. Da Silva moved to New York and tried to work in radio, but American Legion posts all over the country assailed his sponsors with so much hostile mail that he was dropped. He was out of work for more than a dozen years, and did not find a major role until 1976, when he was cast in the Broadway musical *1776* — ironically, in the part of the American patriot Benjamin Franklin.

Blacklisted in the early 1950s, Zero Mostel denied that he had ever been a Communist, though he had lent his name to such causes as the National Negro Congress and the Spanish Refugee Appeal of the Joint Anti-Fascist Refugee Committee. His denials did no good, and his acting career was aborted. He turned to painting. He did not attain stardom until 1964, when he portrayed the legendary Tevye in Broadway's *Fiddler on the Roof*. Even more pathetic was the case of John Garfield. Born in the Bronx, he had sweet-tough good looks and a street-wise manner that had made him a major film star in tough-guy roles. By all accounts, Garfield was not very bright, and in his HUAC appearance his behavior was neither tough nor heroic. Meekly pleading that he had never been a Communist, and could therefore name no names of party cell members, he nonetheless tried to ingratiate himself with the committee by thanking it for the good work it was doing protecting innocent citizens from the "Red Menace." His denials cut no ice with the Hollywood establishment. Blacklisted, he could find no one who would hire him. He turned to Broadway, and worked for as little as a hundred dollars a week. But HUAC was not through with him. He was called before the committee again in connection with some canceled checks supposedly written by him to the Communist party. Though this evidence was never presented, Garfield decided on the mea-culpa approach and hired a public-relations expert to try to clear his name. A confessional article for *Look* magazine was ghosted for him, called "I Was a Sucker for a Left Hook," in which he took the position that he had been unwittingly duped into joining leftist causes. Before it was printed, John Garfield died of a heart attack at the age of thirty-nine.

The most tragic case was that of the actor Phillip Loeb. By 1948, "The Goldbergs," starring Gertrude Berg, had become radio's longest-running daytime serial. It had been on the air since 1929. In 1949, "The Goldbergs" moved from radio onto the television screen, and became one of television's earliest hits. Phillip

Loeb had played Molly Goldberg's husband from almost the beginning, and by 1950 he was making thirty thousand dollars a year and had been voted by the Boys' Clubs of America "Television's Father of the Year." But that same year his name appeared seventeen times in *Red Channels*, a listing of alleged Communists employed in the television industry that was published by an independent group of professional Red hunters.

Phillip Loeb had been a veteran of World War I, and had served in Europe with the U.S. Army Medical Corps. His most political activity had been, as an actor, in his union, Actors Equity. But in 1940 the Dies Committee had charged that Equity was run by Communists, to which Loeb had responded, "I am not a Communist, Communist sympathizer, or fellow traveler, and I have nothing to fear from an impartial inquiry."

"The Goldbergs" struggled through the 1950–1951 season, but was under heavy pressure from its sponsor, General Foods, to drop Loeb from the cast. Gertrude Berg, without whom there would have been no show, talked with her co-star and came away persuaded of his innocence. Together, they decided to fight back. But in 1951, General Foods fulfilled its threats and withdrew its sponsorship, and the show was dropped by CBS. David Sarnoff, certain that both the show and Phillip Loeb's career were salvageable, quickly picked it up for NBC, but by then no other sponsors could be found. Reluctantly, Gertrude Berg decided that it was better to fire one actor from her show than to close it entirely, and put some forty other actors out of work, and offered Loeb eighty-five thousand dollars for the balance of his contract. Loeb refused the money, but agreed to leave the show. In 1952, "The Goldbergs" returned to the air with another actor, Harold Stone, in the role of Jake Goldberg. But the old chemistry of the two actors was not the same. The ratings declined, and the show went off the air in 1955.

Phillip Loeb, meanwhile, could have used the money. A schizophrenic son in a private mental hospital was costing him twelve thousand dollars a year, and now not only HUAC but the Internal Revenue Service was after him, investigating possible tax delinquencies. His troubles were also costing him a sizable amount in legal fees. Loeb removed his son from the private sanitarium, and placed him in a Veterans Administration hospital. He could find

no work. For a while, he moved in with his old friends Kate and
Zero Mostel. Deeply depressed, he began talking about yearning
for some "long peace." On September 1, 1955, he checked into
the seedy old Taft Hotel on Broadway under the alias of Fred
Lange of Philadelphia — a name that could be roughly translated
as "long peace." There he swallowed a lethal dose of sleeping
pills.

Through all this, interestingly enough, the kingpins of the entertainment business — the Sam Goldwyns, the L. B. Mayers, the
David Sarnoffs — never had their loyalty questioned, were never
accused of being Reds, and were never blacklisted, though they
were all as Russian-born as Lewis Milestone. It was only the
underlings who were singled out for persecution — the writers,
directors, actors, who took their orders from above. This was odd
because it could be inferred that HUAC assumed that the big
motion picture and television producers were unaware of the kind
of pro-Red propaganda they were turning out, that the studio heads
and television presidents had been subverted by those lower down
the corporate ladder — on the face of it an unlikely possibility.
There was the fact, of course, that the original blacklist had been
drawn up by the studio heads themselves. This meant that they
were policing their organizations against undesirables and disloyal
elements, and that their own loyalties to the flag could therefore
not be questioned.

But there is another fact, more subtle, to be taken into consideration in examining why the tycoons of the entertainment industry
escaped having to account for their politics before groups such as
HUAC, while the punishment was passed along to their salaried
employees. The fact is that most of the industry leaders had crossed
the invisible borderline that separated "Jew" from "American,"
which, in turn, meant Christian. During the HUAC era, and the
McCarthy period that followed closely on its tail, it was better to
be Christian than Jewish. At the hearings, the Christian Savior
was frequently invoked. It was as though the soldiers of Christ
marched under an American banner, while Russia was the anti-
Christ. Hedda Hopper, albeit no doubt unwittingly, expressed this
sentiment when she referred to Lewis Milestone as a "Russian,"
and his wife as an "American." On the surface, it was a ridiculous
distinction. Lewis Milestone was an American citizen in as good

standing as Miss Hopper. But Milestone had not been *born* an
American. It was a case of native versus foreigner.

But then why was Lewis Milestone more a foreigner than, say,
the Russian-born Louis B. Mayer or Samuel Goldwyn? For one
thing, both Mayer and Goldwyn had gone a step farther. They had
not only married native-born Americans, but they had married
non-Jewish Americans. That meant that they were trying harder
to be *real* Americans, didn't it? Their hearts, and their loyalties,
had to be in the right places, while others, like Lewis Milestone,
were just using their token Americanism as a cover-up for nefarious
and alien thoughts and ideologies and deeds. Their citizenship
didn't matter. They were in America, Miss Hopper suggested, only
on some trumped-up pretext that was probably subversive, and
only on borrowed time. If they can't think and behave like the rest
of us, she seemed to say, better to get rid of the lot of them. In
her little gossip-column item, which destroyed Milestone's career,
she was absentmindedly writing a sort of WASP obituary for America's Russian Jews who had not assimilated sufficiently.

By the same token, no one in the 1950s would have questioned
the Russian-born Irving Berlin's American loyalties, and this had
little to do with the blithely patriotic nature of some of Berlin's
most popular songs. He, too, had proved himself by marrying an
American, and Christian, woman. She was a young *New Yorker*
writer named Ellin Mackay, but there was more to her story than
that. She was a granddaughter of an Irish Catholic immigrant
named John William Mackay, who, in the 1840s, had struck it
rich in the Comstock Lode, and found himself a two-fifths owner
of the richest gold and silver mine in the world. His son, Clarence
Mackay, Ellin's father, had gone sailing into the American upper
crust, had married the aristocratic Katherine Alexander Duer, and
had settled down to a life of moneyed leisure at Harbor Point, his
estate on Long Island's North Shore, where, in 1924, the Mackays
had given a memorable private dinner and ball for the visiting
Prince of Wales.

A year after the ball, in an article for the *New Yorker* called
"The Declining Function," Ellin Mackay had written, "Modern
girls are conscious of the importance of their own identity, and
they marry whom they choose, satisfied to satisfy themselves. They

are not so keenly aware, as were their parents, of the vast difference between a brilliant match and a *mésalliance*."

A year after those prophetic words were published, and to the much-publicized consternation of her Roman Catholic parents, she proved she meant what she was saying when she made her mesalliance with the young Russian-Jewish composer. The Berlin-Mackay nuptials created even more stir in the press than the Stokes-Pastor marriage of two decades earlier. But the Berlins' would prove a lasting union.

Of course, one does not stop being Jewish simply by marrying out of the faith, and, by the 1950s, an even more interesting phenomenon had been taking place.

Dorothy Schiff, the former publisher of the *New York Post*, once said, "As to being Jewish, C. P. Snow wrote that once you reach a certain financial level, people don't think of you as anything but rich." Mrs. Schiff happened to be speaking as a German Jew, whose Frankfurt-born grandfather, the legendary Jacob, had emigrated to America in 1865. But by the 1950s it seemed possible that the Russian Jews, who had emigrated a full generation later, had chosen to follow the German mode. The richest Eastern Europeans had become what their parents and grandparents once deplored about the Germans — "only a little bit Jewish." Their Jewishness had been relegated to the privacy of their homes, families, and temples and synagogues, if any. Their public facade was that of Americans — successful, rich Americans. If Ben Hecht had conducted his little three-man survey about David Selznick in the 1950s, instead of the 1940s, he might have got quite a different consensus.

In Hollywood, as we have seen, the great movie producers had deep ambivalence about their Jewishness — particularly once they became rich. Toward the end of his life, Louis B. Mayer, perhaps influenced by his friend Cardinal Spellman, seriously considered converting to Roman Catholicism. As the man who was drawing the highest salary of anyone in the United States, he once commented that he considered himself a good future candidate for sainthood. Harry Cohn, the despotic head of Columbia Pictures, entered life a Russian Jew, and left it a Roman Catholic. Sam Goldwyn's Catholic wife once said that her husband had expressed the wish that they could both become Episcopalians. "After all," he said, "Goldwyn doesn't sound like a Jewish name" — which of course was why he had chosen it. But by the 1950s it didn't matter. He was rich.

In the world of radio and television, this conscious non-Semitic facade had become if anything more pronounced, as though the newer media had decided to follow the de-Semitization guidelines laid down by the Hollywood of old. Though the boardrooms of the three major networks had become largely populated by descendants of Russian Jews, the out-front faces that the public saw would be the Christian ones of Walter Cronkite, John Chancellor, David Brinkley, Chet Huntley, Dan Rather, Roger Mudd, Harry Reasoner, and Howard K. Smith. As a result, the general public would not think of television as a Jewish enterprise — simply as a rich one.

Meanwhile, had Rose Pastor Stokes still been around in the 1950s, and had she been a film star or screenwriter, she would have been a sitting duck for something like the House Un-American Activities Committee. She was not rich (she'd muffed that chance). She'd been an avowed Communist (a founder of the American Communist party), even though her crusade had to be accounted a failure. And anti-Russian sentiments were running much stronger in the United States than they had been when Rose was in her fiery prime. She'd probably have gone to jail, and Hedda Hopper probably would have wanted her deported.

In the long run, of course, Miss Hopper's little obituary for Russian Jews who had not quite "made it" would not be taken seriously. But it would represent a kind of WASP blind spot that other American non-Jews would occasionally reveal. The Jews were *foreigners*, citizens of the United States or not.

James Graham Phelps Stokes's second, and Christian, wife would deliver the same sort of innocent obituary about Rose and her "breed" many years later. Showing the same blind spot, revealing the same misunderstanding of what Rose had been all about, Lettice Sands Stokes would also manage, in her appraisal of Rose, to get some of her facts mixed up.

James G. Phelps Stokes died in 1960, still a member of all his prestigious WASP clubs — the University, the Church, the Pilgrims, the Sons of the American Revolution, the Society of Colonial

Wars. By then his widow could only speak vaguely of Rose's role in her late husband's life. "I would have liked to have *met* her," she recalled,

because she was from all I'd heard a very — *colorful* character, beautiful, with magnificent red hair. But *my* Graham [Mrs. Stokes would seem to make a distinction between her Graham and Rose's Graham] never liked to talk about her much. He was interested in settlement work, and improving living and working conditions on the Lower East Side, and so was she. He admired her, and wanted to help her. But he felt he couldn't just *give* her money and so, to help her, he married her. It was not a passionate love affair, I gather, the way most are. It was more of a meeting of the minds, I suppose. But then she became interested and involved in the Bolshevik uprising, joined them, and went to Russia to fight with them. [Actually, Rose took no active part in the Russian revolution, although she did visit Russia afterward to see how the new system was working.] She came home and tried to obstruct the war effort and the draft — *my* Graham was in the Fourteenth Squadron of the United States National Guard at the time — and she landed in Fort Leavenworth. My Graham had the *devil* of a time trying to get her out. [In fact, Rose was never jailed and was free on bond pending her appeal.] It was very hard on him. Every time either one of them stepped out of doors there were photographers and reporters asking questions. She became a full-fledged Communist. My husband was interested in social problems until the day he died, but never to that extent. He was never a radical. They were separated for a long time, and the divorce was as quiet as he could make it, with no scandal. But it was a tragic story. She was *foreign*, you see, and not accustomed to our ways.

18

"PEOPLE WHO ARE SOLID"

To American Jews in general, in their second and third American generations, there was a new and nagging question of how much commitment to — or rejection of — the new State of Israel was expected of them. There was no doubt that the creation of Israel enhanced American Jews' feelings of self-worth, but there was more to it than that. Along with the guarded new sense of pride in nationhood came a more sobering responsibility, for now Jews everywhere would be asked, or expected, to shoulder the criticism whenever Israel was involved in anything that was less than honorable — Jewish terrorists, for example — and would resent being unjustly asked to share the blame for any of Israel's mistakes. If Israel could be counted upon to be always in the right, that would be one thing. But that was an unrealistic hope for any country, new or old, and if ever Israel seemed demonstrably in the wrong, would that redound to the discredit of American Jews? Alas, it would seem so. This knowledge that Jews would be expected to respond with either patriotism or apology, depending upon how Israel was being perceived at any given moment in the eyes of the rest of the world, would create another subtle reason for Jewish sensitivity, touchiness. If American Jews had already learned to live in two communities, Israel added a third kind of emotional citizenship. It was a large order.

Many prominent American Jews made it a point to take at least one token trip to Israel in demonstration of support for the new country. David Sarnoff's was in the summer of 1952, when the Weizmann Institute of Science presented him with its first honorary fellowship. In 1957, Sam Bronfman donated the Biblical and Archeological Museum to Israel, but did not actually visit the country until five years later, when he presided over the dedication of a new wing for the Israeli Museum in Jerusalem, for which he had given an even million dollars. But his principal benefactions remained on the North American continent, such as the Saidye Bronfman Cultural Center in Montreal, and the Bronfman Science Center at Williams College, in Massachusetts.

Others, however, have been more ambivalent. Typical of these is Jack Rosenthal, deputy editorial-page editor of the *New York Times*, who has said, "I was born in Palestine — but my parents had the sense to get out quickly, when I was three years old. I have no memory of it, and I've never been back. I feel no emotional attachment to Israel — only a kind of abstract curiosity. I feel the same way about Tokyo — another place I'd like to visit someday."

But at least one wealthy American Jew longed for a peaceful refuge in Israel, and, ironically, it would be denied him. This was Meyer Lansky. "America — Love It or Leave It" was a slogan bruited about by certain superpatriotic types in the 1960s, in answer to the demonstrations of the New Left. But in Lansky's case, at least as far as the United States government was concerned, the principle seemed to be, "America — Love It or Stay." He had been accused, both in the press and in the courts, of virtually every heinous crime against society — of drug trafficking, prostitution, running numbers and protection rackets, illegal gambling, art theft, extortion, and, of course, of having ordered the murder of Benny Siegel. He had been called the Chief of Chiefs of the Mafia, the Brains Behind the Mob, and Public Enemy Number One. The government had succeeded in getting Lansky's old friend Lucky Luciano deported to Italy. One would suppose the government would have been equally eager to see Lansky shipped to some even farther distant foreign shore, particularly when he wanted to go at his own expense. But, illogically, the United States authorities seemed determined to keep America's menace firmly in America's midst.

The trouble was that the federal government had been unable to make any of its plethora of charges against Lansky stick. And so, frustrated, it kept trying.

Everywhere he went he was tailed by federal agents. At his

homes in New York and Florida, he had grown accustomed to periodic hammerings on his front door, and cries of "Open up in the name of the law," and to greeting officers with subpoenas and summonses and search warrants. His homes had been ransacked so often that he was resigned to it. When he traveled, he was routinely frisked and searched at airports. When he tried to take a holiday in Acapulco, federal agents followed him there, invaded his hotel suite, searched it, and even cut out the linings of his suitcases looking for contraband. Everywhere, his telephone lines were tapped, his conversations taped, so that for any important telephone call he had to use a pay booth. During one airport search, agents, rummaging through his luggage, came upon a bottle of white pills in his toilet kit. Triumphantly, they shouted, "Drugs!" It turned out to be medication his doctor had prescribed for stomach ulcers, which Lansky had certainly earned in his career. Lansky always tried to be pleasant and cooperative during these intrusions, but his daily life had become something of an ordeal, and that had taken its toll on both his patience and his health.

Also, needless to say, defending the various actions that his government kept pressing against him kept his lawyers busy and kept Lansky paying hefty legal fees. But then his income was considerable, and his books would demonstrate that most of it came from perfectly legal shares of ownership in various Las Vegas casinos and hotels. In addition to the Flamingo, Lansky had interests in nearly every establishment on the celebrated Strip, including the Desert Inn, the Sands, the Stardust, and the Fremont. Yet why, he would complain, would each new legitimate venture of someone like himself invariably be described as an "infiltration" — as though the act of going legitimate were, in his case, somehow subversive.

As for whatever didn't show up on Lansky's books, that information was securely locked in the well-guarded repository that was Meyer Lansky's brain. Without the key to that, all efforts to find evidence of wrongdoing were futile.

Income tax evasion, of course, had been the undoing of many another criminal. It would be the downfall of Mickey Cohen, who would be sentenced to fifteen years at Alcatraz for that offense — causing Cohen to complain that all his troubles had begun when he *started* paying taxes, which was the first signal to the government that he had any income at all. Lansky, however, had always paid his large taxes scrupulously, on the large income he reported. If there was additional income that he was not reporting, the government simply could not find it, and it was a matter of guesswork. The government suspected large amounts of unreported income, but had not been able to come up with a shred of proof.

Furthermore, despite the Master Criminal reputation that now followed him wherever he went, Meyer Lansky had been convicted of a wrongdoing only once. This had occurred in 1953, when Lansky was arrested for operating an illegal gambling casino at the Arrowhead Inn outside Saratoga Springs. He pleaded guilty, and was sentenced to ninety days in jail — a minor charge and a minor punishment. After serving sixty days, he was released for good behavior. Later, Lansky would tell his three co-biographers, Dennis Eisenberg, Uri Dan, and Eli Landau, that he blamed that arrest on "bad timing." There had been gambling establishments throughout the Adirondacks — Lansky was a part owner of at least one other besides the Arrowhead Inn — and they were popular tourist attractions. But the Kefauver Committee had just completed its report on organized crime, and, said Lansky, "I'm sure the reason why the cops in Saratoga suddenly took action was that Governor Dewey ordered an investigation because of the Kefauver Report." That one offense remained — and remains today — the extent of Meyer Lansky's criminal record.

Of course one reason why it was difficult to pin anything on Meyer Lansky may have had something to do with his physical appearance and personality. The trim, diminutive fellow just didn't match anyone's mental picture of a master felon. He didn't sport loud neckties, flashy jewelry, white-on-white shirts, and pin-striped suits with wide lapels. In appearance he looked no more dangerous or threatening than anyone's family dentist. In manner, he was kindly, grandfatherly. (Mickey Cohen was given to frequent bursts of temper and foul language, and his smashed-nosed face looked as though it had been designed for a post office WANTED poster.) Most people who met him immediately liked him, including the FBI men who were assigned to follow him and who occasionally, if somewhat shamefacedly, let him buy them drinks or take them out to dinner at restaurants where Lansky, a generous but not extravagant tipper, was always a favored customer. At Imperial

House in Miami Beach, where Lansky and his wife had a large and comfortable but not ostentatious condominium, the Lanskys were considered ideal neighbors. In fact, his presence in the building gave the other tenants an added sense of security. One neighbor, who knew him slightly, recalls him as "a perfectly *darling* little man." Public Enemy Number One had no noticeable vices. He didn't drink, though he did chain-smoke. He was a faithful husband, a devoted father to his three children. He loved animals, and curbed his dog, a tiny Shih Tzu, whenever he walked it, with the usual FBI men a few respectful paces behind, waiting to catch him in some felonious act.

His personal life was almost entirely free from scandal. When, in one Bureau report, Lansky's daughter Sandra was described as "a divorcee of doubtful reputation resident New York City," Lansky was outraged. It was true that his daughter was divorced, he protested, and of course he had been saddened by that, but that did not make her reputation "doubtful." Sandra was a law-abiding housewife, a fine, upstanding Jewish woman. The closest thing to scandal to touch the Lanskys' lives was the murder, in 1977, of one of his stepsons, Richard Schwartz, who was shot in his car behind a restaurant he owned in Florida. Schwartz had been about to stand trial for the alleged murder of a young man named Craig Teriaca four months earlier when the two, in a barroom argument over who was going to pay the check, became violent and Schwartz pulled out a gun and shot Teriaca in the chest.

The press, making much of the Jewish and Italian names, called Schwartz's murder a gangland-style revenge murder, and Teriaca's father was said to be a Mafia member. This may have been true, but Lansky had another explanation. "You see, Richard had been drinking too much. He was really an alcoholic — and carrying a gun when you're drinking is crazy, never mind that his was licensed. Several months before he died he had started swinging his gun around a lot. I think it went off accidentally and killed the man he was drinking with. Richard had four children — one of them spent two years in a kibbutz in Israel, by the way. I'm sure his death wasn't vengeance by the Mafia. It was probably suicide, a straightforward family tragedy."

By 1970, meanwhile, Lansky had begun to weary of the constant surveillance under which the government was keeping him. He was sixty-eight years old, his heart had been giving him a bit of trouble, and there was the recurring problem of his stomach ulcers. Over the years, he had been very generous to Israel — not only with personal contributions, but also by regularly turning over his Las Vegas hotels and casinos for Bonds for Israel rallies. Israel continued to offer itself as a land of refuge to Jews of any nationality. Lansky's grandparents were buried there. There, he decided, he and his wife would go to live out their twilight years in peace. Though the United States government was still fruitlessly pressing a number of different charges against him, Lansky had begun to fear that his luck might be running out. He had become convinced that, if he remained in the United States, the FBI would find some way or other to get him behind bars. He had begun to see himself, rightly or wrongly, as a victim of anti-Semitism — and it was true that a number of FBI reports on his activities had mentioned him as part of "the Jewish element" in organized crime. Lansky applied for, and received, an Israeli tourist visa, and flew with his wife to Tel Aviv, where he planned to apply for Israeli citizenship. His visa was good for two years.

Lansky spent his two tourist years in Israel pulling every string, using every contact and connection he could muster to try to gain his citizenship. He even had a friend who was on good terms with Golda Meir take his case directly to the prime minister. Mrs. Meir was sympathetic, and agreed that the one gambling charge for which Lansky had been convicted was definitely minor. But she refused to commit herself. The original blanket invitation to all Jews had been given a bothersome amendment in 1950 to bar any Jewish "undesirable." It was in this category that the FBI insisted that the Israelis place Lansky in order that he could be returned to the United States to face the various indictments it had waiting for him.

In the end, according to his biographers, Lansky became a bargaining chip in an international power maneuver that was being played out between Israel and the United States. The Six Day War was over, but Russia had begun selling missiles to the Egyptians, and Mrs. Meir was worried about an arms buildup in the Sinai. France, meanwhile, had declined to sell Israel any more of the Mirage jets that had been so helpful in the war. But a deal was about to be struck with Washington whereby Israel could purchase a number of 1140-E Phantom fighter-bombers. So determined was the FBI to have Meyer Lansky back within its jurisdiction, incredible though it seemed, that part of Washington's price for the planes was the return of Meyer Lansky. Israel was advised that if it gave Lansky asylum, the planes might not be forthcoming. And Golda Meir wanted her fighter planes more than she wanted to help Meyer Lansky.

In November, 1972, a few days before his visa would expire, Lansky realized that his cause was hopeless. If Israel did not want him, he decided, he would leave the country voluntarily. Armed with a clutch of airplane tickets and entry visas to a number of South American countries that he hoped might take him in, he headed for the Tel Aviv airport. He had no sooner passed through Passport Control, however, than he was joined by FBI agents, who followed him on a zigzag journey halfway around the globe — to Geneva, Rio de Janeiro, Buenos Aires, Paraguay — where, at each stop, he was denied entry despite his valid documents. His last hope was Panama, for which he also had a visa. Alas, he was denied entry to Panama. The FBI had done its advance work well. The next stop was Miami.

The irony was that, during the decade that followed, in none of the cases that the government had arrayed against him was the government able to obtain a conviction. Millions of dollars of American taxpayers' money were spent, only to have case after case dismissed for insufficient evidence. And so, in the end, officially declared innocent of all his crimes, Lansky was allowed to live out his life in retirement at Imperial House, forbidden to leave the country, his passport revoked, forbidden to go to Israel — the man who may have been the most successful criminal in American history sentenced to life imprisonment in Miami Beach. At the time of his forced return, Lansky was both bitter and philosophical. "That's life," he told reporters. "At my age, it's too late to worry. What will be will be. A Jew has a slim chance in the world." He died in Miami in January, 1983, at eighty-one.

Asked once what he considered his greatest feat, Lansky did not mention his bootlegging millions, his contributions to Israel and its war of independence, or even his extraordinary ability to stay out of federal prisons. He did not mention his knack, in a business where lives were often cut off exceptionally early, of staying alive until a ripe old age. Nor did he mention his son, the West Point graduate, or his daughter, the suburban matron, or his law-abiding grandchildren. Rather, he felt that his most significant contribution had been in striking blows against social anti-Semitism in America. "Bugsy and I could never stand hypocrisy," he told his biographers. "People would come to our casinos and gamble and then go back to Washington or New York and make pious speeches about how immoral gambling was. But they didn't make speeches about something I think was a lot worse. When we started out, most of Florida and many resorts in other parts of the country were out of bounds to Jews. Before the Second World War, Jews were forbidden to step inside some hotels and casinos and apartment houses. Our casinos were pleasant places and open to everybody. Jews, Christians, Arabs, anybody could come and gamble."

Seated in the blue-and-white living room of the Imperial House apartment overlooking Miami Beach, Meyer Lansky's widow, whom everyone in the building affectionately calls Teddy, reminisces about her husband. Still petite and pretty in her mid-seventies, she sits surrounded by a collection of Lalique and Steuben crystal objects, a particular enthusiasm of hers. Books on Lalique glass adorn the glass-topped coffee table. Teddy Lansky thinks, perhaps understandably, that her late husband was much misunderstood by the public, much maligned by the press. "Most of what they wrote about him was fiction," she tells her visitor, "including how rich he was. Hundreds of millions! What hat do they pull figures like that out of? One of his troubles was that he handed out money to anybody who asked. Oh, I suppose my life with Meyer may have seemed difficult, but it wasn't difficult for me because I loved the man. Once, when I was coming back from Europe, a lady reporter from I think CBS stuck a microphone in my face and asked me how it felt to be the Godmother. I'm afraid I did a very unladylike thing."

Teddy Lansky shows her visitor her ultramodern kitchen. One of her hobbies is cooking, and friends have urged her to write a cookbook. When her son was living, she and her daughter-in-law used to do all the baking for the restaurant, called The Inside, that Richard Schwartz ran, and Mrs. Lansky still contributes baked goods to this establishment. Another hobby is horticulture, and the apartment also houses many lush, tropical plants. "Still, people come to me and want to talk about Murder Incorporated," she says. "That was another invention of the media. One reason why the government couldn't make any of its cases against him stick was that he told the truth. In one case, I was called as a witness, and the government lost the case simply because I told the truth." She produces a photograph of her late husband, taken when he was in his fifties, and says, "Tell me what you see in this face." Then she answers herself. "Character. Strength of character. Integrity. He wasn't a great talker, but he had a dry, quiet wit. He was the kind of man who could be in a room full of people, with everybody talking, and Meyer would say something, and everybody would stop talking, just to hear what he had to say. You could hear a pin drop. Yes, he was a small man — small in stature. But he was also a *big* man — big in every other sense. Was he bitter about the way the government treated him? Never! It was all political, you know. He understood that, and he forgave."

Of Mr. Sam Bronfman's four children, "the artistic one" was the younger of his two daughters, Phyllis. She had graduated from Vassar, where she had majored in history, and been briefly married to a suave European-born financier named Jean Lambert. But by the early 1950s, while her older sister, the Baroness de Gunzburg, was busily carving a place for herself in Paris high society, Phyllis Bronfman Lambert was a reclusive divorcée living in a modest Left Bank atelier and studying painting and sculpture. Minda de Gunzburg had become a regular at the showings of French couturiers, but Phyllis's uniform was a pair of carpenter's bib-topped coveralls and scuffed sneakers. Her father fretted that she was turning into a wealthy, expatriated beatnik.

In 1954, to give her something to do as much as for any other reason, her father sent Phyllis an architectural rendering of a new Seagram's world headquarters building he planned to erect on property he had acquired at 375 Park Avenue, opposite New York's elite Racquet and Tennis Club, and asked her what she thought of the drawings.

Phyllis leaped to the bait. She thought the design for the new building was atrocious, and she dashed off a lengthy critique to her father explaining just why she thought so. Impressed, her father put her in charge of the new building's design, and for the next three years Phyllis had a full-time job.

She researched contemporary architects, visited their studios, interviewed them, studied their models and sketches, and explored their buildings. She consulted with museum heads and city planning experts, pored through volumes of architectural books and magazines. She signed up for courses at the Yale School of Architecture. In the end, she decided that only one man must design her father's new office building — the master himself, Ludwig Mies van der Rohe. Van der Rohe agreed, and was given free rein with the forty-one-million-dollar project. Mr. Sam offered only one injunction, which was to "make this building the crowning glory of your life as well as mine." A slight hitch was encountered when it was discovered that the celebrated Mies, then at the peak of his career at sixty-eight, had no license to practice architecture in New York State. He had been completely self-taught, had not even attended high school, but in order to obtain the necessary building permits the architect had to be licensed, and in order to obtain a license Ludwig Mies van der Rohe would have to take a state-administered test, like an ordinary civil servant. Huffily, the great man refused to comply with this demeaning bureaucratic condition. But the problem was solved — by Phyllis — by having the New York architect Philip Johnson named as Mies's collaborator.

When the bronze and glass Seagram tower opened its doors in 1957, it was hailed by art and architecture critics all over the world as not only the crowning glory of Mies van der Rohe's career but as the crowning glory of New York City and perhaps one of the most strikingly beautiful office buildings in the world. Lavish — even wasteful, economically — in its generosity of outside space, the building is set back from a huge public plaza of marble and pink granite, made inviting by a brace of fountained reflecting pools. Through most of its main floor, which a less generous designer would have given over to shops and other commercial space, runs the spectacular block-long Four Seasons restaurant. There were even unexpected design benefits. Again, with Phyllis supervising the interior details — including the furniture — the windows of the restaurant facing the street and plaza were strung with thousands of yards of bronze and gold watch chains, looping festoons to give the effect of Austrian shades. When the air-circulating system was turned on, it was discovered that this caused the tiers of chains to shiver and shimmer in perpetual movement, an effect that was as delightful within the restaurant as it was to passersby outside. "This building," declared Edgar Bronfman proudly — he had that year been named president of Joseph E. Seagram and Sons — "is our greatest piece of advertising and public relations. It establishes us once and for all, right around the world, as people who are solid and care about quality."

Well, yes, in a sense that was so, though Edgar Bronfman still seemed to be brushing at the spiderwebs of raffishness and scandal that had clung to the family and its business since the old days of Prohibition and bootlegging. There were some who might have argued that there seemed to be something in the Bronfman family temperament that kept giving the family unwanted headlines, and with each new one some diligent reporter would hark back to the unsolved murder of Paul Matoff in 1922. In 1965, for example, Phyllis Lambert's ex-husband's partners were involved in a complex variety of deals that culminated with the seventy-five-million-dollar bankruptcy of the Atlantic Acceptance Corporation, which Jean Lambert had helped organize. By then, he and Phyllis had been divorced for more than a decade, and Lambert himself was absolved of any involvement in the debacle, but it was a fact that Lambert's seed money in his enterprises had been a million-dollar loan from his then wife.

There were also events in Edgar Bronfman's life that a purist would probably not regard as the acts of the kind of "solid people" Edgar aspired to be. Like his father, Edgar Bronfman seemed to have a quick temper and to wear more than a small chip on his shoulder. At Williams College, where he had enrolled with the class of 1950, Edgar had started out as an attractive and well-liked freshman, and most of his classmates were unaware — since Edgar appeared to have very little spending money — that his family was wealthy. In fact, to earn extra pin money, Edgar worked as a caddy at a Williamstown golf course. The impression of him changed drastically, however, when his parents arrived on the campus to take their son home for the Christmas holidays — in a chauffeur-driven Rolls with a footman, and a mink lap robe spread out on the backseat. Thereafter, the bar at Edgar's Delta Phi fraternity house was generously supplied with Seagram products, courtesy of Mr. Sam.

No one knew exactly what caused Edgar's blowup in his junior year in 1949. There was a rumor at the time that one of his fraternity brothers had made an anti-Semitic remark (unlikely, since Delta Phi was a predominantly Jewish fraternity), or a comment to the effect that "we only took you in because your father gives us booze." In any case, Edgar responded by going on a late-night motorcycle spree, not only through the surrounding countryside but also through the rooms of the fraternity house, causing considerable damage and otherwise disturbing the quietude of the New England college town. The next morning, he was asked to leave. Mr. Sam tried to intercede by calling on James A. Linen, then the publisher of *Time* and a Williams trustee. Linen's intervention saved Edgar from official expulsion, but it was agreed that he would continue his education at McGill University, where he was given a degree in 1951. Some years later, his $3.5 million gift to Williams of its Bronfman Science Center was taken as his peace offering to the school.

By the early 1970s, Edgar's marriage to the former Ann Loeb was in difficulties. But since his college escapade, with the exception of one or two defiant gestures, Edgar had remained very much under his father's thumb. When the possibility of a divorce was brought up, his father would not hear of it. He had set his dynastic hopes on Edgar. Edgar and Ann Bronfman had produced five handsome children, four of them sons. Besides, one divorce in the family was enough. "I've set it up much better than the Rothschilds," Sam once said. "They spread the children. I've kept them together." By this he meant that he had kept the money, and the power, of the family firmly in his own direct line. His brothers, and their children, were permitted only the leftovers.

But the patriarch was growing old, and he was ill and losing his grip. By 1970, even he knew that he was dying of cancer. He died in the summer of 1971 — unknighted, still an outsider to both the U.S. and Canadian social establishments he had spent his life trying to join.

The mantle fell upon Edgar, then forty-two. He responded by almost immediately kicking up his heels in ways not usually associated with "people who are solid." But then, no doubt he felt that he had earned his stripes, and now that he was his own boss, had the right to exercise the perquisites that went with heading a great family business.

His first priorities were personal, however. He immediately took steps to divorce his wife, and the marriage was terminated in 1973. Soon after that, his name was sensationally in the newspapers. He was engaged to marry a beautiful, blond twenty-eight-year-old titled Englishwoman, Lady Carolyn Townshend. Lady Carolyn was described as a descendant of Viscount Townshend of Raynham, who introduced scientific farming to England in 1730 by feeding his cattle turnips during winter months, which had earned him the sobriquet "Turnip Townshend." Lady Carolyn had been married, and divorced, once before, and she and Edgar had known each other since 1968, when she had gone to work in Seagram's London offices.

Edgar's premarital settlement on Her Ladyship, who explained that she liked financial security, was generous, and well publicized. She would receive $1,000,000 in cash; the deed to Edgar's country estate in Westchester County would be placed in her name; she was allowed to select $115,000 worth of jewelry; and she was to be given — in addition to all expenses of running a household — an allowance of $4,000 a month as personal pocket money to spend as she chose. A lavish wedding took place in December of 1973 at the Saint Regis Hotel in New York. But the aftermath was considerably less cheerful, according to court testimony that followed soon afterward.

On their wedding night, Lady Carolyn banished Edgar to his Manhattan apartment, and refused to join him on their nuptial bed. This situation continued, according to Edgar, during their honeymoon in Acapulco. Thus rebuffed, Edgar took Lady Carolyn to court to break the premarital agreement. The testimony was spicy, to say the least. In Acapulco, declared Lady Carolyn, Edgar had spoken bluntly of his desires, which Lady Carolyn did not consider a very gentlemanly or romantic approach. "I told Edgar he was not being very affectionate with me," she testified. Edgar denied this, and in turn testified that his bride "had a hangup about sex after the marriage" — adding that she had shown no such sexual inhibitions during the courtship period. The impression grew that Lady Carolyn had lost interest in sex as soon as the prenuptial agreement had been signed. In the end, the court took Edgar's side, and Lady Carolyn was ordered to return the million, the deed, and the jewels. Edgar agreed to alimony of forty thousand dollars a year for eleven years. Naturally, there were some people who expressed surprise that the young president of Seagram's would go to court to air his sex life in such a public way but, as Edgar explained it, "I hate to be taken."

The next Bronfman sensation occurred barely a year later, in the summer of 1975. His twenty-three-year-old son, Samuel Bronfman II, left the family's Westchester estate one evening to visit friends and a few hours later telephoned the family butler to say, "Call my father. I've been kidnapped!" For the next few days, the Bronfman estate was the storm center of frantic comings and goings of police cars, helicopters, and FBI agents, while hundreds of newspaper reporters set up camp outside the gates. At length, a ransom demand was received — for 4.5 million dollars in twenty-dollar bills, the largest ransom ever asked in American kidnapping history. Raising the money, Edgar Bronfman announced, would be no problem. The problem was logistical, since that much money in small bills would fill fourteen ordinary-sized suitcases. Presently, the ransom demand was cut in half, to 2.3 million, and on an August night Edgar handed this amount, stuffed into two large garbage bags, to a solitary figure near New York's Queensborough Bridge who quickly drove off with the money. The next day, tipped off by a limousine driver named Dominic Byrne, who had been a part of the scheme but who had got cold feet, police found young Sam, bound and blindfolded, in the Brooklyn apartment of a fireman named Mel Patrick Lynch. The youth was unharmed.

In the lengthy trial that followed, the story grew more lurid and bizarre. Lynch claimed that he had first met young Bronfman in a gay bar in Manhattan, and that the two had become homosexual lovers. Together, with an assist from Byrne, they had cooked up the kidnapping scheme as a means of extracting money from young Sam's father. Young Sam hotly denied this, and claimed that he had spent his days in Lynch's apartment lashed to a chair with rope, unable to move, and in terror of his life. But the story began to seem less than likely when a juror asked to examine the rope with which Sam, a strapping six foot three, had been bound. When the juror picked up the rope, it fell apart in several places. Why hadn't Sam, who had been left alone for several periods, been able to wriggle free? Then there was the puzzling matter of the tape-recorded message that had come from young Sam to his father, imploring Edgar to pay the ransom as quickly as possible. At the end of this entreaty, the youth was heard to turn to his captors and say, in a normal tone of voice, "Hold it, I'll do it again." In the end, the jury acquitted both Lynch and Byrne of kidnapping, but found them guilty of the lesser charge of attempted extortion.

Immediately after the trial, Edgar and young Sam held an angry press conference in the Seagram Building, during which they defended young Sam's honor, his heterosexuality, his lack of a motive — he had all the money in the world already, young Sam pointed out — and condemned everyone connected with the trial: the judge, the jury, the police, the FBI, and, for good measure, the press itself.

Three days later, the Bronfman kidnapping story ended with a touch of soap opera — the gala wedding, in Westchester, of Edgar Bronfman to Miss Georgiana Eileen Webb. Like the previous Mrs. Bronfman, she was younger than her husband — just two years older than young Sam — and English, though her background was somewhat different from that of Lady Carolyn Townshend. Her father ran a pub in Finchingfield, northeast of London, where the bride had worked as a barmaid. The pub was called Ye Olde Nosebag, and the press had a good time with "liquor baron weds barmaid" stories. The new Mrs. Bronfman announced her intention of converting to Judaism to please her husband. Meanwhile, someone had come up with the discovery that old Mr. Sam Bronfman's estate in Tarrytown had been sold to, and converted into the American headquarters of, the Reverend Sun Myung Moon.

Not long afterward, young Sam Bronfman himself was married to a Jewish girl named Melanie Mann.

While the Bronfman family's private lives were taking on something of an air of a three-ring circus, Edgar Bronfman was also demonstrating an ability to make headlines in the financial pages. He had always been more than a little stagestruck and, in the 1960s — against his father's wishes — he had joined forces with producer Stuart Ostrow to form Sagittarius Productions, which had as some of its more conspicuous hits the musicals *1776*, *The Apple*

Tree, and *Pippin,* along with some better-forgotten failures. Then, in 1967, Edgar decided to buy Metro-Goldwyn-Mayer — another decision his father strongly opposed. After Seagram's had laid out some forty million dollars in the takeover attempt, Mr. Sam nervously called his son aside and said, "Tell me, Edgar, are we buying all this stock in MGM just so you can get laid?" To which Edgar breezily replied, "Oh, no, Pop. It doesn't cost forty million dollars to get laid." Though Edgar briefly succeeded in getting on the MGM board, the takeover eventually failed, and how much the company lost in the process has never been revealed, though the financial press placed the figure in the neighborhood of ten million dollars.

By 1981 Mr. Sam Bronfman was dead, and that was the year Edgar decided to take another giant plunge, and placed himself at the center of one of the great corporate takeover battles of that year. Seagram's, it seemed, found itself with the embarrassing sum of 3.7 *billion* dollars lying about and waiting to be invested. The target Edgar decided to go after was the smallish but very lucrative oil company known as Conoco. Another giant corporation that also had its eye on Conoco was DuPont of Delaware. In the battle of giants that ensued, Seagram bought twenty-seven percent of Conoco's stock before being outmaneuvered by DuPont. But the fight ended in more or less a draw, and Edgar was not altogether unhappy with the outcome. Nor were Seagram's losses what they had been in the case of MGM. With the conversion of Conoco to DuPont stock that followed the acquisition, Seagram wound up owning twenty percent of DuPont — more than any single member of the du Pont family,* and enough to send Edgar Bronfman sailing onto DuPont's board of directors.

Today, Edgar Bronfman continues to swim upstream in the riskiest financial waters, taking his wins and his losses with the same almost brash élan. Like his father, who once quipped that mankind's greatest invention was not the wheel, but interest, Edgar is the author of the oft-quoted monetary epigram: "To turn a hundred dollars into a hundred and ten dollars is work. To turn a hundred million into a hundred and ten million is inevitable." Thus the

---

*Which does not capitalize the *d* as the company does.

rich get richer. At the time of the Conoco fight, with all that Seagram money burning holes in his pockets, he told a reporter he had asked himself, "What would my father do?" Then he promptly answered his own question with, "Hell, he never had three-point-seven billion!"

19

FROM POLAND TO POLO

THOUGH they seemed blessed — or cursed, depending on how one looked at it — with extraordinary longevity, the founding Russian-Jewish moguls, the men who, as they said, had made it from Poland to polo in one generation, were going one by one. In January, 1973, Adolph Zukor sat in a suite at the Beverly Hilton Hotel in Los Angeles waiting to go downstairs to join the gala dinner party that Paramount Pictures was tossing to honor the founder's one hundredth birthday. No expense had been spared for the party — for such items as seventy crates of rose petals, thirty gross of balloons, and a fourteen-foot-high birthday cake made, appropriately enough, of frosting-coated plywood.

Understandably, in the months of preparation and planning that had gone into the event — making sure that such people as Jack Benny and Mary Livingstone, Anne Baxter, Liv Ullmann, Jimmy Stewart, Barbara Stanwyck, and Bette Davis would all be there — there had been some apprehension on the part of Paramount's board of directors that the elderly honoree might not make it to his own centennial. And, upstairs in his suite, Mr. Zukor was cross. Though he moved slowly, he was able to move about — to make it unaided from his car, two or three times a week, into the card room of the Hillcrest Country Club, where, though he himself no longer played, he liked to watch his friends play bridge and gently kibitz from time to time. His health was fine, he insisted. But now, in their precautionary state, the men who ran his company were insisting that he make his entrance onto the stage in a wheelchair, like an invalid. Furthermore, lest he become overexcited, his entrance was to be delayed until the moment when the huge cake would be rolled in. Zukor was being required to watch the rest of the festive proceedings on a closed-circuit television screen. Furious, he watched as his guests sipped cocktails and otherwise disported themselves in the ballroom below. Finally, Adolph Zukor would have no more of it. Banging his cane on the floor he cried, "God damn it, if I'm supposed to be the star of this show I'm not going to spend all my time waiting in the wings! *Take me down!*" He was taken down. He died four years later, at a hundred and four.

Meanwhile, a whole new Russian-Jewish generation was moving up to fill the shoes, and eventually eclipse the accomplishments, of the oldsters. Brash and young, ambitious and daring and willing to try for the long shot, not all these new entrepreneurs were heirs to great family fortunes like Edgar Bronfman. Some were starting, just as their predecessors had, from scratch, with nothing more than a bright idea and a gambler's nerve. Once again, assimilation was the goal, and, as the older generation had found, assimilation seemed to involve financial success first, and then, it was hoped, some degree of social acceptance by the American establishment. But, once again with this younger generation, assimilation would prove to be a double-edged sword, involving, as it did, the emotional choice of how much Jewishness to retain and how much to abandon on one's journey of upward mobility. Sometimes, in order to assimilate into a new culture or new economic stratum it is necessary to totally deny the old, and in the process, something precious may be lost — a sense of who one really is, or where one came from. To assimilate, after all, means to make oneself similar, to adapt, to blend in, to assume the tone and style and coloration of one's surroundings. But what are the limits of assimilation? At what point does the assimilationist become the apostate? At what point does the assimilationist say good-bye, for instance, to his grandparents or even to his parents? These are questions that many young and successful American Jews of Russian descent would find it difficult to answer in the 1970s.

Ralph Lauren, for example, would much rather talk about his considerable success as a designer than whether he is, or is not, Jewish. "I'm so sick of being described as a poor little Jewish boy from the Bronx who's made good," he says. "Yes, I was born in the Bronx — but in the nice part, the west Bronx, the Mosholu Parkway section, near Riverdale, and I had a wonderful childhood. My parents weren't rich, but they weren't poor either." His father was a painter who specialized in *faux bois* and *faux marbre* work, and did an occasional industrial mural. "And I'm sick of hearing about how I changed my name. The name was Lifschitz. Do you know what it's like growing up as a kid in New York with a name like that? It has 'shit' in it. And *I* didn't change the name. My older brother suggested the change when I was sixteen. We all changed. Still," he adds, "I'm told that the name Lifschitz is a very distinguished name in Russia."*

After graduating from City College, where he majored in business, a major he hated — "My mother wanted me to be a doctor or a lawyer or at least an accountant" — he worked as a clerk in various New York stores, including Brooks Brothers, where he was able to buy classically styled clothes at a discount.

Meanwhile, as the youngest of three boys in the family, Ralph Lauren was often given hand-me-down clothes to wear. Though these outfits were sometimes out of style, Lauren learned to make the most of this fact. An old belted Norfolk jacket, for instance, could, with an upturned collar and the addition of a jaunty scarf, be made to look snappy and debonair. Pleated slacks might have become passé, but with the right belt, shoes, shirt, and other accessories, the young Ralph Lauren — with his close-cropped dark hair, his blue eyes, perfect teeth, and lithe build — could make them look both sporty and sexy. Girls, in particular, began to tell him they liked the way he dressed because he looked "different." All this was in the late 1950s. While his contemporaries were wearing leather jackets, driving motorcycles, and listening to rock music, Lauren was embracing an earlier tradition — that of the 1920s, and *The Great Gatsby,* and the Ivy League look. He was already, like Helena Rubinstein a generation earlier, proving himself a clever adapter — a aster of juxtaposition and pastiche, taking old styles from the American past and from English country and hunting fashions, and giving them new flair.

*Lauren has not been altogether consistent in explaining the name change. Not long after telling this writer that his older brother changed it, he told a reporter for the *New York Times Magazine* (issue of September 18, 1983, page 112) that their father was responsible for the change.

His first job with a manufacturer was with Beau Brummel Ties, which made inexpensive snap-on bow ties. Lauren, whose fashion idols were such vintage movie stars as Fred Astaire, Douglas Fairbanks, Jr., and Cary Grant, along with such public figures as John Lodge, John F. Kennedy, and the Duke of Windsor, asked Beau Brummel if they would let him experiment with marketing wide neckties, such as the Duke of Windsor had made famous. Beau Brummel agreed, and Lauren and his brother Jerry sat up late one night at the kitchen table tossing around ideas for names. "We wanted something that sounded tweedy, sporty, elegant, English, expensive," Lauren says. The choice of names began to narrow down to those of upper-crust sports. Cricket, rugby, fox hunting, and quail shooting were considered and rejected. Finally, Jerry Lauren suggested polo, the most upper-crust, expensive, exclusive international sport in the world. At first, the sales of Ralph Lauren's Polo line of neckties were poor. Narrow neckties were the fashion then, and his were a full four inches wide. In his secondhand Morgan sports car — with a wide leather strap across its bonnet in the manner of the old MG — Lauren tooled about the North Shore of Long Island with his ties in a suitcase, trying to convince shop owners that these were the ties Jay Gatsby would have worn. Then Bloomingdale's hove into view with a small order. The Polo ties were no sooner displayed than they were snapped up.

Ralph Lauren is the first to admit that, at the time, the four-inch-wide ties did not look quite right with the then-prevailing fashions in men's wear. "I saw that you needed shirts and suits to go with the ties," he says. But he was also not really a designer. His drawing ability was amateurish at best. He knew nothing about the sizing of garments. He could not sew, and could not even pin up a hem. He needed someone to execute his ideas. But Beau Brummel, a conservative, old-fashioned firm, was reluctant to branch out into anything beyond neckwear. And so, in 1969, still working out of a drawer — "not an office, a drawer" — in New York's garment district, Lauren approached Norman Hilton, an established men's-wear manufacturer, with the idea of producing a full line of men's clothing under the Polo label. Hilton responded by offering Lauren fifty thousand dollars' worth of credit and a partnership in the business.

The parting with Beau Brummel was friendly, and Ned Brower, the company's president, cheerfully let Lauren take the Polo name with him, along with a small inventory of neckties. Today, of course, Ned Brower looks back on his 1969 generosity with a certain amount of rue. "Given hindsight, considering what's happened since," he says, "I wish I'd asked for five percent of the action. Still, if I'd kept the name and lost the man behind it, it might not have been the same."

What happened, according to Ralph Lauren, "is that I got the chance to do my own look. No one had ever done a whole line of men's wear before me, there were no men's designers in the United States before me." And when, in 1973, Ralph Lauren launched his line of clothes for women, he became the first designer to go from men's wear into women's wear, and not the other way around. Other popular men's-wear designers — Pierre Cardin, Bill Blass, Oleg Cassini, Calvin Klein, Yves St. Laurent, and Hardy Amies — started out designing clothes for the opposite sex.

The rapid rise from itinerant tie peddler to his current preeminent position on the fashion scene was not without its bumpy passages for Lauren. Theoni V. Aldredge, for example, is a well-known costume designer for the Broadway stage and films. When it was announced that she would be designing the clothes for the 1973 remake of the film *The Great Gatsby*, starring Robert Redford, Lauren's star was just beginning to rise, but the movie seemed a natural for him. He telephoned Miss Aldredge and asked for an appointment. They met, she admired his clothes, and he was given the assignment of turning out the men's clothes for the movie, including Jay Gatsby's famous pink suit. Miss Aldredge says, "I did *all* the designs, selected *all* the colors and fabrics. I got a full-frame credit as costume designer, and an Academy Award to prove it. Ralph Lauren got a much smaller credit — 'Men's clothes executed by. . . .' There's a big difference between designing and executing someone else's designs." The trouble was that the film was one of those in which the clothes got more critical praise than the actors' performances. According to Miss Aldredge, Ralph Lauren tried to capitalize on this by claiming that he had "created the Gatsby look." So much publicity to this effect began appearing in the press that Miss Aldredge had to complain bitterly to Paramount and Lauren to get them to stop it.

Nor has Ralph Lauren's climb to huge success been without emotional rough spots. Both he and his wife, Ricky — whom he met when she was working as a receptionist for his eye doctor — insist that they are total perfectionists. When they acquired their vast Fifth Avenue duplex with its commanding view of Central Park and the reservoir, Ralph Lauren confessed to a friend that he "practically wound up in a hospital with a nervous breakdown," because of his inability to come up with a design solution for so much space. At length, the interior designer Angelo Donghia was brought in, and the result is starkly minimalist, all white, mirrored, with glass and chrome furniture, many banana trees, and empty spaces. "The apartment seems all wrong for them," says another friend. "Perhaps because they're both quite small, they seem lost in it, like aliens from another planet. They argue over which oversize white sofa they ought to sit in. But they try very hard. When *Architectural Digest* was photographing the apartment, Ralph made Ricky change her clothes — as though what she was wearing was all wrong. I've never seen two people trying to lead such *relentlessly* perfect lives."

Meanwhile, what started as a suitcase enterprise has expanded, in barely a decade's time, to include complete lines of men's and women's clothes and shoes, boys' wear and girls' wear, lines called WesternWear and RoughWear, luggage and small leather goods, men's and women's fragrances and cosmetics, and home furnishings — sheets, towels, pillowcases, and even glassware. Franchised are some twenty-two Polo by Ralph Lauren retail stores across the country, concentrated in such wealthy watering places as Carmel, Beverly Hills, and Palm Beach, and more are on the drawing boards. This sudden Lauren empire has provided Ralph and Ricky Lauren and their three children with, in addition to the extraordinary apartment, a getaway house in the Hamptons — "East Hampton, the best Hampton," Lauren points out; a winter retreat in Round Hill, Jamaica, that formerly belonged to Treasury Secretary Douglas Dillon; a sprawling horse and cattle ranch in southwestern Colorado, which Lauren admits he has no idea what to do with; and a private jet to carry the Laurens between these places.

One wonders what Lauren's Russian-born parents, who emigrated to the United States after the revolution, think of what has become of little Ralphie Lifschitz who used to play stoopball and stickball in the Bronx. But despite repeated efforts on the part of journalists to find an answer to this question, Ralph Lauren's parents remain an area of his life that he is reluctant to discuss.

Of course one could argue that Ralph Lauren, at forty-four, has not yet had time to grow into, and adjust to, the role of business tycoon. And though there was perhaps not that much difference between Lauren peddling neckties in a secondhand car in the 1960s and David Sarnoff peddling newspapers in a converted packing crate in 1900, David Sarnoff had become by the 1960s a suave and self-assured paterfamilias of the radio and telecommunications industry, had ripened to his position. His personal trademarks had become the heavy gold watch chain draped across his ample front, the large cigar in the ivory holder that was invariably clenched between two plump fingers, and in his lapel, one or another of the ribbons and decorations he had been awarded by American and foreign governments, including those he had received as a brigadier general in World War II, when he had served as General Eisenhower's chief of communications. In the process, he had also developed an enormous ego.

As he moved toward the end of his life, he had begun to think of it as a kind of parable, or Aesopian fable, in which every event had a neat moral attached at the end. There was the strange story, for example, of the mysterious woman who had handed him two hundred dollars to buy his first newsstand. The tale had its payoff, many years later, when Sarnoff himself had become a philanthropist, when dozens of colleges and universities had bestowed honorary degrees in the arts and sciences on him, and New York's Stuyvesant High School had presented him with an honorary diploma to make up for the one he had never earned. One evening Sarnoff was attending a Jewish philanthropic gathering, and suddenly "found himself staring at a sweet-faced, gray-haired woman, evidently a social worker." He recognized her as his benefactress from Monroe Street.

She explained how it had all come about. At the time, she had been a secretary "to a wealthy, big-hearted man who wanted to help people anonymously." She had been dispatched to the Lower East Side to seek out worthy recipients. Sarnoff's name had been supplied to her by none other than school superintendent Julia Richman, who had been impressed by young Sarnoff's spunky stand against the English teacher who had inveighed against the "Jewish traits" of Shylock. Typically, when he told this tale, Sarnoff never supplied a name for either the "social worker/ secretary" or her "big-hearted" employer, but the moral was clear: he who stands firm against bigotry will reap spiritual and material rewards.

Nor, in his role of moralist — or perhaps fabulist — did he forsake his role as prophet. In 1958, he told *Wisdom* magazine what he foresaw for the year 1978, which he himself would not live to reach. Among other things, he predicted the effective harnessing of solar energy; global, full-color television; automation (including men working only two hours a day and robots taking over nine million clerical tasks); the "farming of oceans for nutritive products"; a life span "within hailing distance of the century mark"; the end of the Soviet republic and the Communist hierarchy; universal communications and speedy transportation shrinking the whole world into a neighborhood; the outlawing of war as an instrument of international policy; and, above all, "as a reaction against current cynicism and materialism, there will be an upsurge of spiritual vitality."

But Sarnoff the visionary also remained to the very end Sarnoff the canny businessman. In 1965, when Bennett Cerf and Donald Klopfer, the heads of Random House publishers, wanted to sell their company, Sarnoff decided that Random House, which had published such distinguished authors as William Faulkner, Robert Penn Warren, and George Bernard Shaw, would be an elegant capstone to RCA's communications empire. Naturally, he wanted to acquire this little gem for as little money as possible.

His first offer was half a share of RCA stock for each share of Random House. This was rejected by Cerf as too low. Sarnoff soon came back with another offer — three-fifths of a share of RCA stock for each Random share, a sixty percent offer instead of fifty, and a considerable increase. But this still did not satisfy Cerf and Klopfer, who asked for sixty-two one-hundredths of a share instead of sixty one-hundredths. Two one-hundredths of a share might not have seemed much to haggle over, but in money it amounted to more than a million dollars.

Negotiations remained at a standoff for several weeks. Then a High Noon confrontation was scheduled at Sarnoff's town house on East Seventy-first Street for a Sunday in December. Cerf arrived for the meeting to find Sarnoff's wife watching a boring and unimportant football game on NBC. Cerf reminded her that the good game that afternoon was on CBS. "I don't watch CBS," Lizette Sarnoff replied loyally, and then, remembering Bennett Cerf's long affiliation with the rival network, added, "The only thing I watch on CBS is *What's My Line?*"

Then the two businessmen got down to the matter at hand. Sarnoff was adamant. Sixty percent was as high as he would go. Cerf was equally firm. Sixty-*two* percent was as *low* as he would go, and, Cerf added, since things seemed to have reached a stalemate, they might as well forget the deal and sit back and enjoy the game. Sarnoff paced the room, silently fuming. Finally he exploded.

"You may not realize it, Bennett," he shouted, "but you're dealing with a very arrogant and egotistical man!"

Cerf replied calmly, "General, I'm just as arrogant and egotistical as you are. Let's watch the game."

"We had better talk tomorrow," said Sarnoff, to which Cerf replied that there was really no point in further discussion, and besides, he was leaving the next day for California and a holiday.

Sarnoff was flabbergasted, and said, "You mean to say that with this deal hanging fire, you're going to go off on vacation?"

Cerf reminded him that there was *no* deal hanging fire, since he had already rejected Sarnoff's final offer.

There followed several weeks of silence from the board chairman of RCA, during which Cerf began seriously to wonder if he had overplayed his hand and, in the process, lost a sale that would have amounted to some forty million dollars. But a few weeks, it seemed, was the face- and ego-saving period required of Sarnoff before he could capitulate. In the end, Sarnoff came back, grumbling that Cerf was being very difficult, and offering him, as a magnanimous gesture, what Cerf had been asking for all along — sixty-two percent.

Using the royal first-person plural, Sarnoff said loftily, "We're not going to argue with you over that two one-hundredths of a share."

*   *   *

Ego — it could almost take the place of a religion. Since it was not possible, or even theologically appropriate, to attribute to the Deity the bountiful good fortunes that had fallen upon the shoulders of these Eastern European immigrants, what remained to celebrate was the Self. One could not even credit ancestors, or the importance of good genes, when one looked back at one's life and saw the awesomeness of everything that had happened. The ancestors, in nearly every case, had been poor, not arrogant, for more generations than anyone could count, and lay in unknown weedy graveyards with their Hebrew inscriptions tipped askew above their heads, in places whose names were no longer on any map. Who else could the self-made man worship but himself? "A very arrogant and egotistical man. . . ." The closest things to religious holidays became the anniversaries of the self — the birthdays, the wedding commemorations, the funerals.

For Mr. Sam Bronfman's funeral in 1971, Jewish tradition was abandoned altogether. Judaism treats death as a very private affair, frowns on pomp and oratory, and particularly opposes the public displaying of the remains of the deceased. But Mr. Sam lay in state, in a silver shroud and an open coffin, in the center of the great rotunda of the Montreal headquarters of the Canadian Jewish Congress. At the funeral services, eulogy followed eulogy from prominent laymen, in defiance of Jewish custom, which dictates a simple homily delivered by a rabbi. The Seagram executives who had planned the ceremony also saw to it that the mourners included as many Christian leaders as possible from both Canadian and U.S. business, political, and academic communities, the irony being that many of these men and women had snubbed him all his life.

In California, Frances Goldwyn had given lavish birthday parties for her husband for nearly fifty years, and the big house at 1200 Laurel Lane had been the scene of many other grand entertainments. Winston Churchill had dined there, as had President and Mrs. John F. Kennedy, not to mention the movie royalty — Mary Pickford and Douglas Fairbanks, Gloria Swanson, George Cukor, Katharine Hepburn, Spencer Tracy, and on and on. But by the late summer of 1973, the manicured croquet court at the foot of the sloping lawn lay empty and the house was strangely silent. The only sounds were the periodic beeps of the electronic surveillance system that patrolled the grounds, and the whispered comings and goings of the round-the-clock nurses and doctors who attended the ninety- (or, more likely, ninety-three-) year-old man who lay in an upstairs bedroom, incontinent and uncomprehending: Sam Goldwyn. He had been unable to attend — and had probably not been aware of — the hundredth birthday party of his onetime partner Adolph Zukor, earlier that year. He had lain this way for more than five years.

Downstairs, Frances Goldwyn, greeting a few friends who had dropped in for a brief call, tried to put as cheerful a face on things as possible. "Oh, we have our little excitements," she said. "We try, on most nice days, to wheel him out onto the upstairs deck for a little fresh air and sunshine. The other day, when the nurses weren't looking, he toppled out of his wheelchair and cut himself. Oh, yes, there's always something going on. He wouldn't be Sam if there weren't." Some months before, President Nixon had come to the house to present Sam Goldwyn with an achievement medal. It had been possible to get the old producer dressed and photographed with the President, receiving the medal. There were even occasional flashes of the old fire, brief moments of lucidity when the old man would seem to realize what was going on — and there were even touches of humor in these. Richard Zanuck had come for a visit, and Goldwyn had suddenly begun berating him for making "a piece of filth like *Hello, Dolly!*" Bemused, Zanuck replied that while he did indeed plan to produce *Hello, Dolly!*, filming had not yet begun, and why should Sam describe a light-hearted musical as "a piece of filth"? Sam was insistent — *Hello, Dolly!*, he said, was "cheap pornography." Finally, Zanuck thought he saw a connection, and said, "Sam, are you talking about *Valley of the Dolls*?" And Sam, true to his wife's observation that, though you could be right, he *could not* be wrong, snapped back, "That's right — *Hello, Valley of the Dollies*."

In 1972, when Charlie Chaplin had ended his twenty-year self-exile from America, and returned to Hollywood to receive a special Oscar from the motion picture academy, he was then eighty-three and aged into near senility himself. His picture had appeared in the *Los Angeles Times*, and a copy of the paper happened to be lying beside the bedridden Sam Goldwyn's bed. Suddenly Goldwyn noticed it, sat up, and said hoarsely, "Is that Charlie? Is that

Charlie?" Then, collapsing back into his pillow, he muttered, "He looks terrible."

For years, during the golden era, Sam and Frances Goldwyn had represented one of the most durable partnerships in Hollywood, a town not known for long and stable marriages. He, she often said, made "all the lordly decisions, and I see to it that all the bits and pieces are in good order." With uncharacteristic modesty, Sam declared that this was too limited an appraisal of her role. "I'd be lost without Frances," he said. "She's the only real, close partner I've ever had." It was true that she was one of the few people in Hollywood with whom he was able to get along. But the later years had not been easy. In 1969, after experiencing a series of circulatory ailments, Goldwyn named his wife to take over the operation of his studio and the management of his personal fortune, estimated then at twenty million dollars. A court order in Los Angeles approved a petition naming Frances Goldwyn as her husband's conservator and placed Samuel Goldwyn Productions in her hands — none of which pleased the couple's only son, Sam Jr. An eventual accord was reached. But from then on, relations between mother and son were strained.

"Shall we go up and see him?" Frances Goldwyn suddenly suggested to her visitor. They mounted the curved staircase together and entered Sam Goldwyn's dimly lighted bedroom. He lay — a huge man, grown obese from lack of exercise — hands folded on his stomach, gaze fixed on some indefinite space, flanked by life-sustaining apparatus. "It's me, Sam," said Frances. There was no visible response.

Later, sipping one of her special martinis that she would allow no one else to fix — a special proportion of gin and water that only she understood — she said, "The doctors say that his heart is as strong as a twenty-year-old boy's. Of course I think it's mostly guts and pride that's keeping him alive. This could go on for years and years." Then, turning her back to be unzipped, Frances Goldwyn prepared to go upstairs again, change into a robe, and have her supper on a tray beside her silent husband.

It did not go on for years and years. Within the year, Sam Goldwyn died in his sleep. Friends who had hoped that Frances would now be able to enjoy some well-earned freedom and travel were shocked when, not long after her husband's death, she had a heart attack. Now it was she who lay speechless and immobilized in the upstairs room with nurses around the clock, able to communicate only by writing notes on slips of paper. She died two years later, in the summer of 1976, at seventy-three.

Not long before her death, she had said to a friend, "Just think — more than thirty million dollars in the estate! He had a lot to be proud of. I always thought that everything we had was owed to Mr. Giannini's bank!"

Acknowledgments

THIS book has been in various stages of preparation for more years than I care to count, and the list of individuals who have contributed thoughts and impressions to it is long. But there are a few people to whom I would like to extend a special word of thanks.

For their recollections of the great, gone motion picture moguls of Hollywood, I am grateful for the hours I was able to spend with George Cukor, King Vidor, Adolph Zukor, Minna Wallis, Roddy McDowall, Lucille Ball, Sam Marx, Ava Gardner, John Huston, Gail and Howard Strickling, Lillian Hellman, Elizabeth Taylor, and, most particularly, Frances Howard Goldwyn.

In New York, one of the few remaining people to have a tenuous impression of the sad-fated Rose Pastor Stokes was Mrs. Lettice Sands Stokes. I am also grateful to Mr. and Mrs. Richard Roth, Sr., who supplied me with the unpublished memoir of Mr. Roth's father, Emery Roth, which is herein quoted. Other New Yorkers who deserve thanks are Mrs. Anna Potok, Jack Rosenthal, John Schiff, the late Walter E. Sachs, Robert LaVine, Ralph and Ricky Lauren, Peter Carlsen, John L. Loeb, Jr., Ruth Proskauer Smith, Patrick O'Higgins, Theoni V. Aldredge, Dina Abramovicz of YIVO, and the particularly helpful Rabbi Ronald B. Sobel of Temple Emanu-El.

A special word of thanks to Phillip Applebaum of Detroit. Although I have had personal and business dealings with members of the Bronfman family over the years, I am indebted to longtime Bronfman observer Peter C. Newman of Toronto, who was generous with insights and whose book *Bronfman Dynasty* (published in the United States as *King of the Castle*) was an important source. This book also owes much to Allen and Beverley Gasner of Bethesda,

Maryland; to Robert and Helen Gould of Cincinnati; to Isaac and Dian Levine, also of Cincinnati, for their recollections of Dr. Levine's father, Calman Levine; to Rabbi Alfred Gottschalk of Hebrew Union College; to Mrs. Meyer Lansky of Miami Beach; and to Dr. Edward Lahniers, for psychological insights. In the process of its preparation, the book was fortunate to be taken into the hands of two splendid editors at Little, Brown: my late friend Harry Sions, and the superb Genevieve Young. As always, I am indebted to my friend and agent, Carol Brandt, for her cool guidance and support of the project from the beginning. While all of these people have helped enormously with the book, I alone must be held responsible for any errors or shortcomings.

S.B.

Source Notes

PREFACE

xii–xv   Figures on Christian and Jewish wealth: *Jewish Living*, vol. 2, no. 3 (Sept./Oct., 1979), pp. 41–47; reprinted in Siegel and Rheins, pp. 98–103.

   xiv   Mr. Annenberg's fine: Siegel and Rheins, p. 59.

    xv   Lansky's worth: *Jewish Living*, p. 47; reprinted in Siegel and Rheins, p. 103.

    xv   Mayer's worth: Howard Strickling to author.

1. UPTOWN FIREBRAND

    4   Jewish migration figures: Liebmann Hersch, "International Migration of the Jews," *International Migrations*, vol. 2 (New York: Macmillan, 1931), pp. 490, 496, 501, 504, 507.

 4–5   The Adenoids Riot: *New York Tribune*, June 28, 1906; reprinted in Schoener, p. 132.

    5   "excitable, ignorant Jews . . . nearest 'Yiddisher' ": ibid.

    7   "Julia, I'm pretty . . . will know my name": memorial pamphlet by Addie Richman Altman and Bertha Richman Proskauer; privately printed; no date.

    7   "Julia, take everything off": ibid.

    8   "But we can't do anything": ibid.

    9   "It is much easier": ibid.

   10   "Every time she visits": *Jewish Daily Forward*, Feb. 12, 1911.

   10   "years of": Altman and Proskauer pamphlet.

   13   "the dominion of reason": Rabbi Alfred Gottschalk to author.

14–15   Population figures: Howe, p. xix; *Universal Jewish Encyclopedia and Reader's Guide* (New York: KTAV Publishing, 1944), vol. 7, p. 547.

15–16   Population figures: Oscar Handlin, *Adventure in Freedom* (New York: McGraw-Hill, 1954), p. 84.

   18   Population figures: Report of the U.S. Immigration Commission, vol. 15, 1911, pp. 476–477.

   19   "Rent money and landlord": Applebaum, p. 10.

   20   Baron de Hirsch fund: Manners, p. 193.

   21   Schiff's contribution: ibid., p. 97.

23–24   "peace, liberty . . . Occidental Civilization": Rabbi Ronald B. Sobel to author.

   24   "Are we waiting": ibid.

   24   "thoroughly acclimated American Jew": ibid.

   25   The 1907 syllabus: Howe, p. 276.

   26   Jewish school population: ibid., p. 274.

   26   "thirst for knowledge . . . debatable questions": ibid., p. 276.

   28   Pushcart licenses: Manners, p. 239.

   28   "You don't want to be too hard": ibid., p. 240.

   29   "It is not astonishing": Theodore A. Bingham, "Foreign Criminals in New York," *North American Review*, Sept., 1908, pp. 383–394; quoted in Howe, p. 133.

   29   *Harper's Weekly* article: issue of Nov., 1907.

   30   "sensational methods": Manners, p. 243.

   30   "a Jacob Schiff" and other *Tageblatt* quotes: Manners, pp. 244, 241–242.

31   "Dear Mr. Editor": *Jewish Daily Forward*, Feb. 8, 1906; reprinted in Schoener, p. 247.
31   "In the old country": Dr. Isaac Levine to author.

2. WHY THEY CAME

33–35   Gelbfisz's boyhood and emigration: Frances Howard Goldwyn (Mrs. Samuel) to author.
37   "The purpose in educating": Lucy Dawidowicz, *The Golden Tradition: Jewish Life and Thought in Eastern Europe* (New York: Holt, Rinehart and Winston, 1967), p. 30.
38   Jews arrested or exiled: Howe, pp. 6–7.
39   The cossacks at the station: Lyons, p. 24.
41   Harris Rubin's story: *American Jewish Archives*, vol. 33, no. 1 (Apr., 1981), pp. 10–11.
42   "a sweeping plague": *New York Times*, Jan. 29, 1905; reprinted in Schoener, p. 28.
42–46   Isaac Don Levine's impressions: "Letters of an Immigrant," *American Jewish Archives*, vol. 33, no. 1 (Apr., 1981), pp. 53–61.
46   immigration figures: Oscar Handlin, *Adventure in Freedom* (New York: McGraw-Hill, 1954), p. 84; also *Encyclopaedia Britannica* (1957), vol. 15, p. 466.
47   *oysesn*: *Jewish Daily Forward*, July 14, 1903.
47   Vacations "have become a trend": ibid., June 30, 1904.
47   "God sent us the Victrola": ibid., May 9, 1904.
48   "There are pianos": ibid., Oct. 16, 1904.

3. A JEWISH CINDERELLA

52   "Some pray to marry": John Bartlett, *Familiar Quotations*, 13th ed. (Boston: Little, Brown, 1955), p. 906.
53   Rose's aphorisms: *Tageblatt*, Aug. 13, 1903, Oct. 25, 1905.
54   "Mr. Stokes is a deep, strong thinker": quoted in *New York Times*, Apr. 6, 1905.
54   "If I thought as much": ibid.
54   "love at first sight": ibid.
55   Stokes telegram exchange: Cleveland Amory, *The Last Resorts* (New York: Harper and Brothers, 1952), p. 16.
55   "a descendant of families": *New York Times*, Apr. 6, 1905.
57   "She might have been the model": Lillian Baynes Griffin, "Mrs. J. G. Phelps Stokes at Home," *Harper's Bazar*, Sept., 1906.
57   "I wish the Times would correct": *New York Times*, Apr. 6, 1905.
58   "inspired religion . . . teacher and guide": Griffin in *Harper's Bazar*, Sept., 1906.
58   "The only difference": ibid.
59   "As she talks": *New York Times*, Apr. 6, 1905.
59   "very interesting": ibid.
59   "It was a hard struggle": ibid.
59   "If our life": Griffin in *Harper's Bazar*, Sept., 1906.
61   "we have no definite plans": *New York Times*, July 20, 1905.
61   *Hebrew Standard* editorial: reported in ibid.
62   "closer to the Christian sentiment": *Hebrew Standard*, July 21, 1905.
62   "Fame!": Rose Harriet Pastor, *Tageblatt*, July 26, 1903.
63–64   Description of Stokes apartment and interview with Rose: Griffin in *Harper's Bazar*, Sept., 1906.
67   "For the future": *Universal Jewish Encyclopedia and Reader's Guide* (New York: KTAV Publishing, 1944), vol. 10, p. 67.
68   production of shirtwaists: Howe, p. 298.
68   "I am a working girl": ibid.
69   "If I turn traitor": Barbara Mayer Wertheimer, *We Were There: The Story of Working Women in America* (New York: Pantheon Books, 1977), p. 301.
69   "The girls": McAlister Coleman, "All of Which I Saw," *Progressive*, May, 1950, p. 25.
70   "You are on strike": Howe, p. 299.

71 "A common social and cultural background": Will Herberg in *American Jewish Year Book* (Philadelphia: Jewish Publication Society, 1940), p. 36.

72 "to make room": memorial pamphlet by Addie Richman Altman and Bertha Richman Proskauer; privately printed; no date.

72 "[The fire] taught": Julia Richman and Isabel Wallach, *Good Citizenship* (New York: American Book Company, 1908), p. 76.

73 "The desire to save money": ibid., p. 93.

73 "worse . . . than slovenly": ibid., p. 103.

4. AN OCCUPATION FOR GENTLEMEN

77–78 Meyer Lansky's memories and quote: Eisenberg, Dan, and Landau, pp. 24–28.

78–80 Lansky stories: ibid., pp. 33–38.

80–82 Goldwyn's early years in the United States: Frances Howard Goldwyn (Mrs. Samuel) to author.

82–85 Beginning of Goldwyn's film career, including quotes: ibid.

85–87 Involvement of Zukor with Goldwyn et al.: Adolph Zukor to author.

87 "Adolph didn't think": Frances Goldwyn to author.

88–89 Zukor and *Queen Elizabeth*: Adolph Zukor to author.

89–90 The Goldwyn-Zukor partnership: ibid.

90 "If I hadn't suggested": Frances Goldwyn to author.

90–91 Goldwyn family and business life: ibid.

91 "I didn't think": ibid.

92 "A self-made man": *International Celebrity Register* (New York: Celebrity Register Ltd., 1959), p. 297.

5. HEROES AND HEROINES

93 "David has all the luck": Lyons, p. 38.

93–97 Sarnoff's boyhood: ibid., pp. 29–38, 44.

97 U.S. Navy and radio: ibid., p. 42.

98 "That's nice": ibid., p. 56.

98–99 Sarnoff joins Marconi: ibid., p. 39.

99–101 Sarnoff and the *Titanic*: ibid., pp. 57–60.

101 "brought radio to the front": ibid., p. 60.

103 "Love —": Rose Harriet Pastor, *Tageblatt*, July 26, 1903.

103 Rose's homilies: ibid., Aug. 13, 1903.

104 "The Anglo-Saxon coldness": Yezierska, *Salome*, p. 248.

104 "I am a Russian Jewess": ibid., p. 65.

104 "the oriental": ibid., p. 209.

105 "I felt the deep world-sorrow": Rose Harriet Pastor, *Tageblatt*, Mar. 24, 1903.

105 Yezierska at school: Yezierska, *Ribbon*, p. 39.

105 "A woman alone": ibid., p. 217.

106 "Here I am": ibid., p. 73.

106 Headlines: ibid., p. 40.

106 "laughs and a happy ending": ibid., p. 82.

106 "screaming and yelling": ibid.

107–108 Yezierska and Goldwyn: ibid., pp. 72–73.

108 Fox offer, including quotes: ibid., pp. 84–87.

110 Deportations: James Trager, *The People's Chronology* (New York: Holt, Rinehart and Winston, 1979), p. 791.

110–111 Race riots and strikes: ibid.

113 "So she's back": *Kansas City Star*, Mar. 18, 1918.

114 "To the Star": ibid., Mar. 20, 1918.

114 "I felt it was a matter": quoted in transcript, U.S. Circuit Court of Appeals, Eighth Circuit, no. 5255: Rose Pastor Stokes vs. U.S.A., in New York Public Library.

115–130 Details of Rose's indictment, trial, and appeal: ibid.

131 "Life is strange": quoted in Zosa Szajkowski, *Jews, War and Communism* (New York: KTAV Publishing, 1972), p. 285.

132 Vladeck's embarrassment: Vladeck–Louis Marshall letters, American Jewish Archives, Cincinnati.

132n Immigration figures: Yaffe, pp. 8–9.

133 "Former Prisoners": Howe, p. 326.

133–134 Bank closings: ibid., pp. 136–137.

6. THE JEWISH LAKE AND OTHER CREATIONS

139 "witty and interesting": Carola Warburg Rothschild to author.

140 "They must be Russians": ibid.

142 Lansky-Luciano friendship: Eisenberg, Dan, and Landau, pp. 52–53; Gosch and Hammer, p. 24.

142 George Raft's gangster friendships: *International Celebrity Register* (New York: Celebrity Register Ltd., 1959), p. 606.

143 Jewish gangsters: Siegel and Rheins, pp. 60–63.

146 "If you have a lot": Gosch and Hammer, p. 35.

148 The ambush: Eisenberg, Dan, and Landau, pp. 108–109.

149–150 Bronfman family background: Newman, pp. 66–73.

150 "The Langham's bar": ibid., p. 69.

151 "If they were": ibid., p. 73.

151 "Bolshevism flourishes": pamphlet, Anti-Saloon League of New York, 1919, in New York Public Library; quoted in Newman, p. 82.

152 Recipe and labels: Newman, pp. 84–85.

152 "Distilling is a science": *Leadership* (pamphlet), Seagram Distilling Company, New York, 1972, unpaged.

153 Production and profits: Newman, p. 86.

153 Lansky-Bronfman relationship: Mrs. Meyer Lansky to author.

154 "Rum running has provided": Newman, p. 87.

155 The platform: Samuel Bronfman to author.

155 Bronfman marriages: Newman, p. 95.

156 "was bootleggin' enough whiskey": Gosch and Hammer, p. 41.

156 "the Jewish lake": Eisenberg, Dan, and Landau, p. 79.

7. FITTING IN

157 "Take the Fisher Freeway": Phillip Applebaum to author.

159 "I was ashamed": Emery Roth, untitled, unpublished, and undated memoir, supplied by Mrs. Richard Roth, Sr. (Mr. Roth's daughter-in-law) and quoted with her permission, p. 1.

159 "I attended balls": ibid., p. 10.

160 "I was rather surprised": ibid., p. 32.

162 "By boat": O'Higgins, p. 78.

162–163 The uncle in Melbourne: ibid., p. 146.

163 "The sun was strong": Rubinstein, p. 23.

163 "My new friends": ibid., pp. 23–24.

163–164 Crème Valaze: O'Higgins, p. 151.

164 "Mlle. Helena": ibid., p. 152.

164 "WHAT WOMEN WANT": ibid.

165 "masterful adapter": Patrick O'Higgins to author.

166 "The first thing I noticed": Rubinstein, pp. 57–58.

167n "It's made of a wonderful mixture": O'Higgins, p. 151.

168 "a beautiful area": Howe, p. 132.

168 "In certain strata": ibid., p. 133.

169 "enable the social life": quoted in *New York Times*, Oct. 6, 1982.

170–172 Details of City College: Howe, pp. 280–283.

8. MINSTRELS AND MINSTRELSY

173–174 Carrie Jacobs Bond story: Woollcott, pp. 130–132.
176 Pelham Café: ibid., pp. 40–43, 46.
176 Berlin's musical ability: ibid., pp. 35, 37.
177 Prince Louis: ibid., p. 51.
178 "about an Italian girl": Mary Ellin Berlin Barrett to author.
178 "I suppose you've got a tune": Woollcott, pp. 71–72.
179 Michigan: ibid., p. 76.
180 "whattle": ibid., p. 76.
180 Appraisals of Berlin's music: *International Celebrity Register* (New York: Celebrity Register Ltd., 1959), p. 73.
180–181 Jewish performers: Howe, pp. 556–558; Bermant, pp. 84, 100.
184 Douglas Fairbanks's Jewish mother: Frances Howard Goldwyn to author.
184 Jewish performers who changed their names: Siegel and Rheins, pp. 14–16.

9. HIGH ROLLERS

185–198 Details of Sam Goldwyn's life and career: Frances Howard Goldwyn (Mrs. Samuel) to author.
186 "Is Sunday a legal day?": ibid.
188 "the most colossal fake": ibid.
190 "And this time for good": ibid.
191 "A producer should not be hampered": *International Celebrity Register* (New York: Celebrity Register Ltd., 1959), p. 297.
191 "Mr. Godsol is no longer with us": ibid.
192 "because Metro isn't": Frances Goldwyn to author.
192 "Leo is *my* birth sign": ibid.
198 "quality . . . clean things can be done": ibid.
200–201 Lansky's modus operandi: Eisenberg, Dan, and Landau, pp. 91–92.
201 Profits: Gosch and Hammer, p. 74.
201 Prohibition statistics and arrests: Newman, p. 83.
202 The numbers game: Eisenberg, Dan, and Landau, p. 150; Gosch and Hammer, p. 75.
202 Laundering money: Eisenberg, Dan, and Landau, pp. 250–251.
203 "It was like we had a printin' press": Gosch and Hammer, p. 367.
203–204 Bronfman's modus operandi: Based on author's experiences while working in an advertising agency for Seagram's.
203–204 Bronfman quoted on types of liquor: Samuel Bronfman to author.
205 Bronfman's social climbing: Newman, pp. 24–25.
205 "Our company": ibid., p. 62.
208 The second Mrs. Stokes: Lettice Stokes to author.
208 "language instructor": *New York Times*, June 21, 1933.

10. LITTLE CAESARS

210–211 Class change and anxiety: W. H. Auden's introduction to Yezierska's *Ribbon*, pp. 16, 15.
211–212 Bronfman's temper: author's experience.
212 "I don't *get* ulcers": Newman, p. 29.
212 "The damn fool": ibid., p. 39.
212 "It's expensive!": ibid., p. 40.
213 "Mary": ibid., p. 33.
213 "I don't want my sister to know": ibid., p. 40n.
213 "Interest . . . office boy": Samuel Bronfman to author.
213 "Imagine the secrets": O'Higgins, p. 50.
214 bought the building: ibid., p. 58.
215 "Stella's, of course!": ibid., p. 105.

216   The Lehman Brothers story: ibid., pp. 93–95.
216–222   The Goldwyn stories, Goldwynisms, and so on: based on author's interviews with Frances Howard Goldwyn, George Cukor, Roddy McDowell, Sam Marx, Ira Gershwin, Lucille Ball, Lillian Hellman, Minna Wallis, and others.
222   "I have in mind a plan": Lyons, p. 71.
223–224   The Dempsey fight: ibid., pp. 100–101; Dreher, pp. 72–73.
225   Corporate jealousies: Lyons, pp. 90–91.
225   "on the bridge": ibid., p. 11.
225   "birth of the electron": ibid., p. 14.
227   "Woe to America!": Yezierska, *Ribbon*, pp. 216–217.

11. DEALS

229   Aging whiskey: Newman, p. 133n.
230   Price of Rossville distillery: ibid., p. 134.
231   The naming of Seven Crown: Dr. Isaac Levine (son of Calman Levine) to author.
232   "I always like to have money": ibid.
232n   "Very Own": Newman, p. 107n.
233   Men of Distinction: ibid., p. 137n.
233   Morgenthau and the tax bill: Eisenberg, Dan, and Landau, p. 80; Newman, p. 64.
233–234   The Rosenstiel stories: Cooney, pp. 225–227.
235   Bronfman-Rosenstiel partnership: Newman, p. 134.
235   Nicknames: Cooney, p. 226; Robert Gould to author.
235–236   Card-playing among industry rivals: Frances Howard Goldwyn to author; similarly, Helen Gould to author.
236   Seagram brands displayed: Newman, p. 39.
236–239   The Julius Kessler story: Dr. Isaac Levine to author.
238   "But you're an old man": Newman, p. 157.
240   "This is so much bullshit": ibid., p. 143.
240–241   Rose Stokes's last days, funeral: *New York Times*, June 21, 1933.
241   Rose's memorial service: ibid., July 25, 1933.

12. WAR

243   Joseph P. Kennedy story: Hecht, p. 520.
244   Kennedy and RKO: Lyons, pp. 143–144; Dreher, pp. 111–112.
244   "Sarnoff's grand design": Lyons, p. 143.
244   "A banker?": Adolph Zukor to author.
244–245   Kennedy stories: Frances Howard Goldwyn (Mrs. Samuel) to author.
245   "tough customer": Samuel Goldwyn files.
245   "de-Semitization": Howe, p. 567.
246   "No writers": Frances Goldwyn to author.
246–247   Hecht's involvement with Bergson et al.: Hecht, pp. 529, 532, 536.
247–251   Jewish army fund-raising: ibid., pp. 538–543; also *New York Times*, Feb. 19, 1983.
248   "I called on David": Hecht, pp. 539–540.
249   "accept with pleasure": Frances Goldwyn to author.
251   "We're here to contribute": Hecht, p. 543.
252   "an investigation of propaganda": *New York Times*, Aug. 19, 1941.
253   "The Zionists . . . turning in my grave": Bergson quoted in *New York Times*, Feb. 19, 1983.
254–255   Impressions of Hillcrest Country Club: author's.
255   "in this business": Sam Marx to author.
257   "You will probably think it strange": Goldwyn files.
257   "Please stop crying": ibid.
257   Lansky and Jewish refugees: Eisenberg, Dan, and Landau, p. 297.
258   Bronfman's philanthropy: Newman, p. 46.
258–260   Goldwyn and Danny Kaye: Frances Goldwyn to author.
260   "In dealing with my husband": ibid.

260–262 "The Vanishing Jew": Henry Popkin in *Commentary*, July, 1952, pp. 46, 51.
262 "This originates not in hate": ibid., p. 46.

13. AT LAST, A HOMELAND

263 Siegel in Hollywood: Eisenberg, Dan, and Landau, p. 176.
263–264 Plans for Las Vegas: ibid., p. 225.
264 Cohen's cleanliness: Cohen, pp. 255–256.
265 "not good for anyone's image": ibid., p. 1.
265 "a three-card Monte dealer": ibid., p. 234.
265 "We were insured": ibid., p. 45.
266 "Knockin' their own proposition": Hecht, p. 610.
266 "Who the hell is Ben Hecht": Cohen, p. 89.
267 "This guy got me so goddamn excited": ibid., p. 91.
267 "Jewish people": ibid., p. 93.
268 "America is our Zion": Rabbi Alfred Gottschalk to author.
268 "When one has ten million dollars": Doris Lilly to author.
268 Cohen's party: Cohen, p. 91.
269 Lansky's helpers on the docks: ibid., pp. 92–93; Eisenberg, Dan, and Landau, p. 296.
270 Cohen's orders to kill British officers: Cohen, pp. 91–92.
270 "To me, he was the greatest man": ibid., p. 92.
271 Figures on Jewish deaths: Siegel and Rheins, p. 153.
271 "We had been talking": Dalia Lamport to author.
273–275 Apfelbaum family history: Anna Potok to author.
275 "We loved it here": ibid.

14. TOUCHES OF CLASS

277 "he's just a little old movie producer": Frances Howard Goldwyn (Mrs. Samuel) to author.
277 Madame Rubinstein's nomenclature: Patrick O'Higgins to author.
278 Bronfman children's upbringing: Jack Clifford to author.
278 No business outside Canada: Edgar M. Bronfman, "Name Your Brand — In Any Market in the World," *Columbia Journal of World Business*, vol. 4, no. 6 (Nov./Dec., 1969), p. 31.
278 "How long do you think": Newman, p. 65.
278–279 Mayer's life-style: Gail and Howard Strickling to author.
280 Goldwyn's misspellings: Goldwyn files.
280 Goldwyn's malapropisms: Frances Goldwyn to author.
280 "Find out how many stars": ibid.
281 "How long have you and I": Frances Goldwyn to author.
281 "A kind of love song": ibid.
281n Parsons's column: *International Celebrity Register* (New York: Celebrity Register Ltd., 1959), p. 573.
282–284 Gloversville story: ibid.
284–286 Lansky / Las Vegas story: Eisenberg, Dan, and Landau, p. 226; Gosch and Hammer, p. 316.
287 Siegel / Virginia Hill story: Eisenberg, Dan, and Landau, pp. 225, 237; Gosch and Hammer, p. 331.
287–292 Siegel, Hill, and the Flamingo: Eisenberg, Dan, and Landau, pp. 226, 235–241; Gosch and Hammer, pp. 316–319, 329–331.
288 "the situation": Gosch and Hammer, p. 315.

15. ALL THAT MONEY CAN BUY

297–298 German opposition to changes at Emanu-El, including quotes: Rabbi Ronald B. Sobel to author.
298 The Sidney Weinberg story: Walter E. Sachs to author.

299   The Harmonie Club story: Rabbi Sobel to author.
299–301 David Sarnoff's house: author's impressions.
301   "I believe that television": Lyons, p. 207.
302   "Think of your family": ibid., pp. 207–208.
302   "If we let our imagination": ibid., p. 208.
302   RCA Pavilion: ibid., p. 216.
303   "Good evening": ibid., p. 275.
304   "Father of American Television": ibid., p. 268.
304   "I don't think this television thing": Frances Howard Goldwyn (Mrs. Samuel) to author.
306–309 Five Towns and Woodmere Academy: Beverley and Allen Gasner and Sue Kaufman Barondess to author.
307   "a golden ghetto": Sue Kaufman Barondess to author.
307   "Be civil": Beverley Gasner to author.
309   "And your grandfather and I worked so hard": ibid.

16. CROWN PRINCES

313   The obituary: *New York Times*, Sept. 1, 1967.
314–317 The Calman Levine story: Dr. Isaac Levine (Calman's son) to author.
314   "WE WHO MAKE": Newman, p. 137.
315   The Willkie dispute: Dr. Isaac Levine to author.
315   "*I am company policy*": ibid.
315   "*You go to my enemy*": ibid.
317   "This call is not welcome": ibid.
318   "But Father, don't you know": Newman, p. 174.
318   "But those Bronfmans": Mrs. Arthur Lehman to author.
318   "the son of that Russian": Mrs. J. L. Loeb to author.
319n   Robert Sarnoff's prediction: *International Celebrity Register* (New York: Celebrity Register Ltd., 1959), p. 666.
320   "Find Marshall": Newman, p. 28.
320   "Sam was sitting": ibid.
321   "My God!": Sam Marx to author.
321   "See him": Newman, p. 35.
322   Rubinstein will: O'Higgins, pp. 279–280, 288, 293.
323   Bronfman/*Holiday* story: author's recollection.
323–324 "If you're saying": Newman, p. 183.
324   "In real estate": Robert Gould to author.
324   "We had a code of ethics": Cohen, p. 183.
325   "Where are they going": Mrs. Meyer Lansky to author.
326–327 Lansky's family life: Eisenberg, Dan, and Landau, pp. 256, 230–231, 284–285.
326–328 "Don't you know": ibid., pp. 230–231.

17. WITCH-HUNTING

329   "pervasive shaper of American thought": James Trager, *The People's Chronology* (New York: Holt, Rinehart and Winston, 1979), p. 999.
330   Hellman's income: Siegel and Rheins, p. 447.
331   "Let's take a look": ibid., p. 449.
331   Dalton Trumbo story: Trager, p. 999.
331   "always had something to say": Siegel and Rheins, p. 450.
332   Zero Mostel story: ibid., p. 451.
332   John Garfield story: ibid., pp. 453–454.
332–334 Phillip Loeb story: ibid., pp. 454–457.
335   "Modern girls are conscious": *New Yorker*, Aug. 10, 1925.
336   "As to being Jewish": Dorothy Schiff, quoted to author by John Schiff.

336   "After all": Frances Howard Goldwyn to author.
338   Lettice Stokes on Rose Pastor: Mrs. Stokes to author.

18. PEOPLE WHO ARE SOLID

340   "I was born": Jack Rosenthal to author.
340–342   Lansky's harassment by U.S. officials: Eisenberg, Dan, and Landau, pp. 284–285.
342   "bad timing . . . because of the Kefauver Report": ibid., p. 288.
343   Sandra Lansky story, including quote: ibid., pp. 290–291.
343   "You see, Richard had been drinking": ibid., p. 322.
344–345   Lansky as bargaining chip: ibid., pp. 313–314.
345   "That's life": quoted in *New York Times*, Jan. 16, 1983.
346   "Bugsy and I": Eisenberg, Dan, and Landau, p. 324.
346   "Most of what they wrote about him": Mrs. Meyer Lansky to author.
347–349   Phyllis Bronfman story: Newman, pp. 165–166.
348   "make this building": ibid., p. 166.
349   "This building": ibid., p. 167.
349   Atlantic Acceptance bankruptcy: ibid., p. 164.
350   Edgar's college escapade: author's recollection.
350   Linen asked to intercede: Newman, p. 159.
350   Sam's opposition to divorce: John L. Loeb, Jr., to author.
350   "I've set it up": Newman, p. 21.
351   Edgar's premarital settlement: ibid., p. 189.
351   "I told Edgar . . . after the marriage": ibid.
352   "I hate to be taken": ibid., p. 190.
352–353   Sam II kidnapping, including quotes: ibid., pp. 190–191.
354   "Tell me, Edgar": ibid., p. 187.
354   Conoco takeover story: *People*, Dec. 28, 1982 – Jan. 4, 1983, pp. 62–63.
354   "To turn a hundred dollars": Newman, p. 19.
355   "What would my father?": *People*, Dec. 28, 1982 – Jan. 4, 1983, p. 63.

19. FROM POLAND TO POLO

356–357   Adolph Zukor story: Frances Howard Goldwyn (Mrs. Samuel) to author.
357   "God damn it": Robert LaVine to author.
357   "I'm so sick": Ralph Lauren to author.
358   "My mother wanted": ibid.
359   "We wanted something": ibid.
359   "I saw that you needed": ibid.
360   "Given hindsight": Ned Brower to author.
360   "I got the chance": Ralph Lauren to author.
360   "I did *all* the designs": Theoni V. Aldredge to author.
361   "practically wound up in a hospital": Ralph Lauren to author.
361   "The apartment seems all wrong": Peter Carlsen to author.
362   "found himself staring": Lyons, p. 34.
362   "to a wealthy, big-hearted man": ibid.
363   Sarnoff's predictions: *Wisdom*, Sept., 1958.
363–364   Random House story: Cerf, pp. 286–287.
364   "I don't watch CBS": ibid., p. 286.
364   "You may not realize . . . off on vacation": ibid., p. 287.
364   "We're not going to argue": ibid., p. 287.
365   Bronfman funeral: Newman, p. 151.
365–367   Goldwyn's last years: author's impressions.
366   "Oh, we have": Frances Goldwyn to author.
366   The Goldwyn-Zanuck exchange: ibid.
366   Goldwyn on Chaplin: ibid.
367   "I'd be lost": ibid.
367   "The doctors say": ibid.
368   "Just think": ibid.

Selected Bibliography

Applebaum, Phillip. *The Fishers: A Family Portrait*. Detroit: Harlo Press, 1982.

Bermant, Chaim. *The Jews*. New York: Times Books, 1977.

Cerf, Bennett. *At Random*. New York: Random House, 1977.

Cohen, Mickey. *Mickey Cohen: In My Own Words*. Englewood Cliffs, N.J.: Prentice-Hall, 1975.

Cooney, John. *The Annenbergs*. New York: Simon and Schuster, 1982.

Dreher, Carl. *Sarnoff: An American Success*. New York: Quadrangle, 1977.

Eisenberg, Dennis, Uri Dan, and Eli Landau. *Meyer Lansky: Mogul of the Mob*. New York: Paddington Press, 1979.

Fishman, William J. *Jewish Radicals*. New York: Pantheon Books, 1974.

Gosch, Martin A., and Richard Hammer. *The Last Testament of Lucky Luciano*. Boston: Little, Brown, 1975.

Hecht, Ben. *A Child of the Century*. New York: Simon and Schuster, 1954.

Howe, Irving. *World of Our Fathers*. New York: Harcourt Brace Jovanovich, 1976.

Lyons, Eugene. *David Sarnoff*. New York: Harper and Row, 1966.

Manners, Ande. *Poor Cousins*. New York: Coward McCann and Geoghegan, 1972.

Newman, Peter C. *Bronfman Dynasty*. Toronto: McClelland and Stewart, 1978.*

O'Higgins, Patrick. *Madame*. New York: Viking Press, 1971.

Rubinstein, Helena. *My Life for Beauty*. New York: Simon and Schuster, 1965.

Schoener, Allon, ed. *Portal to America: The Lower East Side, 1870–1925*. New York: Holt, Rinehart and Winston, 1967.

Siegel, Richard, and Carl Rheins. *The Jewish Almanac*. New York: Bantam Books, 1980.

Woollcott, Alexander. *The Story of Irving Berlin*. New York: G. P. Putnam's Sons, 1925.

Yaffe, James. *The American Jews*. New York: Random House, 1968.

Yezierska, Anzia. *Salome of the Tenements*. New York: Boni and Liveright, 1923.

———. *Red Ribbon on a White Horse*. New York: Scribner, 1950.

*Published in the United States under the title *King of the Castle*, in somewhat different form, by Pocket Books, 1979.

Index

THE GRANDEES

Stephen Birmingham

In medieval Spain and Portugal, to which they trace their ancestry, the Sephardic Jews considered themselves the elite. In the United States they still do.

From the arrival of twenty-three Sephardim in 1654, the impact of this wandering band of exiles on America has been immense. They made fortunes in the fur trade long before the Astors, they dealt in slaves, they lent money to the infant Republic, they joined the Navy, the Army, High Society. They managed to combine assimilation with a stubborn Orthodoxy. They were horrified when the hordes of their German – and later their Eastern European – co-religionists descended on the New World. To this day they have remained aloof.

Stephen Birmingham, who chronicled the German Jewish society of New York with such power and success in 'OUR CROWD', here presents a tapestry of extraordinary Americans, spiced with gossip and the gentle rattling of family skeletons, a portrait of a proud, haughty – and quite fascinating – people.

FUTURA PUBLICATIONS
NON-FICTION

ISBN 0 7088 3089 7

'OUR CROWD'

Stephen Birmingham

New York's great Jewish banking families – aloof, mysterious, clannish, even arrogant. Considering themselves an elite, for generations the families married only within 'our crowd'. Today, the branches of the family trees interlace endlessly.

'OUR CROWD' provides a fascinating, insider's view of one of the richest segments of a rich city Jewish upper-class life in New York – vibrant, exotic, romantic, special. A city within a city: where sixty sat down for dinner attended by as many footmen; chateaux on Long Island, castles in Westchester; private railway cars, vast art collections; power, culture and the determination never to invade, or seem concerned to invade, the gentile 'Establishment'.

Remarkable individuals, resplendent dynasties – out of the opulent fabrics of their lives Stephen Birmingham has fashioned a superb social history.

FUTURA PUBLICATIONS
NON-FICTION

ISBN 0 7088 2835 3

DUCHESS

Stephen Birmingham

Her marriage divided a nation, her life has fascinated the world

The full and revealing biography of Bessiewallis Warfield, Mrs Simpson, The Duchess of Windsor.

She was never pretty. But then beauty isn't everything: she had charm, she had grace, she had dreams. She craved for fame and fortune — and found it. But the price was high.

From her genteel childhood in Baltimore to her isolated widowhood in a Paris apartment she has faced — and outfaced — the troubles of life. Scandal, abdication and exile haunted her fairytale marriage to the Prince Charming of her dreams, and cast dark shadows on her glittering life.

And then the hectic years of feverish pleasure-seeking, chasing happiness across the globe, searching for it in drink, party-going, and an entourage of bizarre hangers-on; rootless and restless she longed for love.

At last, accepted by the Royal Family, then widowed and alone she found a kind of peace.

She died on April 24 1986.

Thoroughly researched, brilliantly told, DUCHESS is the compelling and candid biography of a dazzling woman.

FUTURA PUBLICATIONS
NON-FICTION/BIOGRAPHY

ISBN 0 7088 3073 0

ADVENTURES IN THE SCREEN TRADE

William Goldman

'This is the real Hollywood' *Daily Telegraph*

After more than twenty years in Hollywood, Oscar-winning screenwriter William Goldman has written a sparkling memoir as entertaining as the films he's helped create. From the writer of BUTCH CASSIDY AND THE SUNDANCE KID, ALL THE PRESIDENT'S MEN, MARATHON MAN and many more comes an intimate view of movie-making, of acting greats like Redford, Olivier, Newman and Hoffman, of the trials and rewards of two decades inside the most exciting business there is.

'It's the most knowledgeable book ever about the irresistible spell of the cinema. Read it.' *Sunday Telegraph*

'It is refreshing to read his realistic, funny but affectionate guide to Hollywood.' *Sunday Telegraph*

'fast and witty . . . a brave and very funny book.' *Time Out*

'irreverent, vastly entertaining . . . his text studded with insider's gossip, wild anecdotes and behind-the-scene dramas, Goldman makes enough provocative statements in every chapter to keep any reader engrossed.' *Publishers Weekly*

FUTURA PUBLICATIONS
NON-FICTION/AUTOBIOGRAPHY

ISBN 0 7088 2596 6

RUSSIA
BROKEN IDOLS, SOLEMN DREAMS

David K. Shipler

A new classic on the Soviet world – its people, their daily lives and the political realities. David K. Shipler was the *New York Times'* chief correspondent in the USSR from 1974–9; he came to his subject free of prejudice and open to every nuance of the population within whose midst he was charmed, tricked, tempted and disabused of preconceptions. In this vastly entertaining book he covers every aspect of contemporary Russia and brings vividly to life a society far more complex than appearances – and much Western commentary – would suggest.

'Essential reading for anybody interested in the Russian people: a profoundly perceptive study, written with a novelist's eye for anecdote and the telling detail' *Standard*

'An observant and beautifully written account ... sensitive and compassionate' *New York Times Book Review*

FUTURA PUBLICATIONS
NON-FICTION

ISBN 0 7088 2723 3

All Futura Books are available at your bookshop or newsagent, or can be ordered from the following address:
Futura Books, Cash Sales Department,
P.O. Box 11, Falmouth, Cornwall.

Please send cheque or postal order (no currency), and allow 55p for postage and packing for the first book plus 22p for the second book and 14p for each additional book ordered up to a maximum charge of £1.75 in U.K.

Customers in Eire and B.F.P.O. please allow 55p for the first book, 22p for the second book plus 14p per copy for the next 7 books, thereafter 8p per book.

Overseas customers please allow £1 for postage and packing for the first book and 25p per copy for each additional book.